# Quality Problem Solving

Also available from ASQ Quality Press

*Creativity, Innovation, and Quality*
Paul E. Plsek

*Root Cause Analysis: A Tool for Total Quality Management*
Paul F. Wilson, Larry D. Dell, and Gaylord F. Anderson

*Mapping Work Processes*
Dianne Galloway

*Quality Quotes*
Hélio Gomes

*Let's Work Smarter, Not Harder: How to Engage Your Entire Organization in the Execution of Change*
Michael Caravatta

*The Change Agents' Handbook: A Survival Guide for Quality Improvement Champions*
David W. Hutton

*Understanding and Applying Value-Added Assessment: Eliminating Business Process Waste*
William E. Trischler

To request a complimentary catalog of ASQ Quality Press publications, call 800-248-1946.

# *Quality Problem Solving*

by

## Gerald F. Smith

**ASQ Quality Press**

**Milwaukee, Wisconsin**

*Quality Problem Solving*
Gerald F. Smith

**Library of Congress Cataloging-in-Publication Data**
Smith, Gerald F., 1947–
    Quality problem solving/Gerald F. Smith.
      p. cm.
    Includes index.
    ISBN 0–87389–394–8
    1. Quality control.   2. Problem solving.   I. Title.
    TS156.S62   1998
    658.5′62—dc21
                                    97–44035
                                      CIP

10  9  8  7  6  5  4  3  2  1

ISBN 0-87389-394-8

Acquisitions Editor: Roger Holloway
Project Editor: Jeanne Bohn

ASQ Mission: To facilitate continuous improvement and increase customer
satisfaction by identifying, communicating, and promoting the use of quality
principles, concepts, and technologies; and thereby be recognized throughout
the world as the leading authority on, and champion for, quality.

Attention: Schools and Corporations
ASQ Quality Press books, audiotapes, videotapes, and software are available
at quantity discounts with bulk purchases for business, educational, or instruc-
tional use. For information, please contact ASQ Quality Press at 800-248-1946,
or write to ASQ Quality Press, P.O. Box 3005, Milwaukee, WI 53201-3005.

For a free copy of the ASQ Quality Press Publications Catalog, including ASQ
membership information, call 800-248-1946, or access http://www.asq.org.

Printed in the United States of America

♾  Printed on acid-free paper

**American Society for Quality**

Quality Press
611 East Wisconsin Avenue
Milwaukee, Wisconsin 53202

**To Juliet, with love**

# ■ Contents ■

# ■ Preface ■

This book was conceived on April 10, 1992, at a rest stop on the Ohio Turnpike. My family and I were driving from St. Paul, Minn., to Philadelphia to participate in a celebration for the 50th anniversary of my wife's parents' wedding. While at the rest stop, I picked up a copy of *USA Today*. A cover story announced the winners of the RIT/USA Today Quality Cup, awarded to teams of workers in five organizations who "made stunning improvements in their workplaces, rejuvenated morale, slashed bureaucracy, and eliminated waste." The paper's account of what these and other quality teams had done was detailed enough that I could identify generalizable problem-solving insights, lessons of potential value to other organizations. If enough cases of this kind could be discovered, I surmised, lessons extracted from them might form the basis of a book. I spent much of the next year digging usable cases out of past issues of *Quality Progress* and other journals, out of the many books on quality management that had been published during the preceding decade, and from any other sources I could find. These cases and the lessons derived from them are the heart of this book.

The book has other, deeper, origins as well. I entered academia in the fall of 1979 by beginning a Ph.D. program at the University of Pennsylvania's Wharton School. I had qualms about pursuing an academic career, the major one being that I thought academic research was "academic," irrelevant to practice. My driving goal in life was to make the world work better, and I was not sure that an academic career would serve that objective. But, I reasoned, business schools must be different since their core constituencies are managers and organizations. As I was soon to learn, this belief was mistaken. While at Wharton, I got involved in a field of study—managerial problem solving, the thinking managers do in response to complex organizational issues—that was intellectually interesting and, I felt, had great practical significance.

My academic career has had its ups and downs. Managerial problem solving has proven to be a fascinating and challenging topic for both teaching and research. While I have written papers on the topic that have been published in the best academic journals, the publication process has always been a struggle. Managerial problem solving does not lend itself to mainstream research methods, and I opted not to conduct traditional studies that, while readily publishable, would produce little knowledge of real significance. In part as a result of my experiences, I have come to the conclusion that business school research is not really about producing knowledge that can be used in practice. My belief that such knowledge can be developed, in a scientifically respectable way, is an underlying motivation for this book.

The purpose of this book is to improve the thinking done as part of quality improvement activities in organizations. That thinking is problem solving, hence the book's title, *Quality Problem Solving*. It has been written for use by anyone who wants to make organizations work better. Thus, the book's target audience includes managers at all levels and employees in all kinds of organizations: public and private, for-profit and not-for-profit, government, manufacturing, and services, large and small. While it will be useful to quality engineers, inspectors, and other quality professionals, the book offers even more to general managers and employees, people without technical training in quality who are concerned with organizational improvement. *Quality Problem Solving* is also intended for students, providing durable knowledge and hands-on advice that can help them have an immediate impact on the performance of organizations that employ them.

Before describing what the book is, I should say something about what it is not. Two points deserve emphasis. First, *Quality Problem Solving* is not a completely comprehensive, everything-anyone-could-conceivably-care-to-know treatment of its titular topic. Quality problem solving, as defined herein, encompasses far more than could be covered in-depth by a one-volume publication of this kind. In writing the book, I decided only to mention, and not to discuss, topics that were well covered by the quality literature. If I had nothing of importance to add, I chose not to repeat what others had already said so well. As a result, while the book's treatment of quality problem solving is comprehensive, most of its contents will be relatively new for most readers.

A second and related point concerns problem-solving tools or methods. *Quality Problem Solving* is not a "tool book." A number of books have been written with the expressed intent of teaching readers the many techniques that can be used in solving quality problems. Since these books succeed admirably in their intent, there is no need for another book of that kind. However, techniques play an important role in quality problem solving and must be addressed by any comprehensive treatment of the topic. Accordingly, descriptions and discussions of relevant problem-solving methods are included in the book. I have focused on the best known techniques and on a few that will be new to quality practitioners. As compared with the content of "tool books," *Quality Problem Solving* says less about the nuts-and-bolts mechanisms of techniques and more about their strengths and limitations.

Indeed, I am of the opinion that problem solving, both in general and with regard to quality improvement, has become excessively concerned with techniques. Too often, rather than thinking carefully about a problem, people mindlessly apply methods that have been drummed into them at training sessions and workshops. These tools become substitutes for thought, driving out what they were supposed to support. Thinking is hard; applying a technique is easy. Methods are easy to teach; effective thinking about real-world problems is not. This book takes on the hard task. It tries to teach readers how to think effectively about quality problems. The use of problem-solving methods is part of that thinking, but there is much, much more, little of which has been addressed by previous work in this area.

How does this book purport to teach problem solving beyond the techniques? What is its distinctive content? The book's most significant content has already been alluded to. It is the hundreds of insights and prescriptions derived from analyses of published cases of quality problem solving. These insights extend far beyond what might be discovered through the application of problem-solving techniques. Whereas many books include cases to illustrate their points, *Quality Problem Solving* is distinctive in that the many pieces of advice it offers were actually extracted from the cases being cited. The book's contents were not developed through my years of practical problem-solving experience. No one person could accumulate through experience as much knowledge as is contained in this book. The experiences that produced the book were lived by people like you, the reader. The best testimony that its lessons are useful and valid is the fact that these people felt good enough about their problem-solving efforts and outcomes that they were motivated to write them up for publication.

But the book's content has other sources as well. Much of it comes from the years I have spent teaching and thinking about real-world problem solving. From students in an evening MBA program, I learned that insightful thinking about problems includes much more than can be encompassed in the seven-step models of decision-making texts. I learned that complex real-world problems are conceptual constructs and that the language we use to think about these issues has an enormous effect on our ability to solve them. I learned that problems have structures. Their parts are related in certain ways, and these structures can be identified through careful analysis of the situation. This kind of analysis often leads to a solution. And I have learned that problems, like people, are simultaneously different and the same. Recognizing commonalities among problems is essential if experience from similar instances in the past is to be applied to the current situation. But recognizing the differences among problems, the distinctive characteristics of each, is also critical, since the devil, or an angel, can lie in the details.

A final source of the book's content is the work of scientists and practitioners in fields outside quality management. I have drawn on far-flung domains of research and practice, collecting material that will deepen and expand the reader's understanding of quality problem solving. From philosophical arguments about causality to cognitive science research on the mind, from the diagnostic insights of physicians to those learned by equipment troubleshooters, from theories of human error to the theories and techniques that inform architectural design, much that is here has been borrowed from other fields.

Hopefully it has all been rendered in language that will be understandable to a thoughtful, motivated reader. I do not expect that everything in these pages will be easily accessible to every person who opens the book. I do believe that this book will provide ample returns on an investment of time and effort made by anyone who really cares to read it. The book's organization is explained in Chapter 1. Briefly, in addition to two opening and one closing chapters, there are four chapters that discuss problem-solving functions—problem definition, diagnosis, and so forth—followed by five chapters, each addressing a particular type of quality problem—for instance, efficiency and product design.

And now for the acknowledgements, about which I have long been somewhat apprehensive. Obviously, there are many people at Quality Press to be thanked: Roger Holloway, Jeanne Bohn, and outside reviewers, among others. It is their job to turn manuscripts into books, and they do it well. I also want to thank my colleagues in the

University of Northern Iowa's Department of Management, not for specific help with or contributions to the book, but for their acceptance of and kindness toward me during the final several years of the book's creation. Beyond these people, however, I am at a loss. My manuscript did not pass through the hands of helpfully evaluative colleagues, nor did diligent typists labor long hours in its production. Primarily owing to my characteristic tendency to go it alone, this book, much more than most, has been a one-person production. Happily, this absolves me of the duty of absolving others for any errors herein: They are indisputably my own.

There is no harm in dreaming, so I have at times imagined that *Quality Problem Solving* would initiate or play a prominent part in a much needed "second wave" of writing and research about quality. The revolutionary manifestos have been written; the airy generalities have all been spoken *ad nauseam*. Now comes the task of making quality happen in very concrete ways, in every aspect of our lives. This book is dedicated to that task. Finally, in dreams that are wilder still, I have imagined that this book might contribute to a reorientation of academic research in business schools and elsewhere, a shifting away from abstract theories, coupled with a commitment to research that addresses the real problems and needs of people and organizations.

# ■How to Use This Book■

Like any other book, *Quality Problem Solving* can be read from front to back. It will provide readers with a comprehensive and reasonably deep understanding of real-world problem solving, especially that performed for quality improvement purposes. Having read the book in this traditional way, readers can use it as a resource, referring back to chapters and topics that seem pertinent during future problem-solving endeavors.

For some readers intent on going through the book from cover to cover, Chapter 2 on Problem-Solving Fundamentals may pose a stumbling block. Not only is it one of the longest chapters, it is also one of the most dense. It contains a practitioner-oriented summary of scientific knowledge and research pertinent to problem solving. Much of this material is conceptual, some would say theoretical. The chapter is the author's concession to his academic side: Before getting into the fun applied stuff, you have to develop a solid conceptual foundation. Most readers who study this chapter will be rewarded for their efforts by a deeper, more complete comprehension of what follows. At the same time, one could skip Chapter 2 entirely and still learn a tremendous amount from the book. I suggest that you try to read and understand this chapter, but if you do not have the time or willpower to get through it, move on to the less conceptual, more applied chapters that follow. Maybe Chapter 2 will make more sense later, after you have a better feel for the book.

But *Quality Problem Solving* is not just meant to be read in the traditional cover-to-cover way. The book can also be of immediate problem-solving value to people who have not read it all, but who need help solving difficult problems they are currently addressing.

The first step in using the book as part of ongoing problem-solving efforts is to read Chapter 1, a short introduction that orients the reader and outlines the book's content. The latter part of this chapter describes the problem-solving functions and problem types addressed in the book.

After reading Chapter 1, you should be able to say what kind of problem you are dealing with and/or the problem-solving function that is posing difficulties. Doing so enables you to identify one or two chapters directly relevant to your needs. You may also be able to target the most promising sections or subsections within these chapters.

For instance, a team that is having trouble coming to grips with a broad, messy, amorphous situation might benefit by reading Chapter 4 on problem definition, especially the section on The Situation Definition and Analysis Method. A group tasked with reducing costs in its operational area would look to Chapter 9, Efficiency Problems, for advice. Different members of the group might explore suggestions offered in different parts of the chapter's "Prescriptions" section. One person could consider equipment-related efficiencies, as another examines ideas for eliminating unnecessary activities and a third studies ways of reducing waste-related costs. Finally, a quality engineer faced with the challenge of eliminating a recurring product defect should read Chapter 7 on conformance problems and Chapter 5 on diagnosis, the key challenge in solving conformance problems.

Thus, while *Quality Problem Solving* is certainly intended as late night reading material, the kind of thing that invariably puts most people to sleep, it has also been written to be used in "real time" problem-solving situations. However it is read or used, this book offers state-of-the-art problem-solving insights and advice, most of which were derived from the practical problem-solving efforts of people like you.

# chapter 1

# Problem Solving and Quality Management

## Chapter Outline

**The Quality Movement: Fad and Fundamentals**
Principles of Quality Management

**Solving Quality Problems**
TQM's View of Problem Solving
The Stakeholder View of Quality
Quality Problem Solving: A Broader Perspective
Types of Quality Problems
Conformance Problems
Unstructured Performance Problems (UPPs)
Efficiency Problems
Product Design Problems
Process Design Problems
Quality Problem Solving: A Deeper Account
Problem-Solving Functions
Problem Identification
Problem Definition
Diagnosis
Alternative Generation
Case-Based QPS

**Overview of the Book**

The title of this book is ambiguous. Its ambiguity lies in the fact that "Quality" can be read as a characteristic of "Problem" or of "Problem Solving." The ambiguity is intended. This book is about solving certain kinds of problems—quality problems—and it is about solving problems in a certain way—with excellence, goodness, or quality in one's thinking.

Something else about the book's title: It is a union of two less-than-promising parts. "Quality" evokes memories of the late 1980s, of top management memos and speeches, pricey consultants, interminable training sessions, and countless read-alike books. "Problem Solving" has also been burdened by too many authors with too little to say. Even more, it has been stigmatized as the mark of failure, what you do when things go wrong. The implication is that they would not have gone if you had been smarter in the first place.

In this chapter I want to redefine and rehabilitate both these notions—"quality" and "problem solving." Newly conceived and combined, they represent a topic of enduring significance to anyone who wants to make the world, or their small part of it, a better place. The chapter also explains how this topic, quality problem solving, is developed in the chapters that follow.

## The Quality Movement: Fad and Fundamentals

In government, education, industry, and other sectors of our society, the life cycle of programs for change is depressingly familiar. Many "new and improved" ways of achieving long-standing goals are proposed. A few are blessed by successful implementations that receive media attention. The more attractive of these achieve "promising new movement" status and a much larger burst of publicity. The movement's initiators are anointed as gurus. They are soon joined by hundreds of true believers, people who write books and undertake training and consulting engagements to spread the word (and the wealth). Soon the movement has spawned an industry. It also acquires detractors, people who are invested in the status quo, who have had bad experiences with the new approach, or who are simply making the safe bet that this too will pass. Indeed it does. Any complex program for change inevitably has failures. These provide fuel for the debunking phase of the life cycle, a ritualized performance in which what had seemed so promising is now labeled a mere fad, perhaps even a hoax.

Though the naysayers play a part in this demise, most movements suffer more from their friends than from their enemies. The people on the bandwagon over-sell and create expectations that could not possibly be satisfied. They overapply the program, taking it into areas it was never intended to address. They are responsible for the extra bells and whistles, frills that increase implementation costs without increasing effectiveness. What began as a crisp program for change ends up as a bloated monstrosity that deserves to be deflated.

Yet this rise-and-demise cycle is only part of the story, the best known part but not always the most important. Most programs for change express a few sound insights and principles. These are the basis for its success and, if developed and preserved, will be its legacy after the fad. Thoughtful individuals and organizations extract these kernels of wisdom, adapting them to their purposes. Even after the movement has become unfashionable and disappears from public attention, it lives on. In some organizations, some things are done differently, perhaps much more effectively, as a result of that now-forgotten program for change. No movement lives in the limelight for long. But a movement can have widespread and long-lasting effects if it expresses sound principles that have been developed into operational prescriptions for improvement.

The quality movement, most widely known as Total Quality Management (TQM), has been through these changes. The "discovery" of quality was the most important development in management thought and practice in the 1980s. TQM was introduced in all kinds of organizations and received national visibility through the Baldrige Award. Companies like Xerox, Ford, and Westinghouse became corporate role models by virtue of their quality improvement activities. Then, predictably, the counterrevolution began. In a 1992 story subtitled "Business sours on 'Total Quality Management'," *Newsweek* discussed companies where TQM efforts ended in failure, concluding that "seminar organizers, consultants, and book publishers . . . reaped the biggest quality rewards of the 1980s."[1] A 1988 article in *Fortune* cited a survey of electronics companies in which 85 percent of respondent firms had adopted a quality control program, but less than a third reported significant quality and productivity improvements.[2] By the early 1990s, the quality movement had lost the affections of managers to reengineering, a newer, more glamorous paramour that has since lost favor as well.

Though TQM has suffered in the buzzword wars, it has achieved considerable success in its attempt to change organizational practices. In the United States and other industrialized countries, there are few organizations that have not been positively affected by the quality movement. Companies keep in closer touch with their customers, organizational processes have been streamlined, and employees are utilized as sources of improvement ideas. The magnitude and persistence of TQM's influence derives from the validity and significance of the principles on which the movement was founded.

## Principles of Quality Management

Seven foundational claims for the quality movement are summarized in Figure 1.1. Not all of these were first proposed by TQM, but each received new attention and application due to its TQM endorsement.

The first principle proclaims the importance of quality or excellence in human activities and creations. The Greeks valued *arete,* or excellence, for its own sake. Modern cultures tend not to do so. Excellence is especially important in economic activities. Modern production methods fragment work into simple operations having partial and temporary outputs. It is hard to take pride in a well-tightened bolt. In addition, the post-World War II American economy, driven by pent-up demand, rewarded companies that got goods out the door, irrespective of quality. Industrial economists argued that defective products should be tolerated, since the costs of preventing defects exceeded the benefits of doing so. The quality movement successfully challenged this assumption. Its claim that "quality is free" is based on evidence that the costs of poor quality are greater than had been assumed and that significant quality improvements can be achieved.

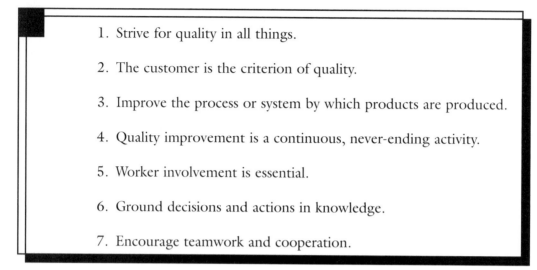

1. Strive for quality in all things.

2. The customer is the criterion of quality.

3. Improve the process or system by which products are produced.

4. Quality improvement is a continuous, never-ending activity.

5. Worker involvement is essential.

6. Ground decisions and actions in knowledge.

7. Encourage teamwork and cooperation.

**Figure 1.1**  Underlying principles of TQM

TQM's second principle is that the customer is the criterion of quality. In an exchange economy, most of what one produces is produced for others. Product users decide whether a product is of acceptable quality. A quality product satisfies pertinent user needs. This principle can be taken too far; consumer evaluations are not the only consideration in assessing a product's quality. Nonetheless, the precept has altered manufacturers' traditional focus on engineering specifications. Products are manufactured according to specifications assumed to define an output that will be attractive to customers. Alas, the history of modern commerce is rife with Edsels, New Cokes, and other creations that people refused to buy, even though the products met specifications. TQM's second principle highlights the fact that product specifications are only a surrogate criterion for quality. While necessary for manufacturing purposes, if specifications don't reflect the needs of product users, they define a failure.

A focus on the process or system by which products are produced is TQM's third principle. Earlier quality control efforts centered on the inspection of final outputs. Realizing that "You can't inspect in quality," TQM shifted attention to the upstream activities by which products are made. TQM tries to prevent defective products from being manufactured, rather than inspecting for defects and correcting them after the fact. The quality movement, and W. Edwards Deming especially, argued that poor quality usually results from systemic failings and consequently is the responsibility of management, not workers. While this transformed traditional labor bashing into *au courant* management bashing, it drew attention to the systems and processes by which things get done in organizations.

The fourth fundamental claim of TQM is that quality improvement is a never-ending activity. The claim is expressed by the Japanese word *kaizen*, by the fifth of Deming's celebrated "fourteen points,"[3] and by the overused aphorism, "Quality is a journey, not a destination." The ultimate goal of zero defects cannot always be

reached, but one can always come closer. Even if all product defects were eliminated, there would still be costs to reduce. Japanese quality circles have demonstrated that significant progress can be achieved through an accumulation of large
and small advances. The quality movement promotes a culture of continuous improvement, an unrelenting commitment to doing better.

TQM's fifth principle is the need for worker involvement. Efforts to improve
quality may start with top management, but to be successful, they must involve all
members of the organization. TQM implies a participative style of management,
one that removes barriers between workers and overseers, encouraging people to
manage themselves. In this respect, the quality movement conforms with trends in
management practice. Worker involvement improves motivation: People work
harder when they feel they are important parts of the organization. More importantly, workers know what is going on, how the system operates, and how it can be
improved.

Sixth is the demand that decisions and actions be grounded in knowledge. TQM
promotes knowledge-based management, encouraging organizations to learn. Surveys help determine customer needs; experiments identify optimal settings of product and process variables. When defects occur, their causes must be diagnosed
through intensive data collection and analysis, proposing and testing causal hypotheses, and evaluating action alternatives for their effectiveness and potential side
effects. Possibilities suggested by gut feelings must be confirmed by facts. It is no
accident that the saying "In God we trust, all others need data" came out of the
quality movement.

TQM's seventh and final foundational principle is the need for teamwork and
cooperation. This need exists at several levels. Teamwork must prevail among line
employees, where work groups can help each person perform effectively. Equally
important is the need for teamwork among organizational subunits. Cooperation
between labor and management is needed within organizations. Each side must
renounce the "blame game" and work with the other for the benefit of the whole.
Finally, TQM endorses teamwork across organizational boundaries, with suppliers,
customers, and other outside stakeholders. Companies should develop long-term
relationships with suppliers, helping them learn how to satisfy company needs.
Firms should develop closer relationships with their customers, keeping abreast of
changing product requirements. TQM tempers unwarranted competitiveness in our
economic system, recognizing that cooperation often enables mutual gain.

These seven foundational principles of TQM are a significant contribution to
management thought and practice. If they sometimes got lost beneath the hoopla,
they are nonetheless what quality management is all about. Every organization can
profit from adherence to these principles.

## Solving Quality Problems

That overview aside, this book is not about TQM. It is about problem solving, or
more specifically, quality problem solving (QPS). Traditionally defined as a gap
between the existing state and a desired state, a problem is more broadly viewed as
a situation that bears improvement. Problem solving is the thinking one does in

trying to improve things. It is relevant to quality management, to management in general, and, indeed, to life in general. Good thinking is more likely to result in effective action, action that achieves one's goals, that improves things. Excellence in thinking—one meaning of "quality problem solving"—is a virtue all might aspire to.

## TQM's View of Problem Solving

The quality movement has always been concerned with problem solving. That concern is evident in the prominence of problem-solving books and training sessions among TQM products. Assuredly, much effective problem solving has been conducted in organizations under the auspices of quality management. These contributions notwithstanding, the quality movement has adopted an overly narrow view of problem solving and has failed to develop its problem-solving methodologies in sufficient depth. These failings prevent TQM and its problem-solving efforts from achieving their potential.

The dominant, though not the only, view within TQM is that problem solving is what you do when things go wrong. This view reflects an assumption that organizational activities are or can be standardized. Products are defined by specifications; rules and procedures state how activities should be performed. Most QPS methods reflect this conceptualization. They deal with situations in which a system, well defined by standards, is not performing acceptably. The methods help determine why things have deviated from standards. Problem solving becomes a matter of finding and fixing deviations or defects.

Not surprisingly, given this conceptualization, problems and problem solving have negative connotations within quality management. A problem is a failure of the system, something that should never have happened. The way to handle problems is to prevent their occurrence through process improvement. Problem solving is a reactive response to failure, a necessary evil that would not be necessary if TQM was totally effective. It is putting out fires, and as Deming noted, "Putting out fires is not improvement."[4] Some TQM experts, notably J. M. Juran, have a more positive attitude toward problem solving, but theirs is a minority view.

Problem solving is also thought to be rather simple. Imai claimed that most quality problems can be solved by common sense.[5] Per Crosby, "You can create solutions to complicated problems by being the only one to break that complicated problem down to its basic causes. Once these causes are exposed, a creative solution appears—if you can recognize it."[6] It is assumed that problem solving is no big deal. Just do such-and-such and, *voilà*, "a creative solution appears." The belief that problem solving is simple reflects the assumption that activities and outputs are standardized. The existence of standards makes problem solving easy: To identify a problem, compare actual performance with the standard. To remedy the situation, simply enforce the standard, returning things to the way they are supposed to be. Problem solving can also seem easy when practitioners focus on easy problems, "picking the low hanging fruit."

As a result of these misconceptions, QPS has not been well developed by TQM. Practitioners assume that learning to solve problems is a matter of acquiring techniques or tools. Problem solving is the application by a group of the most popular methods. Rarely is it a matter of intense thought.

This book develops an account of quality problem solving that is both broader and deeper than that just described. Being broader, the account is more general. It responds to a larger set of situations and makes QPS a more important part of management. Being deeper, the account is more powerful. It enables the development of stronger methods and provides more effective problem-solving prescriptions.

## The Stakeholder View of Quality[7]

The first step towards a sufficiently broad account of QPS is to develop an adequate notion of quality. TQM has defined quality in terms of a product's ability to satisfy user needs. Juran's definition of quality as "fitness for use" reflects this orientation.[8] This consumer-side conceptualization of quality adopts what is certainly the most important usage of the concept in market economies: Quality as a consumer's evaluation of a product's acceptability. However, this is not the only way the term *quality* can be applied, nor does it fully express the concept's meaning. The best single-word synonyms for *quality* are terms like *goodness* and *excellence*. These concepts suggest no special focus on customer needs. Moreover, quality is a property that can be ascribed to any entity, not just products created for use by others.

Organization theorists use the notion of **stakeholder** to refer to any party having an interest, financial or otherwise, in an issue or organization. The stakeholder concept can be used to achieve a broader view of quality. Degree of quality can be assessed according to various standards and stakeholder perspectives, not just those of product users/consumers. A product can be regarded as excellent or of high quality by its manufacturer, the workers who made it, environmentalists, and other parties who are interested in the product. This stakeholder perspective resolves a latent confusion within the quality movement. From its inception, TQM has included efforts at cost reduction and productivity improvement. Such activities are not implied by a customer-focused definition of quality, since they benefit producers, not consumers. If a stakeholder view of quality is adopted, cost reduction and productivity improvement efforts are easily encompassed within quality management. They make the product more profitable, hence of higher quality from the manufacturer's perspective.

The stakeholder view of quality is consistent with progressive thinking within the quality movement. Per Rummler and Brache, "Whether the concern is quality, customer focus, productivity, cycle time, or cost, the underlying issue is performance."[9] Quality management isn't only about quality from the perspective of product users. It is about achieving excellence in all organizational products and activities.

## Quality Problem Solving: A Broader Perspective

An expanded notion of quality implies a broader view of quality problem solving. It is not something you do because you did not get things right the first time. It is more than finding and fixing defects. Quality problem solving is also more difficult than had been assumed. Even when limited to finding and fixing defects, it is mentally challenging. Case studies demonstrate how difficult it can be to identify the causes of unacceptable outputs. Every product and process is infinitely detailed, having many attributes not covered by specifications. Minor changes in material formulations, environmental conditions, or employee performance can be virtually unnoticeable, yet result in rejects. In addition, some processes cannot be proceduralized, making it impossible to identify failures as deviations from standards. There is, for instance, no one right way of selling life insurance. When sales efforts are unsuccessful, determining the problem's cause is not simply a matter of comparing actual behavior with prescribed procedures.

## Types of Quality Problems

What then is the proper scope of QPS? As developed in this book, QPS involves five types of problem situations, each addressed by TQM practitioners. Three of these types are performance problems, situations in which an existing system is not performing acceptably. Two are design problems, situations requiring that something new be created. The five types of quality problems are identified in Figure 1.2.[10]

***Conformance Problems.*** This is the set of traditional quality problems. In such situations, a highly structured system having standardized inputs, processes, and outputs is performing unacceptably from the standpoint of product users. Most exist-

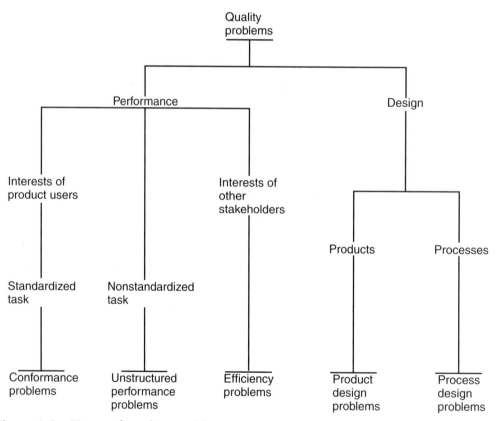

**Figure 1.2** Types of quality problems

Adapted and reprinted with permission from *Quality Management Journal*, Fall 1994.

ing QPS techniques address conformance problems. The existence of standards aids problem identification. System inputs, processes, and outputs can be compared with standards and problems identified when variations are excessive. The major challenge posed by conformance problems is diagnosis, determining the cause(s) of nonconformities. Once this has been done, remedial action is often simple: Return the system to its specified performance routine.

***Unstructured Performance Problems (UPPs).*** Problems of this type involve systems or processes that are not well specified by standards and that are not performing acceptably from the standpoint of product users or other stakeholders. Sales below budget is a typical UPP. The absence of standards can reflect system immaturity or the need for performance flexibility. Service delivery and knowledge work cannot usually be fully proceduralized. Problem identification is more difficult for UPPs, since one cannot simply monitor for deviations from standards. The major challenges in solving unstructured performance problems are determining customer needs and diagnosing the causes of poor performance.

***Efficiency Problems.*** This category of performance problems reflects the interests of system owners and operators. Operations can be more costly than system owners desire or can pose unsafe or undesirable conditions for workers. Cost efficiencies are the most common concern of this kind, hence the category's name. The identification of efficiency problems is driven more by employees than customers. Employees know more about wasteful and unsafe production practices. Solving efficiency problems centers on identifying and eliminating unnecessary activities and finding less costly ways of performing needed functions.

***Product Design Problems.*** This category involves the design of products that satisfy user needs. Users may be internal or external to the organization. Though product design work can be initiated as a result of product inadequacies, problem solving usually occurs as a natural part of organizational life in a competitive market environment. Quality management's product design efforts have focused on one major problem-solving challenge—determining customer needs. Another challenge, devising viable product concepts that satisfy those needs, can be addressed with methods developed in engineering, architecture, and other design fields.

***Process Design Problems.*** A process is an organized set of activities, a way of doing something. Process design problems involve the development of new processes and the revision of existing processes. Problem identification is prompted by recognition of performance inadequacies and of emerging technological capabilities that enable improved processes. New process design may be prompted by the initiation of programs and activities, such as the introduction of a new product. The key problem-solving challenge is generating high-level design concepts that can be developed into effective processes. Quality management and the reengineering movement have made process design a permanent agenda item for managers in modern organizations.

## Quality Problem Solving: A Deeper Account

There is little value in proposing a broader perspective on quality problem solving unless that account is  developed in-depth so useful advice can be given to practitioners faced with quality problems. Historically, only mathematical and statistical techniques have received this kind of attention. The technical literature on quality includes research pertaining to experimental design, statistical process control, acceptance sampling, and other quantitative aspects of quality management. Researchers propose new methods or variations on methods for dealing with situations that could be encountered in practice. Unfortunately, the practical significance of this research is limited. Mathematical and statistical techniques are applicable to only a small proportion of real-world problems. The quality gurus all agree that too much work has been devoted to mathematical and statistical methods. Not enough has been done in devising effective qualitative methods for solving problems.

## Problem-Solving Functions

This book pursues two approaches in developing an in-depth treatment of quality problem solving. The first involves the elaboration of problem-solving functions. A function is a step or task performed as part of problem solving. Many problem-solving methods are simply ordered lists of functions. This book discusses four functions deemed critical to the solving of quality problems: problem identification, problem definition, diagnosis, and alternative generation.

*Problem Identification.* Problem identification is the means by which one comes to believe that a situation is problematic. This function is applicable to all problems and is necessarily the first step in problem solving. The identification process consists of noticing certain stimuli, interpreting this information, and prioritizing the situation as problematic or not, in light of its nature and importance. In organizations, problem identification is aided by organizational roles and procedures, including performance monitoring, internal auditing, and others. Though no technique can reliably identify every kind of problem, statistical process control is an effective method for discovering many conformance problems.

*Problem Definition.* Problem definition is a matter of mentally representing a problem situation. This representation can be communicated to others by verbally stating what the problem is or depicting it in a diagram. Problem definition is a necessary function for all problem solving. Definitions of real-world problems are necessarily complex and evolve during the course of problem solving. They may refer to a pertinent problem category, the goals of relevant stakeholders, the means by which goals might be achieved, obstacles and constraints, and potential causes of a failing. Problems can be defined at different levels of generality and include more or less of a set of related concerns. No existing definitional methods are guaranteed to produce adequate definitions for all problems.

*Diagnosis.* Many problems involve existing systems—a production line or the human body, for instance—that are not performing acceptably. Diagnosis entails determining the causes of such performance deficits. Though not performed in every instance of problem solving, when it is required, diagnosis is typically the key problem-solving task. Solutions based on a faulty diagnosis are rarely effective. The diagnostic process includes activities for generating causal candidates and testing their validity. Because diagnosis is a critical function in solving conformance problems, the quality movement has contributed significantly to the development of diagnostic methods. Cause-effect diagrams are the most familiar. Experimentation is a powerful method for testing causal hypotheses.

***Alternative Generation.*** Alternative generation is the means by which possible solutions or courses of action are identified. Input to alternative generation is the problem situation as currently understood, especially knowledge acquired through diagnosis. The function's output is a set of possible solutions. Often equated with creativity, the alternative generation process is not well understood. Alternatives are typically generated through analytical thinking, recall from memory, or imaginative consideration of possible worlds. Many creativity methods support alternative generation, though most are weak and unreliable.

## Case-Based QPS

Another way of developing an in-depth account of quality problem solving involves case-based reasoning (CBR), a methodology devised by artificial intelligence researchers. "A general paradigm for reasoning from experience,"[11] case-based reasoning is often employed when problem solving cannot be based on scientific laws or principles. Lacking such, solutions to problems are derived from experiences with similar situations. A CBR system consists of a database of cases and a procedure for retrieving cases pertinent to the task at hand. Such systems have been used in negotiation, planning, and design tasks, among others.

Case-based QPS, a strategy for solving quality problems, parallels the approach adopted in CBR systems. Prior experience is used to identify problem-solving insights and solution alternatives. As depicted in Figure 1.3,[12] lessons learned from experience have different levels of generality. A situation can suggest general rules—for instance, identify all possible causes—as well as specific lessons applicable only

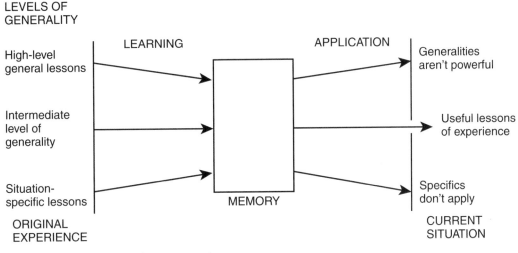

**Figure 1.3** Learning from experience

Adapted and reprinted with permission from *Quality Management Journal*, Fall 1994.

to the case at hand. Useful insights usually occur at an intermediate level of generality. In contrast to case-specific lessons, these are applicable to situations other than those in which they were learned. Unlike high-level generalities, intermediate lessons offer real problem-solving power. Some useful lessons of experience are more or less general than others, but most occupy this intermediate range.

Case-based QPS involves three activities:

1. A large and varied set of experiences of quality problems and problem solving is accumulated.
2. Lessons with a useful level of generality are abstracted from those experiences.
3. The lessons are organized to make them accessible to practitioners.

Performance of the first task is facilitated by the large literature of QPS cases, published reports of attempts to solve quality problems. Cases can be found in practitioner journals, in books on quality management, and in organizational records of activities by internal problem-solving teams. Although some published QPS cases are not detailed enough to support the needed analysis, many satisfy the requirements for the second step. Here the task is analytical: Think through each case, identifying lessons that could be applied in other situations. Many cases offer no such insights. Their lessons are either situation-specific or obvious and general. But some cases yield noteworthy problem-solving insights.

Over a thousand cases published in hundreds of sources were read in preparation for writing this book. Case sources are identified in Appendix A. Many of the cases were relatively mundane or lacked detail needed to support the required analysis. Ultimately, 719 cases drawn from 242 sources were written up and analyzed, forming the research base for the book's findings. These figures do not include a much smaller set of unpublished cases, perhaps a dozen, drawn from the author's personal experience, which appear sporadically in the text. Most of the 719 cases were cited in the book; some offered multiple lessons and were cited more than once.

Lessons drawn from cases were organized into chapters defined by problem types and problem-solving functions. Within chapters, lessons were organized in a manner appropriate for the topic. It quickly became apparent that there is no right way of organizing the material, either within or across chapters. Nor is there a "correct" location for individual cases within an organizing scheme. Lessons to be learned from a case could be variously construed, suggesting different places for the case to be cited in the text.

## Overview of the Book

The purpose of this book is to develop a broader and deeper account of quality problem solving that will be of value to people trying to solve complex, real-world problems.

This purpose is pursued in various ways. The book includes evaluative discussions of the QPS literature with special emphasis on popular problem-solving methods. The book tries to improve the reader's understanding of problems and problem solving, as through a discussion of human cognition. It implements a detailed functional and problem-driven account of QPS that is built on insights developed through case-based reasoning.

Chapter 2 covers problem-solving fundamentals. Cognitive, functionalist, and problem-driven approaches to problem solving are discussed. This chapter provides readers with a solid understanding of problem solving. Much of the material is conceptual and somewhat demanding. While Chapter 2 is a foundation for the treatment of QPS that follows, readers who skip this chapter will still be able to understand and profit from the book.

Chapters 3 through 6 address important functional demands—problem identification, problem definition, diagnosis, and alternative generation—posed by quality problems. Chapters 7 through 11 each deal with one of the five types of quality problems. These nine chapters include descriptions and assessments of QPS techniques pertinent to each function or problem type. The chapters also include discussions of cases illustrating useful problem-solving insights and tactics. Chapter 12 is a brief concluding statement that suggests additional means of improving quality problem solving.

## NOTES

1. *Newsweek,* 7 September 1992, 48–49.
2. *Fortune,* 10 October 1988, 80–88.
3. W. Edwards Deming, *Out of the Crisis* (Cambridge: MIT Center for Advanced Engineering Study, 1986).
4. As cited in: Mary Walton, *The Deming Management Method* (New York: Perigee, 1986).
5. Masaaki Imai, "Solving Quality Problems Using Common Sense," *International Journal of Quality and Reliability Management* 9, no. 5 (1992): 71–75.
6. Philip B. Crosby, *Quality is Free* (New York: Penguin Books, 1979): 129.
7. The stakeholder view of quality was proposed in: Gerald F. Smith, "The Meaning of Quality," *Total Quality Management* 4 (1993): 235–244.
8. Joseph M. Juran, "The Quality Function," sect. 2 in *Juran's Quality Control Handbook,* 4th ed., Joseph M. Juran and Frank M. Gryna, eds. (New York: McGraw-Hill, 1988).
9. Geary A. Rummler and Alan P. Brache, *Improving Performance* (San Francisco: Jossey-Bass, 1990): 2.
10. Figure 1.2 is an adaptation of material in: Gerald F. Smith, "Quality Problem Solving: Scope and Prospects," *Quality Management Journal* 2 (1994): 25–40.
11. Stephen Slade, "Case-Based Reasoning: A Research Paradigm," *AI Magazine* 12, no. 1 (1991): 42–55.
12. Figure 1.3 first appeared in: Gerald F. Smith, "Quality Problem Solving: Scope and Prospects." See note 10.

# Problem-Solving Fundamentals

---

## Chapter Outline

This chapter is a mini-course on problem solving. Few of its contents are specific to QPS, and one can read and understand subsequent chapters without having read this one. The chapter is intended primarily for readers who want a broader, deeper understanding of problem solving on which to build their understanding of QPS. Problem solving is considered from three perspectives. First is the cognitive approach, which views problem solving as an individual thought process. The cognitive account of thinking underlies most current psychological research on problem solving. The second perspective is functionalist, conceiving problem solving as the performance of certain tasks or functions. Since most problem-solving methods are function-based, the chapter includes a discussion of problem-solving techniques. Finally, the chapter outlines a problem-based approach to problem solving. It considers how problems can be characterized and classified in ways that enable effective responses. The chapter provides readers with a working language for thinking about problems and problem solving. Important terms in this language are printed in bold when introduced.

# Cognitive Processes

## Cognitivism

During the past four decades, researchers from many fields, including psychology, artificial intelligence (AI), philosophy, and neuroscience, have developed the cognitive account of human thinking.[1] **Cognitivism** has had an enormous impact on problem-solving research, providing a sophisticated scientific understanding of mental structures and processes.

Cognitivism holds that whenever one is thinking about something, a **mental representation** of that thing is being processed in some way. The notion of mental representation may seem strange, but it is difficult to conceive of thinking without it. Thoughts are about things; they have content. One can think about Abraham Lincoln, a neighbor's dog, or how to machine a tightly toleranced part. While thinking presumably goes on in one's head, whatever one thinks about cannot be there for the event. This apparent paradox is resolved by assuming that not Lincoln himself, but something that stands for or represents Lincoln, participates in the thought process. Thus, the "stuff" of dreams, hopes, ideas, imaginings, and other thoughts are mental representations.

Computers illustrate this notion. Computers process data and instructions that are symbolic representations of something else, such as the balance in your checking account. For this information, initially represented in the English language and decimal system, to be processed, it must be translated into electronic states that symbolize the information's content. Cognitivists assert that minds, like computers, represent and process symbolic information.

If mental representations are the content of thinking, what is the thinking process like? Many cognitivists simply claim that thinking is **information processing**, activity in which informational inputs are transformed into conclusions. Others make the bolder assertion that thinking is a **computational** process, essentially the same as processing performed by computers. Minds and computers possess the same information processing capacities, embodying them in different physical media. The claim that minds and computers are fundamentally of a kind underlies artificial intelligence attempts to program computers to behave intelligently. During the 1980s, **connectionism** emerged as an alternative account of mental processing. Looking to the brain rather than computers for insight, connectionists model the mind as a dense network of simple processors. Knowledge is mentally represented by patterns of activation over this network. Connectionism reflects the convergence of cognitive science with neuroscience, the physiological study of the brain.

Theoretical disputes have not kept cognitivists from addressing practical questions. Cognitive scientists have studied the diagnostic activities of physicians, the design efforts of computer programmers, and the processes by which securities analysts forecast stock prices. Some of this research is reflected in **expert systems**, computer programs using AI methods and knowledge elicited from human experts to perform mentally demanding real-world tasks. Most cognitive research addresses relatively well-structured tasks in areas having clear boundaries.

## The Life of the Mind

Cognitive scientists view the mind as encompassing a variety of contents and activities. The most important of these are listed in Figure 2.1. They are the usual chapter titles for cognitive psychology texts and the research areas with which scientists identify. Each concept will be explained and its role in practical problem solving considered.

*Perception.* **Perception** is the process by which people acquire information from the outside world. It includes all the senses, though research has focused on visual and speech perception. The perceptual process begins with **sensation**, the pick-up of energy, such as light waves, by a sense organ. It culminates in **recognition**, matching a perceptual input with information stored in memory. Recognition is context-sensitive: We perceive stimuli as things that make sense in that situation. Thus, perception is affected by prior beliefs and expectations, though scientists disagree about the extent of these influences.

Perception permeates human activity, including problem solving. Its role is critical in problem identification, where failure to pick up relevant information or to

**Perception:** The process of acquiring information through one's senses.

**Attention:** A limited store of conscious capacity that is allocated to selected stimuli and activities.

**Memory:** The physical store in which knowledge is held and related processes for adding to and retrieving from that store.

**Knowledge Representation:** The different ways in which knowledge might be represented in the mind.

**Categories:** The mental distinctions or concepts we use to understand the world.

**Learning:** The process of increasing knowledge or acquiring a skill.

**Motivation:** The goals or values that inspire human activity.

**Judgment:** Weighing and combining relevant factors to reach a conclusion.

**Reasoning:** Inference, a means of using evidence or arguments to reach a conclusion.

**Creativity:** Imagination, the ability to conceive of things or possibilities that do not exist.

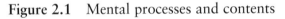

**Figure 2.1**  Mental processes and contents

recognize a situation as problematic can be disastrous. Perceptual powers can be exploited by diagrammatic techniques that help one see important problem elements and relationships. Though people cannot be told to see better, they can be trained to develop reasonable expectations, to know what to look for in certain situations.

*Attention.*   Attention is a resource or capacity, often identified with **consciousness** or **awareness. Intuition** is best viewed as unconscious mental processing. Psychologists have traditionally regarded attention as a filter that provides "overload protection" against the "blooming, buzzing confusion" of multiple perceptual inputs. It functions as a gatekeeper deciding what gets in the door. Attention has an output-side role as well, coordinating activities one is undertaking. **Controlled processes**—writing a report, for instance—require conscious attention. **Automatic processes** use few attentional resources so multiple tasks can be performed simultaneously, such as walking and chewing gum. Activities become automated with practice; tasks requiring minimal attention from experts demand the total concentration of novices.

Attention failures can delay problem identification. With many issues vying for attention, it is easy to ignore something that should be addressed right away. Attentional capacity can not be increased, but it can be supported by memory aids that keep issues from falling into oblivion. Inattention during routine performances can be countered by mistake-proofing devices that prompt desired behaviors.

***Memory.*** Intelligent agents must be able to store and use information acquired through experience, hence the existence of **memory.** What kinds of information are stored in memory? Scientists distinguish between **declarative** and **procedural knowledge,** "knowing that" and "knowing how." They also differentiate between **long-term** and **short-term** or **working memory.** Long-term memory has an effectively infinite capacity (No, Johnny, your brain won't run out of room from too much studying!). However, it can take considerable effort to store information in long-term memory, and it may be difficult to recall the information when needed. In contrast, short-term memory is like a convenience store: Easy in, easy out. What it lacks is storage space. The term "seven plus or minus two" refers to the approximate number of information items that can be held in short-term memory at one time.

Most knowledge used in solving real-world problems comes from personal experience. Consequently, memory retrieval is a critical activity. Many problem-solving techniques are retrieval cues, devices that aid recall. Some books on problem-solving prescribe mnemonic techniques for improving memory. These may bolster one's ability to remember specific items of information—the names of new acquaintances, for example—but they are unlikely to help one recall general experiential knowledge for problem solving purposes.

***Knowledge Representation.*** The view that thinking involves the processing of mental representations raises the question of how knowledge is represented in the mind. Declarative knowledge might be organized into **semantic networks** that connect different items of information by relational links. Semantic networks shade into **schemas,** elaborate knowledge structures that people activate in relevant situations. One has a schema for cat, for living room, for political campaign, and so on. **Mental models** are powerful ways of representing certain kinds of knowledge. The notion of **mental imagery,** seeing with the "mind's eye," has inspired controversy over whether a special representational system supports this capacity.

Conceivably, problem solving could be improved if knowledge was represented appropriately when taught. Unfortunately, it is difficult to determine what the right representations are.

***Categories.*** Closely related to schema is the notion of **mental concept** or **category.** Concepts are the simplest elements of thought. They correspond to words in a natural language and to kinds of things in the world. **Concept formation** is the process by which people develop a new notion or unit of meaning. It was long believed that our concepts have strict definitional lines. For example, a bachelor is an unmarried, adult male; whatever satisfies these criteria is a bachelor. Cognitive research suggests that criteria for concepts are flexible. Is the Pope a bachelor? It has been proposed that concepts are formed around prototypes, instances possessing typical features of things in that category. Some things are better instances of a concept than others by virtue of being more like the prototype. Because of its size, a peach is a more typical fruit than a watermelon.

Concepts are important in problem solving due to the likelihood that people develop problem categories. Physicians use disease categories when diagnosing and treating patients. Categorization can be an effective problem-solving strategy if categories reflect key features of related problems. The problem-based approach to problem solving, discussed later, tries to develop more powerful problem categories for managerial problem solving.

*Learning.*   **Learning** is the means by which people increase their knowledge and improve their skill. One can learn explicit declarative knowledge (such as the capitals of countries) as well as broad concepts and generalizations (such as the meaning of justice). One can also acquire procedural knowledge or skill. In rote learning, the content to be learned is directly available to the subject. In learning by example or analogy, the content must be abstracted from instances. **Skill acquisition** is a multistage process. Performance improves from a halting, error-prone activity to one that is effortlessly automatic as effective procedures are developed and refined. Practice is the *sine qua non* for acquiring a skill.

People learn how to use problem-solving methods. Those frequently exposed to certain kinds of problems develop related skills. However, the range of managerial problems is too great, compared to the limits of personal experience, for anyone to become skilled in dealing with all such situations. Alternatively, one can learn from the experiences of others, as through the case-based learning approach adopted in this book.

*Motivation.*   The English language includes a rich vocabulary of motivational concepts: need, desire, want, value, preference, utility, goal, objective, and purpose. Loose distinctions can be made among these. Wants, needs, and desires usually refer to motivations with a physiological basis, such as the need for food and warmth. Values typically derive from social and cultural influences. Economists speak of individual preferences and use utility as a general measure of value. Managers think of goals and objectives as consciously adopted performance targets, goals being more specific.

Motivations are highly relevant to problem solving, which involves changing reality to match one's desires. Two key functional demands—identifying relevant objectives in a situation and evaluating alternatives in light of those objectives—derive from the motivated nature of problem solving.

*Judgment.*   **Judgment** is a process in which information on pertinent factors is weighed and combined to reach a conclusion. Consider the judges in diving competitions: They look at aspects of a contestant's performance, trading off strengths and weaknesses to arrive at a score for that person. Though guidelines for reaching conclusions can be specified, judgment involves subjective weighing and combining activities that cannot be fully proceduralized.

Its importance in problem solving, especially decision making, has inspired prescriptive research aimed at improving human judgment. Some argue that human judges should be replaced by mathematical models, an approach that can be effective in certain circumstances. Attempts have been made to train people to avoid flawed judgmental practices, but few have achieved lasting results.

*Reasoning.*   Also called **inference, reasoning** is an overt, verbal means of drawing conclusions from data. One states reasons or arguments supporting a conclusion. Scientists have historically been concerned with **deduction,** a strict, logical means of drawing conclusions from premises. Deductive reasoning is guaranteed to yield true conclusions if the rules of logic are correctly applied to true premises. **Induction** is reasoning that moves from instances to a general rule. Having observed many crows, all of which were black, a person might inductively conclude that all crows are black. **Practical reasoning** is the means by which people draw conclusions in daily affairs. Also referred to as **informal logic,** it encompasses inductive, causal, and analogical reasoning, and much more. For instance, in trying to predict how employees will respond to a new compensation plan, a manager might adopt a means-ends form of reasoning that considers employees' goals and the means they can use to achieve their goals.

Reasoning has a prominent role in real-world problem solving. Witness the argumentative content of group problem-solving sessions. Participants make claims about a problem's nature, causes, and potential solutions, supporting their claims with reasoned arguments. People are susceptible to inferential errors, including the **fallacies of informal logic.** Critical thinking courses try to improve students' reasoning skills. Because it is a conscious verbal process, reasoning is amenable to improvement efforts.

*Creativity.*   An important, if poorly defined, notion, associated with **imagination, creativity** is the means by which humans conceive possibilities. Creative performances are not proceduralized; the process does not follow a recipe. Creativity is evident when the products of such activity are both original and valuable. Cognitivists argue that creative thinking involves the same mental contents and processes as normal thinking. Rather than being a unitary process, creativity employs various mental capacities, including associative memory, mental imagery, and analogical reasoning. Stage theories of creativity have been proposed. One theory, for instance, lists preparation, incubation, illumination, and verification.[2] Other accounts emphasize the need to overcome mental blocks and barriers.

Creativity is important in solving real-world problems. In addition to generating solution alternatives, problem solvers conceive possible causes, goals, and constraints pertaining to the problem situation. Discussed in Chapter 6, creativity techniques are numerous, but often ineffective. Better understanding of the mental underpinnings of creative thought may enable development of more powerful methods.

## Belief Processing

One can view most conscious mental activity, problem solving included, as belief processing, developing beliefs that reflect the way the world is or will be. **Beliefs** are mentally represented statements claimed to be true. One believes on the basis of **evidence;** strongly supported beliefs are regarded as **knowledge.** Belief processing employs evidence from perception and information recalled from memory. Conclusions can be reached by observation, through judgment, or by reasoning.

Erroneous beliefs and faulty belief processing activities can doom problem solving to failure. Consider the following cases:

---

**case 2.1**

Samples drawn from a facility producing a blended catalyst exhibited high variability. A study revealed that it took 16 hours to mix the product. Operators had been sampling after 12 hours of mixing, mistakenly believing the product would be fully blended by then.

---

**case 2.2**

A company selling consumer durables experienced declining sales of service parts. Competitors used general retail outlets to sell generic parts at lower prices. Despite warnings from distributors, company management persisted in its belief that the firm faced minimal competition in the service parts market. Sales declines were attributed to alleged improvements in the durability of original equipment.

---

Mistaken beliefs can cause problems to occur (Case 2.1), delay their identification (Case 2.2), and short-circuit diagnostic activity. Erroneous beliefs can reflect false assumptions (Case 2.1), or they can occur if people fail to revise existing beliefs in light of new information (Case 2.2). They can also result from faulty mental activities.

Psychologists have demonstrated that people use mental **heuristics**—informal, quick-and-dirty methods—to reach conclusions.[3] Though often effective, heuristics can lead to erroneous beliefs. The representativeness heuristic uses similarity as a basis for drawing conclusions: A job applicant might be rejected because he reminds the interviewer of an obnoxious colleague. Using the availability heuristic, one assesses the likelihood of an event by considering the ease with which past instances can be recalled. This can be misleading if unusual events are more memorable than common ones. People make estimates by starting from a salient initial value, or anchor, and adjusting in the direction deemed appropriate. This tendency reflects the anchoring-and-adjustment heuristic. The asking prices of real estate and automobiles are anchors that potential buyers adjust downward, often insufficiently, when making offers.

Figure 2.2 lists common mental mistakes. Everyone is vulnerable to these pitfalls, and their practical impact can be substantial. Corporations can acquire poorly performing companies when executives operating under the **illusion of control** mistakenly assume they can turn things around. **Groupthink** has been implicated as a

**Attribution errors:** Explaining the behavior of others in terms of individual dispositions, while explaining one's own behavior in terms of situational factors. Attributing good outcomes to skill and bad outcomes to uncontrollable external factors.

**Belief perseverance:** Persisting in one's beliefs despite evidence showing them to be mistaken.

**Biases due to the organization of memory:** The structure of memory makes some things easier to recall than others, affecting their judged likelihood.

**Confirmation bias:** Looking for evidence that will confirm a hypothesis, rather than looking for disconfirming information.

**Conjunction fallacy:** Thinking it more likely that two events will occur together than that just one of the events will occur.

**Escalation of commitment:** Persisting in a course of action that has no real chance of success.

**Framing effects:** The way a problem or situation is framed or verbally represented can influence preferences among alternatives.

**Groupthink:** Striving for unanimity, group members fail to realistically evaluate proposed courses of action.

**Hindsight bias:** After the fact, overestimating the degree to which one could have predicted an outcome. The "I knew it all along" illusion.

**Illusion of control:** Overestimating the influence one has over events and outcomes.

**Insensitivity to base rates:** Ignoring prior probabilities in favor of data that is less informative.

**Insensitivity to sample size:** Overestimating the validity of conclusions based on small sample sizes.

**Insufficient adjustment:** When making judgments, not adjusting enough from an initial anchor in the likely direction of the actual value.

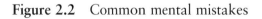

**Figure 2.2**   Common mental mistakes

**Misconceptions of chance:** Committing the "Gambler's Fallacy" of thinking random processes have a memory and assuming that sequences of random events will look random.

**Overconfidence:** Being overconfident in judgments; thinking one knows more than one really does.

**Regression to the mean:** Failing to realize that extreme performances tend to be followed by performances closer to the average.

**Selective perception:** Seeing what one expects to see, what one hopes to see, and the kinds of things that roles and training lead one to look for.

**Vividness and recency biases:** Events that are striking and that happened recently are more easily recalled, so their likelihoods tend to be overestimated.

**Wishful thinking:** Allowing hopes and desires to improperly influence one's beliefs about the future.

**Figure 2.2** (*continued*)

cause of military and governmental decision-making mistakes, including President Kennedy's Bay of Pigs fiasco. New product and systems development projects, as well as bank loans and other investments, frequently give rise to **escalation of commitment:** Rather than admitting failure, people throw good money after bad. **Attribution errors** are evident in corporate annual reports that blame poor company performance on a hostile environment, while crediting good results to management excellence.

But these mental shortcomings are only part of the story. There is a long tradition, dating to the classical Greeks and Romans, that studies errors in practical reasoning. Figure 2.3 identifies common fallacies of informal logic. These too have practical implications. The **slippery slope** fallacy was evident in the "domino theory" used to support U.S. intervention in Vietnam. Corporate executives have justified diversification moves with the **false analogy** that a company, like a stool, needs at least three legs to be stable. People overreact to atypical events as a result of **hasty generalization.** The fact that a valued employee has quit does not imply that a company's compensation program is inadequate.

The most common weakness in practical reasoning, as in problem solving, is incompleteness. Poor outcomes result not so much from the mistakes we make as from the possibilities we overlook. When developing a position on an issue, people

**Accent:** Uncertainty about where stress should fall or what tone is intended creates uncertain meanings.

**Amphiboly:** Poor sentence structure yields unintended meanings.

**Appeal to authority:** Citing an authority that has no special knowledge.

**Appeal to fear:** Using threats to advance one's claim.

**Appeal to ignorance:** Improperly shifting the burden of proof by insisting that the inability to disprove one's position is proof of its validity.

**Appeal to moderation:** Adopting a compromise or middle road alternative, irrespective of its merits.

**Appeal to novelty:** Assuming something is good or right because it is new.

**Appeal to pity:** Exploiting sympathy to gain support for one's claim.

**Appeal to tradition:** Assuming something is good or right because it is old.

**Apriorism:** Certain principles, assumed to be beyond dispute, overrule observed facts.

**Begging the question:** Arguing for a claim by advancing evidence having the same meaning as the claim itself.

**Bifurcation:** Presuming that a classification is exclusive and exhaustive, typically that only two alternatives (either/or) exist.

**Complex questions:** A loaded question presumes that a prior question has been answered in a certain way.

**Composition:** Assuming that what is true of the parts must be true of the whole.

**Division:** Assuming that what is true of the whole must be true of the parts.

**Figure 2.3** Fallacies of informal logic

**Equivocation:** The meaning of a key term shifts during an argument.

**False analogy:** Inferring on the basis of irrelevant similarity.

**False cause:** Claiming, without evidence, that events are causally connected.

**False dilemma:** Assuming that there are only two possibilities, neither of which is acceptable.

**Genetic fallacy:** Rejecting an argument because of its source.

**Hasty generalization:** Reaching a general conclusion on the basis of a small sample or exceptional instance.

**Irrelevant thesis:** Trying to prove a conclusion other than the one at issue.

**Non-anticipation:** Assuming that everything worth doing has already been done.

**Personal attack:** Challenging the character or credibility of one's opponent.

**Poisoning the well:** Making a nonfalsifiable claim, such that any evidence could be interpreted as supporting one's position.

**Reification:** Treating an abstraction as if it were a real thing.

**Sweeping generalization:** A general rule is applied to an exceptional case.

**Slippery slope:** An alternative is assumed to be the first step in an inescapable progression towards an undesirable outcome.

**Special pleading:** Adopting a double standard vis-à-vis one's opponent.

**Unobtained perfection:** Rejecting an achievable improvement for an unachievable ideal.

**Figure 2.3** (*continued*)

propose only one or a few arguments supporting their side. They do not consider many other arguments that could be developed for and against their position. Problem solvers often adopt narrow problem definitions that exclude relevant concerns. They fail to recognize other stakeholders and values implicated in the situation and do not generate an adequate set of solution alternatives. Warning people against mental shortcomings and inferential mistakes is a good start, but they must also be taught to pursue a broad, open-minded course in their thinking and problem solving.

# Problem-Solving Functions

Problem solving is usually described in terms of certain tasks or **functions.** Functions are more abstract and problem-centered than cognitive processes. When a function is the key challenge a situation presents, it can define a problem type. Architects and engineers talk about design problems, because this functionally defined problem type is prominent in their professional practices. Most problems pose multiple functional demands.

Some have argued that problem solving involves a standard sequence of functionally defined activities, so that the process can be represented as a stage or phase model. Figure 2.4 is typical. The claim that problem solving follows a strict functional order may be motivated by the conceptual necessity of certain sequences: A problem must be formulated before alternatives can be generated, alternatives must be generated before they can be evaluated, and so forth. However, experience suggests that problem solving is not a strict linear process, and research has not found a strong sequence of activities. Information received from memory or external sources can prompt a return to functions previously addressed. Most functional models now contain provisions for backtracking.

A more modest claim is that problem solving consists of a standard set of functions. Proponents might argue that every problem-solving activity falls under one of the four elements of Figure 2.4. Such claims can be hard to refute when functions are loosely defined. Problem formulation is a messy concept that can be construed to include almost any problem-solving activity short of finding the solution. If functions are defined more precisely, the claim is surely false. A function like diagnosis can be the key requirement for solving certain problems (such as sales below budget), but be totally irrelevant to others (like locating a new plant). Real-world problems are varied. Some functions are performed in all cases; many only pertain to certain kinds of problems. Thus, while problem solving can be viewed as the performance of functions, there is no strong sequence of functions nor is any set of functions necessary and sufficient for the solution of every problem.

Figure 2.5 lists significant functions performed as part of practical problem solving. Four of these—problem identification, problem definition, diagnosis, and alternative generation—were discussed in the last chapter. The others are reviewed here.

**Research.** It is often necessary when solving problems to collect information beyond that available from memory. Such activities comprise the **research** function. The research process consists of data collection and analysis. Primary research collects original data; secondary research uses existing information, such as might be

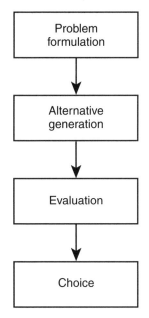

Figure 2.4   Functional model of problem solving

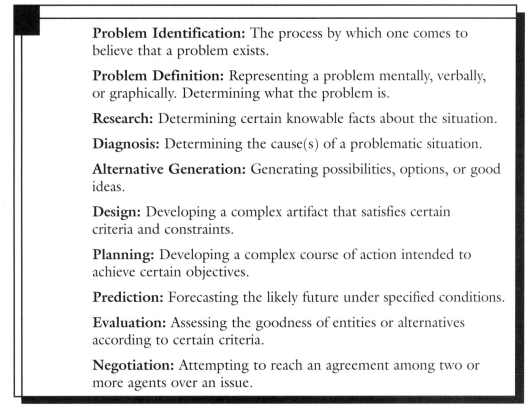

**Problem Identification:** The process by which one comes to believe that a problem exists.

**Problem Definition:** Representing a problem mentally, verbally, or graphically. Determining what the problem is.

**Research:** Determining certain knowable facts about the situation.

**Diagnosis:** Determining the cause(s) of a problematic situation.

**Alternative Generation:** Generating possibilities, options, or good ideas.

**Design:** Developing a complex artifact that satisfies certain criteria and constraints.

**Planning:** Developing a complex course of action intended to achieve certain objectives.

**Prediction:** Forecasting the likely future under specified conditions.

**Evaluation:** Assessing the goodness of entities or alternatives according to certain criteria.

**Negotiation:** Attempting to reach an agreement among two or more agents over an issue.

Figure 2.5   Problem-solving functions

found in a library. Problem solving employs the same research methods as science. The most important is direct observation, consciously attending to the phenomenon of interest. Experimentation can be used to diagnose causes and design products. Quality practitioners use surveys to determine customer needs and employee attitudes. Data analysis is facilitated by check sheets, scatter diagrams, run charts, histograms, and other graphic means of displaying data.

***Design.***   In some situations, **design,** the development of a system or artifact, is the key problem-solving task. In others—corporate acquisitions, for instance—it is totally absent. A designed artifact must satisfy the needs of users as well as constraints imposed by the context of use. The design process is decompositional: A designer generates a high-level design concept, a sense of what the artifact should be like, and breaks that down into components and subcomponents, solving design subproblems as they appear. Designers usually do not create the artifact, but rather a plan for its construction. Design methods support the identification of user needs, the decomposition process, and the generation of alternatives. This book treats design as a problem type. Product and process design are discussed in Chapters 10 and 11 respectively.

***Planning.***   Closely related to design, **planning** is the development of complex courses of action. It is difficult because of the need to coordinate activities to achieve a goal in the face of uncertainty about the environment and action-outcome relationships: If we do this, what will happen? Like design, the planning process uses decomposition, breaking goals into subgoals and devising subplans for their achievement. Quality problems rarely include planning as a significant activity, so planning techniques are not often used by QPS practitioners.

***Prediction.***   The **prediction** function is concerned with forecasting future states of affairs. Some problems, such as forecasting commodity prices, are prediction tasks pure and simple. Others involve no noteworthy predictive activity. Prediction tasks are addressed by forecasting techniques, most of which use historical data and mathematical models. Lack of needed data or knowledge can require the use of subjective forecasting methods. Like planning, prediction is rarely a critical function in solving quality problems.

***Evaluation.***   Solution alternatives must be assessed for goodness or compared with each other so the best can be selected. This is the role of the **evaluation** function. Evaluation is the key process in solving decision problems: Which candidate should we hire? It presumes the existence of criteria for assessing alternatives. Evaluation is a judgmental process, a matter of weighing and combining an alternative's scores on individual criteria into an overall measure of worth. The paramount evaluative difficulty in real-world problems is identifying pertinent criteria. Evaluation is addressed by decision techniques and is discussed in Chapter 6.

***Negotiation.***   The **negotiation** function pertains to situations in which two or more parties must try to reach an agreement. A relatively specialized function, less prevalent than the foregoing, in some situations it is of the essence. The negotiation process is one of bargaining, or trading concessions, and persuasion, or convincing people to adopt certain beliefs. Scientists have developed negotiation techniques and heuristics of practical value. Negotiation tasks often appear when solutions to quality problems are being implemented. They are rarely found during quality problem solving itself.

# Problem-Solving Methods

This section takes a prescriptive look at problem solving, discussing issues regarding problem-solving methods. The terms **method** and **technique** are used interchangeably. A **heuristic** is an informal method or piece of advice that is easy to use but not always effective. The term **strategy** denotes a high-level approach to solving a problem.

At bottom, every problem-solving method is a means of performing one or both of two tasks: collecting information and drawing conclusions. By collecting information, one constructs a mental representation or definition of a situation on which basis conclusions are drawn about how to act. Different kinds of information are collected and conclusions are drawn for different purposes, such as identifying the problem, diagnosing its causes, and designing alternatives. Information can be collected from the outside world or from the memories of individuals. Conclusions can be drawn through judgment and reasoning or according to formal procedures.

Every problem-solving method has a language, a set of concepts with which it represents problems and solutions. Some languages are technical, their terms employed almost exclusively by the technique. Because real-world problem solving is shaped by the experiential knowledge of participants, most methods are devices for eliciting knowledge from memory. These methods use natural language terms that connect to relevant experiences.

## Evaluation Criteria

Like the patent medicines of yesteryear, problem-solving methods are not subject to independent performance reviews. A technique can be promoted on the mere claim that, once upon a time, it was applied with seemingly beneficial effects in the Alpha Division of Beta Company. Never mind the unreported occasions on which the technique was used to no avail. Lacking an Underwriter's Laboratory to certify that problem-solving methods meet substantive performance standards, practitioners must become more sophisticated consumers of these products.

The first step in doing so is to recognize three criteria for evaluating methods: generality, power, and operationality. **Generality** refers to the size of a method's domain, the number and variety of problems to which it applies. General methods can be productively employed in many situations. Like broad-scope antibiotics, they are useful in treating all sorts of maladies. Most methods are only applicable in certain situations. Instructions for using techniques should identify the types of problems to which they can be usefully applied.

**Power** is a method's ability to deliver solutions for problems in its domain. It has several dimensions: the likelihood the method will solve a problem in its domain, the quality of the solutions it delivers, and the amount of resources (time, effort, etc.) needed to achieve these results. A perfectly powerful method would find optimal solutions for every problem in its domain at virtually no cost. An example would be a cheap drug that always cures a particular ailment quickly and with no side effects.

A third criterion, **operationality,** applies when user contributions are part of a method's implementation. Operationality is the degree to which people can reliably perform tasks assigned them in a way that yields acceptable results. Sometimes a method is not operational because it assumes the availability of information that cannot be collected by feasible research efforts. More often, methods are not operational because they require exceptional mental performances. "Identify all possible causes." How? "Creatively envision alternatives." Tell me more.

An almost inevitable trade-off exists between generality and power. To be powerful, a method must exploit certain problem characteristics. In doing so, it loses generality. Consequently, there are no strong general methods for solving problems. If one existed, it would be universally taught and applied, and all our problems would be solved. The relationship between generality and operationality is much the same. General methods consist of abstract, all-purpose instructions that cannot be reliably discharged.

These trade-offs underlie the **Functionalist Dilemma,** which applies to general problem-solving methods and to standardized functional descriptions of problem solving. Standard, one-size-fits-all models ignore the fact that different problems require the performance of different functions and that given functions be performed in different ways. Lacking an adequate account of problems and a way of tailoring prescriptions to the demands of the problem at hand, methodologists are faced with an unappealing choice. They can prescribe vacuous generalities (for example, "synthesize a solution"), or offer pointed advice that will be wrong for most problems. The way out of this dilemma is to characterize problems in ways enabling one to devise powerful, operational methods suited to the demands of particular situations. This requires a problem-driven approach, described later in the chapter.

Of the three criteria for evaluating methods, only power can be measured with precision and then only for certain formal techniques. Nonetheless, it is helpful in deciding whether to learn or use a problem-solving method to make informal assessments against these criteria. With regard to generality, one should assess the size of a method's domain and the kinds of situations to which it applies. For power and operationality, an overall evaluation should be complemented by considering specific areas of inadequacy: situations in which solutions are likely to be of low quality, critical instructions that consistently exceed users' abilities, or types of problems that make excessive resource demands.

## Cognitive Strategies

**Cognitive strategies** are high-level mental practices used in solving problems. First identified through studies of people solving structured tasks, they are weak, but general, methods that informally guide much of our thinking. The simplest is **generate-and-test.** Also known as *trial and error,* it involves generating a candidate solution and testing to see if it works. The strategy can be effective if there are a limited number of possibilities that can be readily generated and easily tested for acceptability. If a combination lock can be opened by one of, say, a hundred settings, it is easy enough to try each until the correct setting is found. If the lock has a million settings, the strategy loses appeal.

Problem solving is often thought of as looking for a solution in a large "search space" of possibilities. Generate-and-test methods explore this space naively, as if there were no reason to consider some possibilities more promising than others. With **heuristic search,** knowledge is used to steer search in auspicious directions. One can use results of initial trials to decide if alternatives of that kind are promising. When one way of performing a task seems almost right, we explore near-variations, homing in on the solution.

**Hill-climbing** is a version of heuristic search in which one keeps moving in the direction of greatest improvement until no better move is possible. The top of the hill has been reached. If you are driving in a strange city and want to get downtown, you might stop at each intersection and proceed in the direction that seems busiest. In some problems where the goal state is known, the difficulty is to find a sequence of steps getting from here to there. Such cases lend themselves to **working backwards.** Say you have to perform errands before catching a plane. The easiest way to decide when to leave is to work backwards from the flight time, allowing time for errands and arrangements at the airport.

**Decomposition** is a common cognitive strategy that breaks complex problems into simple components. It is often used in design tasks. **Means-ends analysis** achieves a goal by decomposing it into subgoals and finding means to attain each of these. A teenage boy, intent on going to the prom, might set up such subgoals as successfully asking a girl for a date, learning how to dance, renting a tux, making dinner reservations, buying a corsage, arranging transportation, and acquiring the funds to pay for it all. He will consider different means—get a job, use savings, beg from parents—to achieve subgoals, and these will be further decomposed, if necessary, into activities that can be reliably performed.

Other heuristics have been proposed.[4] If the problem involves spatial relationships or a time sequence of events, draw a figure. Try solving a simpler problem, as by relaxing a constraint faced in the situation. Think of analogous problems. Try to solve part of the problem. Analyze the goal or unknown. Try to solve a more general problem. These are informal strategies used by expert problem solvers.

## Comprehensive Problem-Solving Methods

One family of problem-solving methods consists of multistep procedures for performing all activities needed to solve some or all problems. These are prescriptive versions of the descriptive stage models discussed earlier. Such methods claim that problem solving should follow a strict sequence of steps, though backtracking and iteration may be allowed. Among quality practitioners, the best known of these is the PDCA cycle, consisting of four steps: Plan, Do, Check, and Act. Methods with 13 or more steps have been proposed.

Most of these techniques include steps requiring one to identify the problem, define the problem, collect data, analyze data, generate causal candidates, test causal candidates, take corrective action, monitor results, and institutionalize improvements. Some methods are more detailed and consequently have more steps. Major differences arise when methods pertain to different kinds of problems. Most multistep techniques found in the quality literature apply to conformance problems. Those dealing with efficiency or design problems require different activities.

Comprehensive problem-solving methods tend to be highly general, applicable to any problem. As always, generality is purchased at the expense of power and operationality. With each of these methods, one can follow the prescribed steps with fanatical fervor without reaching a solution. The methods do not provide specific instructions for performing needed activities. The PDCA cycle exhibits this short-coming. "Plan" is a nebulous way of prescribing front-end problem-solving tasks, which presumably include identifying and defining the problem, collecting and ana-lyzing data, and generating causal hypotheses. The PDCA cycle may provide a framework within which problem-solving activities can be conducted, but the cycle does not describe in useful detail what these activities should be.

Elaborations of the PDCA cycle and similar methods have been proposed, but here we encounter the Functionalist Dilemma. As the specificity of its instructions increases, a method's generality decreases. Particular ways of defining problems, analyzing data, or testing hypotheses are not applicable in all situations. If you tell me in detail how to "plan," I will find that your instructions are often irrelevant or misleading. General problem-solving methods, like general functional models, are thwarted by the diversity of real world problems and the consequent need for a diversity of methods.

## Function-Specific Techniques

Most problem-solving methods address a particular functional part of problem solving, proposing a more or less detailed account of how to perform tasks like problem identification, diagnosis, and design. Because not all functions pertain to all problems, a technique may not be applicable in every situation. This book was not written to be a toolbox of QPS techniques, but it does refer to a sizable set of problem-solving methods. Many of these are briefly mentioned; some are explained and evaluated in detail. Figure 2.6 identifies many of the methods cited in later chapters, including all that receive significant attention. The methods are organized by function.

Each technique adopts a conceptualization of tasks with which it is concerned and employs particular strategies to aid task performance. As noted earlier, many techniques for solving real-world problems are prompts for eliciting experiential knowledge from memory. Some methods are built around diagrams. They prescribe the construction of graphic representations highlighting key problem elements and relationships.

Being function-specific, techniques of this kind are less general than compre-hensive problem-solving methods. It is important for methodologists to specify the functions and problem types to which a method pertains. In one reported case, diag-nostic techniques were used by a team trying to improve a manufacturing process. Team members became frustrated because there seemed to be no problem to diag-nose. There was a problem, a process design problem, but it did not entail diagnos-tic activity. The limited generality of function-specific techniques suggests that they are more powerful than comprehensive methods, and this is usually true. However,

**Problem Identification**
  Statistical Process Control
  Benchmarking
  Kokai Watch

**Problem Definition**
  Affinity Diagram
  Concept Map
  Situation Definition
    and Analysis Method

**Research**
  Stratification
  Check Sheet
  Histogram
  Run Chart
  Scatter Diagram
  Pareto Analysis

**Diagnosis**
  Experimentation
  Shainin Techniques
  Concentration Diagram
  Cause-and-Effect Diagram
  Kepner-Tregoe Method
  Why-Why Diagram
  Root Cause Analysis

**Alternative Generation**
  Brainstorming
  Nominal Group Technique
  Analytical Bootstrapping
    Creativity (ABC) Method

**Product Design**
  Quality Function Deployment
  Design for Manufacturing
  Concurrent Engineering
  Design for Reliability
  Failure Mode Effects Analysis
  Design for Maintainability
  Value Analysis
  Experimentation
  Taguchi Methods

**Process Design**
  Flow Chart
  Process Analysis
  Reengineering
  Benchmarking
  Soft Systems Methodology

**Evaluation**
  Prioritization Matrix
  Multi-Voting
  Force Field Analysis

**Figure 2.6** Problem-solving methods by function

real-world problems are ill-structured and the functional demands they pose can rarely be addressed by algorithmic procedures. All these techniques are low in power when compared with methods for solving structured problems. "Silver bullet" situations, in which a method will reliably deliver first-class solutions to difficult quality problems, are rare.

## Group Problem-Solving Methods

Problem-solving methods can be intended for group or individual use, and many can be employed in either way. One benefit of group problem solving is increased knowledge made available through multiple participants. In situations involving several specialized knowledge domains, group members collectively possess more relevant knowledge than any individual. But groups are advantageous even when the problem only involves everyday experiential knowledge. The reason: Having knowledge is not the same as being able to access it. While in a group, you often hear someone bring up a fact or insight that you knew yourself, but had not thought of. Having multiple problem solvers multiplies the chances of recalling knowledge held in common.

The major benefit of using groups to solve problems is improved memory recall and idea generation due to interactions among members. Where most problem-solving methods use questions to elicit knowledge, group methods use the participants. One person's ideas stimulate ideas of others. Members may have different perspectives on an issue, defining the problem in various ways, perhaps in terms of different problem categories. Someone who regards a situation as a communications problem will recall different knowledge than one who views it as an ethical dilemma. Both perspectives may be valuable. Differing views of a situation promote critical evaluation of assumptions and inferences made in reaching conclusions. Few people can effectively criticize their own ideas. In groups, each member provides a reality check on the thinking of others. In addition, the use of groups helps participants understand and buy into the chosen course of action, easing implementation.

Group problem solving has risks. When more than one person is involved, problem solving becomes a social process in which goals other than finding a solution may be paramount. Members may be motivated by a desire to make friends, to score debating points, or to curry favor with superiors. Never mind solving the problem. If infected by groupthink, the group can become a mindless bunch of cheerleaders, uncritically supporting an apparent consensus position. The group leader plays a key role in insuring that benefits of group problem solving are realized while potential costs are avoided.

The quality movement has promoted the use of problem-solving groups, from quality circles in Japan to cross-functional teams in the United States. Unfortunately, the legitimate benefits of groups are sometimes transformed into a myth of "group magic." Group performance ultimately rests on the performance of individuals. People generate and evaluate ideas and perform other thinking tasks; groups per se do not. Many group methods are weak devices that rely solely on interpersonal interaction. Group methods can be misapplied, as when voting is used in lieu of a critical evaluation of alternatives, which might be called "problem solving by democracy."[5] While groups should often be used in QPS, much can be done to improve group problem-solving performance.

# The Problem Side of Problem Solving

Effective problem solving is responsive to characteristics of the situation. Analysis of the problem can yield important insights, including structural similarities to previously encountered situations. A good solution to a problem is not good by accident. Rather, it exploits possibilities the situation allows. Such solutions are more likely to be recognized if one thinks about the situation and the possibilities it contains. The problem-centered strategy outlined in this section is distinctive compared to existing problem-solving research and practice in TQM and elsewhere.

## Problems and Their Structures

A problem-centered strategy promotes access to experiential knowledge. This is essential with real-world problems, where experience is the primary source of information. Experiential knowledge is not neatly stacked away in long-term memory to be readily accessed on demand. To recollect relevant knowledge, one needs to characterize the current situation in ways that cue memory recall. Problem analysis provides the needed characterization. It can suggest that the problem is of a certain type or possesses certain structural features, prompting recollection of similar past situations and problem-solving responses. Expert problem solvers perform in this way: They perceive situations in terms of problem types, activating knowledge pertinent to that type of situation.

Is a problem-centered strategy feasible? If every problem were unique, there would be no categories or structures to support analysis. Real-world problems are varied, and minor details can have dramatic solution effects. This diversity notwithstanding, problems exhibit significant commonalities. The existence of those commonalities is apparent in the application of problem-solving methods to many different situations and by the role problem categories play in expert problem solving. They appear in everyday discourse when people say things like, "This is a communications problem." Problems are like people: Different in many ways, they share commonalities as well.

Other reasons for believing in fundamental problem types and structures derive from the nature of human and social reality. People have basic needs and capacities. We all need to eat, sleep, and be warm, and we are all capable of certain mental and physical behaviors. These needs give rise to recurring and fundamental problems. In many parts of the world, the problem of finding food is a major task for most people every day. Add human capacities and new problem types are born. One person's hunger can be relieved by stealing from others, hence the problem of crime.

Consider the implications of a market economy, the institution in which agents exchange goods and services at prices set by the market. Though it promotes abundance through specialization and initiative, this institution gives rise to certain problems. Organizations encounter the product/market mission problem ("What should we make and to whom should we sell it?") and the revenue problem ("Sales are below budget"). Individuals face the parallel challenges of choosing a vocation and finding a job. Because organizations purchase costly inputs to create products for sale, they also experience the generic cost control problem of holding input costs as low as possible.

The fact that certain problems are similar is reflected in the notions of **problem type** and **problem category,** used interchangeably. Relatively broad ways of characterizing a problem, they refer to the situation as a whole. Categories are often indicated by labels, such as an "ethical dilemma." Problems are sometimes categorized in terms of their manifest content, or what they are about, such as a "morale problem." Some classifications are based on functional demands posed by a situation; a design problem is one example. Other types reflect a situation's structure, as in occasions on which someone is assigned responsibility but lacks authority needed to get things done.

The notions of **problem structure** and **situational structure,** also used interchangeably, refer to distinctive patterns or arrangements of the elements of situations. Structures may or may not be problematic, and they may only refer to part of the overall issue. Structures can be the basis for problem categories. For instance, a resource allocation problem (a problem type) is a situation in which an agent has one or more resources in limited supply to allocate over two or more uses. That describes the problem's structure.

A rarer structure, termed *pernicious procrastination,* can be described as follows: An agent faces an undesirable task or challenge that can be put off. The situation grows worse as a consequence of delay, causing the agent to continue delaying, perhaps indefinitely. My most memorable encounter with a situation like this was on a ski slope. An untutored amateur, I found it easy to head straight down the mountain, but hard to "christy" back and forth to control my speed. The more I delayed attempting a turn, the faster I went and the harder it was to turn. Fortunately, when I crashed, only a ski was broken. This structure is apparent in some people's relationships with their dentists. It also shows up in problems the IRS has with people who do not file tax returns.

**Problem analysis** is the thinking done and methods employed while pursuing a problem-centered approach to problem solving. The concept is deliberately open-ended, since a comprehensive problem analytic program has yet to be developed. The next section provides the beginning of such a program.

## Problem Analysis

---

**case 2.3: The Publishing Company Case.**

A publishing company has contracted with a husband and wife who have completed their first book, a finance text. To secure their commitment, the acquisitions editor promised the authors more-than-normal input into production decisions, including cover and text design. Now that the book has entered the editorial phase, difficulties have arisen for the production editor, who is responsible for finalizing the book's design and having it printed. The authors have been making numerous revisions to the text, often on the basis of seemingly whimsical aesthetic preferences. The production editor has been trying to limit the authors' changes, which increase costs and threaten to delay publication past the prime marketing season. As a result, the relationship between the production editor and authors has deteriorated. The authors are threatening to back out of the contract, claiming that the company has not done an acceptable job of producing their book.[6]

---

Certain generic issues can be raised in the analysis of this or any problem. Who are the stakeholders, what are their goals, what constraints prevent these goals from being achieved? One can also ask whether the situation is of an identifiable problem type. The Publishing Company Case is a negotiation problem, a disagreement between two parties, authors and publisher, a conflict they are trying to resolve.

Having identified a problem category, one can reflect on common concerns for such problems and on how this situation is distinctive from other problems of its kind. Some negotiation problems involve the allocation of costs or benefits, as in wage disputes between labor and management. Many, including the abortion controversy, involve incompatible goals. The disagreeing parties in the present case share the overriding goal of publishing a successful book. Their disagreement is about means—what must be done to make the book a success.

Difficulties often arise when people have invalid beliefs. The authors may be overestimating the impact of aesthetic factors and underestimating the importance of timely publication on the book's prospects for success. Since the company knows more about book-selling it should help the authors understand the importance of timely publication. As we know from experience, rancorous personal relationships can keep parties from reaching a mutually beneficial agreement. Someone other than the production editor should handle discussions with these authors.

It is often wise to ask how a problem came about: How did we get into this mess? The present situation resulted from a systemic failing. The acquisitions editor gave the authors more-than-normal control over production decisions, creating difficulties for the production editor. This larger problem is of a kind with situations common in organizations: One part of the organization does something that makes its job easier, while making work more difficult for other organization members. Sales promises delivery dates that Manufacturing must satisfy. R & D designs a product and "throws it over the wall" to Manufacturing, which must figure out how to build it. These "I'll buy now, you pay later" situations result from the interdependence of organizational activities. Upstream processors claim benefits for which downstream processors must bear costs. Having recognized the type, people can recall standard organizational responses. In the current case, one might require the acquisitions editor to obtain production editor approval before making special agreements with authors. The company could institute project teams that included all participants in the publication process. Incentives could be based on total project success, rather than individual performance. Thus, problem analysis leads to identification of a larger problem and of responses that can prevent the recurrence of situations like this.

Problem analysis is not a problem-solving method in the conventional sense. No seven-step procedure provides a rigorous analysis of any problem. It is a general approach to problem solving, fleshed out with specific aids and advice. The overall strategy is simple: Think about the problem! To operationalize this, problem analysis provides three kinds of mental tools: ways of characterizing situations, pitfalls to avoid during problem solving, and heuristics that aid the search for solutions.

Problem analysis starts with an attempt to characterize the situation. This provides insights that drive other analytic activities. Problems can be characterized in terms of basic components (agents, goals, constraints, causes, and so forth), situational structures, and more encompassing problem categories. Some components are applicable to all problems. For instance, every problem involves at least one agent and a related goal. Problem structures and types are more situation-specific.

Some apply in few instances, while others are quite general. A situation can contain more than one structure and can be understood in terms of more than one type. It is also important to recognize what is distinctive about the situation. How does it differ from problems of its kind? What are its defining features, characteristics that might be responsible for it being a problem in the first place?

Given a characterization of the problem, two kinds of analytic moves naturally follow: negative prescriptions, or potential mistakes to avoid in situations of this kind, and positive prescriptions, things to do in trying to solve such problems. These prescriptions are termed *pitfalls* and *heuristics*. The mental shortcomings and fallacies identified earlier are pitfalls. Other mistakes are more specifically associated with problem solving.

Connections between problem characteristics, pitfalls, and heuristics can be more or less strong. To illustrate their interweaving, consider perceptual problems. A perceptual problem is a situation that is unsatisfactory because of an agent's mistaken belief, or misperception. Companies often attribute lagging sales to perceptual problems: The market misperceives the quality of our products. While some situations truly are perceptual problems, the notion is often abused. It can be a rationalization that diverts attention from one's own failings. Thus, the problem type has an associated pitfall, the error of defining a situation as a perceptual problem when other inadequacies are at fault. An internal auditor claimed that her department suffered from a perceptual problem: Internal audit recommendations were ignored, arguably because management misperceived the quality and relevance of the department's work. But might there not have been an element of truth amid these misperceptions? A related heuristic is that if a situation is described as a perceptual problem, one must identify the alleged misperception and consider whether it has a basis in fact.

## Problem Types and Structures

Problem structures reflect characteristic relationships among a problem's components. Problems can denote an incompatibility between two or more elements, none of which is intrinsically bad or deficient. Marriages can be problematic in this way. Other situations are marked by an inadequacy or imbalance. The demand for something exceeds its supply. Many problems involve trade-offs between goals. In some cases, a system's performance is not acceptable; in others, the system has broken down or ceases to function. Problems can be defined around situations in which something of value has been or could be lost.

There are also general problem types or categories. One is a negotiation problem, exemplified by The Publishing Company Case (2.3), a situation in which two or more parties must try to reach an agreement. Performance problems are situations in which a system is not performing acceptably. These can give rise to design problems, the need to develop or recreate a system or artifact. Identifying problem types, structures, and components helps solve the problem. For instance, in addressing a performance problem, consider whether the performance target is reasonable. If so, diagnose the cause of the inadequacy before proposing courses of action. In situations of incompatibility, ask whether incompatible elements can be changed or replaced.

Some problem types and structures involve systems phenomena. The category known as **start-up difficulties** consists of situations in which a new system is initiated or an existing system is significantly changed. Ensuing troubles often fade away as "bugs" are worked out and people adapt to new circumstances. **Side effects** arise when a change has unanticipated repercussions. Manufacturers of cardiac pacemakers conduct extensive investigations to identify side effects that might result from a change in product specifications. **Delayed feedback** problems stem from time lags between input activities and a system's response.[7] Excess production of goods—automobiles or office buildings, for example—can occur if manufacturers keep responding to demand that would be satisfied by product already in the system. **"I'll buy now, you pay later,"** apparent in The Publishing Company Case, is a systemic problem that results when upstream processors make their jobs easier at the expense of those downstream. **Thrashing** occurs when so much time is spent managing a system's tasks that not enough is left to perform them. Process logs and databases are maintained because the process takes so long . . . because logs and databases are maintained.

Another cluster of problem structures and types is concerned with resources. Resource scarcity is a generic problem, indeed the defining fact of economic life. It gives rise to **resource allocation problems,** situations in which a scarce resource, such as investment capital, must be allocated among competing uses. **Success to the successful** denotes situations in which a claimant's initial successes allow it to capture more resources at the expense of competitors. In organizations, financial, human, and other assets gravitate toward projects that show early progress. Since resources are scarce, an opportunity cost is incurred when they go unused, thus the problem of **underutilized resources.** On the other hand, free or inexpensive resources tend to be overused. This situation is common with public goods, such as parks and recreational areas that don't charge user fees. It is also why organizations have charge-out mechanisms for information systems and staff services. The **Tragedy of the Commons** occurs when users of a free resource are motivated to exploit it to the fullest, so that the resource is harmed by overuse.[8] Overgrazing of communal pasture lands and excessive demands on a typing pool are examples.

Many problems involve **value trade-offs** in which achievement of one goal requires sacrifices with respect to another. Trade-offs can involve the goals of a single party, as with food preferences: The most appealing foods in terms of taste seem to be the worst from a health standpoint. A conflict may exist between the goals of different parties, as in public policy disputes. The gun control debate matches public safety against the right to bear arms. The abortion controversy pits the life of the fetus against a woman's right to choose. An **ethical dilemma** occurs when one or more of the values is a moral imperative, others being matters of self-interest. Another common trade-off is between short- and long-term interests. Corporate executives are often criticized for sacrificing long-term welfare for short-term profits. Many trade-offs reflect a natural order. Relatively few members of any population will be excellent by any criterion, hence the **quality-quantity trade-off.** Lower quality comes with higher quantity. Bankers know that rapid growth in loan volume invariably leads to a reduction in the quality of credits. Somewhat similar is the

**speed-accuracy trade-off.** When you type faster, you can expect more errors. An airline trying to satisfy customers by reducing times between connecting flights found that shorter connect times led to more errors in the form of lost baggage and missed flights.

Another group of problem types and structures centers on the evaluation function and the related challenge of assessing costs and benefits. Some organizational activities—public relations, for instance—fare poorly in such assessments because their costs are more obvious than their benefits, exemplifying **discrepant cost-benefit visibility. Parasitism** occurs when an activity that is not cost-justified is perpetuated by being lumped in with worthwhile endeavors. The most successful parts of a company usually make the most wasteful expenditures, these being parasitic on profitable activities. **Cost-benefit displacement** occurs when the costs and benefits of an activity accrue to different agents. Salespeople for an industrial products company were reluctant to spend time needed to get their product "spec'd in" as required components by manufacturers. Too often, subsequent sales were captured by other salespeople. If one party incurs the costs of an activity while others enjoy the benefits, the activity will not be performed.

Cost-benefit displacement could be viewed as a motivational or incentives problem, another cluster of issues. The most common is **inadequate incentives,** in which rewards/punishments are not strong enough to produce desired behaviors. Parts of a company's product line may not receive sales force attention if commission rates do not justify the required sales effort. Another structure, **improper incentives,** covers situations in which incentives are misdirected or diffuse. Organizations often encourage teamwork by basing incentives on group performance. This can backfire if individuals become demotivated, believing they cannot affect group outcomes. The fact that each organization member does many different things, some on an ad hoc basis, underlies the problem of **unrewarded activities.** If a task is not included in performance assessments, it tends to be ignored or done carelessly. This is especially true if incented activities are time-elastic; more time can always be spent on them, with consequent performance improvements. Salespeople dislike having to complete paperwork. They would rather be selling. Some faculty regret spending time in the classroom. They would rather do research.

Other noteworthy problem types and structures are listed in Figure 2.7.

## Pitfalls

Confronted by problem situations, people are liable to make various mental mistakes. Some of these are general, while others are situation-specific. People can err by setting goals that are overly demanding and demotivating as a result. Or they can set goals that are too lax, insufficiently challenging. **Infallible goals** is the pitfall of regarding goal levels as absolute, possessing an objective, two-tables-of-stone validity. **Inflexible goals** is the mistake of pursuing a goal that has become unrealistic. Young companies often strive unreasonably to maintain high initial growth rates. Labor unions don't make wage concessions despite declining company competitiveness.

Goals can be revised too readily. **Eroding goals** is the mistake of lowering objectives without good reason. The problem goes away if goal levels are set so the status

**Adverse selection:** Inadequate screening of customers leaves one serving the least appealing segments of a market.

**Cannibalization:** A new activity initiated by an agent is successful at the expense of the agent's initial set of activities.

**Centralization vs. autonomy:** Difficulties owing to the way authority is dispersed throughout an organization.

**Chicken and egg:** Situations in which one must have X to get Y, but also needs Y to get X. Example: Subscribers and advertisers for new media products.

**Cooperation and coordination:** Situations requiring the cooperation of multiple parties or the coordination of different activities.

**Escalation:** Two or more competitors successively "up the ante" in attempting to outdo the others.

**Excessive control:** Counterproductive restrictions on the activities of agents.

**Falling between two stools:** An entity or activity trying to satisfy multiple demands or goals fails for not doing any one thing well enough.

**Free rider:** Agents who are able to use certain goods without having to pay for them. Example: People who watch public TV but do not contribute.

**Front-runner's burden:** Any competitive disadvantage that falls on front-runners. Example: Wind resistance experienced by the leader in a bike race.

**Knowledge asymmetries:** Interagent relationships in which one party has more relevant knowledge. Example: Buyers and sellers of used cars.

**Make vs. buy:** Situations in which agents must decide whether to perform tasks themselves or contract with outside parties.

*Continued*

**Figure 2.7**  Problem types and structures

**Power imbalance:** Interagent relationships in which one party has more power, often because the other has a greater need to maintain the relationship.

**Resistance to change:** An agent's unwillingness to try new things or to accede to change.

**Responsibility-authority split:** Situations in which an agent is held responsible for task performance but lacks the authority needed to get the job done.

**Slippery slope:** Making an exception to an established rule, inviting requests for ever more dramatic exceptions.

**Standardization vs. customization:** Situations involving a trade-off between the benefits of uniformity and those of customization to local needs.

**Success breeds failure:** Ways in which success, especially growth, gives rise to countervailing forces.

**Unclear contracts or responsibilities:** Inadequate specification of the responsibilities of parties to an agreement.

**Weakest link:** A system or activity involving multiple parts will be successful only if each of the parts performs effectively.

**Figure 2.7** (*continued*)

quo is acceptable. A commodity producer had difficulty meeting customer delivery requirements. Rather than improving its processes, the firm redefined its market to exclude customers who required delivery within six weeks of an order. **Monomania** is the trap of being obsessed by a single goal, failing to recognize that many values must be pursued. R & D units get wrapped up in cutting-edge technology and forget about market objectives. Internal auditors lose sight of performance for the sake of compliance with procedures. Government agencies like OSHA and the EPA have reputations for monomanic pursuit of, say, health without regard for economic consequences.

Many pitfalls involve mistaken beliefs. The assumption that waste is inevitable can forestall improvement efforts. Actions are sometimes justified on the grounds that "things can't get any worse." Not surprisingly, they get worse. "If it worked before, do it again" is a valid general strategy. However, the pitfall of "going to the well once too often" is that repeated efforts deplete a critical resource, such as running down the battery while trying to start a car. People hold beliefs that are true in general, but which have exceptions. They overgeneralize, not making key distinctions when applying their knowledge. For instance, while one should defer to the opinions of experts in specialized domains, this rule should be set aside if experts might be motivated by self-interest. Thus, it would not be wise to give physicians control of the U.S. health care system or to allow attorneys to redesign the legal system.

**Scapegoating** can thwart problem identification. One blames others, especially those unable to defend themselves, for troubles. Customers are the classic scapegoats for product quality problems. **The tail wagging the dog** occurs when a proposed solution is of a magnitude far beyond that of the original issue. A label manufacturer experienced raw material losses due to wastage when jobs were set up for production. One suggestion was that the company pursue larger orders to reduce the frequency of job setups and consequent losses. This proposal requires a substantial, and probably infeasible, change in marketing strategy, a move not justified by the problem's magnitude.

## Heuristics

Heuristics are positive prescriptions, what one should do in trying to solve a problem. As with structures and pitfalls, they are of varying generality. Consider the problem faced by an airline. Rather than having a seamless interface for passengers connecting from its feeder lines, customers suffered lost baggage, missed connections, delayed flights, and other inconveniences. This problem consists of many instances of something going wrong. Such problems can be addressed by **stratification,** a heuristic familiar to QPS practitioners. Stratification involves analyzing a set of instances along various dimensions to locate prominent sources of trouble. In this case, one could stratify by type of mistake, such as lost bags, and by feeder line, airport, and flight number. Stratification might disclose that missed connections often occur on certain flights.

Another heuristic, **How did we get into this mess?,** was cited in discussing Case 2.3. It recognizes that problems come about in different ways. Some result from environmental changes, while others occur because someone made a mistake. Many problems result from nearsighted decisions that ignored long-term impacts. In other cases, problems arise from reasonable risks that were consciously assumed. Knowing how a problem arose can suggest measures to prevent its return. This heuristic is most valuable with problems that result from systemic failings. By fixing the system, one can prevent such problems from recurring.

**Conceptual analysis** is valuable when thinking about abstract concepts. For instance, the notion of "inadequacy" implies a mismatch between supply and demand. If capacity is inadequate, one should look for ways to increase its supply and/or reduce demand. **Value of information** heuristics pertain when a costly research activity, such as conducting an experiment, survey, or other study, has been proposed. Strictly speaking, information only has value if it changes one's course of action. Studies are often conducted unnecessarily to support alternatives that would have been pursued anyway.

The problem-solving approach adopted in this book is highly problem-centered. Heuristics, pitfalls, problem types, and structures are often cited in the chapters that follow. The account is by no means complete, not even for quality problems. Much remains to be done in developing the problem side of problem solving. Nonetheless, this is a promising strategy for improving human thinking in complex, real-world problem situations.

## NOTES

1. For a readable introduction to cognitive science, see: Howard Gardner, *The Mind's New Science: A History of the Cognitive Revolution* (New York: Basic Books, 1985).
2. G. Wallas, *The Art of Thought* (New York: Harcourt, 1926).
3. Kahneman, Daniel, Paul Slovic, and Amos Tversky (eds.), *Judgment Under Uncertainty: Heuristics and Biases* (Cambridge, England: Cambridge University Press, 1982).
4. G. Polya, *How to Solve It,* 2d ed. (Princeton, N.J.: Princeton University Press, 1973).
5. Keki R. Bhote, "Design of Experiments Offers Powerful Tools for Quality Improvement," *National Productivity Review* 11, no. 2 (1992): 231–246.
6. This case first appeared in: Gerald F. Smith, "Managerial Problem Solving," in *Encyclopedia of Library and Information Science,* vol. 53, sup. 16, Allen Kent, ed. (New York: Marcel Dekker, 1994): 210–236.
7. This is one of several problem structures identified in: Peter M. Senge, *The Fifth Discipline* (New York: Doubleday, 1990).
8. Garrett Hardin, "The Tragedy of the Commons," *Science* 162 (1968): 1243–1248.

# Problem-Solving Functions

This section of four chapters develops a functional account of QPS. It expands and deepens our understanding of functional demands posed by quality problems. In contrast, the next section of the book (Chapters 7–11) adopts a problem-centered approach, analyzing five types of quality problems.

The distinctions defining these sections and the chapters within them are not always clear-cut. Problem types and problem-solving functions lack the crisp boundaries that differentiate, say, chemical elements. For instance, design is an important problem-solving function. However, in a TQM context, it is better viewed as a problem type, indeed as two problem types—product and process design. Some topics, such as customer relations, could be addressed under several functions or problem types. I have consolidated discussions of these in the most appropriate chapter. Boundaries between functions can be discretionary; a chapter may address more than one function. Chapter 5 is concerned with problem identification, a topic that blends into problem definition. Chapter 6, primarily devoted to problem definition, also discusses data collection and analysis. Related methods—Pareto diagrams, for example—are often used as tools for diagnosis, the topic of Chapter 7. Chapter 8 considers both the generation of solution alternatives and their evaluation.

# Problem Identification*[1]

---

## Chapter Outline

---

*This chapter is an adaptation of material first published by Carfax Publishing Limited, P.O. Box 25, Abingdon, Oxfordshire, OX14 3UE, United Kingdom, in *Total Quality Management*. Used with permission.

1. Actively look for problems.
2. Go to Gemba.
3. Note and explain surprising observations.
4. Exploit precursors and natural symptoms.
5. Anticipate and prevent problems.
6. Pay extra attention to likely trouble spots.
7. Develop lines of communication with informants.
8. Get close to customers.
9. Identify potential problems through planning.
10. How did we get into this mess?
11. Make comparisons.
12. Eliminate slack.
13. Learn from experience.
14. Use attention and memory aids.

Managing Problem Identification

Problem identification (PI) is necessarily the first step in problem solving. This chapter explains the nature of problem identification and describes the identification process. Methods and practices used to identify quality problems are evaluated. The chapter considers ways identification can fail, factors making it difficult to identify certain problems, and common identification mistakes. It concludes with prescriptions, documented by case study evidence, for improving PI performance.

# What Is Problem Identification?

Viewing problems as existing state-desired state gaps or, more broadly, as situations that bear improvement, problem identification is the means by which someone comes to believe that a problem does or will exist, that a situation deserves attention, thought, and action. It has also been called problem finding, problem sensing, and problem recognition. To illustrate the notion, consider three examples of PI, drawn respectively from personal experience, a popular movie, and the quality literature.

## case 3.1

At 4:45 in the afternoon of a brisk, early March day, a man rode the elevator to a subterranean level in a parking garage. Having conducted a daylong workshop on "Quality Problem Solving," he was in a hurry to get to the university, two miles distant, where he was scheduled to teach a 5:30 class. After the usual misdirections, he made it to his car, unlocked the door, and got in. He inserted his key in the ignition and turned the switch. Nothing happened. Several more tries produced the same outcome. When he noticed the position of the headlight switch—the lights had been left on—he realized his car was not going to start.

---

■ **case 3.2**

In the movie *The China Syndrome,* a shift supervisor in a nuclear power plant (a role played by Jack Lemmon) notices his coffee rippling after an incident caused by an earth tremor. Puzzled by the timing of the ripples, he hypothesizes that they result from a secondary source of vibration in the plant. The supervisor's investigation discloses that critical equipment has not been properly inspected prior to the plant's commissioning. He concludes that the plant might have structural flaws that could result in unparalleled disaster.

---

■ **case 3.3**

Each night, an employee at Central Bank and Trust in Denver pushed a cart loaded with $7 million in cash into a vault. He wondered why the money was not put to some use. When the bank created a quality circle, he shared this concern. After investigating, circle members concluded that the bank only needed to keep $1.5 million on hand. Thereafter, the extra $5.5 million was transported to the nearby Denver Federal Reserve, where it earned overnight interest.

---

These cases demonstrate the variety of problem identification. In the first, the problem virtually makes itself known, albeit through a nonevent: Nothing happened when the key was turned. In contrast, Case 3.2 illustrates the sustained thinking and investigation required if certain problems are to be discovered. It also shows how serendipitous observations can provide evidence for identification purposes. The third case concerns the discovery of a chance to make better use of a resource, an opportunity. It suggests how routine practices can blind organizations to potential improvements.

While PI can be simple and direct, as in Case 3.1, it is often more difficult. Some difficulties derive from the nonphysical nature of problems. People come to believe a problem exists after seeing evidence to that effect. Seeing is believing, but problems cannot be directly perceived, since they involve desired states. Equally troublesome is the sheer variety of problematic situations. Because they exist in so many forms, problems have no standard attributes to look for to identify them. It is easy to tell if an elephant is in the room. The massive gray body, large floppy ears, long trunk, and enveloping odor are dead giveaways. No physical evidence is equally informative as to the existence of a problem, since problems are manifested in so many different ways.

Other complications arise as well. Goals can be unclear or unknown, making it difficult to identify related problems. The levels at which goals are set can be unreasonable or arbitrary. What level of background radon emissions in basements should be taken as problematic? Even assuming clear criteria for the desired state, there may be uncertainty about the existing state. Some things—the benefits of public relations activity, for instance—aren't susceptible to reliable measurement. Problem identification is compromised when the current state cannot be accurately assessed. Things are worse regarding problems that could occur in the future. To identify such concerns, one must make convincing predictions as to how things will turn out. The global warming controversy indicates how difficult this can be.

Because of these difficulties, identification claims are fallible. Like Chicken Little, one can mistakenly insist that a situation is or will be problematic. Often there is no way to establish conclusively that a problem exists, so different parties can justifiably maintain opposing views on the matter. One person's problem can, to another, seem neither difficult nor important enough to deserve the name. Disagreements about relevant goals, current conditions, and future forecasts can foster conflicting conclusions about problem existence. These differences of opinion are important in organizations, where a problem becomes fully real only when it is acknowledged by management. Then too, identification claims are revisable. New evidence can come to light, suggesting that a seemingly benign situation is serious or that an ongoing problem-solving effort is much ado about nothing.

Problem identification is a necessary prerequisite for problem solving. One will not attend to, think about, or act on a situation unless it has been identified as problematic. Early identification can prevent potential problems from happening and enable the exploitation of opportunities. As with malignant tumors, when problems are identified quickly, they may be easier to remedy and produce less serious effects. PI sets the agenda for action in organizations. It determines the topics people think about and act on in trying to make improvements.

## The Identification Process

Problem identification has been defined as the process by which someone comes to believe that a problem does or will exist. An account of this process will indicate how evidence of a problem is generated, acquired, and used to reach such conclusions. It will explain why some problems are identified successfully while others are not. Problems are not all identified in the same way. They come to be discovered by various paths. The primary source of PI process variation is the problem itself.

Consider how two companies might learn of product quality inadequacies that escaped in-house detection. Company A, which manufactures personal computers, finds out about its quality problem when unhappy customers return defective PCs to retailers. Company B, which produces peanut butter, faces a more difficult identification challenge. Rather than returning jars of rancid peanut butter, customers trash them and switch to another brand. The company experiences declining sales, which it might attribute to many possible causes. Similar problems can pose different identification demands and may well be discovered in different ways.

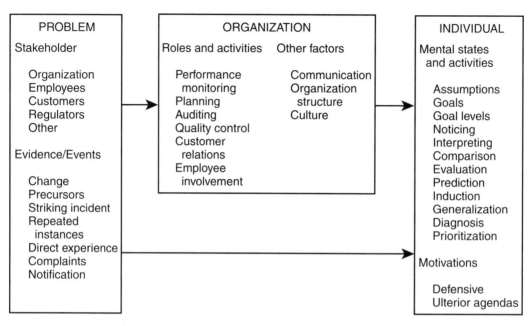

**Figure 3.1** Model of problem identification

Figure 3.1 is a descriptive model of problem identification. It highlights the three key players in the process—problem, organization, and individual—noting ways each can be involved.

## The Role of the Problem

As indicated on the left-hand side of Figure 3.1, every problem involves stakeholders. Someone has to care or the situation would not be problematic. Virtually all problems provide evidence of their existence, often through events they give rise to, necessarily or by serendipity, as in the rippling coffee in *The China Syndrome*. Some problems come to light because they are directly experienced by potential identifiers. People know when their cars will not start, when their workloads are excessive, and when subordinates refuse to perform assigned tasks. Other problems are identified because they affect people who are able and willing to complain. Employees express dissatisfaction over working conditions. Customers let us know that products are not acceptable. Identification can be fostered if organizations solicit stakeholder views. While developing the Taurus, Ford learned from insurance companies how difficult it was to realign vehicles with front-end damage. The Taurus was designed with marks engraved on its frame to facilitate this repair. Certain problems, such as employee theft, resist identification because involved agents are motivated to keep them from being discovered.

Potential problems can be signaled by precursors, similar but less serious events. Earthquakes are often preceded by tremors, heart attacks by angina. The 1966 coal tip slide in Aberfan, Wales—fatal to 144 people, mostly children—was foretold by four major tip slides occurring in the years before the disaster. A problem can be created by change, a noticeable event that prompts PI. After production workers at Fasco Industries learned they would be handling heavier parts, they redesigned the work process to eliminate a lifting task. Some changes are mandated by regulators, who notify affected parties. When a new state law required banks to insure that handicapped people had access to bank lobbies, the official notification made PI simple. Other problems come to light as a result of attention-grabbing incidents. When a Fort Lauderdale worker received a disabling shock from an electrified water meter, the incident led a problem-solving team to develop preventive measures. The Tennant Company became aware of a problem when the Brazilian government held up a Tennant shipment because documentation did not match the contents. What looked like parts smuggling to the Brazilians was recognized by Tennant's management as inadequate shipping procedures.

## The Role of the Organization

Organizational factors play a major role in PI. No company has ever had a Problem Identification Department, but all have institutionalized activities that identify problems as part of their function. Quality control is one example. Process monitoring and testing/ inspection of products uncovers problems. A quality engineer for a computer peripherals manufacturer conducted weekly reviews of subassembly failures. Noting a worsening trend in a PC board assembly, she called up a report on other boards supplied by that vendor. Finding high failure rates in these items, she notified Purchasing. A visit to the vendor disclosed that their high backlog had led to overtime, new hires, and poor quality. Most organizational problems are identified through performance monitoring of individuals, projects, departments, divisions, and the company as a whole. A review of operating results at Colonial Penn Insurance Company cited excessive payments for worker overtime and temporary help. A project team developed a new contracting procedure for temporaries, reducing related costs by $458,000 the next year.

Planning can highlight potential problems and opportunities. A financial services firm conducted weekly reviews of financial markets, looking for trends that would affect its clients. On one occasion, analysts noted a continuing decline in interest rates, a consequential development for elderly clients living on interest income. Acting through its sales force, the company warned clients of an impending drop in interest income, softening the impact of this development. Auditing is another means of problem identification. During a review of an acquired firm, auditors for the Thomas J. Lipton Company found a tea bag filling operation with high fill weight variability and excessive product giveaway. Of great importance are customer relations and employee involvement programs that solicit knowledge of problems from these stakeholder groups.

Apart from relatively formal roles and activities, other aspects of organizations can help or hinder PI. If an organization's structure does not clearly assign responsibilities, problems can go unnoticed and unidentified. Organizational culture is important; effective firms have participative styles that allow honest mistakes. A Wainwright Industries plant experienced recurring damage from materials handling equipment, but operators refused to admit their misadventures. When one finally confessed to damaging an overhead door, the chief operating officer called a plant-wide meeting, described what had happened, shook the operator's hand, congratulated him, and explained that preventive measures could only be taken if such incidents were reported.

Communication practices are influential. Problem identification is promoted when lateral communication enables departments and divisions to share information. Bottom-up communication is critical. The shoot-the-messenger syndrome contrasts sharply with enlightened policies. Vaughn Beals, past president of Harley-Davidson, described how, on a December day in 1976, a mechanic responsible for warranty returns came into his office to ask the company president to come and see "the kind of junk that's coming back from the field."[2] Harley's renaissance owes much to the fact that such communication could happen. By way of contrast, in 1986, managers at a General Motors plant in Mexico learned they were producing defective piston casings, causing a costly recall of engines. Worse yet, the managers discovered that employees had known of the defects six weeks earlier, but had not reported them for fear of getting in trouble.

## The Role of the Individual

Individuals are a necessary part of the identification process. PI involves forming a belief, something that only people can do. The right-most box in Figure 3.1 indicates mental states and processes involved in problem identification. Noticing, having one's attention drawn to something, is critical. For two years, following the instructions of her predecessor, a clerk at the Paul Revere Insurance Companies spent an hour each week alphabetizing cards before giving them to another employee. Then one day she noticed that this employee threw the cards away without looking at them. Comparisons are made in formal performance monitoring—actual vs. budget—and in informal evaluations: How does performance match up against one's sense of what is possible? Induction is used when problems involve repeated occurrences of certain events. A turnover problem can be identified by induction over instances of valued employees leaving the organization. Problems indicated by dissimilar occurrences force identifiers to generalize. By generalizing over instances of communication failure, conflicting activities, and missed assignments, one might conclude that a department has a weak organization structure.

Motivations affect problem identification. People may be motivated not to identify problems that reflect poorly on their performance. The FAA requires airline pilots to report flight safety incidents, but pilots do not always do so because they know investigations can hurt their careers. Similar concerns motivate nurses not to report errors in the administration of medicines to hospital patients. Surprisingly, people can be motivated *toward* the identification of problems that may not exist. Oftentimes in organizations, rather than problems looking for solutions, there are solutions looking for problems. People have pet projects or activities they want to undertake. It may be possible to do so by identifying a problem (real or imagined) and proposing the desired project/activity as its solution. Consider this example: "Since our company suffers from a lack of diversification, we should acquire Acme Corporation."

# Problem Identification Methods and Practices

It is difficult to imagine a highly general problem identification method, one encompassing the many sources of information and interpretive challenges involved in the discovery of real-world problems. In lieu of general methods, specific techniques have been developed, aimed at certain types of problems or at aspects of the identification process. Three methods—statistical process control, benchmarking, and the Kokai watch technique—will be discussed. The quality movement has also promoted problem identification through broader organizational programs, including employee involvement and customer relations activities. This section considers such programs as well as the use of management information systems for PI purposes.

## Statistical Process Control (SPC)

Statistical process control is the quality movement's major contribution to problem identification. The following is an overview of the technique. In addition to the many books on SPC,[3] the topic is often covered in introductory statistics texts.

Every activity is subject to variation in the process and in its outputs. The packaging process at a dairy fills containers with cream. The amount of cream put into a container differs from one container to the next. The process mean is the average of many measurements of a characteristic, such as the average amount of cream per container in a lot of 1000 containers. Due to variability, items produced by a process deviate from the process mean. Most variations are small and are tolerated as process fluctuations that are uncontrollable for practical purposes. Large variations can result in unacceptable products and can indicate that the process is not functioning appropriately.

This is how statistical process control helps identify problems. Historical data are used to determine the normal level of variability in a process. This variability is represented by control limits, upper and lower values for the process characteristic so that it is highly unlikely more extreme values would be observed. For our cream-filling process, these limits might be at 1.05 and .94 quarts, with less than 3 chances in 1000 that the normal process would produce fill volumes outside this range. The process mean and control limits are represented as lines on a control chart (Figure 3.2). This chart is used to monitor process performance, measurements taken periodically and recorded in sequence. Thus, one would record the volume of cream in containers filled by the process, taking sets of, say, five measurements at 30 minute intervals. Twenty data points—each the average of five measurements taken at a given time—are recorded on the control chart in Figure 3.2.

As long as observed values fall within the control limits, everything is fine. The process is in control. The occurrence of an observation outside the control limits— the 18th data point in Figure 3.2—is cause for concern. Because such observations are unlikely to occur if the process is operating normally, when an extreme value is observed, it is reasonable to assume the process has changed. It is out of control. There is a problem with the process that must be corrected so the process will return to its normal, in-control state. The notions of common and special causes have been used to denote sources of normal and abnormal process variation, respectively.

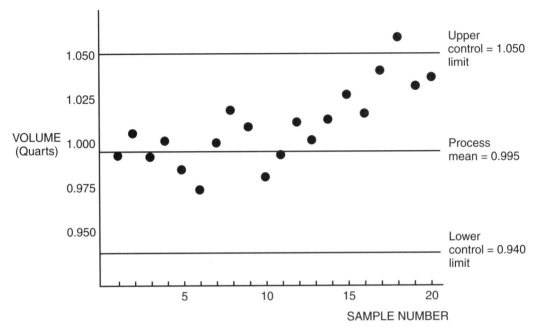

**Figure 3.2**  Control chart

This basic methodology has elaborations. One can plot data on the ranges of sample observations or record the proportion of defects in a sample. Control limits can be augmented with zone boundaries and pattern analysis rules that specify when less extreme observations are cause for concern. But the underlying logic is always the same: SPC identifies problems by monitoring processes for unusual observations, assumed to result from unwanted special causes of variation.

SPC is a powerful problem identification method of limited generality. It is applicable to conformance problems in which a highly structured process yields well-specified outputs. Many manufacturing and some service activities fit this description. SPC is less useful for activities with high levels of natural variability or where characteristics of the process and its outputs are tailored to each situation (unstructured performance problems). Thus, a company that attempted to apply SPC to the activities of a field sales force was unsuccessful. Measuring process variability will not determine if a process is inefficient or if its outputs truly satisfy customer needs. The method elicits little concern over variation due to common causes, though there are good reasons to reduce all variation around target values. While the pattern of observations may suggest what special cause is operating, SPC has limited value as a diagnostic tool. Actually, statistical process control has probably suffered more from its friends than from its detractors. Too many expensive training sessions and unneeded control charts have left organizations skeptical of a technique that has real value when applied within its proper domain.

## Benchmarking

Benchmarking is well described by Robert Camp,[4] a member of the Xerox team that brought the method into prominence. Not strictly a problem identification technique—it will also be discussed in relation to process design (Chapter 11)—benchmarking has an important PI component. It responds to the goal-setting challenge: At what level should performance standards be set when assessing the need for improvement? Every activity can be improved, but one hopes to identify areas offering the largest potential gains. Budgets and prior period results have traditionally been used as performance standards. Benchmarking pursues a different strategy. It identifies performance levels achieved by the best practices employed in other organizations. Benchmarking considers a particular activity, determines which companies are best at that activity, what performance levels they achieve, and how those levels are attained. Xerox used L. L. Bean as a benchmark for order processing. Best practices set the standard for organizational performance, a problem being identified when performance falls too far short of this mark.

Benchmarking is consistent with the philosophy of this book—using prior experience, one's own and others, to direct improvement efforts. The method's limitations are matters of operationality, the difficulty of identifying organizations having best practices and of learning those practices.

## Kokai Watch

This simple technique, described by Walton,[5] illustrates the value of extended, focused observation. During a Kokai watch, a group of people—say, six to eight managers, employees, and outsiders—observes a worker's performance for about an hour. This is done silently, without questioning the worker or disrupting work activities. Observers, who may have no prior familiarity with the operation, note ways of improving performance with regard to quality, efficiency, and safety. They might recognize a need to pre-position tools, improve information availability, install safety guards, or reduce materials handling. After the observational session, group members discuss their findings and propose corrective actions.

The Kokai watch technique is quite powerful. Its only prerequisite is that relevant activities be observable; knowledge work cannot be improved through a Kokai watch. Workers should be assured that their competence is not being questioned and that improvement efforts are aimed at the system, not at individual operators.

## Employee Involvement (EI)

Employee involvement, a guiding value of quality management, is often achieved through organizational programs like suggestion systems and quality circles. Its role in problem identification derives from the fact that most organization members are employees, not managers, who are directly involved in organizational activities. They have an experience-based familiarity with what is going on. This "local knowledge" is usually more valuable for PI than the abstract professional knowledge of managers.

For EI to result in problem identification, employees must know about problems. This condition is often satisfied for efficiency and process design issues. In contrast, few employees outside of sales and customer service personnel have special knowledge of customer needs. Thus, product design and certain conformance problems are unlikely to be identified through EI. The second requirement for EI-based problem identification is that employees can report issues to concerned parties. This boils down to having effective communication channels. Employee suggestion systems are a vehicle for upward communications. Lateral channels are also important. When community-oriented policing was adopted by a police district in Madison, Wisconsin, parking meter monitors were brought into contact with the police and quickly became their best information source.

The final requirement for EI-based problem identification is motivational. Organizations should remove inhibitions to problem identification. They might also provide incentives to promote PI. Progressive companies tolerate honest mistakes and emphasize the system's culpability for performance inadequacies. Positive motivations for PI can be provided through programs that reward employees for improvement suggestions. Teams at the Paul Revere Insurance Companies were motivated to earn lapel pins awarded for improvement efforts. In some organizations, employees aggressively seek out improvement opportunities, with no concern for individual reward or recognition. In others, even lucrative incentives are unable to motivate PI.

## Customer Relations (CR)

Programs that develop and maintain positive customer relations are vehicles for problem identification. From a PI standpoint, customer relations complements employee involvement. Whereas EI enables identification of efficiency and process design problems, CR promotes awareness of product design, conformance, and unstructured performance problems, matters that EI tends to miss. Chapter 10 considers how customer relations supports product design. The present concern is with post-purchase customer relations aimed at identifying user dissatisfaction with a product or service.

The PI effectiveness of customer relations depends on the relationship between producers and users. Dissatisfactions of internal customers, those in the same organization as producers, are discerned more easily than those of external customers. Inadequacies of products sold by contract to individual clients come to light more readily than when goods are marketed *en masse* to faceless final consumers. As with employee-based PI, the critical issues are whether customers are aware of product-related problems and are able and willing to report them.

If customer awareness and motivations are high, the organization need only provide a means for customers to voice dissatisfactions. Product warranty and service programs suit this purpose. Sony collects information from field repairmen concerning customer problems with televisions, analyzing service tickets that report the nature of the problem and what was done to correct it. Customer hotlines make it even easier for users to express grievances.

In other cases—back to our previous example of peanut butter vs. PCs—customers are aware of product inadequacies but are not motivated to complain. To identify problems under these conditions, organizations must solicit customer feedback. This is done through surveys and other outreach devices. IBM-Rochester, a Baldrige Award winner, uses a customer call program to ask users about their product installation experiences. In some situations customers are unaware of product shortcomings or don't recognize that an offering could be better adapted to their needs. People adjust their behavior to the product, treating it as a given. They tend to experience little dissatisfaction with an artifact that could be improved. In such cases, producers must observe the product in use to identify improvement opportunities. A work group in Ford's parts procurement area surveyed dealers, asking how parts should be packed. Team members also visited a dealership, observing the unpacking of parts. The on-site study produced improvement ideas beyond those generated by the survey.

Though it is a valuable PI mechanism, customer relations poses pitfalls. Admitting that each customer's opinion deserves consideration, nonetheless a noncustomized product may not satisfy everyone. The coffee is too strong for some, too weak for others. Some students complain that the course is too demanding, while others lament that they are not challenged. It is impossible to be all things to all people. Not all customer complaints stem from actionable product deficiencies. Another failing occurs when customer complaints are resolved, but information is not used for PI purposes and underlying problems remain unidentified.

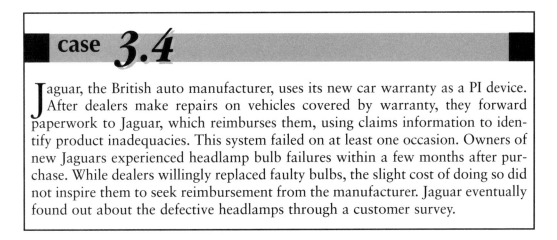

**case 3.4**

Jaguar, the British auto manufacturer, uses its new car warranty as a PI device. After dealers make repairs on vehicles covered by warranty, they forward paperwork to Jaguar, which reimburses them, using claims information to identify product inadequacies. This system failed on at least one occasion. Owners of new Jaguars experienced headlamp bulb failures within a few months after purchase. While dealers willingly replaced faulty bulbs, the slight cost of doing so did not inspire them to seek reimbursement from the manufacturer. Jaguar eventually found out about the defective headlamps through a customer survey.

PI must be acknowledged as a legitimate part of customer relations, and information systems must insure effective PI performance. In addition, customer feedback must be interpreted correctly. Consider the following case, also involving an auto manufacturer.

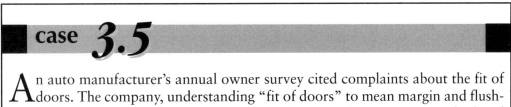

**case 3.5**

An auto manufacturer's annual owner survey cited complaints about the fit of doors. The company, understanding "fit of doors" to mean margin and flushness with the frame, took corrective action. When a subsequent survey disclosed continuing complaints, the manufacturer convened focus group meetings with customers. Here it learned what customers meant by "fit of doors": the amount of effort required to close the door and the sound made when the door shut.

Ambiguity of a key term led the company to identify and solve the wrong problem.

## Information Systems (IS)

Information systems can support the identification of all types of quality problems, though they are more applicable to performance than design issues. IS developers often face challenges in devising PI systems, but the major concern tends to be a matter of *how much* rather than *how*. Some organizations do not make enough use of IS to support problem identification. A study of U.S. and Japanese manufacturers of air conditioners found that the worst U.S. firms collected virtually no information on product defects and field failures.[6] On the other hand, an overabundance of computer-generated information often distracts management from important issues. At Windsor Export Supply, a division of Ford, a critical shipping status report, prepared daily, advised managers of parts that had to be shipped to maintain production schedules at overseas affiliates. A study disclosed that only 20 percent of listed parts were truly critical. Another tendency is to perpetuate PI reports after their purpose has disappeared. When the Bridewell Company experienced production stoppages due to inadequate plant maintenance, a vice president asked for daily reports from maintenance inspectors. The reporting continued for years, even though the VP never read them.

Figure 3.3 summarizes these PI methods and practices, citing their major strengths and weaknesses.

# Identification Difficulties and Errors

This section considers what can go wrong with problem identification, the kinds and causes of PI failure. The discussion is in three parts. First is an account of failure modes for PI, ways in which identification efforts fall short of success. Second, identification difficulties, or factors making it hard to find problems, are discussed. These reflect characteristics of problems and organizations. Finally, the section cites mistakes made by prospective identifiers, mental errors that keep people from becoming aware of problems.

## Failure Modes for PI

PI failure can result from many causes and contributing factors, but they fall into four basic failure modes:

*1. Anticipation Failure.* Such failures reflect the fact that some problems could reasonably have been foretold. General knowledge or specific evidence supports a conclusion that something bad is going to happen. If no one reaches that conclusion, preventive measures are not taken and an avoidable problem comes to pass. Or one can overlook a foreseeable opportunity and be unprepared to exploit the situation when it arises. Clearly, differences of opinion may arise over whether an outcome was predictable. The illusion of 20-20 hindsight must be avoided. But a strong case can be made, for instance, that the U.S. savings and loan debacle of the 1980s was predictable and avoidable. Another case of anticipation failure concerned a company that purchased personal computers for its managers and staff. This was in the mid 1980s, before PC literacy became widespread. Company management, naively assuming the machines would insinuate themselves into work processes, provided

| Method/Practice | Applications | Strengths | Weaknesses |
|---|---|---|---|
| Statistical Process Control (SPC) | Monitoring structured processes having well-specified outputs. | Extremely powerful; good operationality; employs objective data and analysis. | Limited generality; has been misapplied. |
| Benchmarking | Identifying best-practice performance standards for organizational activities. | Quite general, applicable to most organizational processes; adds breadth of perspective to goal-setting. | Implementation challenges can be significant; no help with nonrecurring problems. |
| Kokai Watch | Identifying process improvement opportunities. | Reasonably powerful; highly operational. | Only applies to observable activities; unlikely to catch occasional failings. |
| Employee Involvement (EI) | Encouraging and enabling workers to report problems they are aware of. | Powerful and operational; improves morale; exploits hands-on knowledge of workers. | Not effective with external problems that employees are not aware of; frequent red herrings. |
| Customer Relations (CR) | Encouraging and enabling customers to report product-related problems. | Powerful and operational; increases customer goodwill. | Not effective with internal problems that customers are not aware of. |
| Information Systems (IS) | Monitoring organizational activities. | Fairly general; provides detailed objective data on a recurring basis. | Ineffective with certain kinds of problems; risk of information glut. |

Figure 3.3   Overview of problem identification methods and practices

no training or user support. Most of the computers ended up gathering dust in office corners. This problem was also avoidable.

**2. Late Identification.**   The next PI failure mode applies to situations in which an existing problem goes unrecognized. Bad things have begun to happen, or an improvement opportunity is there to be exploited. Yet the problem is not discovered. Its symptoms are overlooked or dismissed by potential identifiers. Such situations inspire countless domestic quarrels: One spouse admits, and tries to ignore, pains and other symptoms that the other insists are signs of cancer, heart disease, or another life-threatening condition. The loss of competitiveness experienced by American auto and steel producers in the 1970s was not truly foreseeable, but industry executives were unnecessarily slow to recognize and respond to incursions by foreign competitors.

**3. Misprioritization.**   Awareness of a problem is not sufficient. One must also recognize its importance. **Misprioritization,** the third failure mode, occurs when a known concern is not given proper attention. The issue is left to languish in a "To Do" pile, gets mentioned in passing during the final minutes of a staff meeting, or is assigned to a committee that slowly coalesces as the situation sinks into disaster. Correct prioritization takes account of the issue's importance and its likely evolution if left unattended. These are judgmental assessments admitting honest differences of opinion. Subsequent developments sometimes demonstrate that prioritization errors were made. The management of the fastest growing division of a major retailer was unconcerned with slow inventory turnover—until corporate management announced that the division would not receive expansion capital unless its return on assets improved. Wolverine Gasket knew small parts were being lost when they fell through rollers during a coating process. When a quality team addressed the issue, changed the roller design, and saved $45,000 a year, it was clear that the problem had been misprioritized.

**4. Red Herring.**   Each of the foregoing involves an inadequate response to a real problem. **Red herring** is an unnecessary response to a concern that turns out to be overblown or bogus. It is a false positive, an occasion on which an identified problem is seen, in retrospect, not to have deserved the attention it received. Red herrings are common in politics. The "Red Scare" inspired by Senator McCarthy in the early 1950s concerned a nonexistent problem, as did the "missile gap" cited by Kennedy during the 1960 presidential campaign. Health and environmental matters often give rise to red herrings. Remember the furor over alar, the allegedly carcinogenic preservative used to keep apples from rotting in supermarkets? In any organization, if one were to review the histories of all issues that got on top management's agenda of concerns, many "critical" problems would be found that were never solved, but instead faded into oblivion as hot new issues-of-the-month took center stage.

## PI Difficulties

Ultimately, individuals identify problems. A person's success in doing so can be affected by characteristics of the problem and of the organization in which PI is conducted. Some problems are difficult to identify because they do not provide observable evidence. Due to the lack of symptoms, ovarian cancer is seldom diagnosed at a curable stage. An Ore-Ida potato processing factory produced inferior french fries. As it turned out, the 14-foot drops potatoes underwent during the production process resulted in microscopic fractures. The underlying problem was difficult to identify because the potatoes sustained no visible damage. Issues that develop gradually go unnoticed for want of a sharp, attention-grabbing change. Like lobsters in a pot, people acclimate themselves to slow deteriorations.

Assessment limitations may make it hard to identify performance problems. It is hard to evaluate the performance. Is a teacher doing a good job, or a judge, or a marriage counselor? Performances of corporate staff and service units resist evaluation because they lack a natural bottom line. The costs of a public relations office are apparent; its benefits are diffuse and unquantifiable. It is hard to judge if the organization is getting its money's worth from such activities. When relevant information is mixed—some favorable, other unfavorable—people reach PI conclusions more slowly. This has been cited as a factor in the Carter administration's delayed recognition of the threat the Ayatollah Khomeini posed to American interests in Iran.

Potential problems and opportunities go undetected because of the difficulty of forecasting the future. The manager of a small town supermarket would be hard-pressed to predict that a national grocery chain will build a store nearby. Many a killing would be made if one could foresee the next big swing in the stock market. Problems also go unnoticed when needs and goals are not obvious. The need for a safety precaution is rarely noted until after an accident. When the stuff of everyday life, such as marital relationships, are taken for granted, it is easy to overlook signs of trouble. We fail to recognize improvement opportunities because we do not know what is possible. Reengineering reflects belated recognition of business process improvements enabled by modern information technology.

Some kinds of issues are difficult to identify. Peripheral or ancillary activities—materials handling is one example—may not be closely monitored, so inadequacies may go unnoticed. Aggregate measures like "indirect costs" hide components that deserve attention. When parasitism strikes and unjustified activities ride the coattails of worthwhile endeavors, grossly inefficient activities escape detection because they occur in prestigious parts of the organization. Problems that occur as side effects are hard to anticipate since they can be so remote from the precipitating action.

Other difficulties stem from organizational factors. If information needed to identify a problem is spread across individuals and subunits, no one person might have enough evidence to conclude that a problem exists. The United States had more than enough information to expect a Japanese attack on Pearl Harbor in 1941, but the evidence was spread among different parties. Some problems go unidentified because of agenda overload. Management has too much on its plate and declines to consider additional issues, no matter how important they seem. When Khomeini began to incite discontent against the Shah of Iran, the Carter administration was preoccupied with the SALT agreement, a factor that partially explains U.S. inattention to the situation.

Organizational policies and procedures can promote PI, but they may have the opposite effect as well. Partial blame for the Challenger disaster can be attributed to an informal procedural change at NASA. The traditional rule that a launch should be canceled if any doubt exists about its safety was effectively replaced by the rule that "a scheduled launch should proceed unless there is conclusive evidence that it is unsafe to do so."[7] A firm had a policy of charging information services costs to product divisions, but leaving those costs out of bonus computations for division management. When the policy was changed and all costs were included in bonus computations, the divisions erupted in outrage over high MIS costs. Corporate management soon realized that the original policy, coupled with the difficulty of evaluating MIS performance, had allowed empire building by MIS, which had passed costs of new hardware and unneeded systems on to uncomplaining users.

## Identification Mistakes

In problem identification, as in other thinking tasks, mental mistakes can be made. Many were discussed in Chapter 2. The pickup of information for PI purposes can be hampered by biased perception. Trouble lies in only attending to certain sources of data and screening out information that is inconsistent with expectations. Case 2.2 illustrates how belief perseverance—an unwillingness to revise existing beliefs in light of new evidence—can keep one from identifying problems. Because management had always believed that the company had a captive market for service parts, it was difficult for them to recognize that this was no longer true. To preserve long-standing beliefs, people construct rationalizations that explain away discordant information. In Case 2.2, declining sales of service parts were attributed to alleged improvements in the durability of original equipment.

Judgmental heuristics and the fallacies of informal logic can degrade PI efforts. The availability heuristic leads people to be overly concerned with issues that are easily imagined in vivid scenarios. Red herrings often arise as a result of hasty generalization, in which an unusual case is used to conclude that something is fundamentally awry. The fact that a talented employee has resigned does not establish that a company's career development practices are inadequate. The illusion of control can delay PI if managers mistakenly assume they can handle troubles in their areas of responsibility. PI is also thwarted when the cause of a problem is misdiagnosed, so that the true cause or root problem goes unrecognized. A camera manufacturer disappointed with sales of a new product concluded that the sales shortfall was caused by ineffective advertising. Confronted by its client's displeasure, the advertising agency took a closer look at the situation. It found that the product had a "me-too" design and that the company's distribution system was inadequate. Had the company changed agencies, these underlying problems might have gone undetected.

Eroding goals, in which problems are "solved" by lowering aspiration levels to make current performance more acceptable, can prevent PI in the same way. A company's receiving department accepted batches of nonconforming materials. Each decision to accept was based on precedents established by prior decisions. As a result, inspectors effectively ignored deviations between incoming goods and relevant specifications. With scapegoating, problems are blamed on someone who is unable or unwilling to defend himself. As a result, the problem is not addressed. An airline had trouble interfacing its flights with those of smaller commuter lines with which it partnered. Airline managers fell into the habit of blaming lost baggage or missed connections on supposed mistakes by the commuter line involved. The commuter lines were unconcerned because their compensation was volume-based and took no account of service quality. As a result, weaknesses in the customer service system were not addressed. To insure that problems are identified and solved, it is best to assume responsibility for performance, even when it is not wholly under one's control.

# Improving Problem Identification

How can problem identification be improved? Some recommendations are implied by the chapter's contents thus far. SPC and other techniques should be used when appropriate. Beware of red herrings, misprioritizations, and other modes of PI failure. People can guard against mental mistakes that threaten PI. If one is aware of factors that make it difficult to identify certain problems, compensating efforts can be made when such factors are operative. Thus, knowing how hard it is to assess the performance of staff units, organizations should give extra attention to those areas. Organizations should establish and strengthen quality control, internal auditing, planning, and other functions that promote PI. Information systems should be developed to facilitate PI. Organizations must insure that their policies, procedures, and cultures promote awareness and communication of problems, while discouraging cover-ups and head-in-the-sand behavior.

## Prescriptions

In addition to our discussions to this point are 14 other prescriptions. Some of these have been alluded to, but bear further development. Figure 3.4 summarizes this advice.

*1. Actively look for problems.* Organizations and their members must constantly strive to improve things. This is largely a matter of organizational culture and individual attitudes. It is something management can influence by its own example and through reward and recognition practices. The desired attitude was demonstrated by a worker at The Paul Revere Insurance Companies, who questioned the firm's policy of maintaining zero balances in special purpose checking accounts. Upon investigating, the company realized it could save $5000 a year by maintaining defined minimum balances in accounts.

*2. Go to Gemba.* *Gemba* is a Japanese term meaning "where the action takes place." When something goes wrong, managers must get to that place and observe what has happened. Like Sherlock Holmes studying the scene of a crime, put yourself in a position to notice things. The U.S. Air Force improved its response to in-flight equipment malfunctions by stationing maintenance personnel to be ready to debrief crew members when aircraft landed. However, this advice is more general. For managers, the action takes place in the operational areas for which they are

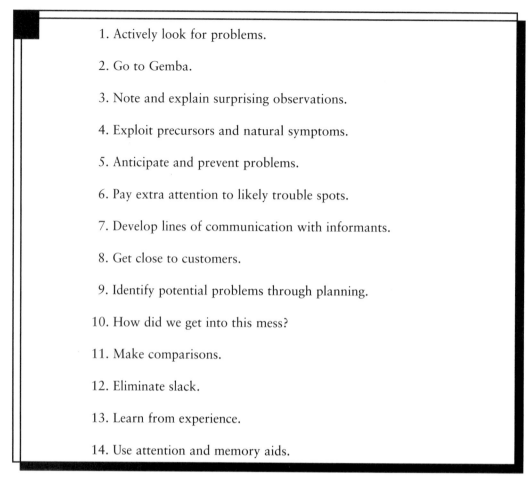

1. Actively look for problems.

2. Go to Gemba.

3. Note and explain surprising observations.

4. Exploit precursors and natural symptoms.

5. Anticipate and prevent problems.

6. Pay extra attention to likely trouble spots.

7. Develop lines of communication with informants.

8. Get close to customers.

9. Identify potential problems through planning.

10. How did we get into this mess?

11. Make comparisons.

12. Eliminate slack.

13. Learn from experience.

14. Use attention and memory aids.

**Figure 3.4**   Prescriptions for problem identification

responsible. Thus, the prescription is also known as "management by walking around." While leading a group of customers on a plant tour, the president of a Canadian snowmobile manufacturer noticed the following: technicians searching for equipment needed to complete setups, operators straining to read blueprints in a poorly lighted area, a welding machine that produced 50 percent rejects due to inadequate maintenance, lack of lubricating oils necessitating shutdowns of machining centers, and mechanics idled because of small parts shortages. Problems do not always make their way to one's in-basket. They must be sought in their natural habitats.

***3. Note and explain surprising observations.***   The Japanese have a term for this too. *Warusa-kagen* are things that are not really problems, but do not seem quite right. It may be the rippling in Jack Lemmon's coffee or a tired feeling the day before you are hammered by the flu. One often experiences such anomalies along with the recognition, several days later, of what it meant: "Oh, that's why such-and-such." It is easy to ignore them (I turn a deaf ear to unusual sounds coming from my car), and most of the time, there is no loss in doing so. Anomalies usually end up as nothing of significance. But sometimes they foretell avoidable problems, and therein lies the justification for attending to *warusa-kagen*. Even if 99 out of 100 of these wells come up dry, the benefit of following up on the winner can justify time spent on the others. Make a habit of taking anomalies more seriously. Do not initiate a full-scale study of every oddity in life, but do not ignore them either.

**4. Exploit precursors and natural symptoms.** Some problems announce themselves with precursors, like the small tip slides at Aberfan, or symptoms that the situation naturally makes available. A telltale sign of speculative lending by financial institutions is above-market growth and yields. These symptoms were observable before the demise of the Atlantic Acceptance Corporation, a Canadian lender that collapsed in the mid 1960s. Determine how particular problems are likely to be manifested, and monitor for these symptoms. Under Florida Power and Light's Condition Assessment program, workers inspect equipment to identify precursors to failure, such as hairline cracks in piping. Ford experienced broken taps during a machining operation for the Taurus. Production engineers rigged a sound detection system that monitored machine vibration, shutting it off before the tap broke.

**5. Anticipate and prevent problems.** Not all problems can be anticipated, and others do not warrant the effort. But an attempt to anticipate and prevent should be made for important issues that could be predicted. Many safety hazards fit this description. A quality circle at Furukawa Electric Company used a "what-if" method to anticipate accidents, determine their likely causes, and implement preventive measures. Breakdowns of critical equipment may also deserve this kind of attention. Prompted by Japanese quality consultants, Florida Power and Light studied trees growing near power lines and developed tree-cutting cycles to reduce the incidence of outages caused by fallen trees.

**6. Pay extra attention to likely trouble spots.** Watch cracks between departments for "orphans," issues ignored because no one takes responsibility. Production problems are often found in high cost operations, areas generating lots of scrap and rework, bottleneck and delay areas, assignments that require extensive walking, and activities that are not proceduralized. In offices, look for overflowing in-baskets and stacks of folders that have not been refiled. Changes cause disruptions and difficulties. Be alert to problems after a change in management, changes in staffing levels, revisions to policies or procedures, or initiation of a new program. PI efforts are wisely directed by an appreciation of problems' common hangouts.

**7. Develop lines of communication with informants.** The most important informants for identifying quality problems are employees and customers. The importance of customer complaints is demonstrated by the well-known story of how Tennant Company learned that its floor cleaning machines had chronic oil leaks. While few American customers expressed dissatisfaction with Tennant's products—they presumably wiped up or ignored the oil—Japanese users had a higher performance standard. Their persistent complaints prompted Tennant to initiate a successful program of eliminating oil leaks. Other sources of information, including suppliers, regulators, and technical experts, should be cultivated. Establish channels that routinely provide PI information. Actively solicit complaints and suggestions.

**8. Get close to customers.** Establishing communication channels with customers is necessary but not sufficient for PI. Product users may not express their dissatisfactions and can be unaware of potential improvements. Thus, you must do more than just listen to your customers. Talk with them. Be with them. Observe the product in use. While accompanying a news photographer on assignment, the general manager of Kodak's Professional Photography Division noticed that the photographer had difficulty opening a film canister while holding his camera. As a result, Kodak developed a container that could be opened with one hand, burnishing its reputation among news photographers. Experience the product the way customers do. When a quality team could not get hospital administrators to approve the installation of privacy curtains in recovery rooms, they had administrators wear surgical gowns over their clothes. Once administrators realized that where clothing showed on them, skin showed on patients, they agreed to the request.

**9. Identify potential problems through planning.** These are called threats and opportunities in the planning literature, things to worry about and things to exploit. No planning method has ever demonstrated an ability to predict discontinuous events, things that seemingly come out of nowhere to affect the organization. No planner has a crystal ball, but planning can integrate disparate pieces of knowledge to project outcomes of current trends and conditions. This can help in anticipating future problems. The city of Sunnyvale, California, used long-term planning to manage the closing of city schools and to justify expenditures for street maintenance. Enacted in plausible scenarios of the future, potential problems become real enough to motivate current actions.

**10. How did we get into this mess?** This question is a heuristic for identifying historical causes and systemic problems responsible for current troubles. Applied to The Publishing Company Case (Case 2.3), it highlighted a systemic problem that deserved attention: Acquisitions editors could create downstream difficulties by giving authors expanded control over production decisions. Virtually all parties to the abortion controversy agree that unwanted pregnancies should be prevented. How did we get into this mess? By not using birth control. The heuristic offers no help in addressing the current situation—it is still a mess—but its use can provoke actions that keep similar situations from happening in the future.

**11. Make comparisons.** Relatively sophisticated comparative methods like performance monitoring and benchmarking are used to identify problems. Simpler approaches can also be effective. People can compare different ways of performing a task in terms of time and expense. An office worker at Toyota observed that a special delivery letter and a regular letter, posted from the same place on the same date, arrived at the same time. After an informal experiment confirmed her finding, the company revised its mailing practices. Workers can compare the time each takes to perform a task. Such a comparison helped another Toyota worker realize she was wasting time sorting documents. Her counterpart in another department received documents that were presorted by the originating office, something they had not been asked to do for her section. Organizations establish comparable operating units, such as retail outlets, or factories, so performances can be compared and the lessons of experience shared. Hewlett-Packard learned about inefficiencies in a production operation when high demand prompted the company to transfer in workers from a similar plant. These workers were appalled at the operation's disorder and disruptions caused by missing parts. Their complaints led to improvements.

***12. Eliminate slack.*** The metaphor of lowering the water level in a lake to expose the rocks illustrates how slack in a system prevents problem identification. There are several variations on this theme. Slack, as inventory, cushions operations so they are not as disciplined as they should be. Slack can show up as a tolerance for mistakes, practices that make errors less bothersome, hence less likely to be eliminated. Workers at Asahi National Electric often broke mirrors when installing them in frames. Actions to improve the operation were only taken when safety stock was eliminated and replacement parts were tightly controlled. Milliken Contract Carpets (UK) gave customers liberal allowances for off-quality product. Though customers were satisfied, the policy didn't motivate Milliken's plant to produce flawless carpeting. When the policy was changed and the plant was forced to deal with customer returns and bear the costs of shoddy product, its quality improved dramatically. Slack can take the form of unneeded workers. A common strategy for improving efficiency is to reduce staffing, forcing remaining people to work harder and smarter and discontinue marginal tasks. Slack can be uncovered by cutting back on service levels or by discontinuing services to see if they are needed. Newspapers drop comic strips and other features to see if anyone cares. In Visalia, California, streets were swept every three weeks. The city gradually stretched this cycle to four, five, and then six weeks before provoking complaints. It settled on a four-week cycle. The same strategy was used to reduce the frequency of grass mowing in city parks.

***13. Learn from experience.*** This prescription, perhaps the central lesson of the book, is especially relevant to PI. What kinds of problems, accidents, errors, and opportunities have been encountered in the past, and how did they make themselves known? Knowing what to look for can help one anticipate issues and detect others as they become evident. An experiential learning strategy has been applied with safety hazards, as through FAA monitoring of incidents during airline flights and the use of experience-based programs to improve workplace safety. It has also been employed to reduce equipment failures, as in Florida Power and Light's practice of analyzing FPL and industry failure data. The approach can be used in less dramatic applications as well. Workers at Stanadyne's Diesel Systems Division developed charts informing each operator of the defects most likely to occur at that station. Warned of potential problems, workers can prevent them from happening.

***14. Use attention and memory aids.*** Recognized problems often fade into oblivion as they lose out in the competition for attention. Managers have more to attend to than they can keep in mind, so things get set aside and, before long, forgotten. The recommendation is to provide attention and memory aids for PI purposes. Information technology (IT) is a key resource in this regard. Some companies have IT-based systems for handling customer complaints. Similar systems can be used to record and track other kinds of problems. These systems include prompting devices, the electronic equivalent of a tickler file, which bring issues up for review at appropriate times. The most valuable practice is to maintain formal agendas of issues for the organization and its subunits. Every manager, conceivably every employee, should maintain a list of problems deserving attention, thought, and action. Items should be added to such lists as they are identified and deleted when the situation has improved or the matter no longer deserves attention. At Cypress Semiconductor, everyone except factory workers and laborers maintains a computer-based list of 10 to 15 objectives, along with due dates. Lists are updated weekly. Managers review lists of subordinates, following up with those who need help.

## Managing Problem Identification

Problem identification is an organizational function that must be managed. Rather than being assigned to a special department, the PI function is the responsibility of every manager, indeed of every employee. Like planning, performance monitoring, and other discretionary activities, PI consumes resources. It requires time, money, and effort. An organization can do too much PI or too little, or it can allocate PI resources ineffectively.

The possibility of doing too much PI is apparent from the chapter. Companies can promote problem identification in so many different ways and so many of these—actively look for problems, anticipate and prevent problems, learn from experience—are bottomless pits, potentially absorbing all of one's efforts all the time. Problem identification cannot be perfected. It is not a target for Zero Defects programs, and there is no economic justification for anticipating everything that could possibly go wrong. Individuals and organizations must be careful not to overdose on PI.

There is also the risk of not doing enough. This risk applies most strongly to a few critical issues for each organization. Product and worker safety are such concerns. Equipment failure is another, especially when large service networks, as in utilities, or public safety, as with airlines, are involved. Other issues warranting special PI efforts include competitor activities, technological threats and opportunities, and international political developments. As part of managing PI, each organization should specify strategic issues bearing closely on its well-being and insure that effective, dedicated PI programs are in place for those issues. The benefits of quickly identifying and preventing problems of this magnitude justify those focused extra efforts.

In most organizations, whether too much or too little is done for PI purposes, what is done could be done better. Too many unnecessary inspections are conducted. Too many periodic reports guard against problems not seen in years. More recently, too many surveys of indifferent customers and employees tell us less and less about how to improve things. This chapter suggests ways in which PI resources can be applied more effectively.

If organizational problem identification is done correctly, a multitude of mostly low-level concerns will be continuously generated by various means. These constitute the improvement agendas for most organization members. More important problems compete for the attention of senior managers, who also receive reports from special PI systems focused on strategic issues. Some low-level problems and improvement opportunities will, no doubt, go undetected. The organization will occasionally be blindsided by strategic developments that may or may not have been foreseeable. Such lapses notwithstanding, every member of the organization will constantly be looking for ways to improve things, and the organization will be making effective efforts to identify matters of concern.

## NOTES

1. Material in this chapter has previously appeared in: Gerald F. Smith, "Identifying Quality Problems: Prospects for Improvement," *Total Quality Management* 7, no. 5 (1996): 535–552.
2. Vaughn Beals, "Harley-Davidson: An American Success Story," *Journal of Quality and Participation* 11, no. 2 (1988): A19–A23.
3. Douglas C. Montgomery, *Introduction to Statistical Quality Control*, 3rd ed. (New York: John Wiley & Sons, 1996).
4. Robert C. Camp, *Benchmarking* (Milwaukee: ASQC Quality Press, 1989).
5. Mary Walton, *Deming Management at Work* (New York: Perigee, 1990).
6. David A. Garvin, *Managing Quality: The Strategic and Competitive Edge* (New York: Free Press, 1988).
7. Randy Y. Hirokawa, Dennis S. Gouran, and Amy E. Martz, "Understanding the Sources of Faulty Group Decision Making: A Lesson from the *Challenger* Disaster," *Small Group Behavior* 19, no. 4 (1988): 411–433.

# chapter 4

# Problem Definition

---

## Chapter Outline

### What Is Problem Definition?

### Defining Managerial Problems

### Techniques
Affinity Diagrams
Concept Maps
Stratification
Check Sheets
Histograms
Pareto Analysis

### Definitional Mistakes
Framing Errors
Focusing Errors
The Wrong Parts
Missed Connections
Mistakes of Style

### The Situation Definition and Analysis (SDA) Method
1. State the presenting problem
2. Analyze the presenting problem
3. Broaden and deepen the analysis
4. Bound the problem
5. Diagram the situation
6. Identify topics requiring further study
7. Develop an overall problem-solving plan
8. Develop a summary account of the situation

---

A not-so-ancient adage holds that a problem well defined is a problem half-solved. But how should problems be defined? What constitutes an adequate definition of a problem? This chapter responds to these questions, developing an account of problem definition (PD) and proposing a definitional method. The chapter includes material on data collection and analysis, which are information-seeking activities that support problem definition. Thus, the chapter is concerned with thinking that occurs after a problem has been identified but before more problem-specific thinking is undertaken.

## What Is Problem Definition?

Having identified a problem, one must determine its nature. Though the two activities—problem identification and definition—often blend together, they are conceptually distinct: Through PI, one becomes aware of an issue; through PD, one comes to understand it.

Thus, a problem definition answers the question, "What is the problem?" That this question is even asked reflects the elusive nature of problems. They are situations that must be defined if they are to be thought about and communicated to others. Adopting the cognitivist view that thinking employs mental representations of whatever one is thinking about (Chapter 2), it follows that problems must be mentally represented or defined as part of problem solving. This mental representation can be expressed in verbal or graphic depictions as well.

Problem definition denotes both a process and a product, the former resulting in the latter. The definitional process develops an understanding of the situation and is sometimes called *situation assessment*. The process has three components:

1. Bounding or framing the situation by specifying what is and is not to be included in it.
2. Characterizing the situation in terms of the elements and relationships that comprise it.
3. Interpreting the situation in light of relevant knowledge.

Problem definition develops a mental account of the situation that directs and informs subsequent problem solving. With real-world problems, this account will usually indicate that the situation encompasses a number of interrelated problems. The effects of PD are especially pronounced on information gathering and diagnosis tasks. Good definitions raise questions to be addressed by such activities; poor definitions foster assumptions that might be mistaken. PD also serves a communicative purpose. By representing the situation with words or diagrams, one can communicate it to others, perhaps as part of securing their support.

One aspect of problem definition—the relationship between problems and symptoms—has been a source of considerable confusion. The issue came to my attention most forcefully once when I was teaching. While talking about my tried-and-true "sales are below budget" problem, I was interrupted by a student who asserted that this might be a problem for an accountant, but for marketing people like himself, "sales are below budget" is merely a symptom of the "real" problem responsible for the sales shortfall. Though initially taken aback by the student's assertion, I soon recognized what was awry. The student's claim reflects the fallacy of bifurcation, or viewing things in either/or terms. People mistakenly assume that problems and symptoms are mutually exclusive categories, like light and heavy. While something cannot be both light and heavy, it can be both a problem and a symptom. A problem is a situation that bears improvement. A symptom is the visible effect of some cause. A situation can be both, as "sales are below budget" demonstrates. One must determine the cause of the symptom/problem to improve things, and this cause may also be a problem. However, it is no more "real" than the obvious problem it produced.

# Defining Managerial Problems

Figure 4.1 reports the Resource Recovery Plant Case, a situation encountered by a public utility, along with problem definitions proposed by managers asked to "carefully state or define the central or primary problem in the case." Their definitions indicate the many ways in which this situation can be defined. The Resource Recovery Plant Case is not unusual in this respect; real-world problems permit great definitional variety. Is there a correct definition, one that gets to the "real" problem? Or are all definitions equally valid so that it matters little which is adopted? These questions are addressed in this section, and the Resource Recovery Plant Case is used to illustrate ways in which managerial problems are defined.

One way of defining a problem is to say what is clearly wrong or in need of improvement, the most obvious existing state-desired state gap. This is known as the **presenting problem**. It is usually what first arouses concern over the situation, though it is not often the only problem or even the most important one. Definitions 1 and 2 in Figure 4.1 are of this kind. Such definitions are rarely very informative. For instance, it would be foolish for a staff person, in a meeting convened to deal with the Resource Recovery Plant Case, to announce with table-pounding fanfare that the key problem was the plant's unprofitable operations. Nonetheless, the presenting problem provides a starting point for thinking about the situation.

A problem definition implicitly or explicitly bounds or frames the situation. This is one source of definitional variety: Different definitions specify different slices of reality, encompassing different problematic parts of the situation. Figure 4.2 includes many elements and issues (nodes or dots) that are interrelated (connected by lines), all a part of a larger sphere of reality (the enclosing figure). To define a problem within this sphere of reality, three kinds of boundaries must be set, indicated by dashed and dotted lines within the figure. First, one must demarcate the target problem from other concerns at the same level of analysis. A company's quality problems may be caused by outdated machinery. A cause of this situation is the firm's financial condition, which results from a declining market for its products. These concerns cannot all be addressed at once. While acknowledging the existence of such problems, a definition must focus on a manageable set of concerns, indicated by the dashed lines in Figure 4.2.

Problem situations must also be bounded from above, where they extend into the larger **macroworld** (Figure 4.2). This is the realm of antecedent historical events

**Resource Recovery Plant Case**

A commercial waste-to-energy resource recovery plant was constructed and put into operation by a major public utility. The plant accepts rubbish and garbage from surrounding municipalities, converting 70 percent into burnable fuel with the remaining 30 percent sent to the land fill.

The plant has contracted to process a certain daily volume of municipal waste. It was projected to make a profit from processing fees and income from recovered fuel material. However, its first year of operation has resulted in sizable losses. Labor costs are high and equipment breakdowns have been frequent. The workforce of 60, three times what was originally planned, is a response to the plant's low processing rate, only 75 percent of rated capacity. Extra people and overtime have been used to try to increase throughput to a level that would satisfy municipal contracts.

Processing difficulties have resulted from the refuse stream, which has included refrigerators, hazardous medical wastes from area hospitals, chunks of concrete from construction sites, and other items that the equipment wasn't designed to handle. Since the union contract forbids layoffs, the plant seems saddled with the excessive labor force, even as efficiency improves to the point where workers are no longer needed.

Corporate management wants to avoid union troubles over a relatively small part of the company. However, management expects this plant to operate profitably.

**Proposed Problem Definitions**

1. "The plant is not operating profitably."
2. "Excessive processing costs."
3. "The problem here was the projections that were made for this plant and on which their contract is based."
4. "Poor operations management is the plant's primary problem."
5. "The problem is that a very inflexible labor contract was agreed to."
6. "The central problem appears to be the excessive labor force."
7. "It seems that the primary problem in this case is the type or stream of refuse the plant is receiving."
8. "The primary problem is that the plant is being used to handle waste types that it was not designed to process."

Figure 4.1   The Resource Recovery Plant Case and proposed definitions

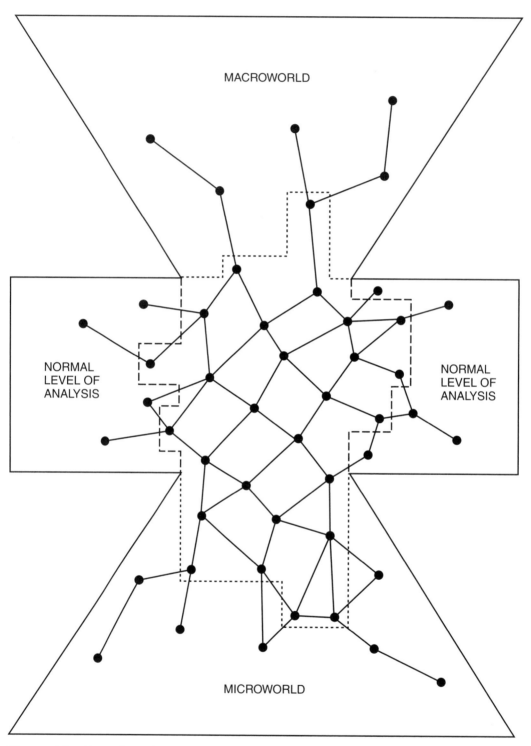

**Figure 4.2** Bounding the situation

and larger systemic causes, issues that come to mind when one asks, "How did we get into this mess?" Definitions 3, 4, and 5 in Figure 4.1 are of this kind. They point to prior activities (poor planning) and general inadequacies (weak management) deemed responsible for the situation. These larger problems should be recognized. Focusing too narrowly on the current situation can leave one in a fire-fighting mode, addressing the same problem over and over again as it is regenerated by a flawed system. On the other hand, one can push too far into the larger system, undertaking a quixotic mission with scant chance of success. When setting this upper boundary, consider your degree of practical influence in the situation and whether evidence justifies concluding that a systemic problem exists. Bound at the lowest level likely to remedy the current problem and prevent its recurrence.

The final boundary to be drawn is the most malleable. It is a temporary fence set up to prevent thinking from getting ahead of knowledge. This boundary extends into the **microworld** (Figure 4.2), detailed characteristics of the situation that can be uncovered through investigation. These characteristics include causes, constraints, goals, and means pertinent to the problem. Definitions 6, 7, and 8 make modest forays into this realm. Here the danger is of moving too far too fast and losing sight of other possibilities. Viewing the labor force as the cause of the plant's unprofitability, one might ignore opportunities to improve refuse processing procedures or to have municipalities prescreen their inputs. Initial PD efforts should be cautious in drawing conclusions about the true cause, critical constraint, or best means in a situation. One should go no further than available evidence allows, developing a broad, open-minded view of the problem.

Characterizing situations in terms of elements and relationships is another aspect of problem definition and source of definitional variety. This characterization can refer to problems, stakeholders, goals, constraints, difficulties, causes, effects, resources, means, facts, beliefs, uncertainties, unknowns, alternatives, costs, benefits, and other conceptual kinds. The elements used to describe a situation reflect what kind of problem it is. Decision problems, those focused on an act of choice, are characterized in terms of alternatives, values, outcomes, and uncertainties. The representation of a conformance problem will emphasize observed effects and their possible causes. Many situations have a history that must be understood. As suggested by Figure 4.1, most problem definitions only cite a few elements and relationships. Since the situation consists of many such elements, different definitions can be proposed. This leads to arguments over the identity of the "real" problem: the goal, cause, or constraint most critical for resolving the situation.

If a definition is to help one understand a problem, it must move beyond specifying elements and relationships. The problem must be represented in broader terms as a recognizable kind of situation. A definition might identify structures manifested in the case or classify the problem as of a certain type. Definition 8 in Figure 4.1 suggests such a structure: The plant's troubles result from a mismatch between its design and the waste stream. The case also demonstrates an example of buy now, pay later: The work force was increased to satisfy short-term needs without regard for the long-term effects of that action. Some managers categorize this case as one of union troubles, a familiar problem type. It can also be viewed as a matter of start-up difficulties, in which a new system has bugs to work out.

Problem definitions are often associated with perspectives, distinct ways of looking at things. Different stakeholder perspectives can be adopted, along with different functional area (marketing, operations) or temporal (short-term, long-term) points of view. Perspectivism can lead to definitional relativism. Some relativists claim that any situation consists of distinct problems reflecting individual stakeholder perspectives. Thus, the Resource Recovery Plant Case includes management's problem, the union's problem, the municipalities' problem, and others. It all depends on how you look at it! But conflicting stakeholder interests are the heart of the issue, and these conflicts must be resolved by an acceptable solution. Saying that each agent has its own problem provides no help in reaching that solution.

Another version of relativism proposes that all definitions are equally valid. Remember, however, that problem definitions direct subsequent problem-solving activity. Many definitions send problem solvers down blind alleys, while only a few direct attention in ways leading to effective solutions. A problem definition can be better or more valid than another by virtue of its positive problem-solving impact.

The belief that definitions matter gives rise to a final definitional fallacy, the view that the situation contains an underlying "true" or "real" problem expressed by the "right" definition. The "real" problem typically states a critical cause, constraint, or means in the situation. On this account, problem-solving failures reflect definitional mistakes: not recognizing the "real" problem and consequently solving the "wrong" one. The fallacy here is the assumption that one can determine, early in the problem-solving process, which definitional path will succeed. A best or true definition may exist, but no one can say for sure what it is, what cause, constraint, or means will be critical. Consequently, the best definition is the most inclusive, the one cutting off the fewest possibilities. During the formative initial stages of problem solving, problems should be represented with comprehensive accounts that include everything plausibly relevant to the situation's resolution. For the Resource Recovery Plant Case, the best definition would include all those cited in Figure 4.1, and then some.

# Techniques

There are no strong general methods for defining real-world problems. Experts in specialized fields have ways of characterizing situations they face, but these methods do not generalize. Managerial problems usually involve open systems subject to many influences, making problem definition more difficult. Heuristics have been proposed. One example is: Characterize the situation in terms of "too little" or "too much" of something. However, few have been tested, and they hardly constitute a comprehensive PD method. Of broader scope are diagrammatic techniques for representing problem situations. Some of these are intended to be general, while others, such as decision trees, only apply in certain situations. After discussing diagrams for representing problems, this section considers data collection and analysis methods. Since this material is familiar to many readers, the topics are not covered in detail.

## Affinity Diagrams

Also known as the KJ Method, this is a group technique for generating and organizing a large set of ideas and information.[1] Items are clustered on the basis of affinity or relatedness. Affinity diagrams can be used for many purposes. They are pertinent to problem definition, which requires that aspects of a complex situation be organized in a coherent representation.

Once a problem-solving team has been established, it can develop an affinity diagram by following these steps:

1. Phrase the issue in general terms.
2. Generate and record information and ideas. Most of these will result from brainstorming, though external research, such as observation and interviews, can be conducted.
3. Write ideas on cards, making them visible and accessible to team members.
4. Sort cards into groups based on affinity.
5. Create header cards that label each group with its defining content.
6. Construct a diagram that organizes groups of cards into a meaningful arrangement.

Figure 4.3 is an affinity diagram that might have been constructed for the Resource Recovery Plant Case.

Generality and operationality are the great virtues of this method. It is easy to use and can be applied in most problem situations. Its major weakness is the notion of affinity itself. Problem situations involve elements in many different relationships, including cause-effect, means-ends, and temporal order. Affinity encompasses all

| Corporate Management | Resource Recovery Plant | Municipalities |
|---|---|---|
| Expects plant to be profitable | First year of operation | Fixed price contract |
| Avoid trouble with union | First plant of its kind | Volume commitment by plant |
| Cake and eat it too? | Small part of company | Many sources of refuse |
|  | Inadequate plant design? | Many kinds of refuse |
|  |  | Don't control refuse |
|  |  | Regard as trash pickup |

| Labor | Equipment | Refuse | Plant Performance |
|---|---|---|---|
| Excessive labor costs | Can't process waste | Troublesome types | Sizable operating losses |
| Excessive workforce | Frequent breakdowns | Refrigerators | Processing at 75% of capacity |
| Union forbids layoffs | Reconfigure? | Medical wastes | Improvements in throughput |
| Workers not needed | Need new equipment? | Concrete | Unrealistic projections |
| High union wage rates | What breaks down? | Screening methods |  |
| Unskilled positions | Questionable selection | Municipalities screen? |  |

Figure 4.3   Affinity diagram

such relationships, making no distinctions among them. A stronger method would recognize different relationships among elements of a situation and allow an item to be connected to other kinds of items. In Figure 4.3, refuse screening methods, listed with the Refuse grouping, might be related to plant performance, labor, and municipalities. Diagramming conventions prevent such relationships from being depicted. As a result, affinity diagrams do not represent problem structures. An important part of the Resource Recovery Plant Case is the mismatch between equipment and the refuse stream. An affinity diagram could report this mismatch, but it could not depict it. Too, the method's idea generation step provides little aid toward recognizing such structures. When used for PD, affinity diagrams are a quick-and-dirty means of generating and organizing elements of a problem situation. Speed is gained at a loss in depth. The method can be used to define problems that do not warrant a full-scale treatment or as a front-end to intensive definitional efforts.

## Concept Maps

This term covers a family of techniques that yield relatively free-form diagrams consisting of nodes connected by arrows.[2] Nodes represent concepts or ideas, and arrows depict relationships, usually of cause-and-effect. Concept maps include relationship diagrams, interrelationship digraphs, cognitive maps, and influence diagrams. They are constructed much the same as affinity diagrams, with brainstorming used to generate elements. Rather than sorting elements into clusters, group members identify causal or other relationships among them. Concepts are arranged so relationships can be depicted by arrows. The result is a network of interrelated concepts highlighting key parts of the problem situation and displaying some of its structure. The Resource Recovery Plant Case is represented by the concept map in Figure 4.4.

Concept maps have a clear advantage over affinity diagrams: They can depict the complex relational structures of problem situations. They are more flexible than cause-and-effect diagrams (Chapter 5), because they are not restricted to causal relationships and are not focused on a single problem or goal. The methodology would profit from explicit recognition of the kinds of elements and relationships comprising problems and labeling these kinds within maps. The major limitation of concept mapping is its lack of generative power. The method offers little help in identifying elements and relationships or in recognizing problem structures. Concept maps are useful ways to represent problem situations, but the methodology provides scant aid in determining what to include in its representations.

## Stratification

A data collection and analysis method, stratification is applicable to problems consisting of multiple occurrences of certain events or those that otherwise involve groups or collectives.[3] Most quality problems satisfy this requirement. Conformance problems, for instance, usually involve multiple instances of defective products. A sales shortfall encompasses the activities of many salespeople trying to sell many products to different customers. Problems consisting of one-time events—the collapse of a bridge or The Publishing Company Case, for example—do not lend themselves to stratification.

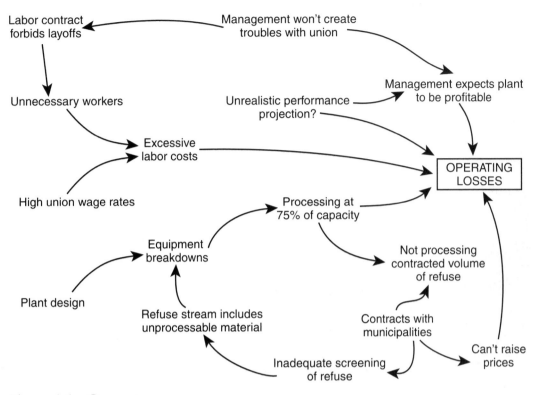

**Figure 4.4** Concept map

Stratification works by analyzing a collective into its component parts, directing attention to critical factors. Identifying bases for stratifying is the key to using the method. Nonconforming products might be stratified in terms of materials, workers, shifts, or time of production. Each is a potential clue to the cause of defects. When switchboard operators at a Japan Steel Works plant investigated complaints that telephones were not being answered promptly, they stratified calls by department and identified engineers as major culprits. After experiencing a 33 percent increase in meter reading errors, Florida Power and Light did a stratification study of errors by reader. They found that one new employee was responsible for 33 of the 79 mistakes.

Stratification is the foundation for check sheets, histograms, and Pareto analysis. It is quite general, reasonably powerful, and highly operational. The most common mistake is failure to stratify on the critical dimension of analysis. Problem solvers usually have reliable intuitions about appropriate lines of investigation. When these intuitions fail, one can adopt a shotgun approach, stratifying around any characteristic that seems relevant. Stratification will not tell you what to do about the critical factor, but simply identifying this factor is often the key to problem resolution.

## Check Sheets

A check sheet is a data recording device, a medium on which problem-relevant data can be entered in a format facilitating analysis.[4] In a typical check sheet, an instance of an event, such as a defective product, is recorded by a mark in an appropriate box. Each box is defined by one or more dimensions—for instance, the nature and location of the defect. A completed check sheet reports the frequency with which different events are observed.

The first challenge in developing a check sheet is to identify dimensions that define different boxes or categories. Stratification addresses this task; in effect, every check sheet is underwritten by a stratification. It is also important to operationalize dimensions so data can be reliably recorded to the correct category. If paint blemishes are categorized as major or minor, operators need verbal classification criteria and visual examples of each category. Finally, dimensions must be organized in a recording instrument—the check sheet—that operators can understand and use. This can be difficult when two or more dimensions are being monitored. Figure 4.5 is a check sheet used to record customer complaints at a restaurant. Check sheets do not always provide useful information. If data entries occur uniformly across categories, one might consider other dimensions of analysis. The technique is easy to implement and can deliver major informational benefits at low cost.

## Histograms

Histograms, a traditional graphic tool for representing data, summarize variation along one dimension in a set of data by indicating the frequency with which different measurements or values are observed.[5] The horizontal or x-axis of a histogram represents the dimension of interest, subdivided into a manageable number of categories. The vertical or y-axis denotes the number of observations within a category. Given a set of data such as the length of steel rods, a histogram can be constructed by:

1. Designating categories or intervals of measurement (one centimeter increments, ranging from 10 to 20 centimeters)
2. Counting the observations in each category
3. Constructing a bar for each category with a height corresponding to the category's observed frequency

Figure 4.6 shows a final product.

One advantage of histograms is their visual power. Compared with check sheets and other tabular presentations, histograms exploit our ability to see patterns in graphic depictions of data. A histogram's shape offers clues to the nature of the process generating the data. On the other hand, a histogram is unidimensional in that it describes its object with only one characteristic. If that characteristic is unimportant for problem solving, the histogram has little value. So, again, the selection of dimensions for stratification is critical. Histograms are also limited by their lack of a time dimension. A trend in the values of observations taken over time will not be apparent. This is unfortunate since time trend can be more significant than the distribution of frequencies.

## Pareto Analysis

A widely used QPS tool, Pareto analysis is based on two claims.[6] First, the Pareto principle holds that many phenomena are unevenly distributed along certain

CUSTOMER COMPLAINTS

| FOOD | | | | | |
|------|---|---|---|---|---|
| **COMPLAINT** | **MENU ITEM** | | | | |
| | A | B | C | . . . | Z |
| Overcooked | | | | | |
| Undercooked | | | | | |
| Portion too small | | | | | |
| . . . . . . | | | | | |
| Overspiced | | | | | |

| SERVICE | | | | | |
|---------|---|---|---|---|---|
| **COMPLAINT** | **SERVER** | | | | |
| | HM | BD | RC | JF | SA |
| Too slow | | | | | |
| Order mistake | | | | | |
| Billing mistake | | | | | |
| . . . . . . | | | | | |
| Discourteous | | | | | |

**Figure 4.5**  Check sheet

dimensions. This is the famous "80-20 rule," which suggests that 80 percent of a firm's sales will be made to 20 percent of its customers. Second, when an uneven distribution occurs in a problem situation, one should focus on the "vital few" and ignore the "trivial many." Concentrate on the most prominent parts of the situation. Pareto analysis is often used as a diagnostic tool, as in helping identify the causes of

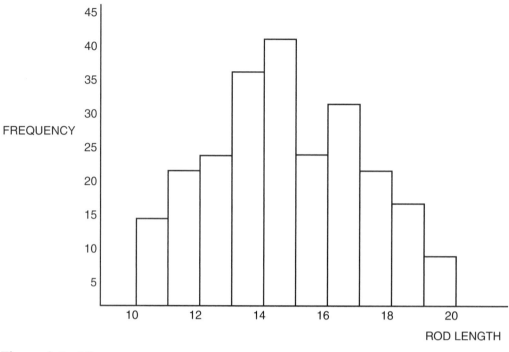

**Figure 4.6** Histogram

defects. More generally, it is a data collection and analysis method. For instance, it might be used to identify market segments offering the largest potential sales increases. Pareto analysis depends on stratification, identifying key dimensions for differentiating within a collective.

Pareto analysis employs Pareto charts or diagrams, which resemble histograms in that frequency of occurrence for a category is depicted by the height of a bar. Unlike histograms, categories are ordered by frequency, usually from left to right descending, rather than by a natural scale on the *x* axis. Categories can also be ordered by their financial impact, with the frequency of occurrences being adjusted by dollar-weightings. Categories reflect the dimension of stratification, often being types or causes of defects. Figure 4.7 is a Pareto diagram that might have been used in the Resource Recovery Plant Case. It categorizes processing stoppages by the kind of refuse responsible for the disruption. A hospital used Pareto analysis to identify the reasons obstetricians performed caesarean sections. Hewlett-Packard's customer support operation discovered, through Pareto analysis, that 80 percent of delays in delivering parts to customers were caused by waits for 20 percent of the parts, most of which came from other H-P divisions.

Pareto analysis is useful if outcomes are unevenly distributed along the chosen dimension. It focuses attention on major areas of concern. As with all stratification-based techniques, categories must be defined appropriately. A wire mill experiencing a high rate of defects due to contamination found that inspectors used contamination as a catch-all for defects that did not fit in other categories. Philip Crosby has been quoted as calling the Pareto chart "pretty much useless."[7] Though too negative by far, this judgment reflects the fact that Pareto analysis does not tell one what

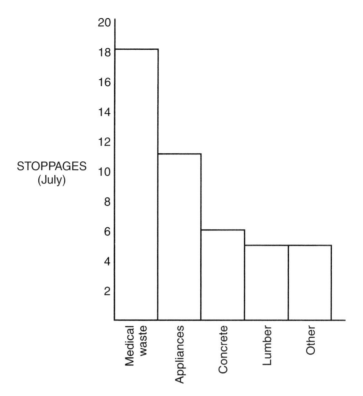

**Figure 4.7** Pareto diagram

to do about identified concerns. It is fair to say that the technique has been overused and is often applied with unrealistic expectations about what can be accomplished.

The foregoing methods are closely associated with quality management, and several are among the traditional "seven tools of quality." Figure 4.8 summarizes their strengths and limitations. Well-known business research methods, including interviewing and surveys, could also be discussed as data collection and analysis techniques. Other methods have been noted in the quality literature. For instance, videotaping is an effective means of studying certain processes. A distribution center used it to determine why one worker could load a rail car with more drums than anyone else. High-speed video can be employed for high-velocity activities. A Baxter Healthcare plant used this tool to determine why gaskets twisted when being applied to bottles by automated equipment. There seems to be an adequate repertoire of data collection and analysis methods for QPS purposes.

The picture is not so bright for problem definition. While concept maps have value, no existing graphical method delivers reliable, insightful problem representations. Though everyday verbal definitions may suffice, they rarely match up to the demands of complex, real-world problems. After considering common definitional mistakes, a method addressing this challenge will be proposed.

## Definitional Mistakes

The notions of Type I and Type II error—rejecting the null hypothesis when it is true, accepting it when it is false—are familiar parts of statistical hypothesis testing

| Method/Practice | Applications | Strengths | Weaknesses |
|---|---|---|---|
| Affinity Diagram | Generating and organizing a large set of ideas. | Widely applicable; easy to construct. | Does not depict relational structure of problems. |
| Concept Map | Depicting relationships among elements of problem situations. | Widely applicable; highly flexible. | Little help in identifying problem elements and relationships. |
| Stratification | Analyzing groups of instances into more useful categories. | Quite general; easy to use; can deliver substantial insights. | Can be difficult to identify appropriate bases for analysis. |
| Check Sheet | Recording frequency data in a multidimensional format. | Easy to use; compact data recording device. | Can be hard to construct; does not indicate trends. |
| Histogram | Representing frequency data in a unidimensional format. | Easy to construct; graphic depiction aids understanding. | Only records data on one dimension; does not indicate time trends. |
| Pareto Analysis | Analyzing groups of instances and directing attention to the most important categories. | Easy to construct and use; graphic depiction focuses attention. | Can be difficult to identify appropriate bases for analysis; not helpful if outcomes are evenly distributed. |

Figure 4.8   Overview of problem definition and research methods

methodology. So it is not surprising that a statistician, John Tukey, invented the concept of Type III error, solving the wrong problem.[8] Type III error is a rather murky concept. Unlike its predecessors, the probability of making this mistake cannot be quantified. It has come to be used as a catch-all term for mistakes of problem identification and definition. This section of the chapter develops a more extensive account of definitional errors.

Problem definition can be thought of as a storytelling activity, wherein one describes a situation to make it understandable. It is similar to what an author does in a novel or a director in a movie, except that the story is true, not fictional. Definitional mistakes parallel those made by storytellers. They are grouped into five categories.

## Framing Errors

Storytellers can err in the way they bound or frame their narrative. A novelist might include too much or too little of the story's context, the histories of major characters, for instance, or the setting within which action transpires. Read *Moby-Dick* and you will learn much that you do not care to know about whales and whaling. These mistakes correspond to questionable settings of situational boundaries depicted in Figure 4.2. A problem definition can encompass too many issues at a given level of analysis, sweeping in concerns that are better dealt with separately. Yes, the U.S. crime problem is related to drug use, urban poverty, and racism, but dealing with any of these is hard enough. Lumping them all together makes the task impossible. Problem definitions can also err in the other direction, leaving out problems that are critical to the situation's resolution. Sometimes you cannot fix what is wrong in Operations unless changes are made in Purchasing as well.

The same mistakes can be made in the macroworld, the larger system within which the presenting problem occurs. A definition can reach too far into this world, assailing the ultimate origins of current troubles. An operator's misinterpretation of instructions inspires a crusade for educational reform. Even admitting the larger problem, the current situation can be addressed more effectively at a lower level. On the other hand, by defining a situation too narrowly, one may be left stamping out fires that reappear because systemic failings have not been corrected. A related mistake is the failure to generalize appropriately, not seeing small problems as parts of a larger concern. A problem like "ineffective management" can only be discerned by generalizing over varied instances of issues handled incorrectly.

The TQM literature warns against framing errors, especially the mistake of overreaching. It has been argued that issues like "worker morale" and "communications" are too complex, abstract, and diffuse to be addressed effectively. Improvement teams at Westinghouse failed to make progress when they took on broad problems. Some of these troubles derive from group mandates. A quality circle consisting of workers from a low-level department should bound problems more narrowly than a cross-functional team that has top management support.

## Focusing Errors

These mistakes relate to the microworld depicted in Figure 4.2 and to how quickly problem-solving attention is narrowed by a definition. A storyteller knows from the start how things will turn out and who the key players will be. Problem solvers do not. As a result, they can mistakenly focus on aspects of the situation—means, goals, causes, constraints—that end up being peripheral. Premature narrowing of focus is the most common and serious mistake in defining real-world problems. Such mistakes result when definitional claims outrun the evidence needed to support them. We know sales are below budget, but do we really know the shortfall is caused by an unmotivated sales force?

The complementary mistake is to not focus quickly or deeply enough. Problem solvers must develop a rich picture of the situation that encompasses many possibilities. Since problem-solving resources are scarce, possibilities cannot all be explored to the same depth. It is necessary, as evidence allows, to attend to promising aspects of the situation while not forgetting matters that have moved to the background. People sometimes persist in treating all factors as equally significant despite evidence to the contrary. This results in inefficient problem definitions that leave one mulling around at the level of the presenting problem.

## The Wrong Parts

Other mistakes concern the specific parts—elements and relationships—included in a problem definition. A definition is a representation. Representations can err by including parts that do not matter, by leaving out parts that do matter, or by picturing a part wrongly.

Problem definitions can overlook relevant stakeholders and goals. Concerned with stock-outs, Marketing might take steps that increase inventory and carrying costs, to the displeasure of Operations. A good definition encompasses both goals— fewer stock-outs, lower carrying costs—and acknowledges the trade-off between them. Even when all stakeholders are represented, it is easy to overlook important objectives. Many bad marriages and career decisions have been made by people who did not know what they really valued.

Problems can be defined in terms of inappropriate goals. Pie-in-the-sky definitions dubiously assert that some abstract aspect of the organization must be improved. "Unclear mission" and "inadequate strategy" are examples. Such issues may merit intense problem-solving efforts, but they often serve as topics of high-minded discussions yielding no discernible betterment. The key to avoiding this mistake is evidence: How do we know our mission or strategy is inadequate? Lower-level problems can be misdefined in terms of nonoperational goals. An automobile manufacturer experienced high defect rates due to wrinkled material in instrument panels. Reject levels dropped sharply when inspectors were given specific descriptions of what constituted a defect.

Another goal-related mistake is the substitution of means for ends. Consider the story of a man whose car has a flat tire. Intent on finding a jack (a means), he does not recognize that another way of raising his car (the goal or end) is available. Similar mistakes happen in organizations. Intent on removing a processing bottleneck, factory managers at Sierra Semiconductor did not realize that throughput was constrained at a different point in the process. Defining this problem in terms of the goal of increased throughput would have helped managers recognize other means of achieving this end.

Constraints are like goals, except that they aren't desired for their own sake. For whatever reason, a solution just has to be a certain way. Constraints are prominent in design problems, where what is being designed must satisfy certain requirements. For example, a personal computer must be compatible with household power supplies. Problem definition can err by omitting pertinent constraints or by including unnecessary ones. The first mistake results in unworkable solution proposals. The second makes it harder to find feasible alternatives. Definitions should challenge assumed constraints. A definition of the Resource Recovery Plant Case should consider the possibility of renegotiating the plant's contract with municipalities rather than viewing the contract as a given.

Definitions also err by presenting misleading causal accounts. The situation may be defined in terms of a false cause, a factor not really responsible for the presenting problem. Or attention could be directed exclusively to a partial cause, one of several contributing to the problem. A quality team defined its problem as "improving engineering response time to problem lots." When members realized that other factors also caused processing delays, they changed the definition to "reducing disposition time of problem lots."

Underlying many errors are false assumptions. One can jump to conclusions or fail to revise beliefs in the face of counterevidence. Studies have shown that most companies believe they are industry leaders in product quality, even after customer surveys indicate otherwise. A problem definition can assume an either-or situation—"Either the market is shrinking or our competitors are selling at a loss"—when other possibilities exist. Mistaken assumptions can result from errors in data collection and analysis. A firm experiencing late deliveries of purchased goods found that 87 percent of incoming shipments were received on time, even though reports indicated only a 69 percent on-time receiving rate. Reporting into the purchasing system was late, not the deliveries themselves. An office equipment company received complaints about late installations of copiers, though internal data indicated a high on-time delivery rate. The company eventually realized that delivery is not the same as installation.

## Missed Connections

Storytellers add resonance to narratives by connecting them to well-known tales. *Moby-Dick* alludes to the biblical story of Jonah. Our enjoyment of *West Side Story* is enhanced by its evocation of *Romeo and Juliet*. Such connections are critical for problem definition, where the intent is to increase comprehension, not enjoyment. We understand something by relating it to existing knowledge, by activating pertinent schemas in long-term memory. Our knowledge of problems is indexed by problem categories and structures. Realizing that the present situation is, say, a problem of resistance to change prompts recollection of similar past experiences and of actions that were effective or ineffective on those occasions.

PD can err by failing to recognize pertinent problem structures or by seeing a situation in terms of an inappropriate category. Customer service representatives for a high technology company received complaints from customers who had unrealistic product expectations. Not surprisingly, salespeople had oversold product capabilities in order to book sales. This situation has the same "I'll buy now, you pay later" structure as The Publishing Company Case (Case 2.3). One part of the organization makes its job easier at someone else's expense. A problem definition that failed to acknowledge this structure would be less effective than one pointing it out. Even more harmful is the use of an inappropriate problem category. The notion of a "communication problem" is applicable when one party (A) does not pass along information needed by another (B). The category is sometimes applied to situations in which party B needs information that neither A nor anyone else possesses. Since the standard response to communication problems—to establish communication channels—will be ineffective in such cases, the misclassification leads problem solvers down a time-consuming dead-end street.

## Mistakes of Style

A final batch of definitional mistakes involves matters of style, the *how* rather than the *what* of a definition. One mistake of this kind is misplaced precision, an unwarranted concern with detail. It has been argued that problems should be expressed in quantitative, rather than qualitative, terms. This is not always true. It is important to precisely state certain facts of the case, typically those relevant to diagnosis, such as the dimensions and timing of rejects. But little will be gained from precise statements of goals that are naturally somewhat arbitrary. Setting quantitative targets in some situations—weak organization structure, for instance—usually results in misdirected efforts. As with dimensional tolerances, precision should only be required where it is really needed.

In the blame game, a definition reproaches someone for the situation: "The problem is that Marketing isn't doing its job." During the course of problem solving, it may become necessary to identify agents whose performance must be improved. But this should not be done as part of problem definition, for fear of alienating stakeholders and turning an impartial study of the situation into a defensive cover-up. The related mistake of prescriptive definitions defines the problem in terms of something that needs to be done. Also described as "framing a solution as the problem," this is analogous to a preachy novel or movie, one that pushes a message. Prescriptive definitions risk pushing the wrong solution by prematurely narrowing the focus.

Finally comes the issue of a definition's length. People tend to define problems with "one-liners" like the definitions found in dictionaries. Though this is convenient for communicative purposes, such definitions cannot encompass the content needed to direct thinking about complex, real-world situations. On the other hand, one does not want a Cecil B. DeMille job, an epic account that loses focus in a welter of subplots and peripheral issues. There is a real conflict originating in PD's dual problem-solving and communicative roles. The conflict can be resolved by developing distinct definitions serving each purpose.

# The Situation Definition and Analysis (SDA) Method

An effective method for defining real-world problems must satisfy the following criteria:

1. It must be applicable to any problem rather than being limited to particular types of situations.

2. The definitions produced should encompass all important aspects of a situation.
3. The method should help evoke relevant experiential knowledge.
4. It must aid the identification of issues that comprise and are connected to the situation and should help bound the problem.
5. The method should highlight needs for additional information, including critical diagnosis tasks.
6. The method should suggest an overall problem-solving plan and possible solutions.
7. Definitions produced should be revisable and expandable.
8. The method must provide both a comprehensive representation and a compact account for communicating the problem to others.

These criteria are satisfied by the Situation Definition and Analysis (SDA) method presented in this section and summarized in Figure 4.9.[9] The method is a sequence of eight steps. While the ordering of the steps makes sense, it is not inviolate. Backtracking to earlier activities is allowed. Each of the steps will be discussed. The method will be illustrated by application to the R & D Case (Figure 4.10). It is assumed a problem-solving team has been formed to deal with the situation.

## 1. State the presenting problem

Problem definition starts with the presenting problem, the triggering issue that aroused concern and which is most obviously in need of improvement. Sometimes this turns out to be the only problem, but more often it leads into a network of concerns. One should validate the existence of the presenting problem, reviewing evidence used to identify it. It may be a red herring created by misinterpretations, so it may not even be cause for concern. Pertinent goals should be assessed for reasonableness. While sales may be below budget, changing market conditions could have turned the budget into an inappropriate target. The presenting problem can be obviated if it expresses a means to a larger goal. When more effective means are discovered, the presenting problem fades away. Problem solving can address other issues, but if the presenting problem is legitimate, it should be dealt with. This step determines whether it deserves attention.

The presenting problem in the R & D Case is that while the R & D lab wants the project to be continued, that may not happen. The issue came to light during the lab's annual planning process, when it reviewed the status of ongoing projects. As things stand, this is a potential problem. The subsidiary hasn't decided on future project funding. While available evidence justifies the lab's concern, it should consider whether its goal of continued project funding is appropriate. The lab may be proposing more work than its client needs.

## 2. Analyze the presenting problem

Valid presenting problems should be analyzed and addressed. Problem solvers often veer off onto other issues without responding to the concern that got things going in the first place. The structure of the presenting problem, the elements and relationships that comprise it, should be delineated. What stakeholders, goals, and

1. **State the presenting problem.**
   Does the evidence justify a belief that there is a problem?
   Are pertinent goals reasonable?
   Under what circumstances might this cease to be an issue?

2. **Analyze the presenting problem.**
   What elements and relationships constitute its structure?
   What type or kind of problem is this?
   What are the distinctive features of this situation?
   What are the possible outcomes and ways of reaching them?

3. **Broaden and deepen the analysis.**
   What stakeholders and goals are involved in the situation?
   What constraints affect the realization of these goals?
   Consider the situation's historical background and current context.
   Identify relevant facts, beliefs, uncertainties, and unknowns.
   What other issues are part of the situation, broadly understood?
   What are the possible causes of the presenting problem?
   Analyze other problems that are important parts of the situation.

4. **Bound the situation.**
   Which issues should be addressed by problem-solving activity and which
      should be set aside?

5. **Diagram the situation.**
   Use multiple diagrams, consistent with the nature of the problem.

6. **Identify topics requiring further study.**
   What diagnosis tasks—determining a problem's causes—need to be
      performed?
   Which uncertainties and unknowns should be targeted for investigation?
   What can be done to resolve questionable beliefs and assumptions?
   Outline potential solutions to the problem and specify related
      information needs.

7. **Develop an overall problem-solving plan.**
   Assign responsibilities and set target completion dates.
   Anticipate possible contingencies and problem-solving outcomes.

8. **Develop a summary account of the situation.**

**Figure 4.9**   The Situation Definition and Analysis (SDA) Method

constraints are involved? Though the situation may be unique, it probably belongs to a problem category. It may also exhibit certain problem structures, discussed in Chapter 2. Evoked categories and structures highlight the situation's distinctive features, which make it different from other problems of that kind. It may be possible to specify the outcome structure, different ways the situation can turn out, and the means by which outcomes can be reached.

**R & D Case**

The R & D laboratory of a large, diversified food producer performs product development work for operating divisions and subsidiaries. R & D project teams are contracted out to users at a cost exceeding several hundred thousand dollars per year, providing these divisions with a full range of state-of-the-art services in food products R & D.

One project team had been contracted for by a small but growing subsidiary, recently acquired by the parent corporation. A new CEO just took over at this subsidiary, quickly making it clear that he would do things his way. He suggests that it may be more economical for the subsidiary to purchase its R & D services from outside the corporation on an as-needed basis rather than committing to another year of expensive, full-service support by an internal R & D project team.

While it has almost completed its primary task under the current project, the R & D laboratory feels that much work remains to be done in this subsidiary, especially in facilitating product transfer to subsidiary operations. R & D would like to have the project team funded for another year of work, but it is becoming worried that might not happen.

The parent corporation has a policy of decentralized decision making. But at times in the past, it has taken steps to insure that divisions and subsidiaries use internal services.

**Figure 4.10**   The R & D case

The R & D Case centers on two agents, the R & D lab and the subsidiary. They have been in an exchange relationship that one may want to discontinue. The parties could have incompatible goals and intentions. Thus, this is a situation of conflict that may be resolvable through negotiation. It might also be viewed as a sales problem: The lab wants to convince the subsidiary, its customer, to buy more of its product. However it is not a typical sales problem since both agents are part of the same corporation. Their transactions are not arms-length and the threat of corporate intervention looms over their negotiation. Since this is not a "first sale," but a continuation of past work, the project's history must be considered. The outcome structure is simple: The subsidiary will purchase some amount of R & D services, possibly none, and it will purchase them from the R & D lab, outside contractors, or some inside-outside combination. These outcomes can be reached by negotiation between the lab and the subsidiary or they can be imposed by corporate fiat.

## 3. Broaden and deepen the analysis

Occasionally the presenting problem is all there is. A definition develops by elaborating its goals, constraints, and causes. Usually the situation encompasses interrelated problems, so a definition must reach beyond the triggering issue. This step, a continuation of its predecessor, forces explicit consideration of other concerns. Problem definition should not be obsessed with the presenting problem. Identify all stake-holders, goals, and constraints. The historical background, including striking events and past occurrences of similar situations, and current context should be examined as sources of relevant information. Pertinent facts, uncertainties, and unknowns should be identified. Identify and question stakeholder beliefs and assumptions. Such investigations and the use of heuristics like "How did we get into this mess?" disclose issues related to the presenting problem. Probing for causes of that problem suggests other concerns, mostly in the microworld. All these issues should be analyzed along the lines indicated in Step 2.

In addition to the lab and the subsidiary, the R & D Case involves the corporation and the subsidiary CEO. Beyond their obvious objectives, these stakeholders might be pursuing the following goals:

R & D lab—May feel a professional need to complete the contract, may be empire-building.

Subsidiary—May want more control over R & D work.

Subsidiary CEO—May want to escape past precedents, may want to establish a cost-cutting mentality.

Corporation—Wants efficient internal services that subsidiaries agree to use.

Note that the corporation's goal of internal contracting encounters a self-imposed constraint, its policy of decentralized decision making. A study of the case's historical background could disclose violations of this policy. It might also disclose incidents in which the use of outside contractors resulted in leakage of sensitive information. Regarding the current context, what is the lab's projected workload and the subsidiary's profit outlook? R & D people may be assuming mistakenly that the subsidiary has been pleased with their performance on the project. The subsidiary CEO might have erroneous beliefs about the cost and quality of outside R & D services.

The presenting problem connects to other issues. It may have been caused by R & D's ineffective marketing. The lab may overbundle its services, selling packages its customers do not want. Its services may be overpriced, perhaps due to inefficient operations. Another issue is the implicit conflict between the corporation's policy of decentralized decision making and its preference for the use of internal suppliers. This is a classic centralization-decentralization trade-off that can also be viewed as a make-buy decision.

## 4. Bound the problem

Having explored the broader situation, it is necessary to limit the scope of current problem-solving efforts. One cannot fix everything that could be improved. Rather than diffusing effort over multiple issues, adopt a more focused approach, one that targets the presenting problem and several closely related concerns. Boundaries set during this step are changeable. Additional information can shift attention toward an issue that had been considered minor, or management might call for a broader problem-solving effort.

An effective response to the R & D Case must address the presenting problem. It must propose a way of dealing with the differing intentions of the lab and subsidiary in terms of project continuation. Depending on the results of its investigations, a problem-solving team might help the lab improve its product and operational efficiency. A team would be unlikely to address the corporate issue in this case. The conflict between decentralized decision making and a preference for (or insistence on) internal contracting is for corporate management to resolve.

## 5. Diagram the situation

The sequencing of this step is discretionary; diagramming can be initiated at various points in the SDA process. Because diagramming evokes elements and aspects of the situation, it can be used early as a knowledge elicitation device. Since it helps organize information, making the situation understandable, diagramming can be used later to shape what has been learned into a coherent whole. Its flexibility makes concept mapping a useful technique for PD. Select or devise a representational format suited to the problem at hand. There is no need to do everything with a single picture. Use different diagrams to depict different aspects of the situation. A diagram consisting of issues that constitute the situation is a useful tool for bounding the problem (Step 4). A representation highlighting uncertainties and unknowns directs research efforts toward critical knowledge inadequacies.

As noted earlier, the presenting problem in the R & D Case is a conflict or disagreement between two parties. Such situations can be depicted by a conflict diagram (Figure 4.11) that compares agents' goals, beliefs, and behaviors. A conflict diagram can be validated by considering whether an agent's observed behaviors are consistent with indicated goals and beliefs. Some goals and beliefs are marked as implicit (I), not necessarily recognized by the agent. Others are designated as uncertain (?),

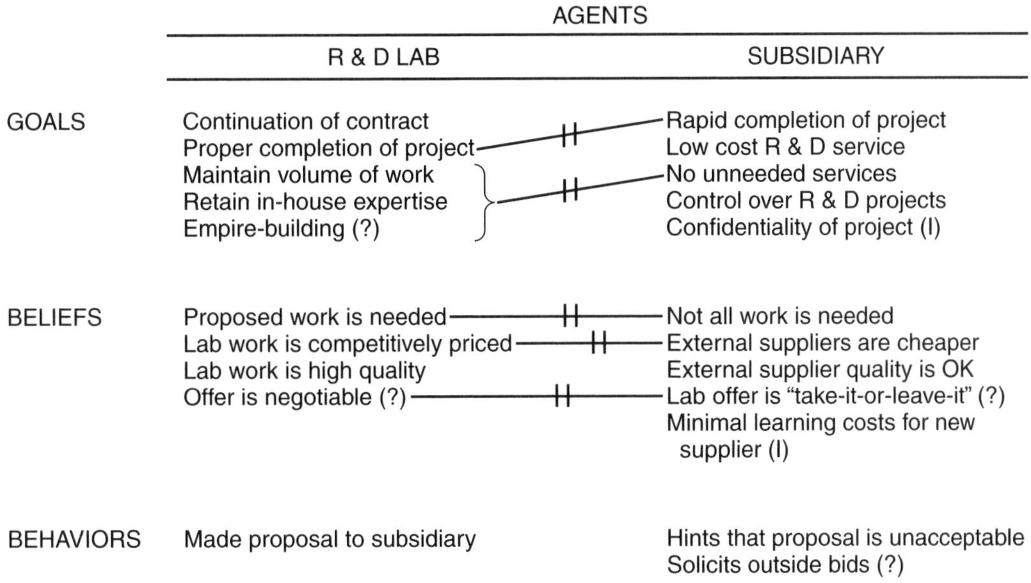

Figure 4.11   The R & D Case: Conflict diagram

because the agent may not truly hold this goal or belief. Points of disagreement are indicated by cross-hatched (ǁ) connecting lines. The diagram highlights matters of dispute and points out goals and beliefs that should be reviewed. Has the subsidiary correctly assessed the risk of leaking sensitive project information through the use of external suppliers? Does it appreciate the learning curve costs of switching suppliers at this stage of the project? Another diagram (Figure 4.12) depicts the situation as a set of interconnected issues. Some of these are well documented; others are speculations resolvable by study. Dotted lines in this diagram indicate how the situation might be bounded for problem-solving purposes.

## 6. Identify topics requiring further study

One function performed by problem definition is identification of knowledge inadequacies: What else must we learn about the situation? Not all knowledge deficiencies can be addressed. It may cost too much or take too long to collect desired data. In addition, purported information needs may be peripheral. But PD should give rise to a flurry of information-gathering activities. The most important of these are diagnostic, determining causes of problems. Since possible solutions create their own information needs, it is appropriate at this stage to suggest solution alternatives and strategies, so their pros and cons can be investigated. In doing so, participants must be careful not to tacitly commit to an option.

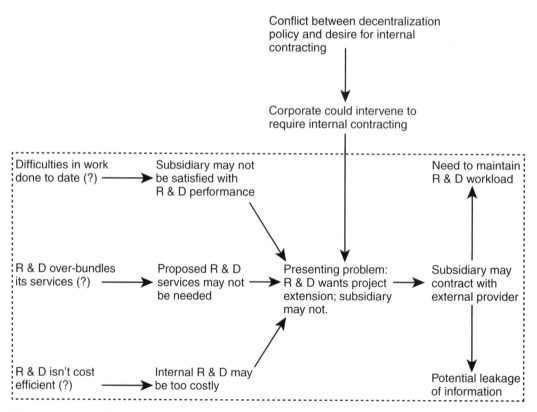

**Figure 4.12** The R & D Case: Problem diagram

The R & D Case does not necessarily pose a diagnosis task, since the cause of the presenting problem seems clear—differing judgments as to the need for further work on the project. It may be useful to study R & D's past performance on the project to determine if it has satisfied the subsidiary's needs and to focus on the efficiency of the lab's operations and cost structure. It is also important to validate the subsidiary's assumptions about the cost and quality of external providers. Clearing up these uncertainties is a prerequisite for productive negotiations between the parties.

## 7. Develop an overall problem-solving plan

Solving a complex organizational problem is a protracted project that must be managed. Formal PD activities should initiate and accomodate project management efforts. Thus, a rough problem-solving plan should be developed. The intent is to clarify where things are going and how to get there. Information-gathering tasks must be assigned to responsible parties. A schedule of target dates should be adopted. Planning of this kind is tentative and flexibility must be maintained. It may be possible to anticipate potential contingencies and problem-solving outcomes and to organize efforts in this light. Looking ahead now can forestall wasted efforts later.

The goal in the R & D Case is for the lab and subsidiary to conduct informed, productive negotiations concerning future project activities. Problem-solving efforts should facilitate this outcome. Ideally the parties will reach an agreement; conceivably the subsidiary will decide to use external suppliers. If so, the corporation may opt to require the use of internal services in this situation. Problem solving should prepare for this contingency, developing options that make corporate intervention less onerous to the subsidiary. One option might be that the corporation pay any price difference between internal and external suppliers.

## 8. Develop a summary account of the situation

The foregoing steps yield a detailed account of the situation in words and pictures that direct and support problem solving. If desired, a comprehensive formulation of the situation as understood can be drafted. A more compact representation is needed for communication purposes. Others will want to know about the situation and what is being done. Responding to this need, the final step in the SDA process develops an "executive summary" of the case. This usually focuses on the presenting problem. Informational value can be added by citing prominent elements of the situation—key causes and constraints—and by outlining the intended course of problem-solving activity.

Assume that a corporate executive heard rumors of trouble between the lab and subsidiary. Were this executive to ask a team member to explain the situation, she might respond as follows: "The lab would like one of its projects with this subsidiary to be funded for another year. The subsidiary feels little additional work is needed and that required services can be purchased more cheaply from outside vendors. The lab may be overbundling or overpricing its services. At the same time, the subsidiary may not appreciate the true costs of external suppliers or the real value of our in-house R & D services. We're collecting information to enable informed discussion and negotiation between the two parties in hopes they can reach an agreement."

The SDA method is highly general, applicable to virtually any problem. Its operationality and power can be improved through identification of a complete set of problem types and structures and development of an expanded repertoire of diagrammatic techniques. The method satisfies the eight criteria for problem definition stated at the start of this section. SDA helps one characterize and bound problem situations and evoke relevant experiential knowledge as part of understanding them. SDA is applied most usefully to complex problems like the R & D Case. Its use would be overkill in some situations, such as conformance problems where problem definition can amount to saying how process outputs deviate from standards. As QPS expands beyond its traditional concerns, techniques like SDA become increasingly important.

## NOTES

1. This technique is described more extensively in: Shigero Mizuno, ed., *Management for Quality Improvement: The Seven New QC Tools* (Cambridge, Mass.: Productivity Press, 1988), and Michael Brassard, *The Memory Jogger Plus+* (Methuen, Mass.: GOAL/QPC, 1989).

2. See Mizuno, *Management for Quality Improvement: The Seven New QC Tools*, and Brassard, *The Memory Jogger Plus+*.

3. See: Kaoru Ishikawa, *Introduction to Quality Control* (London: Chapman & Hall, 1989).

4. For a tutorial, see: "The Tools of Quality. Part V: Check Sheets," *Quality Progress* 23, no. 10 (1990): 51–56.

5. For a tutorial, see: "The Tools of Quality. Part IV: Histograms," *Quality Progress* 23, no. 9 (1990): 75–78.

6. For a tutorial, see: John T. Burr, "The Tools of Quality. Part VI: Pareto Charts," *Quality Progress* 23, no. 11 (1990): 59–61.

7. Marlene Caroselli, *Total Quality Transformations: Optimizing Missions, Methods, and Management* (Amherst, Mass.: Human Resource Development Press, 1991).

8. As reported in: Howard Raiffa, *Decision Analysis* (Reading, Mass.: Addison-Wesley, 1968).

9. The SDA Method was previously described in: Gerald F. Smith, "Defining Real World Problems: The SDA Method," *Minnesota Quality Conference Proceedings* (Minneapolis: Minnesota Section 1203, ASQC, 1995): 294–303.

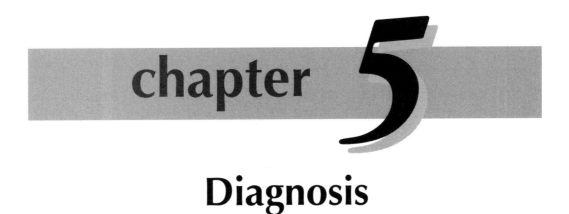

# Diagnosis

---

## Chapter Outline

---

Diagnosis, determining why a system is not performing acceptably, is a key task in many professional practices. Physicians diagnose a patient's condition to prescribe a treatment. Troubleshooters track down faults in electronic equipment so malfunctioning components can be replaced. Scientists seek out causes, using experiments to determine how one variable affects another. In a QPS context, diagnosis is the major challenge in solving conformance problems and one of the difficulties posed by unstructured performance problems.

This chapter begins with a discussion of causality, which lays the groundwork for an understanding of diagnosis. It examines the diagnostic process, using findings from studies of troubleshooting and medical diagnosis. Common diagnostic mistakes are reviewed to arm readers against them. This is followed by a discussion of diagnostic techniques used by QPS practitioners. The chapter concludes with prescriptions for improving the diagnosis of quality problems.

# Causality

Despite its everyday familiarity, causality has been a controversial notion among scientists and philosophers. The controversy traces to the work of David Hume, an eighteenth century Scottish philosopher who pointed out that causality is neither observable nor logically necessary. Followers of Hume regard causation as a matter of regularity, of certain effects consistently following certain causes according to the laws of nature. Others view causation in active, generative terms. Things have causal powers and liabilities that can be activated to produce effects. When a baseball is thrown against a window, its causal powers interact with the liabilities of plate glass, resulting in a predictable outcome. Everyday thinking reflects this view. One can think of causation as the cement of the universe, a link between events that helps us understand and deal with change.

Practically speaking, a **cause** is whatever is responsible for or produces an effect. A single cause can have multiple effects. Smoking causes lung cancer, emphysema, yellow teeth, and burn holes in mattresses. An effect can have multiple causes. Crime results from many causes—poverty, drug use, poor values—several of which may be responsible for a given criminal act. Events can be linked in extended causal chains that resemble Rube Goldbergian contraptions by virtue of their unlikely cause-effect connections.

A less familiar aspect of causality is the distinction between causes and conditions. Whereas a cause is the active, intrusive factor responsible for an effect, a **condition** is an enablement, often a normal state, needed for the effect to occur. House fires are usually attributed to lightning strikes, electrical short circuits, and unextinguished cigarettes, whatever produced the spark that ignited the building. But no house would burn unless it was made of flammable material and was located in an oxygen-rich environment. Though a spark is the cause of fire, oxygen and flammable material are conditions for combustion. Broadly speaking, the cause of fire is the combination of spark, oxygen, and flammable material. Thus, a cause (broad sense) may include multiple causes (narrow sense) and conditions.

## Types of Causes

The notion of causality includes variations, four of which can be traced to Aristotle.

1. **Generative causality,** the most common in daily affairs, refers to that which produces an effect. Example: "The nail caused the flat tire."
2. **Purposive causality** points to the goal or purpose of an action. This notion is often used to explain human behavior. Example: "Joe stayed at work because he wanted to finish the report."
3. **Functional causality,** used in science, refers to an explanatory law or principle. Example: "The period of a pendulum is a function of its length."
4. **Essential causality** explains events in terms of the natures of the things involved, their traits or essences. Example: "The wire bent because it is copper."

**Precipitating** and **underlying causes** can also be differentiated. The former is the factor that sets off an effect. Precipitating causes are usually close to their effects, physically and temporally. An underlying cause is more remotely responsible for the effect's occurrence. If one's car will not start, the failure might be explained in terms of a loose battery cable (a precipitating cause) or by reference to auto industry mismanagement (an underlying cause).

The **root cause** has been defined as "the most basic reason for an undesirable condition or problem which, if eliminated or corrected, would have prevented it from existing or occurring."[1] It has been argued that every quality problem has a single root cause which tends to be a management or supervisory inadequacy. The root cause concept seeks to prevent diagnosis from stopping too quickly. One can identify a precipitating cause as responsible for a problem, but fail to address an underlying cause, which might later produce new troubles. However, the root cause notion may push things too far: Isn't the Big Bang the root cause of everything? What matters is identifying where effective action can be taken to prevent problem recurrence. This may or may not be the problem's root cause. Nor is there any reason to assume that each problem has only one root cause or that management is usually the root cause of quality problems.

A final distinction, fostered by statistical process control (SPC) and promoted by Deming, is between **common causes** and **special** or **assignable causes** of variation in a process. Common causes of variation reflect system design and are regarded as the responsibility of management. Special causes are usually more fleeting, resulting from changes or incidental events. Though it has been argued that control charts are "a good way to differentiate these two types of causes,"[2] control charts actually define the two types, which have no fundamental difference between them. A special cause is whatever produces unusual observations on a control chart. Normal levels of variability are attributed to common causes. Special causes must be identified and corrected, while common causes are accepted sources of variation, at least for the time being.

Consider the case of a manufacturer experiencing high reject rates on certain parts. It turned out that sunshine coming through a skylight caused uneven thermal expansion in a machine tool, resulting in many rejects at certain times on sunny days. Thermal expansion affects every production process. Because its effects are usually insignificant, it is normally lumped among other common causes and ignored. In this case, its effects justified problem-solving effort and corrective action, so here thermal expansion is a special cause. The only difference between common and special causes is the size of their effects in particular circumstances. As for responsibility, management is always responsible for making improvements, as are workers and anyone else who cares about quality.

# Diagnosis Tasks and Strategies

## Diagnosis Tasks

Differences among diagnosis tasks affect strategies, errors, and aids applicable to problem solving. The prototypical task requires one to locate the cause or fault responsible for a system's poor performance. Equipment troubleshooters are classic diagnosticians in this respect. Diagnosis can also be a matter of situation assessment. With this approach, a diagnostician uses symptoms to identify a situation category that connects to an effective response. For example, a physician assigns a patient to the proper disease category.

A fault can be recurring, intermittent, or novel. Recurring faults allow the use of history to determine causes and cures. Intermittent faults are difficult to diagnose and novel failures are harder still. In sequential diagnosis tasks, additional data must be acquired to make a conclusive diagnosis, so actions can be taken for informational purposes. Some diagnostic strategies can only be used with systems—automobiles, for instance—whose performance can be understood. Extremely complex systems, like the human body, thwart efforts of this kind. System structure also affects the process. A system that is structured linearly or permits crisp hierarchical decomposition is susceptible to efficient diagnostic tactics. A system with highly interconnected processes and parts is more difficult to diagnose.

## Diagnostic Strategies

Diagnostic strategies are the primary source of structure in the diagnostic process, but they should not be viewed as algorithms that are followed inflexibly. Diagnosticians behave opportunistically, adjusting their behavior within a strategy and switching strategies in response to new information and insights.

The simplest diagnostic strategy is **trial-and-error** or **random search.** It presumes a set of causal hypotheses, testing them one by one in any order. Despite its mindlessness, random search may be the best that can be done. My kids often beat me at Battleship because I cannot improve much on their random search strategy. If a device consists of many unordered and unclustered components, tracking down a faulty part might entail trial-and-error search. One of the more dubious joys of Christmas is searching through a string of tree lights for the faulty bulb that has shut down the whole string. Equipment troubleshooting affords such a strategy since the causal hypotheses (potentially faulty components) are obvious and easily tested.

The more sophisticated **topographic search** strategy is applicable to structured systems whose parts are organized into groups or stages with a processing order; there is a traceable sequence by which inputs are converted into outputs. Topographic search exploits this spatial structure. A diagnostician can use a "half-split" tactic by making tests, each of which eliminates roughly half the possible causes. An analogy would be asking someone to guess a number between 1 and 1000 and telling the person after each guess whether the number is higher or lower than the guess. Using the half-split tactic, one would always guess at the middle of the active set of possiblities—first 500, then either 250 or 750—to quickly narrow down to the answer. With topographic search, hypotheses are tested for their informational value, not because they are likely causes. One tests the middle element in a sequence, even if that element is not expected to be faulty.

Whereas topographic search exploits the spatial layout of a system, **functional search** analyzes a problem's symptoms to identify troublesome components. A repair specialist, finding that a TV's picture is too low, will regard the vertical deflection generator as a likely cause. Use of this strategy presumes that the system can be analyzed along functional lines and that symptoms offer function-specific information. These conditions are not always satisfied. For example, a fever provides little indication of whether the digestive, respiratory, or another system is causing the illness. Nor does a firm's unprofitability mark a particular functional area as responsible.

The **deep reasoning** strategy derives a diagnosis from in-depth understanding of the system. Knowing how the system works, a diagnostician conceives how observed symptoms could have been generated. An auto mechanic might consider aspects of the vehicle—its age, reported troubles with starting, diminished fuel economy, and so forth—and infer possible causes of the trouble. Deep reasoning supports hypothesis generation and suggests how candidates can be tested. This strategy is applicable to systems that are well understood. Its use is more common among auto mechanics than neurologists. Virtually all diagnosticians make some use of this approach. They think things through, trying to understand why the system failed. However, deep reasoning is rarely used as a stand-alone strategy. It is often applied with novel faults, when experience-based approaches cannot be relied on.

The strategy most associated with expert diagnosticians is **shallow reasoning.** It uses prior experience to generate causal candidates. Having already handled many customer complaints about a certain software function, customer support personnel immediately know what is wrong. Experience can be codified in a diagnostic tree that connects symptoms with problem categories. Or diagnosis can occur through a rapid recognition process in which symptoms evoke the appropriate situation category. Thus, shallow reasoning is less a conscious strategy than a capacity for situation recognition. Use of the strategy presumes that the diagnostician is experienced with situations of this kind. Shallow reasoning does not work with novel faults.

# The Diagnostic Process

Accounts of the diagnostic process focus on three activities: information gathering, hypothesis generation, and hypothesis testing. Figure 5.1, a model of the diagnostic process, allows two variations. Sometimes evidence implies a hypothesis so strongly it is accepted as the problem's cause. More typically, at least for nonexperts, several plausible hypotheses come to mind. These must be tested by collecting further information. Other variations in the diagnostic process are driven by the nature of the system, the diagnostician's knowledge, and the availability of information.

## Information Gathering

A diagnostician must have an informational basis for proposing hypotheses; they do not just come out of nowhere. Problem identification is based on evidence that can suggest the problem's causes. Additional information can be acquired by inspecting the system. Diagnosticians can use process tracing with systems that are still functioning. The following case demonstrates its value.

## case 5.1

In the winter of 1979–1980, Eastern Airline's flight attendants were plagued by a malady known as the "Red Sweat." Most of the 170 reported cases of this rash occurred on flights between New York and Florida. Medical detectives were baffled by the condition until health officials and Eastern supervisors, riding along on flights, carefully observed flight attendant behavior. Investigators noticed that when attendants handled rubber vests during routine ditching demonstrations, flecks of red ink fell from stenciled "DEMO ONLY" letters on the life jackets. These combined with make-up and perspiration to produce what looked like a bloody rash, the dreaded "Red Sweat."

Another source of knowledge is the system's history—a patient's medical records, for instance. Companies that sell complex pieces of equipment, such as computers and copiers, accumulate maintenance and repair histories for each unit. One of the first to do so was Otis Elevator, which developed OTISLINE™, a computer-based system that includes a maintenance history for each elevator installation.

Gathering information is not enough. One must also interpret data correctly, using it to evoke and evaluate possible causes. A study of medical diagnosis illustrates the importance of interpretation. Physicians were given written descriptions of actual cases and asked to propose diagnoses. One case involved an unemployed, 27-year-old, urban male who came to a hospital emergency room complaining of chills and a persistent fever. A medical workup disclosed puncture wounds in the patient's left arm which he said were the result of a cat bite. Physicians who correctly diagnosed an acute bacterial infection of a heart valve recognized, from past

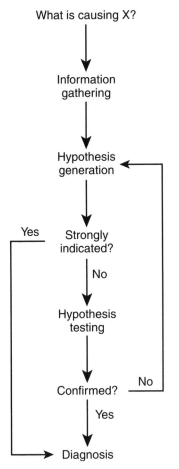

**Figure 5.1** The diagnostic process

experience and everyday knowledge, that the puncture wounds probably resulted from intravenous drug use. Every subject who reached the wrong diagnosis accepted the patient's story about the cat bite.

## Hypothesis Generation

The correct conclusion cannot be reached unless the related hypothesis is conceived. Not surprisingly, given the nature of causality, no strong procedure exists for generating hypotheses. The primary resource is experiential knowledge. Experts may simply recognize what is going on. The cause comes to mind by association with observed symptoms. For instance, a company asked a consultant to investigate a problem involving excessive variation in diameter along the length of a component. While reviewing a process flow chart, the consultant noticed that the component went through an induction hardening process. From experience, he knew that this process could induce significant variation in diameter for such a part.

Much of our knowledge is organized as **causal schemas** that connect patterns of symptoms with likely causes. Observing the symptoms activates a schema and the hypotheses it includes. Relevant schemas create a **causal field,** a sense of the kinds of things that could have produced an effect. Everyone possesses causal schemas for some domains, including the basic situations of everyday life.

In addition, experience has taught us certain **cues to causality** to consider when generating hypotheses. The following are among the most important:

1. **Temporal order.** A cause always precedes its effect in time. One would never propose candidate causes that occurred after the effect. This is a perfectly valid clue, though not very informative.
2. **Space/time contiguity.** A cause must be connected to its effect in space and through time. This cue is also perfectly valid, and much more informative, although the cause-effect connection may be obscure. Isaac Newton struggled with the concept of gravity because it seemed to imply "action at a distance," causality without spatial contiguity.
3. **Similarity in magnitude and appearance.** Less validly, people often assume that causes and effects are similar in magnitude and appearance. This assumption underlies the *doctrine of signatures,* a premodern medical theory that proposed, for instance, that turmeric should be used to treat jaundice because both are characterized by the color yellow.
4. **Statistical correlation.** This cue drives scientific research that seeks to identify potential causal factors that co-occur with an effect, being mutually present or absent on different occasions. Though useful, it can be misleading: Sexual intercourse, the cause of birth, does not always result in birth, so the two are not highly correlated.

While it is good to generate many hypotheses, it is better to generate the most promising. Past experience, normally our most valuable hypothesis generation resource, may hamper efforts to do so. Strong, experience-based causal schemas can dominate thinking, making it hard to conceive of unusual causes that might be operative. Especially for really difficult problems, the critical capacity may be an ability to "think outside the box," to propose alternatives that are not part of normal causal schemas but which make an unusual kind of sense in the situation.

## Hypothesis Testing

Diagnostic hypotheses may or may not be tested, depending on how strongly they are supported by evidence and experience. Hypothesis testing involves producing new information bearing on the validity of hypotheses. Several criteria are used to determine which hypothesis to test: the cost of testing, the likelihood the hypothesis is true, and the informational value of a test. Experimentation is the classic means of testing hypotheses. Being expensive, it should only be used when there are, say, six or fewer plausible hypotheses. Informal experiments—comparisons of how the system works under different conditions—can be conducted more economically.

When diagnosis is unsuccessful, diagnosticians change strategies, perhaps attempting a deep reasoning approach. Often they just take a break, ask a colleague, or wait until the next day before trying again. Another challenge is knowing when to stop. A confirmed hypothesis might cite a precipitating cause, leaving underlying causes unrecognized. Then too, multiple causes can share responsibility for the effect. Figure 5.1 could be elaborated to show that an adequate diagnosis has only been achieved when all underlying and precipitating causes have been identified.

# Diagnostic Errors

Even well-motivated and competently performed diagnostic efforts can fail. The problem's causes might be too unusual. Critical evidence may not be available. Sometimes, however, failure results from avoidable errors, discussed in this section.

The least excusable error is not to perform diagnosis for problems that require it. In one company, supervisors noted burred screws during the final assembly of kitchen stoves and concluded that better screws were needed. A diagnostician segregated data from the three assembly lines and only found burrs on one line, this because of an improperly trained employee. After experiencing problems with undersized eyelets, project engineers at a PC board manufacturer signed waivers allowing use of a slightly larger part. When these eyelets were used on the next lot of boards, they were too loose. Oversized boards, not undersized eyelets, had caused the original problem.

A common mistake is to not acquire available data. A diagnostician can overlook facets of a case by not examining the situation or by doing so when rushed or distracted. People ignore negative information, data that do not match their expectations. Symptoms that have not appeared can be the most telling: Sherlock Holmes solved "The Case of Silver Blaze" by noting that a watchdog had not barked when the crime was being committed.

The most frequent cause of diagnostic failure is inability to generate the correct hypothesis, to conceive of the problem's true cause. This, of course, is not an error, but an understandable consequence of our cognitive limitations. For lack of experience, observed symptoms may not mentally connect to their causes. Sometimes diagnosticians work from an inadequate causal field that narrows their thinking. For instance, in puzzles that ask one to state the next number in a sequence (2, 3, 10, 6, . . . ), one rarely considers that the ordering might not be numeric. The Adolph Coors Company was experiencing excessive scrap on a can manufacturing line. Six months of adjusting and overhauling machines yielded no improvement. Then a production leadman noticed that the problematic machines all ran the same tooling sizes. This led to discovery of a drafting error that caused a tooling mismatch and collapsing cans. The problem could not be solved until the causal field was expanded beyond the machines. A more extreme form of narrowing is binary thinking, viewing the problem as an either-or situation with two possible causes: "Either our workers aren't motivated or they're not adequately trained." Unary thinking—generating only one hypothesis—is worse, except that, for experts at least, that hypothesis is often correct.

Biases for or against alternatives can flaw hypothesis generation. A common bias is toward simple hypotheses. People assume that an effect results from a single, simple cause that involves few enabling conditions. Occam's rule—parsimonious theories are preferred to complex ones—reflects this bias in science. However, reality does not necessarily share our preference for simplicity. As many as 70 percent of clinic patients suffer from combinations of diseases. A diagnostician intent on finding the "one true cause" of a set of symptoms may be doomed to failure.

Another bias affecting explanations of human behavior is the **fundamental attribution error,** in which people explain the behavior of others in terms of personal traits rather than situational factors. An essential cause is cited when a generative cause would be more explanatory. "Why isn't production up to standard? Because our workers are lazy." This hypothesis is easily conceived and not easily disproven, though other explanations, such as poor work methods, may be more valid. Less common, and associated in its extreme form with paranoia, is the **pathetic fallacy.** Here a generative cause is supplanted by a purposive cause. One sees hidden purposes that do not exist. Now production is off because workers are engaged in an unannounced slowdown, conspiring to wring concessions from management.

When Coors began to use recycled lubricant in machines, operators claimed that the lubricant caused tear-off jams. Investigation revealed that the jams were caused by other factors. In this case, operators were naturally suspicious of a change, especially one involving a nonstandard input. But their suspicions went too far. The prior history of jams was ignored, and other possible causes of the problem were overlooked.

In another case, city employees in Fort Lauderdale had to wait in line to make copies. The situation was diagnosed as one of inadequate copier capacity, and the proposed solution was to buy a larger machine. However, a problem-solving team discovered that 95 percent of delays resulted from correctable problems (jams, misfeeds, sorting troubles) rather than an inherent supply-demand mismatch. Inadequate capacity is often a knee-jerk explanation of such situations, as it is when equipment does not produce at required tolerances. Such hypotheses have clear solution implications: Buy new equipment. Since these solutions are expensive, other causes and cures should be considered.

Hypothesis evaluation is judgmental and error-prone. Diagnosticians can be overly tolerant when matching a causal candidate to available information, mistakenly accepting a hypothesis that is not true. Or assessment criteria can be so strict that the real cause is rejected because its expected symptoms do not exactly agree with what was observed. Another mistake is to conduct haphazard tests of hypotheses. I once spent several weekends trying to repair a clothes dryer because of a sloppy check of the power supply. If only I'd opened the fuse box!

Errors in hypothesis testing can result from **confirmation bias,** a tendency to confirm favored hypotheses regardless of the evidence. People often commit to a hypothesis quite early. They look on testing as a mere formality, anointing the chosen one. Asked to diagnose a threatening flight condition, some pilots formed an initial hypothesis, only considered information that supported that hypothesis, and misremembered data in a way that confirmed their suspicions.

Errors in interpreting information can result from schema effects. A situation evokes a causal schema that suggests a certain hypothesis. Related expectations shape subsequent information gathering and interpretation. The **garden path syndrome** is typical: Initial findings plausibly lead one to a causal candidate that happens to be mistaken. Once on the garden path, diagnosticians do not revise their beliefs when conflicting evidence comes to light. Rather, they rationalize, explain away inconsistent data, and find ways to make it seem confirmatory, to make the pieces fit the puzzle. A study of medical diagnosis found that physicians err through overinterpretation, discerning support for their suspicions in data that is truly neutral.

Two interpretive errors deserve special mention. One is the **post hoc fallacy,** the mistake of ascribing causality solely on the basis of temporal order. X happened, then Y happened, so X must be the cause of Y. Remember how Al Gore during the 1992 vice-presidential debate ridiculed Republican claims that their policies had brought about the demise of the Soviet empire: "That's like a rooster claiming that its crowing caused the sun to rise." Think about the many times a change in workers or materials is blamed for unrelated troubles. The other mistake is **confusing correlation with causation.** Correlation is evidence of causality—a suspected cause and its effect tend to be mutually present or absent—but it does not imply causality. People who wear dresses tend to have babies, but wearing a dress does not cause birth.

Interpretation can involve recognizing a pattern in the data, seeing a commonality that suggests possible causes. Pattern recognition is important, but one must not be blinded by it. Coors had problems with internal coating of cans. Defective cans had been processed by a single bank of spray guns, so diagnostic attention focused on that commonality—to no avail. A quality team eventually realized that affected cans shared other commonalities as well. In particular, they went down the same side of the cure oven. The team found that the oven's unbalanced air flow caused the defects.

Diagnostic success can be blocked by **mistaken assumptions,** beliefs so taken for granted as to be held unconsciously, without question. Assumptions must be brought to the surface to assess their validity. A bus company spent six months conducting laboratory analyses to determine the causes of failing alternators. Then an engineer noticed that alternators were located in a position exposing them to environmental corrosion. Investigators had assumed that alternators were in engine compartments, safe from such effects. In another company, a team could not solve a problem caused by an airborne contaminant until they walked around the plant, tracing every air conduit, intake, and exhaust. Inside the clean air zone, they found construction going on that everyone had thought was outside the zone.

A final diagnostic mistake is **stopping too soon.** Diagnosticians may not trace causality deeply enough. The notion of *root cause* helps prevent this error. A worker once confessed to Kaoru Ishikawa, the Japanese quality guru, that he had caused a process to be out of control by using the wrong material. Ishikawa replied that the real cause was unclear labeling, a poorly arranged warehouse, or whatever had led the worker to the wrong material. Of course, if the worker had simply been careless, tracing causality more deeply would be of no value.

The next case illustrates how mistaken diagnoses can result if one accepts a hypothesis without considering other alternatives. It also demonstrates the value of going to where the problem is and of carefully observing the process.

Frequent integrated circuit (IC) failures were experienced in a component designed for satellite usage. Since all failures were observed when the assembly was tested at –20°C, it was hypothesized that uneven thermal contraction of parts resulted in cracks at low temperatures. Luckily, an analyst made additional checks, visiting the fabrication area where parts were cemented to plastic spacers before installation. The adhesive hardened in a few seconds. When the analyst asked how misalignments were corrected, the assembler showed how he used a knife to pry misplaced parts into position. This prying was the real cause of IC failures.

Another form of stopping too quickly occurs when a system has multiple faults but diagnosis ends when the first source of trouble is found. A Japanese manufacturer of automobile radiators conducted leakage tests. On one occasion, a faulty radiator was detected, repaired, and passed on to the painting process where another leak was found. The radiator had had two leaks, only one of which was initially detected and corrected. Diagnosticians can err by disregarding causes lying outside their areas of responsibility. It is wise to consider the extent of one's practical influence in deciding which causes to address, but these practicalities should not constrain efforts to determine a problem's causes.

## Diagnostic Methods

This section reviews and assesses diagnostic methods applicable to quality problems. Each technique is described, though not in detail. References to in-depth accounts are provided. The narrative explains how each method works, discussing its strengths and limitations.

### Experimentation

Experimentation is the traditional scientific means of testing causal hypotheses. Experimental methodology manipulates the presence of suspected causal variables and observes what happens to effect variables. Causal candidates can be tested individually or in combination. While its core logic is simple, experimentation is complicated by the challenge of arranging crisp comparisons. Controls prevent extraneous factors from affecting results; other influences even out through randomization.

More complications arise from the need to test hypotheses efficiently, to learn as much as possible from each experiment. Efficiency is critical when there are many causal candidates with multiple levels, as in food formulations with varying amounts of ingredients. This is where design of experiments (DOE), a technique for devising informationally efficient experiments, becomes useful. DOE prescribes how to organize treatments, or causal candidates, and treatment levels to reach conclusions with the fewest experimental runs.[3]

The importance of DOE implicates a disadvantage of experimentation: It is expensive. Time spent experimenting with an industrial process is time lost from production. Materials used in experiments are usually lost as well. A major consequence is the need to narrow the set of causal candidates—say, to six or fewer—before conducting tests. Of course, if this set does not include the true cause, the experiment is a waste. This trade-off is unavoidable. In addition, experimentation is not always feasible due to practical or ethical considerations. This can be the case when people, as operators or customers, are part of the problem. One may not be able to control for certain variables or use treatments that are unfair or pose risks to involved parties.

Experimentation is a powerful means of testing causal hypotheses. It is most useful when relatively few causal candidates are truly viable and when these are measurable, controllable variables in a well-structured process. Such conditions are often satisfied by conformance problems. Sometimes, though applicable, experimentation is overkill. A company designed an experiment to determine which characteristics of parts were responsible for defective assemblies. While arrangements were being made to conduct these expensive tests, a freelancing employee measured dimensions on parts taken from functional and nonfunctional assemblies. Using statistical regression, he derived target values for each dimension, obviating the need for an experiment. In general, a thorough analysis of existing data using regression and other statistical methods should be performed before using experimentation to collect and analyze new data.

## Shainin Techniques

During his career as a quality practitioner and consultant, Dorian Shainin developed many diagnostic techniques.[4] Viewed as an approach to experimental design, these methods have been criticized by mainstream statisticians for an alleged lack of rigor. This is unfortunate because the methods, for the most part, serve as a front end for experimentation. They offer ways of generating promising hypotheses and reducing them to a manageable number. A multi-vari chart, for instance, is designed to detect common patterns of variation in process outputs, including positional (such as within or across parts, across machines), cyclical (as in batch-to-batch), and temporal (shift-to-shift, day-to-day, etc.). In one application, these charts were used to establish that most variation in the outputs of a molding process was within-mold, thereby eliminating mold-to-mold and time-to-time factors as potential causal candidates. Components search involves swapping parts between good and bad assemblies to determine which part is responsible for a malfunction. When you find the part that turns bad assemblies into good ones and good assemblies into bad ones, you have identified the problematic component. Paired comparisons applies the same logic with items that cannot be disassembled. One compares good and bad items, looking for consistent differences. Variables search uses the half-split heuristic to reduce the set of causal candidates. A process of elimination allows one to quickly home in on the true cause. And the B vs. C technique is an informal means of testing the claim that B, a new process alternative, is better than C, the current way of doing things. One simply compares the outputs of each alternative against pertinent criteria.

I cannot evaluate the technical aspects of Shainin's work on DOE. However, the techniques just described are useful diagnostic methods. Several are based on well-known heuristics, and all have demonstrated their worth through practical applications.

## Concentration Diagrams

A concentration diagram is a picture or drawing of a product that has been of unacceptable quality. Locations of defects are plotted on this picture in hopes of identifying trouble spots or interpretable patterns. Concentration diagrams are often used to localize occurrences of voids in molded products. When dents were found in a part used in the production of TV picture tubes, dent locations were recorded on a concentration diagram. Recognizing that most dents occurred near the part's edges, problem solvers focused their attention on materials handling methods used by untrained personnel.

This is a simple, reasonably powerful, but special-purpose diagnostic tool. It employs the logic of stratification by characterizing events in ways that reveal patterns or clusters. Concentration diagrams stratify on the basis of spatial location. They can only be used if defects are localized. Concentration diagrams are not effective if the paint in a vat is off-color.

## Cause-and-Effect (CE) Diagrams

Also known as Ishikawa diagrams (after their originator) and fishbone diagrams (in respect to their shape), CE diagrams are the most popular technique for diagnosing quality problems.[5] CE methodology has been elaborated into several variations, each with its own bells and whistles.

CE diagrams are a means of identifying the potential causes and effects of a problem and organizing these systematically. Given a problem of unknown cause, a team generates causal candidates through brainstorming. This effort can be aided by the "5 Ms"—man, materials, machines, methods, and measurements—or "4ME"—drop measurements and add environment—generic causes applicable to quality problems. These and other high-level categories are major cause headings under which specific candidates are organized hierarchically. The same generate-and-organize process can be conducted for the problem's effects. Results are depicted in a diagram like that of Figure 5.2.,[6] which addresses the problem of why tables in a restaurant were not cleared quickly. Generation of high-level causes is assumed to promote recognition of detailed causes that comprise them. Reflecting on observed effects can remind one of causes potentially responsible for them. By organizing these ideas, CE diagrams foster a systematic diagnostic effort.

If the method's essence is to generate and organize causal candidates, its effectiveness can be assessed in terms of these functions. As an organizing device, a CE diagram is a simple hierarchical structure. Despite its unique appearance, the diagram is no different from the outline format taught in composition classes. Because the representational format is generic, CE diagrams are prone to misapplication. A quality circle in a hospital used a CE diagram to depict requirements for a training program for phlebotomists. This is a design problem. The diagram was a structured

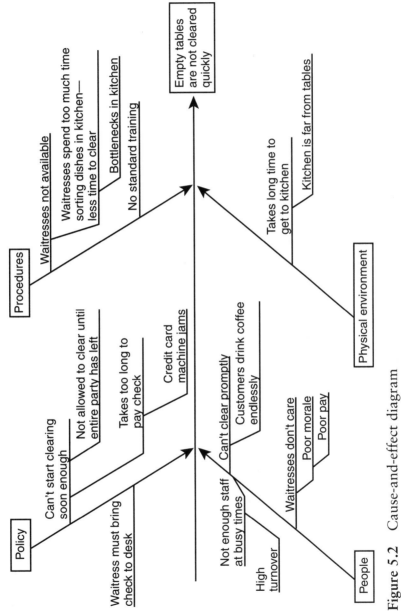

**Figure 5.2** Cause-and-effect diagram
Reprinted with permission from *Quality Progress*, ASQ, Milwaukee, WI, October 1991.

111

list of design requirements that served no diagnostic purpose. CE diagrams can contain whatever one wants: causes of a problem, means to a goal, characteristics of a product, or requirements for a design. No harm comes from using the fishbone structure to organize a set of ideas, but problem solving can be derailed if this is mistakenly viewed as diagnostic activity.

What about the technique's generative power, its ability to identify potential causes of a problem? CE diagrams rely on brainstorming, augmented by the 5 Ms. These devices can be helpful but are not especially powerful. The technique presumes that someone will identify the problem's cause during a brainstorming session. The 5 Ms and group interaction may prompt this recognition, or they may not. The method encompasses little generative machinery and consequently cannot provide much help during the process.

CE diagrams are most useful with recurring problems. Diagnostic experience with a system can be accumulated, recorded on a diagram, and accessed when the system malfunctions. This is how fault trees and diagnostic dictionaries are used—as organized records of frequently observed problem-symptom pairs. Prevailing practice is to develop a CE diagram from scratch each time a problem occurs. Used in this way, the technique's generative inadequacies are a serious shortcoming. These weaknesses might be offset by research that identified a broader, deeper set of standard causes, tailoring these to problem types. This possibility is explored in the next section. In current problem-solving practice, cause-and-effect diagrams are useful but overused.

## Kepner-Tregoe Method

This was one of the first diagnostic methods developed for and taught to managers.[7] Its success in that market resulted from the fact that it embeds useful heuristics in a structured process. After defining the problem, one describes it in terms of identity (what is wrong), location (where the problem is observed), timing (when it occurs), and magnitude (how far it extends). These dimensions are used to compare the problem situation with similar situations that are not problematic. Comparisons can suggest distinctions and changes, what is being done differently than before. Causal candidates that surface through this analysis are tested, leading to identification of the problem's true cause.

A colleague once told me how Kepner-Tregoe had been used on a problem within the telephone company. If you screw up a long distance call, you can contact an operator, admit your incompetence, and receive a credit to offset the charge. Customers who did this did not find the promised credits on their phone bills. Using Kepner-Tregoe, the phone company discovered that operators were using different pencils to record credits. The scanning system could not read marks made by the new pencils.

This case illustrates the importance of looking for changes, a valuable diagnostic heuristic. Other sources of the method's power are its insistence on describing the problem and on making comparisons. Describing the situation is also advised by the 5W2H method, which asks what, why, where, when, who, how, and how much.[8] Comparisons can be made with similar systems, with the system's performance before the problem appeared, or with system design specifications.

Any situation can be described in infinite detail. The Kepner-Tregoe dimensions of identity, location, and the like are unlikely to evoke all critical facts. Comparisons can be informative, but what if there is no useful standard of comparison, as when the baggage handling system in Denver's new airport did not work? Relevant changes can occur gradually, rather than all at once. Changes can be unobservable, as when employee morale slowly goes south. Participants in Kepner-Tregoe training have commented that the technique forces one through a protracted process that can be frustrating. A pair of *Harvard Business Review* articles demonstrated the method by applying it to a hypothetical manufacturer of automobile parts that experienced a sudden increase in defects.[9] The problem was caused by a change in sheet metal, the new alloy being less malleable than its predecessor. The cause was eventually identified by Kepner-Tregoe. But it is hard to believe that a team, using a cause-and-effect diagram with the 5 Ms, would not quickly have realized that the problem was caused by materials.

Kepner-Tregoe is most effective with technical troubles in which a system that has been performing effectively abruptly goes awry due to a single cause. The system and its inputs and outputs should be observable, unlike, say, computer chips or the mental states of human beings. Kepner-Tregoe will not provide much help with problems involving complex behavioral phenomena, though some of its heuristics—make comparisons, look for changes—can be used in such situations as well.

## Why-Why Diagrams

Also known as the "5 Why Method," this simple technique is notable for getting to a problem's root cause.[10] One begins by stating the problem and asking why it exists. This question should evoke possible causes of the problem. These causes are effects of deeper causes, evoked again by asking "Why?" This iterative process of evoking a cause that is used to evoke deeper causes continues until all causal chains terminate with root causes, factors that cannot be explained by anything else. A diagram (Figure 5.3) depicting the emerging causal tree is constructed during the process. In a case at Toyota, a machine stopped because a fuse blew due to an overload. Why? Because of inadequate bearing lubrication. Why? Because the lubrication pump was not working properly. Why? Because the pump axle was worn. Why? Because sludge got in. The solution—attaching a strainer to the lubricating pump—assuredly had more staying power than replacing the fuse or lubricating the bearing.

Depending on the problem, a why-why diagram can resemble a bushy tree or a slender path. Each kind of problem/diagram poses risks. The case just cited would yield a path-like diagram. Here the risk is that one does not identify the problem's true cause. What if the fuse blew for a different reason? Asking "Why?" will not always direct one down the correct causal path. Other problems—the high U.S. crime rate—generate massive tree-like representations. Asking "Why?" evokes numerous responses at each level of inquiry. Here the challenge is to evaluate causal candidates, narrowing down to the critical few. The method provides no help in this regard. Though asking "Why?" can be an effective way of identifying causal candidates, this heuristic will not reliably generate remote possibilities and offers no aid in assessing alternatives. The method's real benefit is preventing premature stoppage. By pushing

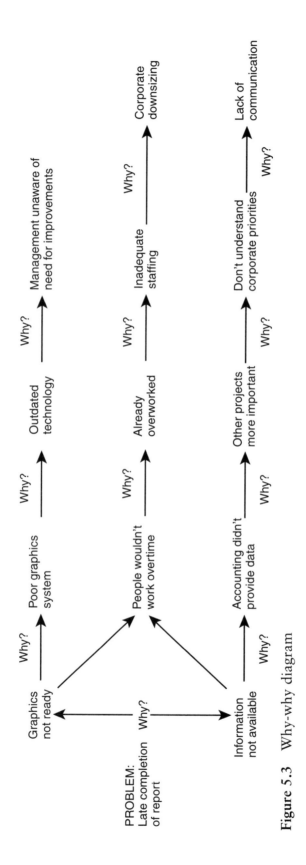

**Figure 5.3** Why-why diagram

inquiry further, it insures that precipitating causes do not keep one from finding underlying causes.

## Root Cause Analysis

Root cause analysis was developed for use in nuclear power plants and other complex, "high-stakes" systems.[11] The method is a relatively unintegrated collection of heuristics, each applicable in certain situations. Change analysis studies the effects of changes. It can be performed before or after a problem occurs. The technique owes much to Kepner-Tregoe, requiring that situations be described and that problematic and nonproblematic conditions be compared. Barrier analysis applies to situations where a hazard must be prevented from reaching a target by placing barriers in the way. Mistake-proofing uses barriers to prevent unwanted events; if a mistake occurs, one should examine the barriers to see how they might be improved. When a problem—an accident, for instance—results from a sequence of activities, it can be studied through event and causal factors analysis. This enables identification of factors responsible for the outcome so steps can be taken to prevent its recurrence.

Root cause analysis demonstrates a more general lesson. While no method will reliably diagnose any and all problems, useful heuristics have been developed. The best approach is to use different methods on an as-needed basis, applying each in situations where its strengths are called for. Figure 5.4 supports this effort, summarizing the virtues and limitations of the diagnostic techniques just discussed.

# Prescriptions

The nature of quality problems prevents the development of powerful diagnostic methods. Such problems usually involve large open systems encompassing the activities of many individuals and departments. The systems are hard to isolate, making it difficult to investigate malfunctions. The number of possible causal influences is beyond imagining. Performance inadequacies usually result from multiple causes. One can often conceive of many potential causes of a malfunction while overlooking the true cause. Few hypotheses can be tested in a convincing way. Rarely is it possible to pull out a questionable component, replace it with a different one, and see if this solves the problem. Due to these characteristics, methods used to diagnose quality problems are relatively weak.

What can be done to improve the diagnosis of quality problems? We can identify, organize, and apply heuristics that underly the effectiveness of existing methods. We can determine what diagnosticians should look for, from specific clues to general categories of symptoms, and which causes are associated with these indicators. We can develop a taxonomy of causes, a hierarchical scheme of factors typically responsible for quality problems. These possibilities are pursued in the remainder of this chapter.

## Diagnostic Heuristics

Diagnostic techniques derive their power from certain heuristics. Since no technique employs more than a few, practitioners may be better off learning and applying the

| Method/Practice | Applications | Strengths | Weaknesses |
|---|---|---|---|
| Experimentation | Testing causal hypotheses. | Very powerful; well-developed methodology. | Expensive; can be impractical or infeasible. |
| Shainin Techniques | Generating causal hypotheses and narrowing down to the most promising. | Quite general due to the variety of heuristic methods employed; good operationality. | Less well known and less rigorous for hypothesis selection than experimentation. |
| Concentration Diagram | Localizing defects by means of a picture of the product. | Easy to use; can yield valuable insights. | Only applicable to physical products with localized defects. |
| Cause-and-Effect (CE) Diagram | Identifying and organizing possible causes of a problem. | Easy to construct; efficient hierarchical organization of possible causes. | Little help in generating possible causes; has been misapplied. |
| Kepner-Tregoe Method | Generating and testing causal hypotheses. | Embeds sound heuristics in a systematic process; good with technical troubles of systems that had been performing effectively | Less effective with behavioral problems, those occurring gradually, or where many causes are involved. |
| Why-Why Diagram | Generating and organizing a deep causal account of a problem. | Widely applicable; easy to construct and use; promotes identification of underlying causes. | Limited aid in generating possible causes; not effective with hard or very broad problems. |
| Root Cause Analysis | Generating causal hypotheses and corrective actions. | Fairly general; well-developed heuristic methodology intended for use in complex, high-stakes systems. | Not as well known as other methods; though useful, heuristics lack cohesiveness and comprehensiveness. |

Figure 5.4 Overview of diagnostic methods

1. Observe the process.
2. Attempt quick fixes.
3. If possible, wait.
4. Expect multiple causality.
5. Identify conditions.
6. Look for interaction effects.
7. Watch out for side effects.
8. Make comparisons.
9. Activate competing and complementary hypotheses.
10. Work from general to specific hypotheses.
11. Shift the causal field.
12. Test hypotheses indirectly.
13. Use appropriate criteria in selecting hypotheses to test.
14. Use negative information.
15. Use all information to assess all hypotheses.
16. Swap components.
17. Do not stop with the first validated cause.
18. Do stop when an effective action is indicated.

**Figure 5.5**    Diagnostic heuristics

heuristics rather than the methods. Some heuristics of great relevance to QPS are listed in Figure 5.5. Each is briefly discussed.

**1. Observe the process.** The first move in diagnosis is to observe the malfunctioning system. The sooner this is done, the better; time destroys evidence. Verify symptoms to insure that a problem exists. You do not want to spend time fixing a device that is not plugged in. Talk with operators, people who know how the system works, people who were there when things went wrong. With some problems—employee turnover, for instance—it may be enough to simply ask people about their behavior. Visually inspect the site. This can require an intensive process trace, starting from the point of failure and moving upstream. When a manufacturer of high pressure hoses asked Shigeo Shingo to find out why steel wire wrapped around hoses often broke, Shingo told company managers to observe the process. In doing so, they noticed that wire fed through a guide was bent at a right angle, which was the cause of breakage. Describing the situation was endorsed by Kepner-Tregoe and the 5W2H method, though their templates for description may not be adequate. Mirroring patient workups conducted by physicians, it is best to have a comprehensive information-gathering protocol tailored to the system. Lacking that, collect any data that seems relevant, erring on the side of completeness.

**2. Attempt quick fixes.** After familiarizing themselves with the situation, experienced diagnosticians run through a repertoire of quick fixes. Troubleshooters "check fuses, adjust controls, push circuit boards firmly into their sockets, clean contacts, clean filters, replace gaskets, vacuum, dust, and bang or kick interlocked doors or cabinets to make sure they are properly seated."[12] If a manufacturing process is producing rejects, check equipment settings, tool wear, fluid levels, and materials. Some quick fixes address likely causes of the problem, such as replacing batteries in a flashlight. Most are easy to do and little is lost if they come up empty.

3. **If possible, wait.** This heuristic is used by physicians when available information is inconclusive and the situation is not serious. Doctors know that time can be their ally. The problem may clear up by itself or the disease's development may generate better evidence. This advice is also applicable with quality problems. Perhaps the system or an operator is new and is experiencing start-up difficulties; hasty intervention can be counterproductive. It may be too soon to tell if subpar departmental performance results from organization structure weaknesses, poor morale, or ineffective management. Sometimes an apparent problem is simply due to normal variation in the process; tampering with the system will only make things worse. If possible, wait and keep a close eye on the situation.

4. **Expect multiple causality.** Equipment troubleshooters routinely assume that malfunctions result from a single cause. This assumption will often be mistaken for quality problems. Note, for instance, that Pareto diagrams depict the frequencies of different kinds of rejects having different causes. In view of the tendency to assume that causality is simple and unitary, the opposite is advised: Assume that the problem results from several factors. Do not stop looking when one cause has been identified.

5. **Identify conditions.** The distinction between causes and conditions was discussed earlier. Causes are active, intrusive factors responsible for an effect; conditions are passive factors enabling its occurrence. Still, a condition is as necessary for the effect as are its causes. While conditions are not often addressed by diagnosis, they can offer effective means of correcting a situation and preventing its recurrence. It may be that guns do not kill people, people do. But guns, the condition, may be more controllable than people, the cause, of this violence. With an eye toward solution finding, diagnosis should identify conditions as well as causes.

6. **Look for interaction effects.** An **interaction effect** results from a combination of two or more causal variables. The effect only occurs if each is present. The most familiar examples involve parts that are supposed to fit together. An electronics company manufactured an hourmeter that had a 20 percent to 25 percent defect rate. A study revealed that defects resulted from an interaction between the mainframe and numeral wheel. Revising the wheel specifications eliminated the defects. Two-way interactions (those involving two causal variables) are most common, but higher-order interactions (three or more variables) can occur. DOE and Shainin methods can identify interactions. Watch for such effects during less formal diagnostic efforts as well. If a problem seems to result from a suspected cause, but only sometimes, look for interacting variables present on those occasions but not others.

7. **Watch out for side effects.** A **side effect** is the unintended result of an action. Drowsiness from taking a medication is a common example. Quality problems can result from side effects. A telephone equipment manufacturer experienced repeated transistor failures. They resulted from inductive transients generated by a buzzer that was being used temporarily to test assemblies for continuity. The Cherry Point

Naval Aviation Depot found that self-locking nuts had damaged Teflon rings. The culprit was a cleaning solution that ate Teflon. All actions affecting a system should be viewed as causal paths for infiltration by harmful side effects. Study each path to see if it is the origin of difficulties.

**8. Make comparisons.** Important in problem identification, comparisons have an equally prominent role in diagnosis. Experimentation is, after all, the controlled comparison of different treatments, all potential causes of an effect. Less formal comparisons are employed by Kepner-Tregoe and in Shainin's method of paired comparisons. Look for ways of comparing one system or component with another. Compare the same system or component to itself before and after the problem occurred. Be alert to noncomparabilities, but remember that even rough comparisons can yield valuable insights.

**9. Activate competing and complementary hypotheses.** Physicians are taught to generate a set of hypotheses that specifically includes diseases that often co-occur with a favored candidate and diseases that are frequently confused with that candidate. Some causes are parts of informal syndromes, tending to be observed with each other. Low morale is associated with compensation inadequacies and poor management. Other causes form natural competitor sets, competing explanations for a given problem. The natural competitor set of diagnoses for human performance problems includes lack of ability, lack of training, and poor motivation. Once a favored hypothesis has emerged from the crowd, problem solvers should try to think of other hypotheses that naturally compete with or complement that candidate.

**10. Work from general to specific hypotheses.** Not always followed by QPS practitioners, this is standard diagnostic practice in other fields. During the early stages of a diagnosis, a physician suggests general disease categories as hypotheses, only offering more detailed diagnoses when additional information is received. A troubleshooter localizes the fault in a module before conducting tests to identify the malfunctioning part within that module. The approach is economical from a memory standpoint. Rather than remembering many specific causes, one encompasses them under a few general hypotheses and narrows down as evidence allows.

**11. Shift the causal field.** When people cannot generate correct hypotheses, it may be because their causal fields are too narrow. They suffer from tunnel vision, only conceiving certain kinds of causes. To overcome the impairment, list, classify, and reflect on hypotheses considered thus far. To what causal categories do they belong? What other kinds of causes are not being considered? Diagrams can be used to evoke different causal categories. In addition to a flowchart modeling the process flow, one might use diagrams that represent information flows, the physical proximity of operators, and interpersonal relationships. Any of these could be affecting performance.

**12. Test hypotheses indirectly.** Experimentation is expensive, and it is not always possible to conduct direct tests of hypotheses. Sometimes the best option is to test hypotheses indirectly through the hypothetico-deductive (H-D) method. The H-D method tests a causal candidate $X$ by deducing its observational implications $Y$. The diagnostician then checks to see if $Y$ is true. If so, and if $Y$ is otherwise unlikely, the validity of $X$ is supported. Medical diagnosis works this way. If the patient has disease X, we would expect to see so-and-so in her blood test and such-and-such in the ECG. When considering causes of a problem, think about indirect evidence that might support their existence. If poor morale is responsible for lagging productivity, what other signs of this cause can we expect to find?

**13. Use appropriate criteria in selecting hypotheses to test.** Being expensive and not always conclusive, tests must be made selectively on the basis of appropriate criteria. These criteria include the ease or cost of a test, its informational value, and the likelihood of the suspected cause. In a quality context, if past defects often resulted from a particular malfunction, check out that cause first. It may not be worthwhile to test for causes that cannot be cured. A physician made this point: "I do not care whether I make a diagnosis of multiple sclerosis. There is little I can do about it anyway. I want to make sure that this patient does not have a tumor of the spinal cord which we can remove surgically and cure the patient."[13] In a QPS setting, this criterion delays pursuit of hypotheses blaming problems on top management or economic conditions. Explore actionable causes first.

**14. Use negative information.** People have a confirmation bias toward positive information, data that is consistent with their hypotheses. Negative information, which tends to be ignored, is of two types: One can observe something that is inconsistent with a hypothesis or fail to observe something that the hypothesis leads one to expect. Consciously relating all observations to hypotheses can offset the first failing: What are the implications of this finding for each causal candidate? To counter the second failing, state all observational expectations up front and check each against the data: My hypothesis led me to expect that X would be observed, but it was not. Why not?

**15. Use all information to assess all hypotheses.** Cognitive limitations force diagnosticians to consider hypotheses sequentially. One rarely entertains more than four possible causes at a time. New possibilities are added as old ones are discarded. This sequential approach is vulnerable to error due to the timing of informational inflows. Diagnosticians fail to assess hypotheses in light of evidence received during "off-hours." New information might not prompt reconsideration of a previously rejected hypothesis, or a new hypothesis may not be evaluated against information collected much earlier. Misdiagnoses can be prevented by maintaining a record of diagnostic activity. Lists of evidence and hypotheses should be compared periodically to detect connections.

**16. Swap components.** This heuristic, the basis for one of Shainin's techniques, is a traditional tactic in equipment troubleshooting: Plug in a part from a unit that works and see if the faulty unit now performs as intended. Not only parts of the product, but parts of the process can be swapped. If you suspect that a worker is causing rejects, assign a different person to that station to see if things improve. Do the work on a different machine or with materials from a different vendor. Obviously, informal experiments like this can only be conducted with interchangeable components. Doctors cannot use the heuristic to see if a patient's lungs are malfunctioning.

**17. Do not stop with the first validated cause.** Working from the assumption that causality is simple, diagnosticians often stamp a case as CLOSED once a hypothesis is backed by strong confirmatory evidence. This exposes them to two errors: There may be multiple causes of the effect, and the identified cause can be the result of a deeper root cause. Premature closure can be prevented by expecting multiple causality (heuristic #4). Physicians are trained to keep searching until a well-confirmed set of ailments explains all case findings. The tendency to ignore underlying causes has been addressed by why-why diagrams and root cause analysis. For each identified cause of a problem, consider whether a deeper cause must be addressed to prevent its recurrence.

18. **Do stop when an effective action is indicated.** The flip side of premature closure is the never-ending search. Diagnosis must be limited by stopping rules that bring things to a timely conclusion. One issue is that of confidence, how strong the evidence must be to conclude that X causes Y. Unlike scientists, quality practitioners cannot insist on overwhelming evidential support for hypotheses. They must act in the face of uncertainty and check to see if results are as expected. Another concern is precision: How specific a cause must one identify? A diagnosis need be no more refined than the actions it implies. If machine malfunctions are corrected by replacing faulty modules, diagnosis can stop at the module level. Finally, there is the question of how deeply causality must be traced. Again, the answer lies in the realm of action. Rather than seeking the ultimate root cause of a problem, diagnosis should pursue causes to a depth where an identified action will correct the current situation and prevent recurrence of similar problems.

## Developing the Symptom Side of Diagnosis

A heuristic left out of Figure 5.5 is Analyze the effects. This advice was omitted because it forms the basis for a program of diagnostic improvements outlined below.

Diagnosis is a movement from effect to cause. Symptoms, evidence, or findings are used to infer causes. Some findings are more informative than others. The medical field classifies symptoms on a continuum of informativeness. At one end are **nonspecific symptoms,** conditions like a fever that could result from any number of causes. At the other extreme are **pathognomonic symptoms,** findings that could only result from one cause. Observing such a symptom, a physician immediately reaches a conclusive diagnosis of the patient's condition. Unfortunately, pathognomonic symptoms are rare.

This suggests a way of developing the symptom side of diagnosis: Identify symptoms indicating certain causes and train diagnosticians to recognize and use these symptom-cause associations. Another way of improving diagnosis exploits the fact that evidence can be found in certain ways. Expert diagnosticians know what questions to ask and where to look for evidence of a problem's cause. Diagnosis can be improved by developing heuristics for evidence acquisition and interpretation, where to look for symptoms and what findings typically mean. Figure 5.6 identifies several heuristics.

1. **Look for patterns.** The search for patterns often uses data from check sheets and control charts. If a dimension of a machined item gradually increases over time, an experienced diagnostician will suspect tool wear. Periodicity, a tendency

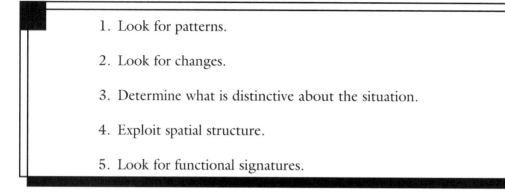

1. Look for patterns.

2. Look for changes.

3. Determine what is distinctive about the situation.

4. Exploit spatial structure.

5. Look for functional signatures.

**Figure 5.6** Symptom-side heuristics

for data values to repeat themselves at predictable points in time, is a valuable clue. A diagnostic study of cutting machine variability only succeeded when someone noticed periodicity in the data. The observed cycle corresponded to the travel time of a conveyor belt feeding the machine, implicating the belt as a causal factor. In another case, surface blemishes on a product were traced to a filter-changing operation. SPC charts revealed that the blemishes had a time period paralleling the timing of filter changes. The multi-vari charts developed by Shainin provide a structured way of searching for certain patterns of variation.

**2. Look for changes.** Used by Kepner-Tregoe and often employed informally, this heuristic should be an official part of every diagnostic effort. It can be applied whenever a system was performing effectively (before) but ended up in an unsatisfactory state (after). Look for changes affecting the system that occurred during the transition from before to after. Anything that changed should be scrutinized as a potential problem cause or as a condition enabling other causes to produce the effect. Some changes are especially suspicious. In diagnosing product abnormalities, look for personnel changes that might have led to a change in work methods.

**3. Determine what is distinctive about the situation.** Identify unusual aspects of a case, how it differs from the norm. This heuristic motivates the patient history-taking performed as part of medical diagnosis: Physicians look for past events (illnesses, operations) or distinctive patient characteristics (allergies) that could explain the current illness or affect its treatment. When International Packings Corporation investigated a problem with receivables, it found that many overdue accounts involved sales of tooling, which are transactions with a lengthy customer approval process. Recognizing the special nature of such sales led to a change in billing procedures and resolution of the receivables problem.

**4. Exploit spatial structure.** A cause is necessarily connected to its effect by a spatial path of interaction. Diagnosticians can exploit the inevitability of this connectedness. The topographic search strategy used to troubleshoot electronic equipment is an example. Diagnosticians trace signals through a series of linked components. Flowcharts support process tracing by depicting connections between system parts. Poor product can be traced from the point of its discovery back up the system to its point of origin. If a suspected part of the system is not the cause of trouble, check if components physically close to it are responsible.

**5. Look for functional signatures.** The functional search strategy discussed earlier is based on the fact that a symptom can suggest the functional identity of its cause. Jaundice is a strong cue, almost pathognomonic, for liver disease. Bloody sputum directs diagnostic attention to the patient's lungs. These symptoms are functional signatures. They reliably point to certain parts of the system, narrowing the set of causal candidates. Diagnosticians can be trained to look for and recognize such signatures.

These heuristics can be augmented by less general, but still useful, symptom-cause relationships. Consider the following case:

---

■ **case 5.3**

During the production of semiconductor-on-sapphire (SOS), the product is heated and then slowly cooled in industrial furnaces. An American manufacturer found that its SOS operations could rival, but not match, the quality of Japanese competitors. In particular, the American firm saw that product coming out of its furnaces during the last run of each day was of substantially lower quality.

---

The pattern here—end-of-day defects—occurred because workers, in a hurry to get home, did not cool the furnace as slowly as they should. Diagnosticians must be alert to behavioral effects of this kind. Another pattern is evident in the next case.

---

■ **case 5.4**

A manufacturer was producing motor shafts that did not fit properly. Believing its equipment could not hold the required tolerances, the company made plans to purchase a new machine. Then a consultant found that variation was minimal after downtime for breaks, lunch, and other work interruptions. This led to a discovery that the machine had been overheating because of a low coolant level. Adding coolant reduced process variation by 50 percent.

---

The lesson: When performance improves after downtime, look for causes involving time strain, such as worker fatigue or equipment overheating. Another insight comes from the case of a wave soldering operation. PC boards on the outer edges of panels had higher defect rates than those near the middle. Processes often exhibit positional variation, with units located at the front, back, or periphery of a lot more prone to trouble. Sometimes the meaning of symptoms can be recognized through personal experience. A foundry was experiencing excessive stagger (dimensional variation) in cylinder block castings. An investigator eventually realized that the problem occurred because molds traveled down an incline after being filled with molten metal. In retrospect, it is surprising that the symptom of stagger did not evoke everyday experiences with liquids in containers, immediately directing attention to the incline.

## A Taxonomy of Causes

If symptom-side developments can aid diagnosis, so can work on the cause side. An organized set of possible causes of quality problems would prove useful for diagnosticians. The value and viability of this approach has been demonstrated by the use of disease taxonomies in medical diagnosis. Troubleshooting also employs this approach when diagnosticians compile fault dictionaries recording the problems, causes, symptoms, and cures experienced with certain systems or equipment.

The task of developing a comprehensive taxonomy of causes is more difficult with quality problems. Whereas all people are liable to the same set of diseases, there is a huge variety of organizational products and systems, each affected by different problems. Two kinds of taxonomies can be created. One is system-specific, like a fault dictionary. The other is a general classification of causes of problems experienced by many different systems.

The envisioned general taxonomy of causes would apply to many systems, but with varying degrees of power. It would be more abstract than a system-specific categorization. The possibility of developing such a scheme is evident in the 5 Ms. These are general cause categories, the rudiments of a taxonomy that could be extended and elaborated. More comprehensive taxonomies have been suggested by others. No one correct taxonomy of causes exists, in part because there is no dominant basis of classification. Diseases are classified in terms of their origins (infections, cancers, etc.), the organ system involved (heart, liver, etc.), and other criteria. In QPS, causes might be classified in terms of the inputs to a system (materials or equipment for instance), the processes that comprise the system (such as receiving or assembly), and the components of products created by the system (engine, brakes, finish, etc.).

Figure 5.7 is a taxonomic framework depicting major categories of causes to consider when diagnosing quality problems. The framework is built around a simple input-process-output structure. Problems can be caused by deficiencies on the

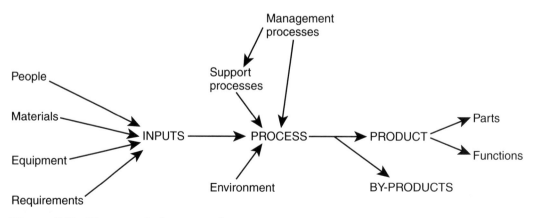

**Figure 5.7** Taxonomic framework

input side; causes can be located in the production process or in supporting processes; and product deficiencies can be traced to particular parts or functions. The framework supports process and product diagnosis. One can try to determine why a manufacturing process is producing defective TVs and investigate what is wrong with the TVs themselves. It also enables causes to be traced deeply. If a product failed due to an inadequate component, responsibility could be traced to purchasing and then to underlying managerial deficiencies.

This framework is fleshed in by Figure 5.8, a detailed taxonomy of causes for quality problems. Possible causes of a problem can be generated by stepping through the list, applying each relevant category to every input, process, and product involved in the situation. Though not complete, this taxonomy suggests far more causal candidates than the 5 Ms. Many of these causes will be evident in the discussion of conformance problems in Chapter 7.

The relevance of the general causal categories in Figures 5.7 and 5.8 varies across situations. Whereas materials and equipment are key inputs to manufacturing processes, they are less significant for administrative systems. Specialized taxonomies tailored to the characteristics of different kinds of systems can be developed. At some point, customization results in a system-specific taxonomy developed within organizations. Diagnosticians should report successes and failures so a formal body of experience is compiled for each system and system type. Compaq Computer has done this with its SMART system, an integrated call-tracking and problem resolution system. SMART contains hundreds of cases of problems experienced by users of Compaq products. It uses case-based reasoning methods to identify cases pertinent to problems posed by customers calling in on a help line. Compaq is also distributing a case base directly to its customers.

## Recommended Diagnostic Method

The following is a series of steps a problem-solving team might take when addressing a diagnostic task. Think of these steps as a diagnostic method, though its heart is in the material already discussed.

1. Verify the problem. Confirm that the system is not performing acceptably, perhaps by recreating observed failures. Establish the need for diagnosis.

2. Collect relevant information. Use methods discussed in this and the preceding chapter.

3. Examine the evidence for special clues and signature symptoms. Do any of the data strongly indicate certain causal candidates?

4. Apply the heuristics presented earlier in this section. These pertain to different stages of the diagnostic process.

5. Use the past history of the system to generate causal candidates. What problems have been encountered previously with this process or product?

6. Generate other candidates by going through a taxonomy of causes. This should enable one to develop a comprehensive set of possible causes.

7. Collect information that bears on the most promising hypotheses, conducting experiments if appropriate. Reevaluate causal candidates as information is received. Continue until one or a few candidates are strongly established.

I. Inputs
   A. People–primarily process operators
      1. Lack of knowledge
         a. Untrained
         b. Inexperienced
      2. Lack of basic skills
         a. Mental—reading, math
         b. Physical—manual dexterity, visual acuity
      3. Unmotivated
         a. Inadequate incentives
         b. Conflicting motives
      4. Carelessness
      5. Boredom
      6. Fatigue
      7. Stress
   B. Materials—physical inputs consumed by the process, including direct and indirect
      1. Improperly specified
      2. Don't meet specifications
      3. Impurities
      4. Inadequately blended
      5. Overstressed
      6. Too fragile
   C. Equipment—includes tools, jigs, and fixtures
      1. Not available
      2. Inappropriate
      3. Miscalibrated
      4. Damaged or worn
      5. Unclean, not maintained
      6. Too complicated
      7. Overheating
   D. Requirements—demands set by product users and other agents
      1. Unclear
      2. Inappropriate
      3. Late and frequent changes
      4. Uneven workload
II. Processes
   A. Production process—core activities that transform inputs into outputs
      1. Work methods
         a. Do not exist
         b. Unclear, unknown

**Figure 5.8.** Taxonomy of causes of quality problems

        c. Not standardized
        d. Inappropriate
    2. Work flow
        a. Scheduling
        b. Bottlenecks
        c. Process stops & starts
        d. Abrupt movements
    3. Demanding tasks
    4. Measurement methods
    5. Excessive work volume
    6. Lack of task information
  B. Support processes—activities that support production
    1. Procurement inadequacies
    2. Poor materials handling
    3. Inadequate maintenance
    4. Product testing/inspection
        a. Sampling methods
        b. Measurement methods
        c. Inadequate equipment
  C. Management processes—management activities that can affect quality
    1. Resource misallocations
    2. Poor planning
    3. Inadequate control system
    4. Weak communications
  D. Environment—factors outside the system that affect quality
    1. Work environment
        a. Inadequate lighting
        b. Heating/ventilation
        c. Excessive noise
        d. Messy work area
    2. Contaminants
        a. Air-born particles
        b. Electromagnetic
III. Products—system outputs
  A. Parts—product components
  B. Functions—what the product and its parts are supposed to do
IV. By-products
  A. Scrap
  B. Waste
  C. Pollutants

**Figure 5.8.** (*continued*)

8. Assess whether other causes might be operative and whether a deeper cause might underlie those under consideration. If so, collect information that would establish or disconfirm these hypotheses.

9. Controlling for the identified causes, conduct a trial run of the system to confirm their effects. If the problem can be turned on and off by this means, the causes are fully validated.

10. Take actions that respond to the problem's causes. As a result of these actions, system performance should again be acceptable.

If, at this point, the problem remains unsolved, your search for causes has probably been too narrow. Get outside the box by consciously reviewing and classifying all the causal hypotheses considered thus far. What other kinds of factors might be responsible for this problem? Generate and explore these more unusual possibilities. If, after doing so, you are still stuck, hire a consultant. At least now you can blame someone else for not having solved the problem!

## NOTES

1. Wilson Paul F., Larry D. Dell, and Gaylord F. Anderson, *Root Cause Analysis: A Tool for Total Quality Management* (Milwaukee: ASQC Quality Press, 1993).
2. William J. McCabe, "Examining Processes Improves Operations," *Quality Progress* 22, no. 7 (1989): 26–32.
3. A standard text on experimental design is: Douglas C. Montgomery, *Design and Analysis of Experiments,* 4th ed. (New York: John Wiley & Sons, 1997).
4. Shainin's techniques are well described in: Keki R. Bhote, *World Class Quality: Using Design of Experiments to Make it Happen* (New York: Amacom, 1991).
5. A tutorial can be found in: J. Stephen Sarazen, "The Tools of Quality. Part II: Cause-and-Effect Diagrams," *Quality Progress* 23, no. 7 (1990): 59–62.
6. Figure 5.2 is taken from: Gaudard, Marie, Roland Coates, and Liz Freeman, "Accelerating Improvement," *Quality Progress,* 24, no. 10 (1991): 81–88.
7. Charles H. Kepner and Benjamin B. Tregoe, *The New Rational Manager* (Princeton, N.J.: Princeton Research Press, 1981).
8. Alan Robinson, ed., *Continuous Improvement in Operations: A Systematic Approach to Waste Reduction* (Cambridge, Mass.: Productivity Press, 1991).
9. Perrin Stryker, "Can You Analyze This Problem?" *Harvard Business Review* 43, no. 3 (1965): 73–78; and Perrin Stryker, "How to Analyze That Problem," *Harvard Business Review* 43, no. 4 (1965): 99–110.
10. See: Howard H. Bailie, "Organize Your Thinking with a Why-Why Diagram," *Quality Progress* 18, no. 12 (1985): 22–24.
11. See note 1.
12. Robert F. Mager, *Troubleshooting the Troubleshooting Course* (Belmont, Calif.: Pitman Learning, 1983).
13. Jack D. Myers, "The Process of Clinical Diagnosis and its Adaptation to the Computer," in *Logic of Discovery and Diagnosis in Medicine,* Kenneth F. Schaffner ed. (Berkeley, Calif.: University of California Press, 1985): 155–180.

# Alternative Generation and Evaluation

---

## Chapter Outline

**Creativity**
    Creative Products
    Creativity (Partially) Demystified
    The Creative Process
    Creative People

**Creativity Techniques**

**Prescriptions**
    The Problem Analytic Strategy
    The Analytical Bootstrapping Creativity (ABC) Method
    Alternative Generation Heuristics

**Evaluating Alternatives**
    Evaluation
    Decision Making
    Group Evaluation

**Implementation**

---

This chapter addresses problem-solving tasks performed after a quality problem has been defined and, if necessary, diagnosed. Though this might seem to encompass most of problem solving, that is not always the case. With conformance problems, for instance, once diagnosis has been completed, it is usually easy to generate and evaluate solution alternatives. In contrast, alternative generation is a critical task in solving product and process design problems. Creativity is discussed in this chapter, as are the evaluation and choice of alternatives and solution implementation.

# Creativity

Discussions of alternative generation invariably focus on creativity and imagination. How does one generate alternatives? Be creative! Use your imagination! **Creativity** and **imagination** are often viewed as cognitive faculties, like perception or attention, that underlie efforts to generate alternatives. Another way to think of creativity is as a collection of mental capacities and behaviors shaped by task and environmental factors.

## Creative Products

Most definitions of creativity emphasize two characteristics of creative products: originality and value. Creative thinking produces novel outputs which have not been seen before. But if just being different, original, were enough, every new rock band and off-the-wall artist would be lauded as creative geniuses. Creative products must also be good according to certain criteria. A building design can be creative by virtue of an innovative structure that satisfies practical needs while appealing to aesthetic tastes. The notion of creativity is sometimes used more broadly to refer to thinking that goes beyond what one knows or can readily infer. Individuals or groups are said to be creative when their thinking goes beyond normal boundaries, even though that thinking might not result in a significant new discovery.

Though creative products must be good or valuable, different fields have different standards of value. Artistic creativity is assessed in terms of aesthetic criteria that are somewhat relative. Van Gogh's contemporaries did not regard him as a great artist, and changing tides of taste affect expert rankings of English authors. In science, creativity must satisfy standards of validity. Beyond being novel, a creative theory must comport with available evidence and be confirmed by subsequent findings.

In problem solving, the standard is practical effectiveness. A proposed solution, however original, is not creative unless it solves the problem. Indeed, except in special domains like advertising, a solution's originality is of no account; practical effectiveness is what matters. Consider the efforts of a problem-solving team trying to improve a company's order processing system: A highly innovative proposal involving cutting-edge technology will invariably lose out to a more traditional process design that is demonstrably better in terms of cost and performance. Why then do we value creativity in problem solving? Because it expands the set of solution possibilities one can consider. Creative thinking uncovers options that can turn out to be more effective than those coming readily to mind.

## Creativity (Partially) Demystified

The notion of creativity has been shrouded in mystery. Cognitive scientists are cutting through this fog, dispelling the "myth of genius" and other fictions enveloping the topic. Much of the mystery centers on our ability to think of things that do not exist. How can this be possible? The answer lies in our capacity for mental representation, discussed in Chapter 2. Our minds process not the actual objects of thought, but mental representations that stand for those objects. Most of our thinking tries to develop true beliefs, mental representations that depict what the world is or will be like. We try to form true beliefs about whether it will rain today, what customers think of our products, and whether we can get across the intersection before that truck arrives. Creative thinking drops this focus on reality. It seeks to produce possibilities rather than true beliefs. The realm of possibilities includes anything that can be conceived using our stock of mental contents and processes. Only some possibilities can be realized, but by taking actions that bring those to pass, we can achieve our goals.

On this view, we cannot imagine anything whatsoever, only things constructed out of existing knowledge. I can imagine an animal with a fish's head, a tiger's body, and the legs of a table, but not an animal that exists outside space and time. Nor can I imagine colors beyond my visual experience. Creativity uses normal mental capacities, rather than being a specialized function only employed for certain tasks. As part of being creative, we compare, recall, evaluate, associate, recognize, and reason, as in other mental performances. However, creative thinking is not bound by the reality constraint. It generates possibilities rather than true beliefs.

The notion of mental representation demystifies creativity by making it conceivable. This is not the same as explaining creativity or the process by which creative products are conceived. Though many theories of the creative process have been proposed, none provides an adequate explanation. Arguably, creativity is too diverse to be captured in a crisp scientific theory. If not a total mystery, creativity remains poorly understood.

## The Creative Process

If one were to perform a creative task—say, writing poetry—by following a detailed recipe, most people would deny that the resulting output was truly creative, irrespective of its apparent merits. Thus, the notion of creativity implies a lack of procedure. Indeed, researchers have yet to discover anything that could be regarded as such. This does not mean that the creative process is an unanalyzable "black box" beyond our powers of understanding. Many useful things can be said about the creative process, and much paper and ink have been expended trying to do so.

One approach to explicating the creative process is to distinguish different kinds of thinking, some of which are viewed as creative and others which are not. This strategy is often marked by the use of catchy names for different categories. Thus we have bisociation, Janusian thinking, and the distinction between convergent and divergent thinking. The usual split is between logical, analytical thought (noncreative) and associative, imagistic thinking (creative). Consider de Bono's distinction between vertical and lateral thinking. Vertical thinking is selective, analytical, sequential; it follows most likely paths. Lateral thinking is generative and provocative; it makes jumps and explores least likely paths.[1] Some of these distinctions reflect the intent of creative thinking: to generate possibilities rather than forming true beliefs. Logical analysis is a different mental activity than associative recall. Unfortunately, these accounts add little to what we already know. They relabel things, pouring old wine into new bottles, without increasing our understanding. Their weakness is evident in the absence of a useful description of the creative process. It is also apparent in the lack of prescriptions powered by the distinctions.

Stage models are another means of explaining the creative process. Wallas's oft-cited model proposes that creative thinking proceeds through four stages: preparation, incubation, illumination, and verification.[2] This model emphasizes the importance of acquiring relevant knowledge (preparation), the value of temporarily withdrawing conscious attention from a task (incubation), and the need to test proposed solutions (verification). However, the core creative process is not explained: How does illumination occur and what does it consist of? Lacking a detailed account of the idea generation process, stage models of creativity beg the question.

Useful accounts of the creative process are emerging from cognitive science research.[3] Several themes are apparent. First, creative thinking is less a special capacity than the application of normal cognitive resources to certain kinds of tasks, those requiring an innovative response. Second, domain knowledge is a prerequisite for thinking creatively within a field. This claim is supported by research on composers and painters that demonstrates that even child prodigies require years of study before they can produce work of the first rank. It suggests that really understanding a problem is the key to generating breakthrough solutions. Finally, though no specific creative process has been identified, strictly speaking, creative thinking is marked by the use of analogies, visual imagery, associative memory, and other cognitive capacities. Heuristics and strategies such as planning, abstracting, undoing, and making ends into means can guide creative thinking. This suggests that people can be helped through training and techniques to perform more effectively in creative tasks.

## Creative People

A contrasting view—that creativity is an inherent trait, relatively immune to training—is endorsed by psychologists who emphasize nature over nurture when explaining human behavior. If creativity is an inherent trait—you either have it or you don't—training programs should be replaced by tests, so creative people can be identified and employed in tasks requiring their talents. Scientists have searched for empirical associations between creativity and other cognitive and personality traits without much success. The characteristic most strongly linked to creativity is motivation, especially *intrinsic motivation,* valuing an activity for its own sake apart from external pressures and rewards.

Two kinds of tests are used to measure creativity. Self-assessment tests ask subjects to describe themselves; their descriptions are compared with profiles of the creative personality. Test results can be biased by mistaken self-perceptions. Most people think of themselves as especially open-minded, innovative, and energetic. When used for hiring purposes, self-assessment tests can be abused by people who respond with "creative" answers rather than ones that reflect their nature. Other tests ask subjects to perform tasks requiring creative skills, such as proposing unusual uses for a common object. Such tests seem like better measures, but they have not been very successful in predicting creative ability.

# Creativity Techniques

Hundreds of creativity methods have been developed, many on a relatively ad hoc basis by organizations and consultants. Since few have been tested for effectiveness, practitioners must select methods without knowing whether they work. Creativity methods can be characterized in various ways. Some can be used by individuals, others must be employed by groups, and many can go either way. Some support **convergent thinking,** thinking analytically about the problem. Most emphasize **divergent thinking,** mentally moving away from the problem into the realm of possibilities. A few combine elements of each.

Beneath the diversity of idea generation techniques lies a substrate of active ingredients, basic devices used to promote creativity. Each method employs one or more of these devices. Three types of active ingredients can be differentiated:

1. **Strategies,** the most significant type, are operative means for generating ideas. Most refer to identifiable mental activities.
2. **Tactics,** the least common type, are stimulatory tools that support strategies.
3. **Enablers** are passive means of promoting idea generation. Rather than directly inspiring creative output, enablers foster conditions within which ideas are more likely to appear.

Devices can be grouped into categories, some of which are discussed below.

***Analytical Strategies.*** These devices demonstrate the value of focused, convergent thinking for idea generation. **Decomposition** is an analytical device that breaks things into their component parts and attributes. Ideas are generated by changing particular parts or attributes. Decompositional techniques are often used to create new product ideas. Another analytical strategy, **abstraction,** asks one to think about the problem in more general or fundamental terms. In one application of a related technique, people were asked to think of ways of stacking things. Their ideas were used to find ways of parking cars.

***Search Strategies.*** These strategies rely on directed retrieval of information from memory. **Association** exploits the mind's ability to move from one concept or idea to another along mental paths of various kinds. The strategy assumes that associative connections between ideas can reflect solution-relevant relationships. Techniques using **analogy** rely on similarity-based searches of memory. Thus, in designing a door hinge, one might consider how the same function is achieved in a clam shell. A Japanese engineer invented a revolutionary device for refining pulp after observing the operation of a tannery.

***Imagination-Based Strategies.*** The strategies in this category require one to imagine elaborate, unrealistic states or to run extended mental scenarios. Using the **fantasy** strategy, a person conceives of states in which reality constraints have been dropped. When trying to reduce deaths caused by automobile collisions with streetlight columns, an engineer's fantasy that columns disappear when struck by cars led to the design of structures that break away on impact. **Identification** requires people to imaginatively become a nonhuman part of the problem. By imagining that they were human hairs, people at Gillette were aided in the development of a new shampoo.

***Habit-Breaking Strategies.*** These strategies are based on the premise that the mind must break out of normal response patterns to think creatively. **Challenge assumptions** questions beliefs associated with a task. **Negation** asks people to assume the opposite of what they currently believe. Using a technique based on **change of perspective,** a problem solver thinks about the problem from the viewpoints of different agents who may or may not be part of the situation. How would Napoleon have dealt with a problem like this?

***Relationship-Seeking Strategies.*** Things have so many characteristics and there are so many kinds of relationships that one can always identify relationships between any two things. Doing so highlights characteristics that might be changed in the problem situation. The **stimulus analysis** technique has people generate a list of concrete terms unrelated to the problem, such as *doorknob.* Then they select a term, decompose it into characteristics, and relate each characteristic to the problem in hopes of finding solution ideas.

***Task-Focused Strategies.*** These devices are analytical but deal with particular parts of the problem. **Boundary stretching** explores extreme values of variables in the situation, something designers do when developing new design concepts. The **combination** strategy asks one to combine elements, attributes, and other aspects of the problem, usually by pairs, in search of ideas. **Rearrangement** alters the structure of a situation by rearranging its parts. A motorist could not get past a flock of sheep traveling down a country lane bounded by high banks. The shepherd refused to move the sheep to the side, fearing some would be struck as the car drove through. A rearrangement of moving and fixed elements solved the problem: The motorist stopped the car while the sheep were driven back around it.

***Development Strategies.*** Ideas generated previously can be manipulated to create better alternatives. The simplest such device is **enhancement,** modifying an idea to make it more feasible and effective. **Integration** combines alternatives into solutions encompassing the virtues of many. With **circumstances,** rather than altering an idea to fit current circumstances, one looks for circumstances that fit the idea. Post-it™ notes originated with a 3M scientist trying to think of applications for a semisticky adhesive.

***Interpersonal Strategies.*** The dominant ingredient in group ideation methods, these devices rely on interpersonal interaction. **Group interaction** is the core strategy in this family. Group members verbalize their thoughts so one person's ideas can spawn ideas in others. Brainstorming is the strategy's classic embodiment. Group members are encouraged to build on the ideas of others. The technique legislates against criticism, asking members to withhold evaluation of ideas until the appropriate time. The **nominal group** strategy tries to capture the synergies of interpersonal interaction while avoiding inhibitions and distractions. Members of a *brainwriting pool* write down ideas and share them anonymously. Some of the spontaneity and energy of a brainstorming session is sacrificed for the sake of focused, uninhibited thinking.

*Stimulation Tactics.* Tactics work within or support a strategy rather than being stand-alone idea generation mechanisms. **Personal experience** involves the problem solver experientially in the problem so he/she can develop a richer understanding of it. An *experience kit* immersed detergent brand managers in the realities of home laundry operations. With the **concrete stimuli** tactic, physical things or pictures are introduced in idea generation sessions on the assumption that such stimuli incite mental activity.

*Mental Readiness Enablers.* Enablers are devices that facilitate, but do not directly provoke, idea generation. This category of enablers promotes a state of mental readiness, as might one's morning cup of coffee. Its most prominent member is **block removal.** Typified by the work of James Adams,[4] it tries to remove mental barriers that inhibit idea generation. The Creative Whack Pack, developed by Roger von Oech, is a set of cards offering admonitions like "Get out of the dogma house." Methods assume that awareness of a block is tantamount to removing it. This assumption may not be valid.

Notwithstanding the value of these devices, the next section argues that problem analysis—carefully thinking about the situation—holds the greatest potential for improving alternative generation.

# Prescriptions

## The Problem Analytic Strategy

As noted earlier, in problem solving, the criterion for an alternative's goodness is practical effectiveness. Solution originality is rarely valued for its own sake, in contrast with creativity in the arts. The preeminence of practical effectiveness has critical implications for creative problem solving. Effectiveness is understandable, at least in principle and usually in fact. A person can understand why one solution works and another does not. Good alternatives have a rationale. They are explicable and make sense.

This implies that, in principle, good solutions can be derived by reasoning. De Bono acknowledges as much: "If a solution is acceptable at all then by definition there must be a logical reason for accepting it. It is always possible to describe a logical pathway in hindsight *once a solution is spelled out.*"[5] His point in emphasizing the last phrase is to assert that logic or reasoning provides no help in finding such solutions in advance.

This conclusion is too pessimistic by far. The prominent roles that reasoning and analysis play in many creativity methods, including some proposed by de Bono, contradict it. Admittedly, formal logic, the manipulation of symbolic expressions according to well-defined rules, provides no help in alternative generation. But reasoning encompasses more flexible means of drawing conclusions, means that we routinely employ in everyday idea generation tasks. In problem solving, reasoning and analysis can be used to understand the situation, and this understanding helps one identify effective courses of action.

This argument motivates the problem analytic strategy for generating alternatives. The strategy is proposed as a complement to traditional creativity methods. The basic premise of the approach is that alternatives and more general solution strategies can be discovered through in-depth, analytical thinking about the problem. Some problems yield more to analysis than others, but with virtually all real-world problems, thinking carefully about the situation will disclose solution possibilities it contains.

Figure 6.1 illustrates the problem analytic approach. The top of the figure depicts the problem solver's challenge when the problem situation is not analyzed.

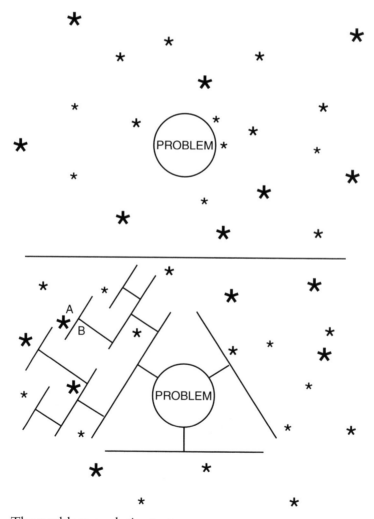

Figure 6.1   The problem analytic strategy

One is aware of the problem, but needs to generate possible solutions not connected to the situation in an obvious way and more or less remote from it. Instructions to be creative are of no help. Techniques asking one to fantasize, negate current assumptions, or look for relationships are not much more effective. Alternatives close to the problem may be discovered by mental association; remote possibilities are much harder to reach.

The bottom of Figure 6.1 indicates how problem analysis ameliorates this challenge. Through careful thought about the situation, the problem solver has identified three basic solution strategies that it affords. If the problem was one of subpar worker performance, the three approaches might focus on worker knowledge, ability, and motivations, respectively. One of these (on the left) has been mentally explored in some detail. The problem solver may have considered fairly specific ways in which worker knowledge can be improved. In effect, the problem solver has extended his reflective, conscious thought out into the realm of possible solutions. He has created a sort of mental scaffolding allowing him to remain connected to the problem, while mentally moving away from it and coming closer to solution ideas. This increases the chances of discovering useful alternatives. It is unlikely that idea *A* would come to mind if deliberations never went beyond the original problem. Once analysis has extended reflective thought to point *B*, however, idea *A* should be readily recognized.

To illustrate the problem analytic strategy, let us apply it to The Elevator Case, a problem often cited in the management literature.

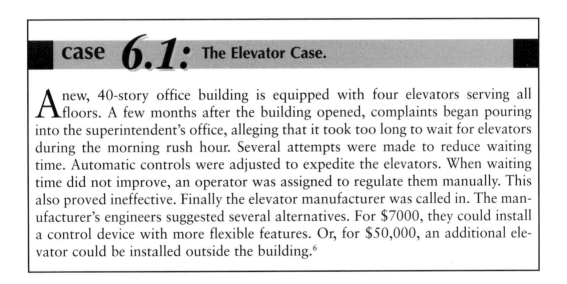

**case 6.1: The Elevator Case.**

A new, 40-story office building is equipped with four elevators serving all floors. A few months after the building opened, complaints began pouring into the superintendent's office, alleging that it took too long to wait for elevators during the morning rush hour. Several attempts were made to reduce waiting time. Automatic controls were adjusted to expedite the elevators. When waiting time did not improve, an operator was assigned to regulate them manually. This also proved ineffective. Finally the elevator manufacturer was called in. The manufacturer's engineers suggested several alternatives. For $7000, they could install a control device with more flexible features. Or, for $50,000, an additional elevator could be installed outside the building.[6]

The people dealing with this problem have implicitly defined it as one of inadequate capacity. Their proposed solutions increase the building's actual or effective elevator capacity. An analysis of the problem suggests other possibilities:[7]

1. Elevator users might have unreasonable expectations, so their complaints may not be justified. A queuing study would indicate if waiting time is indeed

excessive. If not, service expectations must be adjusted by communicating with complainants.

2. The building design may be flawed. If so, the developer/designer should be held responsible for the cost of fixing the situation.

3. Since it is a new building, this may be a case of start-up difficulties. Over time, as people adjust to the system by arriving earlier or walking up several floors, the problem might go away.

4. Inadequate capacity implies an imbalance between supply and demand. Why not reduce demand? There may be high volume tenants on top floors that could be relocated lower in the building. Working hours could be staggered. Or the elevator could only stop on even floors, with one-floor walk downs required of some tenants.

5. While the problem is caused by people having to wait too long for elevators, a condition for the complaints is that people do not like waiting. Perhaps this condition, and the complaints, can be alleviated by making the wait more enjoyable. Install a TV or mirrors in the lobby.

None of these proposals might turn out to be effective, yet each is worth recognizing and considering. Traditional creativity methods are unlikely to generate more than one or two of these possibilities, yet all can be derived through problem analysis. The next case also illustrates the value of an analytic approach.

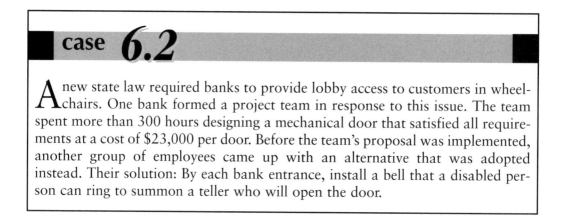

## case 6.2

A new state law required banks to provide lobby access to customers in wheelchairs. One bank formed a project team in response to this issue. The team spent more than 300 hours designing a mechanical door that satisfied all requirements at a cost of $23,000 per door. Before the team's proposal was implemented, another group of employees came up with an alternative that was adopted instead. Their solution: By each bank entrance, install a bell that a disabled person can ring to summon a teller who will open the door.

The law required that handicapped people have access to the bank, not that they be able to open the doors themselves. Access is achieved if a handicapped person can signal someone to open the door.

Different problems require different forms of analysis. A telephone manufacturer in India experienced rejects due to an ineffective process for stamping batch numbers on receivers. Numbers were often smeared and unreadable. Analyzing the function, "how to provide product identification," suggests using other means of labeling. When stamping was replaced by the use of stickers, the problem was solved. Van Gundy described an input-output technique used to design a fire alarm.[8] This is a detection problem: A warning system must sense the presence of inputs (smoke, heat) signaling the existence of a threat (fire), thereby setting off an output alarm. The input-output method exploits the structure of detection problems. A final case illustrates the role of experiential knowledge in problem analysis. A manufacturer of programmable controllers could not obtain a +/– 1% resistor in time to meet scheduled deliveries. Since they could get +/– 5% resistors, they ordered the 5% part and sorted out resistors meeting the 1% criterion, finding enough to satisfy their delivery commitment. Thinking about what is available and recognizing that products often exceed specifications led to this solution.

## The Analytical Bootstrapping Creativity (ABC) Method

The diversity of problems and forms of analysis prevents development of a compact analytic technique for generating alternatives. The problem analytic strategy is more an approach to alternative generation than a well-specified technique. The approach can be partially operationalized in a group setting by means of the Analytical Bootstrapping Creativity method (Figure 6.2). The ABC method relies on two analytical activities. In Step 2, the group is asked to conduct top-down problem analysis as an aid to alternative generation. Members are prompted to think about these and other questions: What kind of problem is this? What is its structure? What are its distinctive features? What kinds of solutions are possible?

In Step 4, the method "bootstraps" analytically off of generated ideas, including those not implied by the problem's apparent structure. Group members try to explain alternatives that do not fit within the recognized solution space. How might this proposal be effective? What is its underlying rationale? Are other possibilities suggested by the rationale? This step is based on the claim that we are not always aware of what makes an idea valuable. By reflecting on ideas, we can discern their underlying insights and use them to generate more proposals. It is as if

Step 1. Group members should privately write down ideas on their own.

Step 2. Collectively analyze the problem, delineating the structure of its solution space.

Step 3. Generate and report ideas resulting from problem analysis along with those produced in Step 1.

Step 4. Analyze ideas and alternatives, especially those not clearly implied by the recognized solution space. Ascertain the rationales for these proposals, augmenting the solution space as appropriate.

Step 5. Generate and report ideas suggested by the enlarged solution space.

Step 6. Consolidate and organize all solution alternatives.

Step 7. Select several alternatives for further evaluation and choice.

Figure 6.2   The Analytical Bootstrapping Creativity (ABC) method

the scaffolding in Figure 6.1 were being constructed from possibilities back to the problem, rather than vice versa. Whereas traditional group methods promote hit-or-miss associative hitchhiking on the ideas of others, ABC enables a thoughtful, thorough exploration of the solution space. The method will be demonstrated by application to the following case:

## case 6.3

Branches of a large commercial bank experienced difficulties processing loan requests under $50,000 from small business people. These applications were handled by business bankers whose average client had a borrowing relationship of $200,000. Studies indicated that a business loan must exceed $75,000 to be profitable. Automobile and other consumer loans were processed efficiently by the consumer banking department. While the bank might refuse small business loan requests, it fulfilled a legal and social responsibility to the community by processing these applications.

People request small business loans to start a new business or to finance or expand an existing one. Many applicants are inexperienced with banks and do not know how to develop a business plan or financing request. Many have not considered how the loan will be repaid or what can be pledged as collateral. Their requests pose a problem to bankers, who spend time listening to proposals, teaching applicants how to develop a business plan, and explaining how loan decisions are made. Though a banker may know right away that an application is not viable, he/she cannot refuse a loan request without taking the time to discuss it and the reasons why the loan cannot be made. Even when loan risk is acceptable, usury laws prevent banks from charging interest rates that would cover the high costs of granting and servicing these loans.

While performing Step 2 of the ABC method, group members might note that this is an efficiency/process design problem, a situation in which process inadequacies may justify significant redesign activity. The process involves delivering a personalized service to customers on a one-at-a-time basis, an expensive delivery mode. Loan applicants may have unreasonable expectations, perhaps believing that their business is valued by the bank. The many unacceptable requests raise the question of how loan processing responsibilities should be allocated between applicants and the bank. A distinctive feature of the situation is the fact that the bank would probably prefer that there were no requests for small business loans. Organizations usually compete aggressively for customers, but that is not the case here.

These insights suggest the following high-level alternatives:

1. Eliminate unnecessary activities in loan processing and servicing systems.
2. Consolidate and depersonalize the service to make it less expensive.

3. Charge fees for some activities, both to recover costs and to reduce demand.
4. Require people to do more themselves before submitting loan requests.
5. Refer applicants to other providers of loans and related services.

Many specific proposals can be derived from these options.

Assume the group had completed its top-down analytic work, generating a sizable set of ideas. Now in Step 4 of ABC, it is considering alternatives that fall outside the recognized solution space. Note how these can be bootstrapped into other possibilities:

Idea: Have a secretary act as a gatekeeper, restricting applicants' access to the bankers. This proposal has two useful implications: It suggests the use of front-end screening to reduce processing volume and the use of less expensive personnel for certain activities. Why not have all loan applicants handled by an administrative assistant, only forwarding viable applications to bankers for their review?

Idea: Process small loans as if they were automobile loans. The value of this proposal lies in its use of an efficient existing system. Though there are substantial differences between the two kinds of loans, some small business loans might be converted to personal loans.

Idea: Find out if any loan officers are really good at dealing with these applicants. This reflects a generic strategy of building expertise. Learn the best way of doing things by studying top performers. Encourage skill development by assigning all small business loans to a few bankers who can develop efficient processing methods.

Idea: Reduce loan monitoring costs by using tax filings as evidence of a borrower's financial condition. Many costs are incurred after a loan has been granted, as part of monitoring the borrower's financial status. This proposal exploits the fact that people and companies prepare financial reports for tax purposes. The bank can save money by piggybacking on these filings. Extending the idea, one can ask if anyone else monitors the financial condition of borrowers. In fact, credit agencies like Dun and Bradstreet (D&B) do so routinely. Some banks have turned small business loans into a profitable activity, in part by using D & Bs as a substitute for internal loan monitoring.

## Alternative Generation Heuristics

The chapter's primary recommendation for alternative generation is to be analytical: Think about the problem to identify possible solutions. The case examples demonstrate that advice. It will be illustrated again and again in the problem-driven chapters that follow.

A second recommendation, implied by the first, is to use idea generation devices suited to the problem at hand. Creativity strategies vary in effectiveness, and much of the variation is problem-dependent. Analysis can suggest the devices,

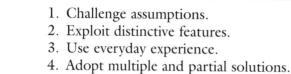

1. Challenge assumptions.
2. Exploit distinctive features.
3. Use everyday experience.
4. Adopt multiple and partial solutions.
5. Avoid premature closure.

**Figure 6.3** Prescriptions for alternative generation

hence creativity techniques, likely to be effective in a situation. If a problem entails design of a radically new system, fantasy-based techniques are helpful. If human behavior is a cause of failed solutions, change of perspective should be used. Issues that involve systemic wholes, like new product design, can be addressed with decomposition and rearrangement techniques. When the task is to find a way of performing some function, use abstraction and analogy-based methods to find out how the function is performed in other domains.

These recommendations can be augmented by five prescriptions of lesser scope, listed in Figure 6.3. Some were anticipated earlier but bear repeating.

**1. Challenge assumptions.** This advice risks becoming a mantra through repetition. It is important nonetheless. The major block to creativity is the tacit assumption that things have to be a certain way because that is how they are now. Improvement opportunities arise when this assumption is challenged. The dramatic economies achieved by Ford's reengineered accounts payable system resulted from an altered assumption. Whereas Ford had assumed that vendor payments should be initiated upon receipt of an invoice, payments are now prompted by receipt of the goods. Ford improved the performance of its truck assembly process by challenging the assumption that assembly lines have to keep moving. Building a brief pause into the line facilitated the mating of body with chassis, improving overall performance.

**2. Exploit distinctive features.** Good solutions are good for a reason, but sometimes that reason is idiosyncratic, an individuated aspect of the situation. Marketing breakthroughs are often based on unique attributes that allow a product to be marketed in a certain way. Within an organization, a good solution might appeal to the pet interests of a key executive. Distinctive features can cut the other way as well, dooming an otherwise promising alternative. When generating solutions, identify aspects of the case that are unusual or distinctive for that kind of problem. Keep these in mind as opportunities to exploit or pitfalls to avoid.

**3. Use everyday experience.** This heuristic remains largely untapped by existing creativity methods. One simply asks, "How do I deal with situations like this in my daily life?" or "What everyday object might satisfy this need?" A company trying to design an inexpensive TV set got the idea for a cabinet from a waste basket seen in a store window. Needing a new solder flux because of environmental restrictions, a process engineer developed a formula using lemon juice from his refrigerator. Unable to keep racks clean when they carried parts coated with a sticky compound, an operator used the no-stick substance sprayed on cooking utensils to solve the problem. A Japanese firm could not find an abrasive to smooth an ebonite surface. One of its workers, the son of a farmer, recalled that his family peeled potatoes by rotating them in unhulled rice. The rice worked on ebonite as well.

**4. Adopt multiple and partial solutions.** Trying to find a single cure, a solution fixing all troubles, can hinder alternative generation. This habit is most harmful for problems that encompass various deficiencies or when many causes produce an undesired effect. Look for solutions responding to some of the troubles. A collection of these may address all known difficulties. Janbridge Inc., a manufacturer of printed circuit boards, solved the problem of unwanted copper plating in PC board holes by developing a decision grid stating which hole-clearing method (such as plugs, tents, or drilling) to use in different circumstances. Sometimes a single solution, though it does not correct all troubles, is better than the status quo. A Japanese manufacturer used four workers to remove fluorescent lights from hooks after a dipping operation. When Shigeo Shingo proposed a different method for removing lights, the plant manager protested, arguing that Shingo's approach only took off 70 percent of them. Yet the new method enabled a 50 percent reduction in the work force. It was implemented successfully.

**5. Avoid premature closure.** Consider a large and varied set of solution alternatives. This may not happen if an individual or group too readily accepts one of the first options proposed. If an alternative inspires favorable comments from group members, it can benefit from halo effects: It seems perfect in every possible way. As a result, people stop thinking of other options. They say "We can't possibly come up with something better than this." Premature closure is common with kids, who have yet to learn life's bitter lessons about glittery things that are not gold. But adults are susceptible as well. One way of countering the tendency is to set a quota for alternatives. Better protection comes with thorough problem analysis.

# Evaluating Alternatives

Once alternatives have been generated, they must be evaluated to identify the best as the chosen course of action. These activities—evaluating and choosing among alternatives—are addressed by decision-making research. The volume of this work dwarfs research on all other aspects of managerial thinking. Decision making has not been a prominent topic in the quality literature, for reasons that will be explained. This section discusses the evaluation task, reviews decision-making research, and concludes with suggestions for improving group evaluation of alternatives.

## Evaluation

Evaluation is a judgmental task. Each alternative has attributes or characteristics relevant to an assessment of its merit. A person buying a car will consider the price, appearance, and reliability of candidate vehicles. Since no alternative typically scores highest on every attribute, evaluators must make trade-offs. Different factors are subjectively weighted to reflect their importance, and weighted attribute scores are combined into an overall assessment of the option, which can be compared with assessments of other alternatives. Though this weighing, combining, and comparing is judgmental, evaluation encompasses other mental activities as well: recognizing important features of alternatives, remembering how things turned out in similar situations, and reasoning about an alternative's likely outcomes.

Two kinds of evaluation tasks are defined in terms of the origin of assessment criteria. **Subjective evaluations** are those in which individual preferences are decisive. The evaluator should choose the option appealing most strongly to his or her desires. Ordering a meal in a restaurant is a matter of subjective evaluation, as are other consumer choice situations. Uncertainty may arise about how alternatives will turn out (Will I really like this new brand of breakfast cereal?), but preference satisfaction is what matters. With **objective evaluations,** external criteria are critical. Merit is measured in terms other than the evaluator's preferences. Performances in diving and figure skating competitions are measured against field-defined standards of excellence. Alternatives in business decisions are evaluated in terms of their financial and other effects on the firm. Neither type of evaluation is objective in the sense of there being a fully specified procedure for determining the best option. Evaluation tasks are intrinsically judgmental, but assessment criteria can have subjective or objective origins.

Evaluation tasks pose several difficulties. One challenge is predicting how things will turn out: If I choose this option, what will be the outcome? Another difficulty is trading off pros and cons. It is often hard to judge whether an option's goods outweigh its bads. Finally, there is the challenge of comparing alternatives, deciding which is best. This task is complicated when options have different value-relevant attributes. It is not hard for a home buyer to compare the asking prices of two houses, but it is difficult to compare the extra bedroom in one with the large porch on the other.

In real-world evaluation problems, the first difficulty—predicting outcomes—is the most imposing. One predictive difficulty arises when alternatives are only contingently linked to outcomes. A given alternative might lead to many different outcomes. Such is the case with an investor who may end up with more or less money, depending on whether the market price of the stock goes up or down. Even when outcomes are selected directly, as in consumer choice situations, there is uncertainty about whether one will like what one has chosen. We are normally confident about decisions over breakfast cereals or restaurant entrees we have tried before. More demanding decisions—first-time choices, those with long-term implications—often turn out badly as we find ourselves unhappy with what we wanted at the time: the utterly unprogrammable VCR, the house next door to impossible neighbors, the career choice that has doomed one to years of discontent.

Some of these troubles arise because of unforeseeable changes in the world or in our preferences. Most result when attributes of an alternative, unknown or ignored during the evaluation process, end up having strong effects on its acceptability. How could you know that the people you would be working with would be jerks? Or that those odd personal habits of a spouse would, over the years, become infuriating? Evaluations are fallible because we do not know what we want until we have got it.

Since dominating alternatives—those that are best on every dimension—rarely exist, evaluators must determine how much of one value (such as price) they are willing to sacrifice for more of another (such as a house's square footage). We encounter many value trade-offs in our daily lives. Some were cited in Chapter 2: ethical dilemmas that pit moral values against self-interest, the trade-off between short- and long-term interests, the quality-quantity trade-off, and that between an activity's speed and accuracy.

Evaluation is also complicated by the potential for **side effects,** peripheral consequences of a choice. Courses of action have both intended and unintended effects. Since our attention is focused on the former and the latter can crop up at unexpected places and times, side effects are hard to anticipate. Public policy decisions often fail for this reason. In the 1980s, the state of Massachusetts tried to reduce homelessness through an extensive assistance program. Its actions had a counterproductive result: Poor people vacated their dwellings to qualify for state aid to the homeless. Side effects are usually to blame in situations where solving one problem creates another. A consumer electronics manufacturer received customer complaints about charred circuit boards. A study revealed that board overheating resulted from a design change made to solve an earlier problem.

Scientists have yet to devise effective means for identifying potential side effects or for determining the value-relevant attributes of complex alternatives. They have addressed the issue of value trade-offs by developing the notion of utility as a fundamental measure of value, a metric for use in establishing comparability among attributes and alternatives. Utility-based evaluation techniques strike a balance among competing values, identifying the option that is best overall. Though this approach has merit, it can be vastly outperformed by strategies that alter a situation's basic structure.

Consider that for many years manufacturing operations were conducted in accordance with the economic order quantity model, an equation that strikes a balance between the costs of carrying inventory and the setup costs associated with producing or ordering goods. Typically, large inventories had to be carried because of high setup costs. Rather than accepting this trade-off, Japanese manufacturers dramatically improved their setup methods, reducing these costs. As a result, they could order/produce in much smaller lot sizes, carry less inventory, and have more efficient and flexible operations. A focus on optimizing value trade-offs can be dysfunctional if it inhibits thinking that improves a situation's basic structure. Rather than making the best of a bad situation, why not improve the situation itself?

Researchers have developed other aids for the weighing, combining, and comparing parts of evaluation. The best known of these is cost-benefit analysis (CBA), a general evaluation method devised by economists. CBA encompasses measurement techniques and practice-based knowledge of the benefits and costs likely to result from certain actions. Another device, less widely used, is the glyph, a graphic means for comparing alternatives along multiple dimensions of value.[9] These aids notwithstanding, it can be difficult to evaluate and decide among alternatives, even assuming relevant attributes and outcomes are known. It is consoling, then, to recall Fredkin's Paradox:[10] The smaller the difference between two options, the more difficult the decision, but the less significant the choice, since neither alternative is likely to be much better or worse than the other.

## Decision Making

Most scientific studies of evaluation have been conducted as part of decision-making research. Much of this research has been performed within schools of management, which have traditionally viewed managers as decision makers. Decades of research have produced a substantial decision-making technology, techniques for selecting among alternatives. However, these prescriptions are not widely used by practitioners.

Psychologically, decision making is viewed as a judgmental process. Individuals make predictive judgments about how alternatives will turn out and evaluative judgments to determine which outcomes are preferred. A major achievement of descriptive research on decision making was the identification of judgmental heuristics and biases. Discussed in Chapter 2, these are informal mental practices by which people draw conclusions, sometimes erroneously, in daily affairs.

Decision theorists have devised procedures for assessing utility curves (Figure 6.4). Plotted on x-y axes, they depict the relationship between the amount of some good, say dollars, and its value, in units of utility, for a given individual. Since most goods have diminishing marginal utility—my second million dollars will mean less to me than the first—utility curves usually have a decreasing positive slope, as in the figure. In situations of decision making under certainty, the outcome resulting from each course of action is known. One simply chooses the alternative leading to the best outcome. This can be difficult when alternatives are valued for more than one characteristic. Multi-attribute utility theory (MAUT) deals with such situations. It prescribes how to compute a composite utility value for each alternative, which is a weighted combination of utilities for each valued attribute of that alternative. Thus, MAUT could be used to identify the personal computer offering the best combination of price, speed, memory capacity, reliability, and other attributes.

But most real-world decisions do not lead to known outcomes. Uncertainty usually exists about the ultimate consequences of a choice. Known as decision making under risk or uncertainty, such situations are modeled with decision trees. These diagrams explicitly represent contingencies that affect how a choice will turn out, using probabilities to quantify related uncertainties. The decision tree in Figure 6.5 depicts an investment situation. A person can invest $1000 in one of three ways: stocks, bonds, or gold. The outcome of this decision, the investment payoff, depends on the state of the economy during the term of the investment. The box or choice node at the left-center of the figure originates the three alternatives. Each leads to a chance node, a circle depicting the contingent economic state. Economic conditions can be up ($U$), steady ($S$), or down ($D$), with unspecified probabilities summing to one at each node. Each investment alternative-economic condition path leads to an outcome, the final dollar value of the investment under the assumed economic condition. Thus, an initial $1000 investment in stock will be worth $2000 if the economy is up, but only $500 if it is down. When probabilities are added to the tree, the worth of each alternative can be computed as the sum of its ultimate outcomes multiplied by their respective probabilities. For instance, if $P(U) = .3$, $P(S) = .4$, and $P(D) = .3$, the expected value of an investment in stock is $1150 [$(.3 \times 2000) + (.4 \times 1000) + (.3 \times 500)$], that of bonds is $1100, and that of gold is $1000. Consequently, a profit-maximizing individual would invest in stock. Decision analysis is

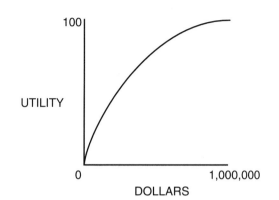

**Figure 6.4** Utility curve

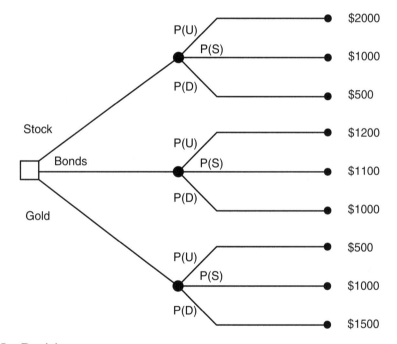

**Figure 6.5** Decision tree

an applied methodology that uses decision trees and other tools to aid decision makers in complex choice situations.

Though decision theoretic methods are useful, their power and generality are often overstated. The technology does not offer much regarding the most critical difficulties in real-world decision tasks. Decision-making methods provide little aid in generating alternatives, determining the value-relevant aspects of alternatives, identifying potential side effects, ameliorating value trade-offs, predicting the ultimate outcomes of a choice, or identifying contingencies that mediate between an alternative and its potential outcomes. As is often true in scientific research, decision theorists have focused on issues that can be addressed rigorously—by proving theorems or conducting experiments—rather than on those of greatest practical importance. As a result, decision theoretic technology often comes off as a sophisticated form of question-begging: It does not help with the really tough parts of the job.

Less powerful than advertised, the decision-making approach is less general as well. It implies that all situations requiring action-oriented thought can be viewed as decision situations and that all decision situations are matters of preference-driven choice. Both implications are mistaken. Preferences are only relevant in subjective evaluation tasks. When other criteria pertain—for instance, the effectiveness of a program or the financial performance of a venture—individual preferences are an indirect and potentially misleading guide to choice. Yes, a decision maker prefers the alternative that will perform the best, but inquiring into his/her preferences will not reliably indicate which alternative that will be. Decision theoretic methods are too strongly focused on preferences to be effective in situations where preferences are not informative.

A greater limitation of the decision theoretic approach is that most situations requiring action-oriented thought are not decision situations. They do not hinge on a final act of choice. The critical task may be to diagnose a problem's cause, to design a system that achieves certain goals, or to negotiate an agreement among contending parties. Virtually every problem situation includes decision tasks, but they should not be viewed as decision problems on that account, since other tasks can be more important. This explains why quality practitioners and the QPS literature rarely mention decision methods: Quality problems, by and large, are not decision problems.

## Group Evaluation

Since quality problem solving is often a team or group activity, issues pertaining to group evaluation and choice should be discussed. In evaluating alternatives, groups have an inherent advantage over individuals: It is easier to evaluate someone else's ideas than to assess one's own. Even honest, thoughtful people have trouble seeing pitfalls in their proposals. Groups obviate individual blindness, providing an evaluative capacity that individuals cannot match.

A social psychological phenomenon known as **groupthink** is a threat to effective group evaluation. Identified by Irving Janis through studies of governmental and military decision fiascos,[11] groupthink describes situations in which group members are so anxious to be agreeable and to reach a consensus that their evaluative capacity is thwarted and goes unused. The occurrence of groupthink is evidenced by such symptoms as collective rationalization of conflicting evidence, self-censorship, an illusion of unanimity, and pressuring of dissenters. Groupthink often results when a group leader, typically the person of highest rank, does not insure that views other than his/her own receive a fair hearing. As a result, group members coalesce around "the boss's proposal," failing to evaluate it critically. To prevent groupthink, assign a devil's advocate to argue against favored proposals. Have informal breaks during meetings so people can discuss issues among themselves. Ask outsiders for their opinions. Require each member to identify a weakness in a favored proposal.

A final issue is that of consolidating individual evaluations into a group decision. How should a group choice be derived from individual assessments of alternatives? Following the democratic tradition, group decisions are often made by voting, so that each member has equal influence on the outcome. One procedure is multivoting: A series of votes are made, the least favored option being dropped after each round. Voting is a reasonable way of arriving at a group decision, but it can be misused. The most serious mistake is for people to vote their preferences when other criteria are at issue. If the group is deciding where to eat lunch, members should vote their preferences. If they are deciding which marketing program to adopt, votes should reflect careful assessments of the effectiveness of each option. Such assessments are not always made before votes are taken. As a result, superficial and irrelevant preferences—"I kind of like this one"—can determine which alternative is selected. Each member, and the group leader especially, must insure that thoughtful evaluation informs any vote among alternatives.

# Implementation

In a way, problem solving ends when one identifies a course of action that is expected to improve a problematic situation. Thinking has identified the right thing to do in that situation. In a broader sense, however, a new phase of problem solving has begun. This is the task of implementation, getting the right thing done. Implementation is part of problem solving because it too depends on good thinking.

Known by various names, including managing change, implementation has been the topic of huge amounts of writing by academics and practitioners. Though its importance justifies this attention, little is known about implementation. No deep theory of change or powerful implementation method is anywhere to be found. I am not alone in regarding the implementation/change literature as unsatisfying. Unfortunately, I have little to add to what has been said. This section provides a brief overview of the topic.

Implementation poses two challenges. First is the need to secure the support of relevant parties. Problem solvers may have reached a conclusion about what to do, but everyone involved in the situation may not agree with or support that conclusion. Implementation is about winning their support. Second, while some solutions can be enacted simply and directly—replacing a worn part in a piece of equipment—others entail complicated courses of action, such as installing a new customer relations program. Implementation becomes a matter of planning and coordinating a complex set of activities.

The first of these tasks, securing the support of relevant parties, comes in several shapes and sizes. One problem is getting management to endorse a proposed course of action. Quality practitioners are familiar with this one—witness their constant declamations on the need to gain top management support for quality initiatives. Equally common is the need to win the support of line workers, people directly affected by a change. This is difficult in situations where union rules, habits, or individual insecurity make *change* a dirty word. Divisionalized corporations encounter implementation problems when centralized staff units try to get operating divisions to enact improvement programs. Line managers may be skeptical of program benefits or feel they have more important things to do. Recommendations of outside consultants often come to naught for want of inside commitment. A final variant is the difficulty technical experts encounter in having their proposals put into practice. This raises questions to consider with every implementation problem. Is the proposed course of action really an improvement? Might uncooperative parties have valid reasons for resisting recommended changes?

Research on the consent/support part of implementation has generated a sizable literature on change management. This literature stresses the need to unfreeze the existing situation and then to refreeze the situation after a change has been made. It has identified "risk factors" affecting the likelihood that implementation difficulties will be encountered. These concerns have migrated into practitioner writings, which emphasize communication, participation, and buy-in by affected parties. Arguably the most beneficial development has been increased use of cross-functional teams whose membership includes multiple stakeholders. Implementation is easier if the solution is devised with input from all affected parties.

The other part of implementation, the planning/coordinating task, is critical when solutions entail complex courses of action. This challenge has been addressed by project management research, which has developed network diagrams and techniques, such as PERT and the Critical Path Method, for scheduling and coordinating sequences of tasks in a project. Related graphic methods—tree diagram, process decision program chart, activity network diagram—have been devised for use in QPS.[12]

Though these techniques are helpful, they do not address key challenges in implementing a major organizational change. Implementation can require changes in individual responsibilities, the organization structure, information systems, incentives, measurement and control systems, and even the organizational culture. Little established wisdom focuses on this, the most difficult part of implementation.

A final phase of problem solving, extending beyond implementation, is post-evaluation. Whereas evaluation, discussed earlier, identifies the best alternative, post-evaluation determines if the implemented solution was effective. Post-evaluation came into its own in the 1960s, when the expansion of government social programs created a need for rigorous performance assessments. Much evaluation research has been conducted over the years, primarily with governmental and educational programs. There still is nothing like a strong technique for measuring the effects of complex interventions. As organizations have learned from trying to assess the effects of training or marketing programs, measurement is difficult when many unidentifiable and uncontrollable factors can influence outcomes. Nonetheless, post-evaluation efforts should be made.

## NOTES

1. Edward de Bono, *Lateral Thinking: Creativity Step by Step* (New York: Harper & Row, 1970).
2. G. Wallas, *The Art of Thought* (New York: Harcourt, Brace, 1926).
3. See, for instance: D. N. Perkins, *The Mind's Best Work* (Cambridge, Mass.: Harvard University Press, 1981); and Robert J. Sternberg, ed., *The Nature of Creativity* (Cambridge, England: Cambridge University Press, 1988).

4. James L. Adams, *Conceptual Blockbusting,* 2d ed. (New York: Norton, 1979).

5. See note 1.

6. Gordon K. C. Chen, "What is the Systems Approach?" *Interfaces* 6, no. 1 (1975): 32–37.

7. This analysis first appeared in: Gerald F. Smith, "Heuristic Methods for the Analysis of Managerial Problems," *Omega* 18 (1990): 625–635.

8. Arthur B. Van Gundy, *Techniques of Structured Problem Solving* (New York: Van Nostrand Reinhold, 1981).

9. Howard S. Gitlow, *Planning for Quality, Productivity, and Competitive Position* (Homewood, Il.: Dow Jones-Irwin, 1990).

10. Marvin Minsky, *The Society of Mind* (New York: Simon and Schuster, 1985).

11. Irving L. Janis, *Group-think,* 2d ed. (Boston: Houghton Mifflin, 1983).

12. These methods are described in: Shigero Mizuno, ed., *Management for Quality Improvement: The Seven New QC Tools* (Cambridge, Mass.: Productivity Press, 1988); and Michael Brassard, *The Memory Jogger Plus+* (Methuen, Mass.: GOAL/QPC, 1989).

# Quality Problems

This section consists of five chapters, corresponding to the five types of quality problems: conformance, unstructured performance, efficiency, product design, and process design. The chapters use a case-based approach to support problem solving. Each presents insights and lessons gleaned from analyses of hundreds of cases of quality problem solving. Chapters also contain discussions of problem-solving techniques, research findings, and other issues pertaining to the target problem type.

Problem typologies are invariably artificial, the current one being no exception. No sharp boundaries differentiate conformance problems from unstructured performance problems. Both kinds of issues, along with efficiency problems, shade into process design. Then too, there are topics, such as worker motivation, pertinent to more than one problem type. Such topics are covered in the most appropriate chapter.

# chapter 7

# Conformance Problems

---

## Chapter Outline

### Fundamentals

### Solving Conformance Problems

### Prescriptions

6. Eliminate troublesome operations
7. Make errors less costly
8. Make errors more costly
9. Work with customers

A conformance problem is a situation in which a highly structured system with standardized inputs, processes, and outputs is performing unacceptably from the standpoint of product users. An assembly line is producing rejects. Mistakes are made in the processing of insurance claims. These are classic quality problems addressed by traditional quality control activities. Though conformance problems usually involve products, services produced by highly structured systems are vulnerable to these difficulties. Most service-related processes are not fully specified, so related troubles are classified as unstructured performance problems, discussed in Chapter 8. Conformance problems can appear in processes that have been free of trouble for years. They can thwart the best efforts of experienced problem solvers.

The key feature of a conformance problem is that there is a known right way of doing things, a prescribed means of achieving desired outcomes. The system has worked before, but now, for some reason, it no longer performs acceptably. Parts of the system, its inputs or processing activities, have deviated from the norm, so outputs are not what they should be. Problem solving is a matter of identifying these deviations and restoring the system to its intended mode of functioning. System complexity, the many variables affecting its performance, make this task difficult.

The chapter's first section discusses basic issues regarding conformance problems. Its second and longest section contains case-based suggestions for diagnosing and solving such problems. The chapter concludes with several general prescriptions.

# Fundamentals

Figure 7.1 depicts the major elements and relationships constituting a conformance problem. The large box denotes the problematic system. This system transforms inputs into outputs. It is tightly defined by requirements—input and output specifications, operating procedures—reflecting customer needs. A disparity between system outputs and user needs signals a conformance problem. This mismatch implies the existence of nonconformities, or deviations from requirements, in the system. Identifying these nonconformities is the primary challenge in solving conformance problems.

## Relationship to Other Quality Problems

Conformance problems blend into unstructured performance problems as system requirements become less clear and complete. Some parts of a system may be well specified while other parts are not. If outputs do not satisfy user needs, one might first check for nonconformities before investigating less structured parts of the system. Conformance problems can co-occur with efficiency problems, as when poor work

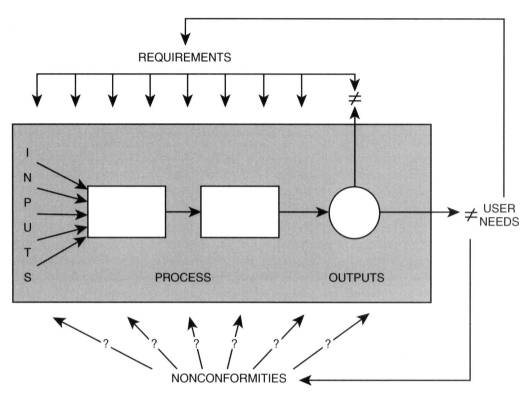

**Figure 7.1** Conformance problems

methods result in defective outputs and excess usage of material. If performance is seriously inadequate, a process design problem might be implicated and it may be necessary to develop a new or substantially revised system. When output requirements do not reflect user needs, the situation is a product design problem.

## Functional Demands

Viewed in terms of problem-solving functions (Chapters 3 through 6), conformance problems are distinctive. The existence of a known right way of doing things strongly affects problem solving. Problem identification is easy since clear output standards presumably reflect user needs. Outputs can be compared with standards and problems identified when mismatches are observed. Statistical process control, which presumes the existence of a structured system with predictable inputs, processes, and outputs, can be used to identify conformance problems.

Problem definition is also straightforward: Identify points of nonconformance and collect relevant information. Determine if the problem occurred abruptly or developed gradually over time. Pertinent aspects of the system's history should be noted. A first-cut problem definition might say that the defect rate for component X produced by line A increased sharply to 3.4 percent between 2:00 and 3:00 P.M. on May 24, going on to report information about workers, materials, machines, the environment, and other system characteristics at that place and time.

Diagnosis is the core challenge in solving conformance problems. Since the system is capable of performing correctly, one must determine why current performance fails to meet standards. Diagnosis is a matter of localizing nonconformities. Since complex systems are involved, this can be difficult. Most failures in solving conformance problems occur because the true causes of nonconformance are not considered or cannot be singled out from other causal candidates. Once a correct diagnosis has been reached, a solution usually follows directly. One simply restores the system to its intended mode of functioning—for instance, by insuring that operators follow procedures.

## Process Variability

A **process** is an organized set of activities devised to achieve some goal, typically production of an output. Variability is inherent in any activity, hence in every process. The notion of process capability indicates the natural level of variability in a process. Conformance problems are often viewed as instances of excessive variation around a target value. This process variability account is useful but can be misleading. It can be overgeneralized and misapplied to other kinds of quality problems.

Another mistake involves statistical process control. SPC directs attention to special causes of variation. As a result, practitioners sometimes assume that variation due to common causes need not be reduced. This is not true: All unintended variation should be minimized by process improvement efforts. The benefits of reducing variation were demonstrated most famously in a case involving automobile transmissions:

---

■ case **7.1**

Unable to keep up with demand, the Ford Motor Company purchased transmissions built to its specifications from Mazda. Months later, Ford realized that customers preferred cars with the Japanese transmissions. Investigating, Ford engineers discovered that the Mazda units had less piece-to-piece variation, using only 27 percent of the tolerance range, compared to 70 percent for Ford-built units. As a result, Japanese transmissions were quieter and had warranty costs averaging only 10 percent of those for their American counterparts.

---

As argued in Chapter 5, the distinction between common and special causes of variation is not fundamental. These causes are differentiated by an arbitrary cutoff employed in statistical process control. Nonetheless, the distinction has been cited in controversies about who is responsible for poor quality. Deming claimed that 94 percent of the troubles and opportunities for improvement in industry involve common causes of variation that are management's responsibility.[1] Worker nonresponsibility was illustrated by his "red bead" experiment in which blindfolded participants drew beads from a mixture of 80 percent white and 20 percent red. Each red bead signified a defect. Though defects can result from factors lying beyond workers' control, Deming's experiment goes to the other extreme: His participants had no control over their performance, implying that workers are equally blameless. Rather than arguing about who is responsible for defects, managers and employees should all make a commitment to improving quality.

Another Deming experiment has fostered confusion about process control. Deming argued that some level of output variation should be accepted tentatively as normal and that process parameters should not be adjusted to compensate for it. This is the error of **tampering** or **overcontrol,** which can lead to *increased* variation. The error was demonstrated by Deming's funnel experiment, in which marbles are dropped through a funnel aimed at a target. Participants who adjust the funnel to compensate for the previous marble's deviation from the target inevitably end up with more diffuse shot patterns than those who keep the funnel aimed at the target. The experiment warns against simple-minded process control regimes. That lesson can also be misapplied. Participants in the funnel experiment do not understand the causes of variability and have no reliable means of compensating for them. In contrast, control regimes built on an understanding of deviations from a target, and which adjust the process based on this understanding, can be highly effective. Such controls are routinely employed in industrial processes. Process control should reduce unwanted variation that is understood and can be adjusted for.

Standardization is the primary means of reducing variability. Companies establish and enforce input specifications and process instructions. Standards reduce operator discretion to perform tasks as each sees fit. Japanese manufacturers have demonstrated how experience-based standards can lead to low variability performances converging on the "one best way" of producing an output. But there is a danger of overgeneralizing this lesson as well. Some activities should not be standardized. There is no "one best way" of selling life insurance, writing advertising copy, or handcrafting fine furniture. Variability in products and processes may be needed to satisfy the desires of different customers and situations. This intended variability should not be curtailed by inappropriate, one-size-fits-all standards.

## Human Error

Little scientific research bears directly on conformance problems. Unlike, say, product design issues, this category has no unifying theme that could productively direct research activity. A notable exception is research on human error. People are a key component of organizational systems, and conformance problems often result from human mistakes. Research that explains the origins of such mistakes and proposes preventive measures would benefit QPS practitioners.

Research on human error has been concerned with operator performance in complex sociotechnical systems with significant safety and economic impacts. Scientists have tried to reduce the incidence of errors made by airline pilots, nuclear power plant operators, air traffic controllers, refinery operators, and others. Compared with typical manufacturing and service workers, these people perform challenging, nonroutinized tasks requiring high levels of education and training. Nonetheless, research on human error can be applied in a TQM context. This section reviews relevant findings.[2]

The notion of human error implies that individual behavior has resulted in an unintended outcome. Errors can be distinguished from violations, deliberate noncompliance with a rule, and from accidents, undesirable outcomes resulting from factors other than the individual's behavior. Errors can be differentiated into mistakes and slips. A **mistake** is a planning failure: An action goes as planned but ends up badly because the plan was misconceived. A **slip** is an execution failure: An intended action was not performed correctly. In football and other team sports, players do the slipping while coaches make mistakes.

Research on human error distinguishes between skill-based, rule-based, and knowledge-based behavior. Skill-based behaviors are highly practiced activities performed fluently with little conscious attention. At the other extreme, knowledge-based behaviors address novel or otherwise demanding tasks requiring careful thought. Different performances are liable to different errors. Operators working at the knowledge-based level are prone to overlook relevant information and to make reasoning and judgmental errors. Operators at the intermediate rule-based level often use ineffective rules and overapply good rules to exceptional cases. An accounting clerk might process a special invoice as if it were a normal purchasing transaction. Errors in tasks performed at the skill-based level can result from inattention or overattention. In *strong habit intrusions,* a highly learned response takes over in situations where it is not intended. Hydraulic and electrical systems have contrasting logics—counterclockwise turns increase energy through a hydraulic valve but reduce it through an electrical valve. A naval vessel almost sank because a technician reverted to his earlier hydraulic experience while operating an electronic system.

Some people are error prone. Their errors derive from an inability to sustain attention or vulnerability to stress. Obviously, such people should not be employed as pilots, surgeons, or other jobs where errors have catastrophic consequences. Other prescriptions try to prevent errors or minimize their effects. One preventive strategy is to design work systems offering few opportunities for error. Error-prone tasks and situations can be highlighted for special attention. Thus, operators should be warned when a procedural change makes it likely that old "strong but wrong" habits will misdirect their efforts. Another strategy is to reduce the consequences of error, as through redundancy in system design and robust methods that are effective despite operator variability. Many prescriptions insure that errors are quickly recognized. Assembly tasks can be shaped by "forcing functions" that prevent workers from proceeding until mistakes have been fixed.

## Solving Conformance Problems

No problem-solving techniques have been devised specifically for conformance problems, which offer few structural "hooks" a method could exploit. Because diagnosis is the critical task, techniques like Kepner-Tregoe and cause-and-effect diagrams are useful. But these methods apply to other performance problems as well.

The importance of diagnosis suggests a problem-solving strategy built around possible causes of nonconformities: Identify everything that could affect system outputs. Investigate and successively eliminate candidates until the problem's causes are

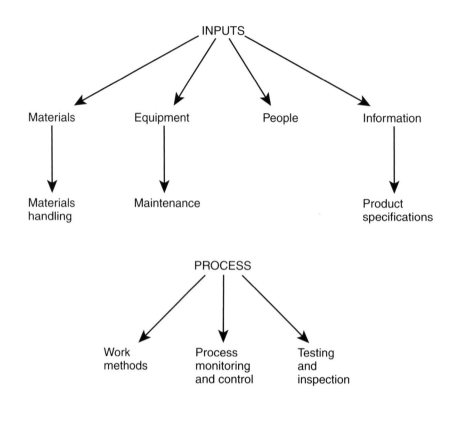

**Figure 7.2** Causal categories

established. This section is organized around a set of causal categories, depicted in Figure 7.2. View these categories as an elaboration of the 5 Ms used in CE diagrams. Each category encompasses specific factors that could be responsible for a conformance problem. Faced with such an issue, a practitioner can review this section to trigger recognition of the problem's causes and possible solutions.

## Inputs

Conformance problems can result from deficiencies in the kind, quality, and quantity of inputs. It is usually easy to detect if an input is of the wrong kind as when a supplier's shipment contains parts other than those ordered. Input quality is less readily assessed, so inadequate inputs often make their way into the process, creating troubles downstream. Input quantity can be greater or less than system needs. Too many inputs increase costs; too few result in processing delays and customer dissatisfaction.

The input quality issue is one of detecting and dealing with deficient inputs before they harm system performance. Equipment and labor pose fewer problems of this kind. Each involves a sizable investment that, being made infrequently, entails intensive front-end qualification and testing, such as probationary periods for new employees. Material and informational inputs, acquired more frequently, are prone to quality deficiencies. These inputs come from three sources: external suppliers, internal processors, and customers. The input source affects the problems faced and ways of dealing with them.

One problem involves handling *close calls*, inputs that are marginally unacceptable.

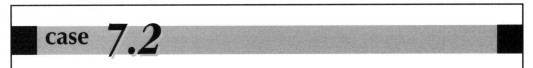

### case 7.2

A bank spent $2000 a month dealing with processing holdouts, computer tickets rejected during processing. Thirty percent of all tickets were holdouts. A study revealed that three clerks, responsible for most errors, were processing tickets with unclear or incomplete information. They were instructed to return such items to their originators rather than pushing them further down the system.

This case illustrates the temptation to make do with faulty inputs, "cleaning them up" so they can be processed. The practice often creates difficulties downstream. Worse, it leaves input originators unaware of their inadequacies and provides no incentive to improve quality. Some IBM departments made the same mistake, reworking, or "off-specing," parts rejected by receiving inspection. Then they realized that their efforts told suppliers that IBM's specs were not important. Ironically, IBM's policy regarding internal processes is to not accept defective work: If a person accepts faulty input from a coworker, he is responsible for correcting it.

Firms can get into this mess via a *slippery slope,* a problem structure cited in Chapter 2. Small, one-time, or special-case exceptions to input requirements lead to increasingly drastic deviations. Exceptions can be made, but be sure they do not become institutionalized as the de facto rule.

Organizations have the most leverage when dealing with faulty inputs from suppliers. The usual response is to return defective goods and request a replacement shipment or credit. If supplier performance is consistently poor, it may be necessary to change sources. TQM encourages companies to work with vendors to correct and prevent defects. When Ford experienced problems with blisters and pits on plastic grille pieces for the Lincoln Towne Car, its employees visited the supplier, analyzed their process, and proposed changes that solved the problem.

Other difficulties arise when faulty inputs come from upstream processors in an organization. Downstream processors do not have the option of buying from someone else. They can, however, reject faulty inputs, as in Case 7.2. Situations like this often degenerate into interdepartmental warfare. To prevent ill feelings, the downstream unit must justify its standards for input acceptability and help suppliers meet those standards. Motivational pressure may be needed as well. Upstream processors can be made to bear the costs of their mistakes. Salespeople will fill out order entry forms correctly if errors result in delayed shipments and unhappy customers. Accounts receivable personnel at Nashua Corporation found that customers refused to pay invoices because of order processing errors made by

Nashua's customer service representatives. When responsibility for dealing with these accounts was transferred to the customer service department, the incidence of errors declined dramatically. Realigning responsibilities is also an option if upstream processors lack skills needed to produce acceptable inputs. The 900 employees in one company averaged 1500 mistakes a day filling out payroll cards. The payroll process is considerably quicker now that payroll department employees perform all computations on cards. The New York City Department of Parks and Recreation addressed this problem by providing supervisors with preprinted labels containing required employee information.

Customers are a challenging source of inputs. Many transactions are initiated by customers providing information. Their inexperience produces mistakes. Because it might alienate them, customers are not penalized for their mistakes. The do-it-yourself option has appeal: Relieve customers of input responsibilities that can be handled by the organization. Alternatively, train customers in proper procedures. The Bank of California educated merchants so they could correctly make deposits by mail and phone. To minimize the effects of faulty customer inputs, screen and correct inputs at the point of contact. At P*I*E Nationwide, a freight company, 63 percent of bills of lading received from shippers contained one or more errors. Seventy-seven percent of the errors could be corrected by drivers during pickup. P*I*E trained drivers to review and correct bills of lading at the customer's loading dock. Within a month the error rate fell to less than 20 percent.

Other prescriptions apply to faulty input problems. Use Pareto analysis to identify the most common errors and error-prone providers. Brand-Rex Cable Systems asked operators to record the supplier's name each time a materials nonconformity was found. Seventy-eight percent of defects occurred in one supplier's materials. When throughput times are long, triage up-front so faulty inputs do not waste time in the process before being returned for correction. Wisconsin Power and Light was disappointed in the time required to process applications for customer rebates earned through energy-saving projects. Half of all applications were missing information. By developing a check sheet for screening applications when received, the utility could immediately return incomplete applications to originators, speeding the approval process. Another strategy was used by the Federal Communications Commission to reduce processing time for FM radio station license applications. The FCC provided better instructions for applicants and redesigned forms to make them clearer. These steps reduced application error rates by two-thirds and improved service speed by 47 percent.

At times input quantity is the trouble. Every company has experienced production delays and shutdowns because of materials shortages. The flip side of this problem, common in some industries, is supplier overshipments. When a customer complained that a packaging manufacturer had delivered 22 percent more than was ordered, the manufacturer investigated. It found that its sales department had a policy of adding 10 percent to each customer order quantity, and that Materials issued up to an additional 17 percent (of the 110 percent) to use up nonstandard base materials. Westinghouse cured its vendors of the practice by informing them that unauthorized overshipments would not be paid for or would be returned at the vendor's expense.

# Materials

Assume that a production system with a long history of effective performance is producing defective outputs at an unusually high rate. What should you do to determine if the system's material inputs are responsible for these troubles?

First, identify every material input, direct and indirect, to the production process. Each is itself composed of material inputs, but identifying the proximate cause of defects may solve the problem. Recognize the potential for input variability: Part of an ingredient might be good, while other parts are unacceptable. Careful sampling insures that conclusions about an input's overall quality are valid.

Following the diagnostic prescriptions in Chapter 5, pay special attention to materials that have changed. The change might be in the supplier, the formulation, even the packaging. Due to the time needed to consume existing supplies, the change might have occurred long before defects increased. Attend to materials having a history of trouble, such as failure-prone components or materials that must be precisely formulated.

Defective components and off-spec ingredients are the most common material causes of conformance problems. After introducing a line of TV sets, a company experienced high customer returns. Repair shop workers recorded malfunctioning components on checksheets. Capacitors were the primary cause of product failure. Do not overlook indirect materials. Though they seem ancillary to the production process, lubricants and cleaning agents can have significant effects on quality.

The presence of a contaminant is a common materials failing, one that can be quite subtle. When IBM experienced high failure rates in thin metal film resistors, its diagnosticians deprocessed a resistor for failure analysis and used x-rays to study the failure area. They found high levels of chlorine which combined with moisture and corroded the metal film. The vendor's cleaning and drying process exposed the resistor core to these contaminants.

Huntsman Chemical Corporation was having trouble producing resin beads of a consistent size. An investigation targeted the peroxide used as a process catalyst. When Huntsman asked peroxide suppliers to test their products, one found an impurity that proved to be the culprit. The IBM case demonstrates the effects of indirect materials; the Huntsman example illustrates how causality can trace down through several layers of material inputs.

Failing to identify a material cause of these kinds, a diagnostician should consider less likely possibilities. Materials could be bogus, something other than labeled. The Defense Industrial Supply Center once found that bolts marked Grade 8—high strength automotive bolts used in weapons systems—were really of much lower quality, which was the cause of field failures. While studying forced outages at a generating plant, Florida Power and Light used Pareto analysis to highlight failures of a superheater end cap. The part turned out to have an incorrect ASME marking and was less capable than the application required. With formulated products, the possibility exists that while ingredients are correctly proportioned, they may not be blended. Union Carbide experienced this problem with a catalyst they produce. The company assumed that blending was complete after 12 hours, but learned the hard way that 16 hours of mixing were needed.

Most materials degrade over time, sometimes imperceptibly. If stock is not rotated, defects can result from out-of-date materials.

---

### case 7.3

A manufacturer of baby pants received field complaints about cracking vinyl. Naturally it suspected suppliers of providing inferior material. When a batch of a supplier's material was compared with vinyl from the manufacturer's inventory, the latter was seen to be inferior. The supplier noticed that inventoried material had dried up and lost its oil. As it turned out, the manufacturer's buyer had ordered enough vinyl for two years, rather than the normal one-month supply. Sitting in storage, the vinyl dried and became prone to cracking.

---

Problems can result from mixed lots, batches containing multiple varieties of a part that are assumed to be interchangeable. At Hewlett-Packard, an automatic insertion machine used to fabricate circuit boards had higher defect rates when plastic and ceramic parts were mixed in the same lot. Parts can interact with each other. The most trouble-prone interactions involve precision-moving parts that fit closely together, like the transmission components of Case 7.1. **Tolerance stack-up** refers to mating failures that result when part dimensions are at incompatible extremes of their tolerance limits.

Component search and swapping methods can test for faulty components and interactions among parts. Failed parts analysis identifies defective components in products that have failed in the field. However, the basic strategy for diagnosing material causes of defects is to identify all direct and indirect materials and to verify that each meets specifications. When a noncomplying part or ingredient is discovered, replace or modify it to solve the problem.

## Materials Handling

A surprising number of conformance problems trace to inadequacies in the physical handling of materials, work-in-process, and final products. Because they do not directly transform inputs into outputs, materials-handling activities are often ignored and not proceduralized. Poor practices increase costs and threaten customer satisfaction. A comparison of American and Japanese air conditioner manufacturers noted that the latter pay far more attention to materials handling.

Materials handling includes storage of material inputs, transport to and within the production process, and packaging and shipping finished goods to customers. Damage can occur during any of these tasks. Ralph's Grocery Company experienced a scenario common in warehouse operations: Stacks of pallets were undermined as stock was removed from lower levels, resulting in breakage. In another company, high levels of scrap and rework prompted investigation of a plating process. Defects were attributed to racks holding pieces being plated. When defective racks were reconditioned or replaced, scrap fell from 1.9 percent to 0.5 percent and rework from 12.4 percent to 2.5 percent of production.

Damage often results from inadequate materials-handling methods. Since tasks seem so simple, workers pack and move things without considering better ways of doing so. Carolina Freight experienced high customer claims for damages because its forklift drivers and dock workers had not been trained in the art of loading a trailer. Some products are vulnerable to damage from seemingly innocuous activities, and workers may not be aware of these vulnerabilities. At Decision Data Computer Corporation, a high reject rate for integrated circuits was due to bent IC legs. These sensitive parts were damaged when workers grabbed them out of bins. At another manufacturer, gaskets damaged during handling caused leaking components that necessitated rework. The materials-handling needs of each input and output should be assessed and provided for in prescribed handling methods.

Since handling always exposes an object to injury and since it is not a value-adding activity, process design should minimize materials-handling operations. Once entered into the production process, materials should be kept at the height of the work flow. This can be done by moving materials on carts rather than pallets. Placing outputs on carts instead of tables eases transportation to the next operation.

Damage can result from inadequate materials-handling equipment: balky forklifts or worn-out rollers and conveyor belts. Sixty-eight percent of paint defects on folding chairs manufactured by MECO Corporation were due to hooks from which chairs hung during the painting process. Weakened by the heat of paint ovens, hooks often broke. By using stronger hooks, MECO reduced paint defects by 87 percent, saving more than $110,000 per year. It may be necessary to design custom equipment to transport sensitive materials. A job shop devised dollies that reduced scratches incurred during handling of soft aluminum plate.

Adequate containers and packing methods are needed when shipping goods to customers. Parker Brothers lost $7000 a month due to damaged cardboard boxes that its supplier shipped on wooden pallets. Moisture from the wood seeped into boxes, making them unusable. Some Japanese firms have packaging laboratories that develop impact-resistant containers. American companies have also discovered the benefits of well-designed containers. Ford developed a reusable shipping rack for Aerostar mufflers, saving $735,000 a year on cardboard boxes and reducing shipping damage by 33 percent. Office equipment manufacturers ship products in reusable containers that promote correct product identification, reduce weight and disposal costs, lessen wasted space in trailers, and require less labor for packing and unpacking. A Japanese auto manufacturer realized similar benefits—a 95 percent decrease in part-counting time, minimization of forklift time, and better control of work-in-process—by developing standardized in-plant containers for parts and in-process components.

## Equipment

Broadly speaking, equipment encompasses everything used but not consumed during a process. We associate the term with large machines—ovens, presses, and backhoes—but equipment includes hand tools, dies, and tooling as well. Many items of equipment are custom-fabricated to serve specific needs. Japanese manufacturers are noted for the extensive repertoire of jigs and fixtures used to improve performance.

A common mistake in diagnosing conformance problems is to blame defects on equipment inadequacies. Machines cannot defend themselves and the implied solution of purchasing new equipment appeals to everyone except senior management and a few accountants. Equipment can be, but usually is not, the cause of rejects. Problems must be carefully diagnosed before resorting to the new equipment option. Case 7.4 illustrates the point.

## case 7.4

Nashua Corporation's process for manufacturing carbonless paper was troublesome. Coating material was not consistently applied to paper at the desired rate, resulting in materials loss, frequent adjustments, and stoppages. The company considered spending $700,000 on a new coating head, but a study revealed that the coating head, when not tampered with, was not a major source of variation. After making improvements in the head, the coating material was modified and other causes of variation were identified. These actions corrected the problem, saving Nashua $800,000 annually on material.

Of course, purchasing new equipment is the best option under certain conditions. Existing equipment may not be suited to its task. Workers at the IRS service center in Cincinnati complained that work carts were too wide for two to pass in the aisles. A quality team designed an improved cart. Equipment can be obsolete. The Packaging Manufacturing Division of R. J. Reynolds Tobacco Company experienced inconsistent color matching in printing operations. A project team identified new equipment that provided consistent ink color mixing. Once installed, the machine saved $161,000 a year by reducing product scrap and production time.

In other cases, equipment should be repaired, not replaced. When Warner-Lambert followed up on customer complaints about unsealed packages, it found a broken bolt in one blister-packing machine and a broken sealing ring in another. Some defects are due to the wrong parts. At Jantzen, the swimwear manufacturer, seven operator stations had problems with new sewing machines that leaked oil. The wrong gaskets had been installed when the machines were built. If equipment is not broken or misconstructed, it may simply require maintenance and adjustment.

A good move when addressing any equipment problem is to take advantage of the manufacturer's expertise. When oil streaks appeared on cloth produced by a textile company, a quality circle traced the oil to the weaving machine. Attempts to modify the machine's lubrication system made scant progress until the team contacted its manufacturer. Other users had experienced the same problem and the company was working on a new pressure valve that ultimately fixed the problem.

Improvements are often achieved through customized devices—tools, jigs, fixtures, and templates—that enhance system performance. Asahi National Electric had high breakage rates when small mirrors were installed in frames. Breakage was even greater if the operation was performed by someone other than an assigned worker. Workers devised a tool with a special cam that allowed even inexperienced workers to push mirrors into their frames without breaking. Welders with the Rotary Drill Division of Ingersoll-Rand used blueprints to lay out parts to be cut with an acetylene torch. Transferring dimensions from prints to fabrications provided many opportunities for error. By developing templates for high volume parts, the company saved $30,000 a year in layout time and error costs.

Companies should insure that workers have adequate tools. As in the military, big ticket hardware purchases look impressive, but the provision of ordinary hand tools often has more impact on quality and productivity. Sometimes tools have been provided but are not available due to lack of control. Tool boards, monitors, and control procedures can keep workers from squirreling away a private supply.

Juran described a historical development that illustrates the mistake of applying a tool beyond its proper domain of use.[3] The ox was the first draft animal. Later, when horses were used to pull things, they wore ox harnesses, even though the poor fit reduced a horse's pulling capacity from 15 units to 4. The Chinese developed a collar specifically for use by draft horses, but it took six centuries for Europeans to adopt this innovation. It is not uncommon to find equipment being used for tasks that could be performed more effectively by other devices.

Finally, not only must equipment be suited to its task, it must also be compatible with the surrounding production system. Interfaces between operations should be seamless so items of equipment must be mutually congruent. Compatibility is usually achieved as rough spots are smoothed out over time. But when they first appear, those rough spots can be jarring. At Mount Sinai Medical Center in Miami, stretchers used to transport patients were as much as five inches lower than x-ray tables. Moving patients from stretchers to tables resulted in injuries to patients and back strain to hospital employees. The hospital eventually purchased hydraulic stretchers with adjustable height levels. Another hospital discovered that its emergency room and critical care unit used different IV pumps. When patients were transferred from ER to CCU, tubing had to be changed to continue IV processes.

## Maintenance

A conformance problem can reflect a need for maintenance. Equipment may require cleaning. Abbott Laboratories experienced errors with bar code readers that accumulated dust. The company reconfigured readers so air blew across the reader face, making it self-cleaning. There may be a need to lubricate equipment and replenish fluid supplies. Maintenance workers correct problems caused by worn parts and tools. Equipment may need to be recalibrated.

An electronics plant suffered with a defect rate of 2500 parts per million (ppm) on an old British pick-and-place machine. A sister plant used a newer Japanese machine, costing $700,000, with a defect rate of less than 50 ppm. When a problem-solving team realized that a maladjusted head caused most of the defects, the plant reduced its error rate to 70 ppm, without making the $700,000 investment.

Problem occurrence will be minimized if maintenance is performed before, not after, things break down. This is the rationale for preventive maintenance. Basic issues in designing such programs are deciding what to do and when to do it. Some activities—clean filters, lubricate, replenish fluids—are included in scheduled maintenance for every piece of equipment. Programs go further by specifying equipment-specific tasks, such as recalibrations, adjustments, and checks or replacements of critical parts. Equipment can be modified to make it easier to maintain. While investigating power outages, a team at Florida Power and Light discovered that dampers stuck because there was no way to lubricate them. The team recommended that dampers be drilled for grease fittings and that damper lubrication be added to the maintenance schedule. As with the bar code reader discussed earlier, equipment can be altered to make it self-maintaining. General Motors redesigned machining equipment to automatically compensate for tool wear.

With regard to timing, a balance must be struck between the cost of maintenance and the cost of letting things go too far. Total Productive Maintenance,[4] a Japanese program, reduces the cost of maintenance by having machine operators perform tasks at opportune times. Losses resulting from inadequate maintenance, including downtime, inefficient and defect-prone processes, and damaged equipment, were evident in a case at the North Island Naval Aviation Depot. A plating shop often had to replace $300 anodes that corroded through use. Cleaning anodes every six weeks instead of every six months resulted in less downtime, improved plating performance, and increased anode life.

The timing of scheduled maintenance can be based on predicted equipment failure points. These predictions focus on wear parts that are replaced when their service lives have almost been exhausted. Refined measures of use can achieve economies. At a Ford plant, cables on heavy-duty cranes were replaced monthly, at a cost of $465 a cable. After a team found that good cables were being discarded, the plant shifted to an hours-of-use replacement policy. Commercial airlines have found that 89 percent of maintainable engine parts do not lose reliability with age, so there is no need to replace them after a specified number of hours of operation.

While most maintenance-related problems result from errors of omission, errors of commission can occur. Maintenance-induced failure accounts for up to 48 percent of failures for some U.S. Air Force equipment. Because they are performed infrequently, maintenance tasks may not be governed by strict procedures, making them error prone. Maintenance is an intervention in normal system processing that is potentially responsible for conformance problems.

## People

People are the most controversial causes of conformance problems. Management's proclivity for blaming mistakes on workers is offset, in some circles, by a tendency to exonerate employees even when they are culpable. A balanced view acknowledges that problems can result from inadequate worker performance. Figure 7.3 identifies five attributes of individuals, each detailed into characteristics that can be responsible for conformance problems.

Individual traits are relatively fixed, usually physical, characteristics that can interact with performance demands to yield problems. After a personnel change at Toyota, a meter was consistently misread because the new operator was shorter than his predecessor. Damaged crankshafts in a factory were traced to an operator

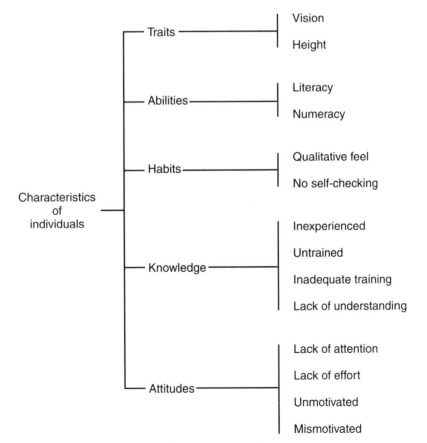

**Figure 7.3** Human causes of conformance problems

who was left-handed. Because the workplace layout was inconvenient for him, this worker occasionally bumped a crankshaft into a conveyor belt. Sometimes people can compensate: A color-blind carpet layer got along by referring to product codes, until he screwed up a job where that information was not available. The best option is to redesign tasks or assign them to better-suited individuals.

Unlike traits, abilities are acquired through training and experience. Companies often assume that workers possess basic literacy and numeracy skills. Problems can occur if this assumption is invalid. A Ford supplier found that an inspector responsible for measuring hoses could not read a ruler. A similar situation occurred in the Campbell Soup Company. Yield problems were traced to a worker who could not read a scale. The employee had gotten by for years by watching the needle and relating its position to a coworker's activities. This strategy was negated when a digital readout replaced the scale.

Over time, workers develop habitual ways of doing things, practices that become unconscious routines. While these habits are generally effective, they may include risky shortcuts and deficient methods that result in error. A quality circle at Japan Steel Works attributed defects to bad habits in reading scales, the use of informal mental calculations, and a lack of worker self-inspection.

Knowledge inadequacies cause errors. Perhaps due to inexperience, an operator may not know everything required for effective performance. Resulting mistakes are usually not the worker's fault. IBM Kingston noted an increase in mistakes on purchasing documents during a week when many buyers were on vacation. People covering for absentees were unfamiliar with their commodities. Automobile manufacturers close their plants for vacations rather than jeopardizing quality by using replacement workers.

Knowledge inadequacies can reflect a lack of training. If a training program is in place, some workers may not have participated. Dow Chemical tracked a problem to an employee who was not properly trained despite years on the job. Paperwork errors in the San Jose Medical Group were ascribed to a part-time worker who was on vacation when training was conducted. Even when all employees receive training, mistakes can occur if instruction is inadequate. In addition, training may not be effective for infrequently performed tasks. When engineers at Florida Power and Light filled out forms to retire obsolete pieces of equipment, 80 percent of the documents had mistakes. Though FPL's accountants gave engineers an eight-hour course on completing the paperwork, the infrequent occurrence of the task suggests that other methods, such as detailed written procedures or centralized responsibility, may have been more successful in reducing errors.

Workers can possess necessary technical knowledge but lack the deeper understanding needed for effective performance. One company manufactured a part with a weight specification of 40.0 grams and a tolerance of +/− 0.5 grams. Though the process capability was 0.1 grams, the full tolerance range of 1.0 grams was being used up. Workers did not realize that inconsistent weights created subsequent assembly problems. Consider the following case:

## case 7.6

An auto screw machine for turning bolts had a 69 percent reject rate. The bolt diameter specification was 0.250 + 0.000 inches/– 0.003 inches. Believing the machine inadequate for the job, management considered buying a new one. A frequency distribution of bolt diameters indicated clustering around the upper specification limit. Operators aimed at that limit to avoid scrap, because oversized bolts could be machined down but undersized bolts were lost. After operators were told to aim for the midpoint of the tolerance range, rework vanished.

Here is a trade-off between over- and under-costs, between doing too much of something and not doing enough. Because operators did not understand the trade-off, their efforts to avoid scrap created rejects.

Many mistakes derive from inattention and attitudinal causes. Instances of wrong patients receiving surgery, wrong limbs amputated, and wrong drugs administered in hospitals result from a lack of attention by responsible parties. Along the same lines are vehicles painted the wrong color in a paint shop. A worker's poor attitude can show up as lack of effort, unwillingness to perform tasks as required. Florida Power and Light had excessive lightning losses of transformers because workers did not drive eight-foot grounding rods into the earth. Knowing their work would not be inspected, operators took shortcuts and fudged on test results. The *Tallahassee Democrat* lost $100,000 a year to advertising mistakes, mostly from carelessness. Ad builders did not take responsibility for error-free production. Some errors are due to motivational conflicts, situations in which other objectives compromise the pursuit of quality. People take shortcuts to avoid unpleasant tasks or to finish work early.

The fact that errors can be traced to people does not mean the implicated individuals are necessarily at fault. Workers cannot be blamed for their physical traits or lack of training. Irrespective of fault, corrective actions must respond to the problem's cause. Some trait-based inadequacies can be cured by adjusting the system—positioning meters so operator height does not affect readings—or by individual aids—getting a pair of glasses. Training and publishing detailed procedures cure knowledge deficits. These can also correct poor work habits. Intractable trait and ability inadequacies can be addressed by selection, picking the right person for the job.

Problems resulting from individual attitudes are among the few conformance problems for which knowing the cause is not tantamount to knowing the cure. If a company's products are of low quality because workers are unmotivated, a simple remedy may prove elusive. Insure that performance is monitored and that individuals are held accountable for quality. The literature is filled with instances of **Hawthorne effects,** situations in which outputs improve once management pays attention to worker performance. In 1983, when rejects at Corning Medical were 12.6 percent of production, a team designed check sheets to accumulate data. When the sheets were collected, they were mostly blank: Operators had virtually eliminated rejects. A purchasing manager achieved an immediate improvement in the error rate on purchase requisitions, from 5.2 percent to 3.1 percent, by making two statements: "I care about errors because they affect our costs and delivery schedules" and "I am going to start to count errors by individual buyers so I can understand the causes."

If performance monitoring does not work, other approaches can be adopted. Mistake-proofing, designing the product or process to prevent errors, is a useful strategy discussed later. Mechanisms that quickly detect and correct errors can be devised. An electronics company developed pictorial guides enabling technicians to easily spot defects. Some motivational problems can be cured by incentive systems, though financial rewards can be expensive. Show workers how their mistakes affect others. Spinners in a textile plant were not using the right knots to tie yarn ends together. Though they disliked their supervisor and had bad feelings for the company, the spinners mended their ways when shown how their knots created troubles for weavers. The ultimate cure for dysfunctional worker attitudes is, again, selection: Fire or reassign employees who will not do their jobs. This is an extreme solution, but one that most workers will support, if used judiciously.

## Information

Information permeates productive processes. We find it in the product specifications and work procedures, specific instructions customizing a job, phone numbers of customer contacts, and addresses where finished goods are sent. With administrative and some service systems, information is the very content of production. Mistakes can result if information is erroneous, incomplete, unclear, or nonexistent.

Administrative processes are often corrupted by data transfer errors, mistakes made transcribing information from one form to another. Miles Laboratories had a customer complaint recording process with three data transfers. The process had a 10 percent error rate, primarily due to extra or missing digits and transpositions. Such mistakes can be reduced by eliminating data transfers.

Conformance problems can result from labeling errors: What you see is not what you get. An average of 17 mistaken runs were made each month in Ohio Bell Telephone's data processing center, because job tickets did not agree with internal labels on tapes. Honeywell Information Systems found that customer orders were sent to the wrong destination because of hard-to-read shipping labels. A team at Campbell Soup traced a series of mistakes to a supplier that had near-identical codes on labels of different products. Indeed, labeling mistakes can be fatal, as in the hospital where a patient was hooked up to an oxygen tank containing $CO_2$.

Customers need information to play their part in the system. A manufacturer of consumer electrical products found that 28 percent of customer complaints were from people who could not assemble handles on an otherwise complete product.

After an instruction sheet was included, only 3 percent of complaints related to handles. After disappointing customers and wasting time with incoming calls and mail that were routed incorrectly, Honeywell Control Systems added contact information to letterheads and advertisements to enable customers to target their communications more accurately.

## Product Specifications

Encompassing blueprints, drawings, bills of materials, and other documentation, product specifications operationalize the goal of the production process: They express the product design. Poor design can render a product liable to breakage during production, creating conformance problems. Mercury Marine had a 12 percent breakage rate for barb fittings on cylinder blocks. A study implicated a thin section on the neck of the part, a flaw corrected by redesign.

Defects result if specifications are erroneous or unclear. A tool manufacturer scrapped 20 percent of its output due to drawing errors. When a manufacturer of aviation instruments investigated a quality problem with its control panel supplier, it found that the supplier had been working from unclear procurement drawings. Jenn-Air, an appliance manufacturer, faced a similar situation with thermostat controls purchased from Robertshaw. Once representatives from the companies got together, they realized that Robertshaw had misinterpreted Jenn-Air's requirements when making its drawings and that Jenn-Air had misunderstood Robertshaw's standard practices in its design work.

Specifications might be out of date. Changes may be made but not recorded on pertinent documents. In one company, an inspector rejected a part that lacked an angle cut. The inspector was using drawing revision $D$, the production floor had used revision $B$, and just three days earlier, the design office had issued revision $E$.

The components, dimensions, and tolerances in a specification are not equally important. Product performance may be unaffected by modest variations in some characteristics, yet be extremely sensitive to deviations in others. Then too, specifications are not all-inclusive. Products can have subtle characteristics, not in the specifications, that show up under certain circumstances. When Toyota needed parts to satisfy demand for a hot-selling car, it ordered them from a new supplier. After insuring that the parts met specifications, Toyota fed them into its production process, only to discover that some parts did not mesh with those from its normal supplier. Specifications must be clear, accurate, and up-to-date, but rarely are they complete accounts of what a product must be like to be acceptable.

This point is reinforced by the case of a machinery manufacturer that experienced many customer complaints. A study revealed that: a customer's requirement for a certificate of conformance had not been included in internal work authorizations; technical manuals did not accompany equipment as required; a release note form that had been used was not the one required by a customer; and a source inspection stamp, required by the purchase order, was not on the paperwork. Products must be construed broadly to include all special customer needs and requests pertaining to an order. Any failure to meet those needs constitutes a defect.

## Process

The notion of process, discussed in Chapter 11, has a prominent role in quality management. Processes differ in their ability to consistently produce acceptable outputs. Process capability can be increased by improving materials, machines, and other inputs. Identifying and correcting process-related causes of error also enhances this capability.

Gryna distinguished between worker, component, information, setup, and time-dominant processes.[5] This distinction points to the factor most critical for achieving quality output. In some situations worker performance is the key; in others the quality of materials is decisive. Whereas some of these factors are inputs, setup and time are aspects of the process itself. They are sources of process-related defects.

Any process can produce bad output as a result of setup errors. In a setup dominant process, correct setup is likely to result in an error-free production run. With such a process, extra checks and measurements should be made to insure a correct setup. Huron Machine Products uses computer simulated trial runs to catch setup errors.

Setup is a matter of tailoring, adjusting process parameters to produce desired output. Not all process parameters need to be adjusted for each job. Some, such as the pressure in a press, might not change from one job to another. But the values of these parameters can shift over time, a phenomenon known as **process drift**. All parameters should be checked periodically and recentered to target values. In a time-dominant process, process drift accrues rapidly as fluids are used up, tools wear down, and heat builds in machinery. Defects result if the process is not monitored and adjusted in the course of a production run.

Processes consist of individual activities or subprocesses. Like a chain, the whole is no stronger than its weakest part. One way to improve quality is to improve weak-link activities in a process. After Campbell Soup Company changed to a microwaveable format for Swanson Pot Pies, they received customer complaints about pies lacking vegetables. Campbell developed a less variable dispensing method. Activities are vulnerable to other kinds of errors. A swimwear line at Jantzen had troubles when operators sewing black garments with black thread could not recognize and correct mistakes.

Processes perform most effectively during steady state operations. Process stops and starts cause poor output. An 11 percent scrap rate in the production of TV screens was caused by machine stoppages. Operators of a wave soldering process at Hewlett-Packard noted higher defects on circuit boards that were on the conveyor during downtime. Stoppages due to equipment breakdowns can be reduced by preventive maintenance. Process interruptions can result from the need to replenish consumables and empty output containers. Assembly processes undergo stops and starts when parts kits are incomplete. Errors in knowledge work result from interruptions and switching between tasks. Work flows with high peaks and low valleys are error prone. Ask any company that has end-of-the-month shipping rushes.

When a process handles different kinds of jobs, such as an assembly line making multiple product models, errors can result from job sequencing. Changeover effects can result if parts of the system do not adjust quickly to new tasks. An Eaton plant that manufactures axles for heavy vehicles received customer complaints about gear sets. Troubles traced to the plant's heat-treating operation. Two heat treatment cycles were used, and though they could be mixed in the furnace, the quality of each was compromised by mixing. As a remedy, production scheduling was revised so the furnace always ran a full week on any cycle.

Errors also occur due to process handoffs, especially when communication is weak. Handoffs create a start-up situation for the receiving party, and the transferring party often fails to pass on needed information. Nineteen percent of customer returns to a consumer durables manufacturer occurred when the sales force sold customers something special but did not notify engineering or manufacturing of required product adjustments. Packing errors on overseas shipments by the Tennant Company were ascribed to a poorly organized process with inadequate communication among work groups. Fulfillment accuracy improved to 100 percent when one person was assigned to gather parts for each shipment.

Some activities are error prone because they are complicated or because too many tasks are assigned to one worker. Such process weaknesses are especially damaging with inexperienced workers or after a change in job assignments. A quality circle in the inspection department of a Japanese manufacturer attributed an increase in inspection errors to changes in work assignments that increased the number of models handled by each person.

Errors can result from delays. Some processes involve perishable, time-sensitive inputs, such as milk, glue, or concrete, so speed is of the essence. Defects in a foundry's pipe production were caused by a pouring schedule that did not get the ladle to a far-off casting machine until the molten metal was dull. In other processes, jobs can be sidetracked. Once out of the normal process flow, they tend to be forgotten and may not be completed correctly when reinitiated. Administrative processes are vulnerable to sidetracking and perishability, the latter if they require information from informants whose memories diminish with time.

Unobservable activities are vulnerable to error because of inspection difficulties. General Motors encountered troubles with an operation that welded nuts to a metal panel. Car parts were later attached to the nuts. A welding machine attached nuts under the panel and out of the operator's sight. Since the machine would cycle even if there were jams or misfeeds, missing nuts might not be detected until it was time to bolt in a part. GM solved the problem by rigging the welder so current would flow and the machine could cycle only if a nut was in place.

Positional effects are common in processes that are spatially extended, such as coating and heat treating. It is hard to insure that all inputs or parts of a large input receive the same treatment. In a wave-soldering operation, boards on a panel's outer edge had more defects than those near the center. Start-up instabilities make the first item in a lot a candidate for trouble. The Willimatic Division of Rogers Corporation uses a slicing machine to cut urethane tubes into "tires." A newly purchased slicing machine had to be shut down when the first tire from each tube was consistently out of spec. Adjusting the knife speed solved the problem.

Finally, activities create defects by overstressing materials. Seventy-four percent of castings produced by a foundry were rejected, in part due to mold breakage that occurred when molds collided and were jerked around before pouring.

## Work Methods

Work methods are the ways operators perform assigned tasks. In a highly structured process, methods are usually delineated by formal procedures, analogous to product specifications. Methods may be inadequate to the task. An electronic assembly shop found that 50 percent of cable defects involved damaged grommets and connectors, due to ineffective grommet extraction methods. When methods were improved, the defect rate dropped from 41 percent to 12 percent, and scrap costs declined from $142 to $29 per cable.

If work methods have not been formalized as procedures, unwanted variation in methods across operators may create output variation. At Union Carbide Chemicals and Plastics, production of a urethane intermediate was plagued by problems with additive levels due to lack of a written procedure insuring that operators measured and mixed additives the same way. Lack of standardized testing methods compromised test reliability at an instrument manufacturer. Of 11 water meters accepted after testing, two had unacceptable performance levels.

Defects can result if methods are outdated or if procedural changes have not been communicated to operators. Fifty-nine percent of paperwork submitted to the personnel office of the State of Florida was incorrect, largely because of an outdated personnel manual and underspecified procedures for completing forms. National Cash Register's Wichita plant experienced production problems due to process changes that were not communicated to assembly workers. The plant established a log book to document changes and made lead workers responsible for insuring that people signed off in the book after being notified of changes.

Quality experts, especially the Japanese, endorse formalizing work methods through written procedures. Written procedures promote uniformity of method, a virtue when individual variations are less effective than prescribed procedures. Written procedures are also a vehicle for worker training and a resource for the inexperienced. At Hoffmann-La Roche, temporary absences of secretarial and support personnel inevitably resulted in mistakes and confusion, because replacement workers did not know their jobs. The troubles were alleviated when employees developed handbooks for each position and for general office procedures. Formal procedures institutionalize work method changes, inhibiting operators from sliding back into old practices.

Like product specifications, procedures are usually incomplete. Manuals rarely encompass all the tricks of the trade, the "knack" found in the practices of skilled operators. When a firearms manufacturer studied a defect affecting 10 percent of its output, it learned that the best assemblers used a file to cut down a dimension on a component. Even these workers did not realize that this unprescribed activity prevented defects. Leaking spigots in the output of a coffee urn manufacturer were traced to a relief person. Instead of using an air hose to blow chips out of a valve, this worker tapped the component on his work table to dislodge the chips. Though the procedures manual was silent on the issue, tapping created nicks that resulted in leaks.

Formal procedures—prescribed work methods—are often associated with bureaucracy, multivolume procedures manuals, and the stifling of individual initiative. The dangers of formalization are that procedures become outdated and institutionalize inadequacies. Formal procedures thwart the search for better methods. Thus, before an activity is proceduralized, insure that the prescribed method deserves to be formalized and that there are means by which even better methods can be discovered. One approach uses CEDAC, a variation of cause-and-effect diagrams: Operators prepare and post cards reporting experience-based improvements in work methods, making one's "knack" a matter of public record.[6]

## Process Monitoring and Control

Processes are monitored and controlled to insure that outputs are acceptable. These activities depend on measurement, the more fundamental topic of this section. Process monitoring and control will be discussed in a process design context (Chapter 11). The current focus is on conformance problems resulting from monitoring and control inadequacies.

Monitoring and control usually require instruments, results being affected by their adequacy. Instrumentation deficiencies can be obvious, as when Carolina Freight's trucks ran out of fuel because broken fuel gauges had not been repaired. Or they can be subtle, as when a sequence plot of data from a manufacturing process showed inexplicable shifts. Lab staff eventually realized that a testing machine could not be controlled at the required temperature. Even if instruments are adequate, they may not be calibrated correctly.

A control variable should be available for each important output characteristic. Case 7.8 illustrates what can happen when this requirement is not met.

---

### case 7.8

Steam is used to cook tea leaves in a tea processing plant. It provides moisture and heat needed to soften leaves. But excessive moisture washes away leaves' taste, aroma, and color. This dilemma was resolved by replacing steam with separate sources of heat and moisture, regulated independently to achieve desired product qualities.

---

Relationships between control variables and output characteristics should be transparent so operators can determine which adjustments to make. In a process for making polyethylene film, these relationships were so complex that workers had to go through an extended "cut and try" process when setting up a run. Control adjustments should not be uncomfortable to make. During the summer in a plant that produced glass bottles, workers neglected a control located next to the furnace because the area was so hot.

Measurement and control devices can lack precision needed to regulate a process. A manufacturer cut sinks to specified dimensions with recurring errors of

0.5–1.0 millimeter (mm). After installing a magnascale, which magnifies readings to improve precision, dimensional variation was reduced to 0.005 mm. A similar case involved final adjustments of television sets during assembly. Skilled workers had to turn an adjustment screw until the desired waveform was obtained on an oscilloscope, a tedious task. By replacing waveforms with numerical voltage readings and adding a circular plate to the screwdriver, which increased the visibility of adjustments, any worker could perform the task in half the original time.

Sometimes measurement methods are inadequate. A producer of wood chips improved on its manual grab-sampling technique, which did not always provide valid evidence of chip quality. Managers at a manufacturer were suspicious when an operator's data sheets indicated that all 3.5-foot-long rubber gaskets were cut and notched exactly at nominal. Misunderstanding the measurement process, the operator stretched and contorted gaskets to match nominal markings. Well-defined measurement procedures and better training would prevent such mistakes.

Errors can result from qualitative assessments, or measurement by "feel." However, sensory impressions do have a role in process monitoring and control. Witness the Toyota worker who detected off-spec material by experiencing a different feeling as she cut plastic parts for a fan shroud. She notified her supervisor, who stopped production. An extensive investigation disclosed that the materials manufacturer was mixing different size grains in its production process. Such discoveries notwithstanding, when possible, quantitative measurement should replace qualitative feel. Operators of a plastic molding process used their hands to check die temperatures, pinched coolant lines to assess flow rates, and adjusted coolant flow by feel. Chronic problems were cured when quantitative measurement techniques were introduced.

Many measurement mistakes, technical and commonsensical, can be made. Conformance problems result if instruments used to test a product are more precise than those employed in its production. Disputes on a construction project occurred because form setters used carpenter levels and rulers to set forms for concrete, whereas sophisticated optical instruments were used to inspect the results. To check a critical but hard-to-measure dimension, an inspector used different gauges to measure two related dimensions, computing the critical dimension as the difference of the two. He failed to recognize that the variance of the difference of two measurements exceeds the variance of each measurement. When a special gauge was developed to measure the dimension directly, out-of-spec production dropped from 15 percent to almost zero.

Walking the thin line between over- and undercontrol is a recurring challenge in process management. Deming emphasized the dangers of the former; process drift warns against the latter. Understanding the causes of variation is crucial. Absent such an understanding, any process adjustment is a shot in the dark. When adjustments are informed by understanding, the notion of overcontrol has no meaning.

One way to reduce measurement error is through automation, what the Japanese call *autonomation*. Toyota builds automatic measuring devices into production lines. These gauge critical tolerances on parts, stopping production if dimensions fall outside specification limits. Self-monitoring and control by operators is facilitated by providing needed information. When bottle weights at a glass container manufacturer were too variable, a study identified the causes as operator adjustments of a gob shear and the pressure of gas used to melt glass. Unable to install automatic gob shear controls, process managers gave operators a chart indicating the appropriate gob shear adjustment for various levels of gas pressure.

A generic strategy, epitomized in the kanban system used by Japanese manufacturers, is use of visual controls. Enable operators to see if products are defective, if more production is required, if consumable levels are low. Headlight switching defects at a Japanese automobile parts manufacturer were eliminated by placing positioning tape on cords so operators would not stretch them too tightly. A ceramics manufacturer suffered from a 39 percent defect rate in the production of fire-flash tile. Most defects occurred when buckets ran out of flashing liquid. Once galvanized buckets were replaced with semitransparent containers, operators could monitor liquid levels and flashing problems disappeared. Finally, remember that measurement is costly. Do not monitor process variables more closely than their importance justifies.

## Testing and Inspection

Testing and inspection are means of assessing products to insure acceptability. Like process monitoring and control, this assessment depends on measurement. Testing and inspection rarely create defects, but mistakes in these activities allow unacceptable products to move downstream, perhaps to end users. Testing and inspection errors can also result in false positives, indications of nonexistent problems. At Adolph Coors Company, an apparent problem in the process by which insides of cans are coated with a protective film turned out to be an artifact of the testing procedure. A test can was used three times to measure coating thickness. Because cans were not fully cleaned between readings, film thickness increased with each test.

Testing errors can result from equipment deficiencies. When Motorola could not find anything wrong with radios rejected by test stations, it launched a team to investigate. Five of seven stations needed modifications. Testing methods are another source of problems. Inspectors may rely on qualitative assessments in lieu of quantitative measurements. A plant rejected up to 56 percent of gearboxes purchased from suppliers due to excessive noise. However, inspectors assessed noise levels subjectively by ear rather than with an audiometer, and testing procedures were not standardized. After test methods were improved, noise rejections fell to 17 percent. This case illustrates another potential weakness in inspection methods—lack of an operational definition of error. Inspectors must know, in perceivable terms, what counts as acceptable versus unacceptable output. When inspectors of automobile instrument panels were given examples and operational definitions of wrinkle defects, rejection rates plummeted from 50 percent to 10 percent in less than a week.

Self-inspection, requiring operators to validate their own work, can increase worker commitment to quality. Simplified versions of checklists employed in formal inspections can make self-inspections more thorough. Each operator should also inspect items received from his/her predecessor. This catches errors early, while they are easy to correct. A potential pitfall is that when a system includes multiple checkers—the operator, her successor, and a final inspector, for instance—people may inspect less carefully, assuming errors will be caught elsewhere in the process. The best processes have reliable self-inspection by operators, reducing the need for final inspection.

The following case illustrates an interesting inspection-related error:

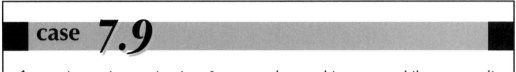

### case 7.9

At an inspection station in a Japanese plant making automobile parts, radiators were submerged in water, and bubbles provided evidence of leaks. On one occasion a leaky radiator was detected later in the process. The unit leaked when first inspected but had been repaired and retested. Since only the repaired part of the tank was submerged during a retest, a second leak in the radiator was not discovered.

The moral is to insure that a repaired item passes any inspections or tests it initially failed before reentering production. Do not let items reenter the process downstream of an inspection on the assumption that repairs have made it acceptable.

Products should be tested under conditions similiar to those encountered when they leave the factory. A computer manufacturer tests memory units on a vibration table, replicating shocks and jolts encountered during transport. Multiple Environment Overstress Testing (MEOST) extends this philosophy, testing products under simultaneous extremes of environmental conditions (temperature, humidity, vibration, etc.) occurring in the field.[7]

Since inspection involves measurement, and measurement is fallible, triangulation is a good policy. Take measurements in different ways. A can-filling line can check for empty cans with height gauges, weighing scales, and air jets that blow empties off conveyors. The advice is especially pertinent for complex and exceedingly critical measurements. The Hubble telescope fiasco was caused by a measurement error that was not detected because no other reliable measurements were taken as cross-checks. The old carpenter's adage should be revised: Cut once, but measure at least twice, each time using a different method.

## Environment

A final potential cause of conformance problems is the environment within which processing takes place. This includes aspects of the facility. For instance, ventilation systems can take in outside vehicle emissions, causing workers to become ill and to make errors.

Lighting can be problematic. While the general level of lighting may be acceptable, task-specific lighting may be less than ideal. Draftspeople in the Norfolk Naval Shipyard suffered from eyestrain until floating arm magnifier lights were provided for each drafting table. Workers at Granville-Phillips made mistakes inserting components into circuit boards. Shigeo Shingo noticed that, while the plant was well lit, holes in circuit boards were not clearly visible. By increasing illumination below the boards, holes were made visible and errors diminished.

Airborne contaminants are a common cause of defects. Because they are especially damaging in the production of computer chips, the computer industry has invested heavily in the development of clean room technology. A more mundane problem is dirt-in-paint, encountered by almost every company that paints its products. When its reject rate for engine cowls rose to 25 percent due to dirty paint, a manufacturer changed filters in the paint system, installed plastic sheets on conveyors, and reduced use of gasoline-powered tow motors because their exhausts created air turbulence. The defect rate dropped to 10 percent. Facing a similar problem at a truck plant, Ford worked with its air filter supplier to improve the plant's air filtration system. It used special sponges to swab vehicles and purchased a laser dirt counter that identified sources of dirt. These efforts reduced dirt-in-paint defects from 6 percent to 1 percent of production.

Another case involves humidity, an airborne contaminant that is not often troublesome. A manufacturer found that humidity degraded insulation used in heater assemblies for hot plates. Units absorbed atmospheric moisture when cooling after being heated in an oven. Filling cooling chambers with low humidity compressed air solved the problem.

## Prescriptions

The previous section identified possible causes of conformance problems, organized around major causal categories. This section offers nine general prescriptions for situations of this kind. Though most conformance problems are relatively easy to solve, a more fundamental challenge is to prevent them from happening in the first place. Several prescriptions, summarized in Figure 7.4, respond to this challenge.

1. Do not accept mistakes as inevitable.

2. Catalog and track recurring defects.

3. Respond to possible causes of "onesies."

4. Watch out for side effects.

5. Error-proof the system.

6. Eliminate troublesome operations.

7. Make errors less costly.

8. Make errors more costly.

9. Work with customers.

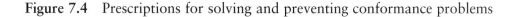

**Figure 7.4** Prescriptions for solving and preventing conformance problems

## 1. Do not accept mistakes as inevitable

Most conformance problems result from mistakes when things are not done as they should be. Mistakes are usually blamed on some part of the system—machines, workers, or suppliers, for instance—that must either be lived with or replaced. Replacement is an expensive long-term solution, so we opt, in the short run, to live with mistakes. Then too, mistakes are part of our everyday experience, something that, to avoid hypertension, we accept as a fact of life.

Recognize, however, that in some domains, such as airline safety or nuclear weapons control, mistakes are not tolerated. Consequently, in these domains, mistakes are rarely made. Many companies—Motorola comes to mind—have demonstrated that errors can be virtually eliminated from certain processes. But this can only happen if everyone becomes intolerant of error and accepts responsibility for eliminating it.

Having made this argument, I must qualify the prescription. Though mistakes are not inevitable, neither are they totally eradicable. Given all the things that need doing in organizations, trying to anticipate and prevent the last defect may not be worth one's while.

## 2. Catalog and track recurring defects

Because they involve established systems, conformance problems offer opportunities to apply experiential knowledge. The breakdowns of a normally reliable system follow Pareto's rule: Most malfunctions result from a few recurring causes. Consequently, it pays to learn the lessons taught by each problem, to understand why it occurred and how it was fixed, and to recall and apply these lessons the next time things go wrong. This advice has been applied widely and to good effect. As a result of efforts to catalog and track defects occurring during final assembly, a manufacturer's defect rate was reduced by 75 percent. A lab unit of Smithkline Beecham required employees to sign off and comment on errors made in lab reports and to suggest ways of preventing recurrences. Florida Power and Light collected failure data from its power plants and those of other utilities. These data were analyzed to identify common failure modes so preventive measures could be taken. FPL has developed a similar system for customer trouble calls. Able to electronically retrieve a record of past problems at a customer's installation, a repairperson may have a probable diagnosis before arriving on site.

## 3. Respond to possible causes of "onesies"

*Onesies* are sporadic defects that appear in only a single output. This makes their causes hard to diagnose: Little evidence remains after the fact as to what went wrong that one time. As a result, normal investigate-and-correct routines do not work and should not be applied. Rather, problem solvers should shift from trying to figure out what caused the problem to thinking of ways it might have happened.

The onesie's existence demonstrates that something went wrong. If one cannot determine what it was, there should nonetheless be a basis for informed speculation as to how the observed defect could have occurred. When plausible defect-generating scenarios have been developed, they can be used to identify cost-justified corrective actions that would prevent the problem from happening again. In this way, over time, the actual causes of onesies will be corrected and the incidence of these defects reduced.

## 4. Watch out for side effects

Cited as a key topic of diagnostic attention (Chapter 5), side effects are unintended consequences of activities or system design. Because these effects are unintended and can be so remote from the initiating activity, related problems are hard to diagnose. When their causes cannot be identified, such problems are often dismissed as inexplicable quirks in the system.

case *7.10*

A company experienced high reject rates due to bare metal exposed after a plated product was polished. Rejects were originally attributed to unskilled polishers or differences in polishing wheels. The company eventually learned that the problem derived from variability in plating thickness. This was traced to heating elements in plating tanks that created an uneven circulation of solution, so articles in a tank's left side were plated less thickly.

Some side effects—for instance, those due to electrostatic discharge—are common and therefore anticipatable. Others, far more rare, are responsible for problems unprecedented in past experience. These can occur as a result of well-intended actions, taken perhaps to solve other problems. Investigators at the Thomas J. Lipton Company traced excessive variation in fill weights of tea bags to defective funnel tips in a filling machine. The tips had been crimped, presumably because they tore bags. Crimping had the side effect of disrupting the flow of tea leaves. To diagnose problems occurring as side effects, it may be necessary to perform extensive process-tracing studies. To prevent such problems, analyze the possible effects of any change to the system, including those made to solve other problems.

## 5. Error-proof the system

Conformance problems can be prevented by characteristics of a product or process that make it harder for mistakes to happen. This simple idea has a long history. It has been applied most effectively by the Japanese, who denote the concept with the term *poka-yoke*.[8]

Error-proofing can be pursued in many ways, reflecting differences in situations and mistakes. The Ford Motor Company's St. Louis plant occasionally received an Aerostar part that had missed an operation in the Van Dyke plant. By designing details into a fixture used at the operation following the omitted one, the part could not be positioned unless the preceding operation had been performed. Here, error-proofing is achieved by a fail-safe interlocking sequence. Processing cannot continue if a mistake has been made. At Matsushita Electric, vacuum cleaners were sometimes packed without certain parts and instructions. These errors were corrected by rigging spring-driven switches to parts containers, only allowing the product box to move ahead if all parts had been inserted. Other ways of error-proofing an operation include: limiting mechanisms (such as a slipping-type torque wrench) that prevent too much of an activity from being performed, providing the exact number of parts needed so workers are cued of an operation's completion, and the military practice of repeating orders aloud to the order-giver, verifying that instructions are understood. Error-proofing mechanisms should not make the process more demanding. Accidents often occur because safety features have been deliberately disabled by operators. Poka-yoke devices should help, not hinder, the worker.

## 6. Eliminate troublesome operations

If a mistake-prone activity cannot be error-proofed, perhaps it can be eliminated by redesigning the process. This more radical approach may be justified if a high error rate resists other improvement attempts. Japanese manufacturers try to automate tasks that are susceptible to error when performed manually.

## 7. Make errors less costly

During the production process in a hosiery company, tights would fall to the floor and be damaged. The company installed protective liners in boxes under work tables so tights would not be damaged if they fell. This solution exemplifies a useful principle: Make errors less costly. Reduce damage consequent upon a mistake. Catch errors more quickly, for instance, by detecting defective products before they are shipped to customers. Products can be designed so mistakes are easier to correct. Obviously, the best course is not to make errors in the first place. But if accidents do happen, the less severe the consequences, the better.

## 8. Make errors more costly

The opposite of its predecessor, this recommendation applies when errors have a motivational origin. People are not trying hard enough to get it right. Making mistakes more costly for responsible parties can motivate improved performance. At Tennant, when the floor space and mechanics assigned to rework faulty products were reduced, people found ways to lessen the number of products needing rework. Systems often contain slack that makes mistakes less costly, hence more likely to occur.

   In addition to removing slack, steps can be taken to increase accountability. After Ford forced individual departments to assume responsibility for reducing water leaks in Escorts, the first-try pass rate for vehicles taking a soak test increased from 40 percent to nearly 80 percent. One firm's final product was packaged in bales that were transported by forklift and occasionally damaged by misdirected prongs. When the company began to identify which lift moved which bale, damage declined considerably. Held responsible for producing defect-free output, individuals and departments find ways of doing so.

## 9. Work with customers

Working closely with customers prevents conformance problems for two reasons. First, customer contact promotes development of interpersonal relationships, motivating operators to avoid mistakes. People do not want their friends and acquaintances to view them as incompetent, sources of shoddy output. Second, increased communication with customers reduces errors due to inadequate information. Both factors were evident in the word processing center at an insurance company. The center had high error rates and slow turnaround times on documents prepared for other departments. Then, as the result of job redesign, word processing operators were assigned to clients. The resulting customer contact gave operators better job instructions and performance feedback, motivating them to take pride in their work. This led to lower error rates and turnaround times.

Conformance problems are not the most difficult situations addressed by quality problem solvers, though they may be the most common. There is, of course, no silver bullet solution method for these issues. Good problem solving takes account of the particulars of a situation. It uses past experience and case-based insights, as presented in this chapter, to diagnose the problem and devise a cure. These tools can also be employed to prevent problem recurrence.

## NOTES

1. W. Edwards Deming, *Out of the Crisis* (Cambridge: MIT Center for Advanced Engineering Study, 1986).
2. This material is drawn from: Jens Rasmussen, *Information Processing and Human-Machine Interaction: An Approach to Cognitive Engineering* (Amsterdam: North-Holland, 1986); and James Reason, *Human Error* (Cambridge: Cambridge University Press, 1990).
3. Joseph M. Juran, *Managerial Breakthrough* (New York: McGraw-Hill, 1964).
4. Seiichi Nakajima, *TPM: Total Productive Maintenance* (Cambridge, Mass.: Productivity Press, 1988).
5. Frank M. Gryna, "Production," sec. 17 in *Juran's Quality Control Handbook,* 4th ed., Joseph M. Juran and Frank M. Gryna, eds. (New York: McGraw-Hill, 1988).
6. Frank M. Gryna, "Quality Improvement," sec. 22 in *Juran's Quality Control Handbook;* see note 5.
7. Keki R. Bhote, "America's Quality Health Diagnosis: Strong Heart, Weak Head," *Management Review,* May 1989, 34–38.
8. See: Shigeo Shingo, *A Study of the Toyota Production System from an Industrial Engineering Viewpoint* (Cambridge, Mass.: Productivity Press, 1989); and Shigeo Shingo, *The Sayings of Shigeo Shingo: Key Strategies for Plant Improvement* (Cambridge, Mass.: Productivity Press, 1987).

# Unstructured Performance Problems

## Chapter Outline

**Fundamentals**
Relationship to Other Quality Problems
Functional Demands
The Absence of Standards
The Product-Service Distinction

**Solving Unstructured Performance Problems**
Problem-Solving Method
Problem Structures
Analyzing UPPs
    Sales Shortfall
    Employee Morale and Turnover
    The Elevator Case

**Service Inadequacies**
Customer Needs
Service Offerings
Initiation of Service Transaction
Waiting Time
Customer Involvement
Service Delivery
Completion of Service
Postservice Evaluation

## Prescriptions
Use Incentives to Inspire Improvement
Develop Expertise
Add Structure Appropriately

---

Unstructured performance problems (UPPs) are situations in which a nonstandardized task is performed ineffectively. The most familiar UPPs are situations in which customers are unhappy with the quality of a service. Most services cannot be standardized. Consequently, problem solving is more difficult than with conformance problems. But UPPs are not just about services. Many organizational activities are relatively undefined by standards and procedures: public relations, the marketing of products, strategic planning. When such activities are not performed effectively, an unstructured performance problem exists.

The chapter begins with a discussion of basic issues regarding UPPs. This enables development of an informal method for solving such problems. The chapter continues by examining an important subset of UPPs, customer service inadequacies. It concludes with general prescriptions for solving unstructured performance problems.

# Fundamentals

A performance problem is a situation in which a system is not performing acceptably. The previous chapter was concerned with conformance problems, performance problems in which a highly structured system produces outputs unacceptable to product users. Unstructured performance problems, the topic of this chapter, involve systems whose inputs, processes, and outputs are not well specified. There is no one right way of doing things. Then too, with UPPs, product users are not the only agents of concern. Performance can be unacceptable to organization members and other stakeholders. Figure 8.1 illustrates this conceptualization.

## Relationship to Other Quality Problems

The differences between UPPs and conformance problems can be seen by comparing Figures 8.1 and 7.1. Conformance problems assume that user needs are known and can be expressed as requirements governing system inputs, processes, and outputs. Problems are identified as deviations from these requirements. With UPPs, system inputs, processes, and outputs are not fully specified by requirements. This makes it difficult to ascertain how performance falls short of expectations. Since the existence of requirements is a matter of degree—some parts of a system can be well specified, others not—the two categories, UPPs and conformance problems, blend together.

Their concern with the interests of stakeholders other than product users connects UPPs to efficiency problems, which reflect the goals of organizational managers and employees. But UPPs are matters of system effectiveness, getting the job

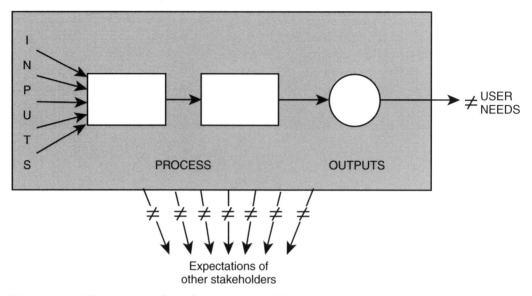

**Figure 8.1**   Unstructured performance problems

done, not efficiency. Most efficiency problems involve clear criteria, such as cost, volume, and safety. UPPs often have unclear goals.

Like other performance problems, UPPs give rise to process design issues when system inadequacies are not susceptible to local fixes. UPPs have less connection to product design. The systems involved in UPPs do not produce standard outputs. Rather, customized outputs are created as a result of design work performed within the production process. Product tailoring or design is an integral part of the process, not a separate, stand-alone activity that might be implicated by performance inadequacies.

## Functional Demands

Diagnosis is a critical task with all performance problems, UPPs included. One must determine why performance is unsatisfactory. Diagnostic efforts are complicated by the absence of standards. Lacking crisp specifications of normal system states and activities, it is hard to determine what is wrong.

Setting performance criteria is another challenge. A sometimes vague sense that things are not as they should be must be translated into specific performance targets and inadequacies. This includes the task of determining customer needs regarding a product. When needs are individualized and changeable, as with personal services, the task is all the more difficult. An apparent performance problem can be a red herring, not a problem at all if expectations are unreasonable. Benchmarking helps insure that criteria are appropriate.

The lack of a known right way of doing things suggests a final challenge, that of determining how to achieve performance goals. With conformance problems, procedures and specifications define a viable way of producing good outputs. These standards have no parallel in unstructured performance problems. A marketing manager needs to figure out how to increase sales. A nurse must determine how to satisfy a patient's special needs. Experience is a valuable resource in such tasks when no general method exists for devising means of achieving performance objectives.

## The Absence of Standards

The quality movement's traditional focus on structured production activities has led some to assume that all organizational processes and outputs can be defined by strict specifications and standards. This is not true. Much of what goes on in any organization cannot be proceduralized. In some organizations, such as small consulting firms, specifications and procedures provide little direction for the production of outputs. Negotiations with clients can fill in some of the void—for instance, public accounting firms use engagement letters to partially define audit processes and products—but invariably much is left unspecified.

Performance standards may not be available for several reasons. Sometimes relevant systems are immature. Not enough knowledge has been accumulated to set standards. Companies accept process and product variability as the cost of learning, moving toward optimal work methods and product specifications.

More commonly, the absence of standards reflects a need to tailor processes and outputs to situational demands. Operators adapt their performances to the needs of the situation. Such is the case with knowledge work. All market research projects draw on a repertoire of tools and techniques. Yet in each study, these methods are applied flexibly, adapted to the situation as the researcher understands it. Such tasks cannot be proceduralized because no standard output would be best in all situations.

Finally, standards can be lacking due to the uniqueness and variability of customer needs. Different people want different things, and a given person may want different things on different occasions. This is the case with personal services. A waiter adjusts his behavior in view of the expressed and anticipated preferences of each customer. If a fixed performance routine were employed, it would clash with the inclinations of some customers and the restaurant would lose their business.

## The Product-Service Distinction

The distinction between products and services is well established in marketing and quality literatures. In contrast to products, services are intangible, heterogeneous, perishable, and are produced and consumed at the same time. The need to insure service quality poses different challenges than those of products. One might argue that the product-service distinction underlies the difference between conformance and unstructured performance problems, between this chapter and its predecessor.

One section of this chapter deals solely with service inadequacies. Nonetheless, while the product-service distinction is important for QPS, it is not fundamental. What matters is whether a system's inputs, processes, and outputs are standardized. Because they involve intellectual activity and produce outputs tailored to customer needs, many services cannot be standardized. Quality deficiencies give rise to UPPs. Other service activities—administrative tasks, for instance—are susceptible to proceduralization. If mistakes are made in processing bank deposits or insurance claims, the situation is a conformance problem. In addition, not all products are produced by a fully specified system. The design and construction of a Gothic cathedral, the handcrafting of fine furniture, a master chef's creation of a special entree cannot be captured in a set of specifications. When things go awry, there is no standard to fall back on. Though service activities often gives rise to UPPs, the product-service distinction does not itself imply different kinds of problem solving.

## Solving Unstructured Performance Problems

No strong general methods exist for solving unstructured performance problems. The category encompasses too many kinds of situations to be susceptible to a single technique. The approach taken with conformance problems—identifying potential causes of poor performance—has less value with UPPs. These problems admit a wider range of possible causes, and diagnosis is but one of several important problem-solving tasks.

As noted in Chapter 2, all problems possess structure. They consist of parts—agents, goals, constraints—related in some way. However, UPPs as a category of problems lack a common deep structure. This makes their solution especially dependent on past experience. Fortunately, many UPPs are generic situations frequently encountered by individuals and organizations. For instance, "sales below budget" is an unstructured performance problem that has confronted virtually every organization and generated a sizable body of experiential knowledge.

Consequently, intensive situational analysis is the key to solving unstructured performance problems. Analysis yields structural insights and prompts recollection of experiential knowledge. It suggests problem-solving heuristics and methods that can be applied to the situation at hand. A general method for addressing UPPs will be proposed. Implementing this method depends on in-depth problem analysis.

### Problem-Solving Method

Assuming an unstructured performance problem has been identified, problem solving should emphasize the following activities.

First, **analyze and identify the problem structure.** What elements and relationships comprise the situation? Is it a member of a common class of performance problems, such as sales shortfall or employee morale? What are its distinctive features? Structural analysis evokes experiential knowledge and directs attention to important aspects of the situation.

Second, **clarify and validate goals.** Whereas the goals of conformance problems involve well-defined, attainable states, the desired performance levels of UPPs can be vague or unreasonable. It is important to specify the intended outcomes of performance improvement efforts, to insure that performance targets are achievable, and to develop valid ways of assessing outcomes. UPPs can be red herrings. Unreasonable expectations foster concern over performances that are not really out of line, drawing attention and effort better spent elsewhere.

Third, **diagnose causes.** Localize the performance inadequacy by identifying parts of the system needing improvement. Identify the situations or transactions for which system performance is weakest, for performance may only be unacceptable in certain cases. Diagnostic efforts should consider causal candidates discussed in Chapter 7 and others relevant to the problem at hand. Whereas conformance problems usually have a single cause, UPPs almost always result from multiple causes. Many aspects of the system might be changed to improve its performance. Consequently, it may be necessary to prioritize and focus improvement efforts on the most significant causes.

Fourth, **devise improvements.** UPPs cannot be solved by enforcing standards. A better way of doing things must be found. Careful diagnosis and analysis of the situation supports this effort, but experience with similar situations is the most valuable resource. Generic problems often have well-known, off-the-shelf solutions that are effective but costly. These options should be considered, but not quickly adopted. Equally effective, less costly solutions may exist, and good problem solving tries to find them.

Finally, **implement the chosen solution and monitor its effectiveness.** The solution might encompass multiple changes to the system, each responding to one or more inadequacy. Because the system is not well specified, one cannot be sure how it will respond to changes. Thus, monitoring the effectiveness of solutions and making adjustments or trying something else if corrective actions do not yield desired outcomes is the most likely path to success.

## Problem Structures

Identifying problem structures is important for UPPs because they lack a common structure that could support powerful problem-solving methods. Many problem structures were cited in Chapter 2. These and others can be discerned by analyzing UPPs. For instance, problems often involve conflicts between values or situational demands. Identifying the conflict is a prerequisite for alleviating it. A systems development department at Florida Power and Light had a poor record of responding to phone calls from internal customers. A study revealed that the department's weekly staff meeting was held when customer calls were at their peak. The conflict was removed by rescheduling the meeting.

Competition is a defining characteristic of some performance problems. Maybe you ran a great race, but someone else ran a better one. Sales shortfalls can result from the actions of competitors. Beyond simply working harder, such problems can be solved by developing a strategy that exploits one's strengths and the weaknesses of opponents. The marketing and strategic planning literatures contain useful suggestions. Other advice can be found in military history and political writings, from Machiavelli to Nixon. During five millenia of practice, the Chinese developed numerous strategems:[1] "Loot a burning house" is the move of attacking when an opponent is most vulnerable. An example might be starting a price war when a competitor is having financial difficulties.

The following case demonstrates another problem structure.

---

## case 8.1

The Compliance Bureau at the Wisconsin State Department of Revenue received inadequate service from its word processing pool. Document turnaround time was slow, mistakes and revisions were frequent, and word processors had high workloads and low morale. A survey disclosed poor customer relations and a lack of communication and trust between word processors and their customers. Another discovery was that half the typing requests were designated as "rush" jobs by customers trying to improve turnaround time and that the pool was handling requests that should have gone to other units.

---

This case exemplifies a *Tragedy of the Commons* situation in which a resource is available to many users, each of whom benefits by using it as much as possible. Unfortunately, excessive demands degrade the resource and make it less valuable. The structure derives its name from the English "commons," village pastureland, available to all residents, that was overgrazed as villagers selfishly added livestock to their personal herds. In such situations, resource utilization must be managed by appropriate mechanisms.

Another structure is apparent in a problem addressed by the IRS district office in Austin, Texas. Tax revenues were lost because people did not file returns; delinquency investigations increased from 2380 in 1984 to 10,897 in 1990. A team found that many nonfilers, fearing prosecution, did not reenter the system after their first nonfiling. The team also learned that nonfilers often overestimated their obligations and did not realize that the IRS would work with them to develop payment plans. This is a case of *pernicious procrastination:* Someone puts off dealing with an undesirable task, which consequently becomes more threatening and likely to be put off again. The temptation to procrastinate perpetually can be countered by active intervention and enforcement, such as prosecuting delinquent taxpayers. Or one can make the challenge less ominous by helping nonfilers get back into the system, which was the approach taken by the IRS in this case.

## Analyzing UPPs

To illustrate what can be done with UPPs, three problems will be analyzed. Two are generic situations; the third and more unique problem is a classic, The Elevator Case, which was previously cited in Chapter 6.

***Sales Shortfall.*** At one time or another, every organization faces the problem of unsatisfactory sales. This and corresponding problems faced by individuals—not making enough money, not having a job—reflect the nature of market economies. Economic agents must sell outputs to customers. Competition is a defining aspect of such situations in which being good is not enough. One's products must be better than competitive offerings. Unlike a foot race, where an objective standard determines who wins, here the customer is the criterion. Products sell because they satisfy customer needs better than competing products. Consequently, one task in addressing a sales shortfall is to determine customer needs and to analyze one's product in comparison with competitors. A quality circle at Pentel conducted a competitive analysis to improve sales of brush pens.

Goal setting is a crucial issue with sales shortfalls, due to the difficulty of insuring that target performance levels are reasonable. Customer purchasing decisions are influenced by many factors, from economic conditions to the idiosyncratic preferences of individuals. Companies almost always want to sell more, but at some point efforts toward this end can be dysfunctional, alienating customers and employees alike. Thus, when sales shortfalls occur, problem solvers should validate the performance target, insuring that it is reasonable in light of market conditions. In reaching the conclusion that brush pen sales were unsatisfactory, Pentel's quality circle noted the many customer inquiries about their product.

As always with performance problems, diagnosis shapes subsequent problem solving. As is common with UPPs, sales shortfalls usually have multiple causes. Many things can be improved, each affecting sales. The marketing literature is a resource for diagnostic purposes. Its 4 Ps—product, price, promotion, and place, analogous to the 5 Ms of CE diagrams—denote generic elements of sales situations that are potential causes of shortfalls. When a team at Xerox investigated lagging sales of a personal computer, it concluded that the problem resulted from a confusing price structure that customers did not understand. Low attendance in hospital-sponsored classes for mastectomy patients at a Columbus, Ohio, hospital was attributed to inadequate promotional efforts. Patients did not always know about the classes.

The salient role of customers suggests a heuristic for diagnosing sales shortfalls: Ask people why they are not buying the product. More generally, when a problem involves a group of people with important information they will share, survey methods should be used. A field sales force could be surveyed while diagnosing a sales shortfall. Stratification can analyze sales by product, customer, region, salesperson, and other dimensions to localize the shortfall and discover its causes.

Sales shortfalls are addressed by a number of standard solutions: lower prices, increase advertising, expand the distribution network, and enhance sales force incentives, among others. Each of these off-the-shelf responses is appropriate in some situations, but they are expensive remedies that should only be used if the situation truly calls for that response. Good problem solvers develop other courses of action, better targeted interventions that respond cheaply and effectively to the problem's causes by recognizing and exploiting the situation's distinctive features.

For sales shortfalls, unique aspects of the product or market may afford corrective action. To solve the problem of low attendance at classes for mastectomy patients, the Ohio hospital exploited a distinctive feature of its situation: Customers all had physicians whose opinions they respected. The hospital educated physicians about its classes, and physicians recommended the service to patients, resulting in a fivefold increase in attendance. Faced with a similar situation—customers unwilling to use automated teller machines (ATMs)—the Fulton Bank in Lancaster, Penn., found its own feature to exploit. A stratification analysis disclosed that most nonusers were elderly people, so the bank had its retired employees come in on Social Security days to demonstrate ATM use to other senior citizens.

***Employee Morale and Turnover.*** Another common problem in organizations, low employee morale leads to high turnover. Many people have worked in a company or department where management gives much less than they ask for, where employees do not get along, where no one takes pride or finds satisfaction in their work. Such situations reflect poor relationships between the organization and its employees or among employees themselves. In either case, management must improve the work environment.

Employee unhappiness often results from a mismatch between individual expectations and perceived reality. People may expect to be promoted quickly, to get large raises, and to have enjoyable working conditions. Morale plummets if expectations are not met. Some problems can be prevented if expectations are kept at realistic levels when people are hired. Morale problems are less likely than sales shortfalls to be red herrings: Organizations rarely set unreasonable goals for themselves regarding employee morale and turnover. Competition, an important consideration in analyzing sales shortfalls, is less relevant here, but turnover can result if other organizations use attractive offers to hire away workers. A problem structure to watch out for is *adverse selection,* in which morale is lowest, and turnover highest, among the best employees, the people who feel unchallenged or unrewarded by the current system. Turnover is not cause for concern if weak employees leave and are replaced by better ones; it is disastrous if the cream departs, leaving the dregs behind.

Like sales shortfalls, morale problems center on a disaffected party. This is a boon to diagnosis, since one can simply ask workers why they are unhappy. Given the anonymity of surveys and the after-the-factness of exit interviews, employees usually respond honestly. Thus, morale problems rarely pose deep causal mysteries. Stratification can be used to determine if certain subgroups are especially unhappy. Age, race, gender, marital status, profession, and supervisor are worthwhile stratification bases. Multiple causality should be expected. The "usual suspects" that are typical causes of low morale include compensation and benefits, opportunity for advancement, hours, and working conditions. Morale problems can result from special conditions: an inconvenient location, insensitive supervisor, obnoxious coworker, or company policies that ignore employee commitments to family, religion, or the fishing opener.

Solutions to morale and turnover problems start with the recognition that employment is an exchange relationship. The parties, organization and employee, provide each other with something of value. Employees quit when they believe they are asked to give too much for too little. Organizations should try to enhance the rewards and alleviate causes for complaint that workers experience from employment. The obvious move, to raise salaries, is expensive and may not be effective. Good problem solving uses an insightful diagnosis of the causes of dissatisfaction to identify changes responding to salient employee concerns. For instance, if workers are bored with their jobs and feel their opinions are not valued, job enrichment and empowerment practices can create benefits for both parties.

Some examples: Hawaiian Airlines experienced low morale among flight attendants. Attendants had been promised training in 10 different functions, such as loading and beverage distribution, but few had been fully trained. This made it difficult for them to cover for absent coworkers, leading to boredom as the same people performed the same tasks on each flight. A quality circle solved the problem by developing a job rotation plan that qualified all attendants for all functions. As their jobs became more interesting, attendant morale increased and absenteeism declined.

Another case involved the new Victorville, Calif., plant of AFG Industries, a producer of architectural glass. The Victorville plant, after eight months of operation, still had an employee turnover rate exceeding 30 percent. An employee team investigating the problem identified three causes of turnover: shift schedules, lack of management responsiveness to employee concerns, and inadequate methods for evaluating potential employees. When the company changed to a 12-hour shift schedule providing longer blocks of employee off-time, turnover fell below 11 percent.

***The Elevator Case.***   This case was reported and briefly analyzed in Chapter 6. This more extensive analysis illustrates heuristics useful in solving UPPs.[2] The case concerns a new 40-story office building, where management has received numerous complaints that elevator service is too slow during the morning rush hour. If elevators had been breaking down, this would be a conformance problem, perhaps caused by faulty components. Since elevators are working, a broader perspective must be adopted, making this an unstructured performance problem. One cannot simply enforce specifications and procedures to get the system operating acceptably.

The situation exemplifies a noteworthy structure: It involves a limited capacity resource subject to varying levels of demand. Morning delays in the lobby are of a kind with time commuters spend in rush hour traffic. A first step may be to examine who is complaining. Though we commonly assume complainants are justified in their dissatisfaction, this is not always true. Stratifying complaints would determine who the complainants are. On what floors do they work? Maybe only a few people are kvetching. Complaints may not be valid in that people might have unreasonable expectations about elevator service. This issue can be resolved by a queuing study, in which one records the time users spend waiting for and using elevators. If the average time spent in this building is consistent with industry standards and times spent in comparable buildings, the elevator problem is a red herring. The real task is to communicate with complainants, convincing them that service levels are appropriate and helping them toward reasonable expectations.

We will assume complaints are valid and that elevator service is too slow during the morning rush hour. This performance inadequacy must be diagnosed. A problem solver should observe system operations and ride along with passengers in the morning. This might reveal that high volume tenants are located on the uppermost floors. Moving these tenants to lower floors might alleviate the situation. Diagnostic efforts also should consider an apparent anomaly: Building occupants arrive during the morning rush hour and leave during the evening rush hour, yet no complaints have been received about elevator service later in the day. Why not? What is different about the evening rush hour? Could this difference be used to relieve congestion in the morning?

Diagnosis can pursue other directions as well. Asking "How did we get into this mess?" directs attention toward larger systemic or historical causes of current troubles. Perhaps they got into this mess as a result of building design errors, which underestimated elevator capacity requirements. If so, building designers/developers should make amends. Diagnosis might note a distinctive feature: This is a new building, only open for a few months. Perhaps they are experiencing start-up difficulties that will disappear when tenants adjust their behaviors to the morning rush. Similarly, long lines of cars created by highway construction projects diminish when people reschedule trips and take alternate routes. The problem might just go away on its own. Problem solvers in the case have defined the situation as one of inadequate elevator capacity. Conceptual analysis discloses that an inadequacy involves a mismatch between supply and demand. Past efforts to improve the situation have tried to increase supply. What about reducing demand?

Our diagnosis has generated possible causes of and related solutions for the elevator problem: If a building design error was made, have developers make things right. If it is a matter of start-up difficulties, wait to see if the problem resolves itself. A demand-side approach to the situation suggests others: stagger working hours to spread peak load demand or set elevators to stop only on even-numbered floors, requiring some users to walk down to their destinations. The trouble with demand-side solutions is that they burden tenants. This may not seem fair and tenants will not be happy about it. If it were an owner-occupied building, such solutions might be more appealing.

Whenever this case has been presented in the literature, it has been resolved by one of a family of "cute" solutions that purportedly follow from seeing it as a behavioral, not a technical, problem. It is not clear that these solutions always work. More importantly, their derivation has been misconceived. The critical insight involves the distinction between causes and conditions, the latter being passive factors that enable, but do not actively produce, effects. People complain because they have to wait for elevators. In the absence of complaints, building management would not be concerned. While complaints are the effect of people's waits (the cause), a condition for this effect is that people do not like waiting. If the wait were more enjoyable, people might not complain about slow elevator service. The cute solutions propose that a television, newsstand, snack bar, or other diversion be located in the lobby to make the morning wait for elevator service less onerous. These solutions attack the condition for, rather than the cause of, the problematic effect. The solutions might work, especially if the problem was situated in a hotel. In an office building, they may prompt employers to complain about employees hanging out in the lobby.

## Service Inadequacies

Though not all UPPs involve service operations, many do. Owing to their intangibility and heterogeneity, the delivery of services tends not to be tightly proceduralized. Consequently, when performance is unsatisfactory, it may not be clear how to improve things. This section focuses on problems with service operations and is organized around elements of the service cycle depicted in Figure 8.2.

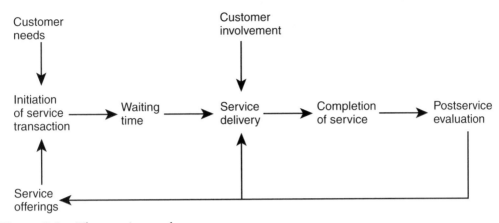

**Figure 8.2** The service cycle

## Customer Needs

Researchers have identified various dimensions of service quality: reliability, responsiveness, competence, access, courtesy, communication, credibility, security, understanding, and tangibles.[3] These are generic attributes of service offerings that always matter to customers. They can be collapsed into two categories: **functional** and **relational needs.** Customers want a service to satisfy the functional purpose motivating the transaction, be it getting a car to start or buying a new suit, and they want personal interactions with service workers to be enjoyable.

Identifying generic customer needs is easy. More difficult is determining what customers desire of specific service offerings. These needs vary from one service to another. Customers want service providers to be competent, but the competence of a sales clerk differs from that of a chiropractor. Companies must determine what their service workers must be good at to be regarded as competent. Some services involve unusual needs. A swimming pool builder sends letters to the neighbors of clients, assuring them that noise, dirt, and hazardous conditions will be minimized during the construction period. This company recognizes that its service can affect customers' relations with their neighbors. In addition, needs vary across customers. One patron calling a mail order company wants fast, efficient, order processing. The next prefers a sedate personal interaction with the order taker. Finally, needs vary from situation to situation. An airline believed its customers placed a high priority on prompt departures. It discovered that for long international flights, food service and clean rest rooms were more important.

Market research methods, including surveys, are the primary means of determining customer needs. Owing to their involvement in service transactions, it may be possible to identify customer needs as the service is delivered. Other interactions with customers can also be informative. Mechanics working for the city of Madison, Wis., rode along on police patrols, learning that squad cars spend more time idling than in high speed driving. This led to changes in the way engines were tuned.

"The customer is always right." This maxim, attributed to Marshall Field of department store fame, has been widely endorsed within the quality movement.

Unfortunately customers do not always deserve this standard of treatment. Expressed customer needs can be arbitrary, unreasonable, and mistaken. The Bureau of Office Services in the Pennsylvania Department of Transportation required customers to enter due dates on print shop orders. Bureau employees eventually realized that many reported due dates did not reflect real needs. Customers set due dates because they were asked to. When a team at Johnson Controls reviewed IRS requests for documents needed for examination, they found unrealistic demands that increased compliance costs. Both parties benefited by staggering due dates for requested information. Lest one conclude that only government agencies make unreasonable demands, consider the merchandise returns retailers are asked to accept. Expensive clothing, crystal chandeliers, and silver tea services are purchased and returned for full credit after an event. Service providers owe it to their many good customers not to accede to the unreasonable demands of a few. Nor should they prompt customers to express needs they do not have.

## Service Offerings

Service design, the development of specifications for services, is less developed than product design. Why? Because services are tailored to individual customer needs, and this tailoring is often performed as the service is being delivered. Service providers try to realize the consistency, economies, and other benefits of standardization without creating rigid, one-size-fits-all offerings that leave customers unsatisfied. The potential for standardization depends on the nature of the service, and level of contact is one attribute that determines that nature. **Contact** is the proportion of service time during which the customer is present. Barbers deliver a high contact service, while VCR repair is low contact. With the customer closely involved, high contact services require more flexibility. Barbers adjust when customers protest that too much is being taken off.

In some ways, service design does resemble product design. Setting service levels is analogous to setting product specifications. How quickly will the order be processed? How close will the bill be to our estimate? How often will we provide the item that was ordered? These are issues customers care about that service providers can measure and control. Just as products include bells, whistles, and other differentiating features, service offerings surround core commodities with auxiliary and nonobligatory benefits. The effects on purchasing decisions can be seen in air travel, where $1000 transactions are swayed by in-flight dinner menus. Like products, service offerings must be designed in view of the organization's capabilities. Do not offer more than can be delivered, but use existing capacities to the fullest. When people at Metroweb, a Cincinnati printer, met to discuss a problem, customer service representatives learned that recently acquired equipment had capabilities that could be exploited to deliver a better product.

Since service workers are a crucial part of the offering, organizations promote development of close customer-worker relationships and allow customers to be served by the workers they choose. Many people have a personal physician, hairdresser, and chef that they favor. Attempting to improve the quality of case management services in Jefferson County, Wis., the county's case workers surveyed elderly and disabled clients. They learned that clients wanted closer, more lasting, relationships with case workers, a preference that prompted the county to redesign case worker roles.

When it is not possible for customers to have a provider of choice, comparable benefits can be achieved through information technology. By recording and storing preferences expressed during a customer's visit, companies can recall and satisfy those preferences on subsequent occasions. The Ritz-Carlton, a chain of hotels based in Washington, D.C., has a computerized customer recognition program that enables its hotels to automatically provide repeat customers with their favorite newspapers, fruits, and other amenities. The Four Seasons Hotel in Toronto uses a similar system to remember, for instance, if a guest needs a foam pillow because of an allergy to down.

A dark side to these improvements in service quality has been called the "Peanut Syndrome," in honor of complaints a Swedish airline received from passengers dissatisfied with the way their peanuts were roasted.[4] In some industries, customer expectations have risen to ridiculous heights. These expectations are often attached to trivial aspects of the service offering. Rising expectations can cause customer satisfaction to decline despite demonstrable improvements in quality. Organizations must manage customer expectations regarding services and focus improvement efforts on what has real value for customers.

## Initiation of Service Transaction

Most service transactions are initiated by customers. The customer decides to eat in a restaurant, to take a course in art history, or to have her house painted. However, service organizations do not wait passively for this to happen. Marketing efforts promote customer awareness. These efforts can capitalize on special situations or selling opportunities. J. C. Penney's catalog division devised a system that flashes a message to the order taker whenever a customer purchases a product requiring batteries. The system identifies which batteries are needed and encourages cross-selling. Items are now sold with batteries more than 90 percent of the time. At Barney's New York, a computer system enables salespeople to track purchases of regular shoppers. A handwritten note prompts a customer when, say, new shirts might be needed.

Some service organizations can initiate transactions, perhaps because service is mandatory. In such cases, customers should be notified as early as possible and arrangements should be sensitive to customer needs. The Preventative Maintenance Inspection (PMI) Program at the Randall's Island garage, a New York City Department of Parks and Recreation facility, had a 40 percent no-show rate for vehicles scheduled for PMI. After the garage changed its procedures so clients could review maintenance schedules a month in advance, the no-show rate dropped to 5 percent.

## Waiting Time

The queue or waiting line is a commonplace of service operations. Lines exist because it takes time to perform services, customers arrive in bunches and at unpredictable times, and service capacity is costly to maintain. Customer waiting time is a generic problem. An obvious solution—increasing service capacity—is flawed by its costliness. Another option—reducing processing time to complete transactions faster—is more promising. It will be discussed as part of service delivery and again in Chapter 11.

Other ways of reducing waiting time merit consideration. Many were tried by the Bursar's Office at the University of Wisconsin (UW) in Madison, which wanted to lessen student waits for financial aid checks at the start of each semester. It found that some things need not be done in person. The Bursar's Office enabled transactions to be completed by mail or over the phone. To relieve congestion, service activities can be dispersed with different things done at different locations. However, this tactic should not be used if it forces customers to visit multiple service sites. The Bursar's Office tried that approach by setting up satellite payment locations but abandoned it when students objected. Activities can be dispersed in time so that certain transactions are assigned specific time periods to spread demand. Customers needing special services might be instructed to come during off-peak hours. Another way of smoothing demand is to let customers know when things are usually busy and slow. The UW Bursar's Office used the student newspaper to inform students about off-peak hours.

Resources should be freed to handle customer demand during peak load periods. When a quality circle at East Jefferson General Hospital in Metairie, La., tried to reduce processing time for CAT scans, it discovered that equipment maintenance was scheduled for Tuesdays, their busiest day. Changing the service schedule reduced customer waiting time. Employees with other responsibilities can be assigned service roles during peak load periods. Florida Power and Light found that customer payments were not processed quickly enough, especially on Monday mornings, when workers were inundated with mail arriving over the weekend. FPL added a Sunday-to-Thursday shift and adjusted the Monday schedules of four employees so they could help with the mail.

To reduce time needed to greet customers and start the service process, provide workers with advance notice of customer arrivals. A task force at Burger King noted that order takers took several seconds to react after a car drove over the bell hose announcing its arrival. When the hose was moved ten feet back, order takers could respond immediately to customer requests.

Another tactic is to put waiting time to good use. Customers should be triaged as they arrive to insure that they can perform their part in the transaction. Unprepared clients should be identified so as not to waste their time or that of other customers. If possible, correct customer-related deficiencies on site. UW students who forgot to bring their bills to the Bursar's Office were given replacements while waiting in line. Some tasks, such as filling out patient history forms, can be completed while the customer waits to be served. Victory Memorial Hospital in Waukegan, Il., reduced waiting time in its emergency department by having triage nurses initiate tests and other activities before patients were seen by physicians.

## Customer Involvement

Depending on whether the service is high or low contact, customers may be more or less involved in the delivery process. Much involvement is information transfer from customer to service worker, as when a tailor takes measurements for a suit. Customers may be expected to perform activities that could be done for them, such as pumping gasoline or preparing drinks in a hotel room. Some customers like this autonomy, while others prefer full-service. Whether demands on them are light or heavy, customers must be prepared to perform their roles in the service system. Their expectations must be managed, and they must be given information needed to do things right.

Customer involvement in service delivery is an opportunity to determine their needs and to tailor services accordingly. We have noted that customers often enjoy having personal relationships with service workers. In addition to satisfying relational needs, experience with a customer enables a service worker to know the customer's preferences, to correctly interpret customer requests, and to adjust service delivery to suit the person's desire for self-service. All these benefits accrued when the word processing center at Lincoln National changed its procedures so word processors had continuing client relationships.

Since customer involvement is critical for effective delivery, service systems must be designed to help customers do things correctly. Customers must be provided with needed information in an accessible format. Forms to be completed by customers should be easily understood. A redesign of forms filed by Arkansas taxpayers helped the state save $5000 each year in salaries and reduced refund processing time by four weeks. Mistake-proofing techniques should be used to shield customers from frustration and embarrassment. As evident in Case 8.2, service systems that are not user-friendly risk losing sales.

## case 8.2

A large consumer products company equipped a facility for use by internal and external clients conducting focus group research on new products. Central to the facility is a meeting room in which focus group members discuss new products and related consumer needs. The facility includes videotaping equipment used to record group meetings. External clients are required to provide their own videotapes and to operate equipment themselves. During one 18-month period, there were three occasions on which the equipment failed to record a group meeting for external clients, who consequently derived no benefits from their expensive sessions. While clients blamed the equipment for the failures, investigations disclosed that they did not operate the equipment properly and, in one case, used defective recording tape. Nonetheless, the incidents tarnished the facility's reputation, prompting some customers to look elsewhere for such services.

To maintain customer loyalty, service providers must go out of their way to insure that customers have satisfying service experiences. If customers play a critical role in the delivery process, the service system must insure that they can consistently perform their part successfully. This lesson is especially germane with expensive service transactions. It has been taken to heart, for instance, by chartered fishing boat operators, who provide bait, tackle, and anything else needed to help their customers have enjoyable experiences.

## Service Delivery

Service delivery must satisfy both functional and relational needs of customers. Owing to the prevalence of indifferent, even rude, behavior by service workers, the quality literature has focused on relational needs, highlighting the "love factor" in service delivery. Service workers should be more than courteous; they must be empathetic and caring in interactions with customers. At the same time, courtesy is no substitute for competence. Satisfying the customer's functional needs is "job one." No amount of service worker caring will compensate for a restaurant's inedible entrees or recurring, post-repair car breakdowns.

Well-trained, highly motivated service workers are key in satisfying customer needs. Customer contact positions should be staffed with friendly people who like helping others. Service workers should be held accountable for customer satisfaction. Policy-service representatives at USAA, an auto insurance firm, are evaluated by auditors who monitor the quality of phone calls. Overloading workers with peripheral tasks can reduce service quality. A patient satisfaction survey at Meriter Hospital in Madison, Wis., disclosed that the staff of a postpartum unit spent so much time on documentation they could not respond to patient needs.

The other key to effective service delivery is the delivery system. Process design, including processes for delivering services, will be discussed in Chapter 11. Several issues deserve current mention. When transactions are lengthy, service providers should keep customers informed of their status. This principle underlies efforts that freight and overnight delivery companies make to inform customers of the location of shipments. The principle was also in evidence at a hospital that devised a system to keep departments informed as to the status of plant and equipment requisitions. Customers want to know if their orders are progressing.

Service can be delivered by various means. For instance, training and education can be provided in person, through books, or with videotape. As with products, service offerings fall along a continuum, with customization and standardization at the end points. Service delivery systems are often designed to efficiently produce standardized outputs while remaining capable of customization upon request, still able, for instance, to "hold the mustard." Service systems should provide for customers who have minimal needs with services like express checkout lanes. Experienced and empowered service workers make handling problems and exceptions easier and reduce the need for supervisory intervention. When mistakes occur, the customer must quickly be "made right" by redoing the transaction or through a compensatory gesture, such as another meal on the house.

## Completion of Service

Service completion usually occurs simply and naturally. The customer or service worker indicates that the transaction is finished, after which the worker makes payment arrangements and suggests and schedules follow-up activities. Problems with service completion arise under two circumstances. First, when a complex service system is involved, different system components must be advised that a transaction is complete to coordinate their activities. Failure to do so causes delays. By providing its pharmacy with early notice of patient discharges, the University of Michigan Hospital had drug prescriptions ready faster. The Greater Laurel Beltsville Hospital in Maryland developed a multicopy discharge form that notified admitting, the cashier, and the pharmacy of a patient's discharge. Use of the form increased notification rates from 25 percent to 95 percent, improving the accuracy of bed counts and facilitating arrangements for payment.

Service completion can also be problematic if customers do not naturally become aware that their transaction is complete. With low contact services, customers may have to be informed that orders are ready. Notification should be made as soon as possible. Boise Cascade's Timber and Wood Products Division had problems with customer order pickup. Customers were not notified of order completion until the day the lumber was ready and waiting in the mill yard. Customers' trucks had to wait as much as five hours to be loaded, and it took more than three days on average before completed orders were picked up. To correct the situation, Boise forecasted order completion dates a week in advance, making this information available to sales representatives who passed it along to customers. Faxes were automatically sent to certain customers, notifying them that orders were ready.

## Postservice Evaluation

Because no set of specifications exists to assess delivered services, postservice evaluation depends on customer responses. One hopes to learn customers' immediate reactions to the service ("Did you enjoy your stay?") and, for some services, their long-term assessments of quality ("Was the course helpful in your work?"). Especially important are customers' reactions to certain aspects of the service. All service providers want to increase the speed and reliability of their offerings while reducing prices. Equally valuable is discovering which discretionary features of offerings are valued by customers and which ones merely add cost. They would also like to identify new features that increase customer satisfaction.

Most customer evaluations are expressed as complaints or through responses to surveys. Complaints are customer-initiated, but are enabled by service providers. Dissatisfactions may not be expressed because customers do not want to offend service workers or be seen as making a big deal out of a small concern. To overcome this reticence, effective complaint systems are convenient and anonymous. If service workers solicit customer evaluations, they should do so in a positive way. Mechanical "Was everything okay?" solicitations are not effective. Complaints must be evaluated and responses made, perhaps through changes in offerings.

Customer surveys are initiated by service providers. This allows them to be comprehensive, to address areas of special interest to providers, and to provide a balanced view. Surveys offer more than the bad news. Encouraged by the quality movement, many organizations have initiated or expanded their use of surveys to assess customer satisfaction. A small consulting industry has emerged to serve this need.

Customer surveys are valuable sources of information, but since they are not customer-initiated, they may impose on customers' goodwill. Surveys should be conducted in moderation and should make it easy for customers to decline to participate.

# Prescriptions

Unstructured performance problems are among the most challenging situations encountered in organizations. Their diversity and relative lack of structure renders them immune to strong solution methods. Nonetheless, some advice can be offered for dealing with UPPs. The most general recommendation is to carefully analyze the problem. This prescription, elaborated earlier, promotes effective problem solving in many ways. Verifying goal levels prevents attention from being wasted on red herrings. Identifying problem types and structures activates experiential knowledge. Focusing on distinctive features alerts one to potential pitfalls or exploitable opportunities in the situation. Careful diagnosis targets corrective actions on major causes of performance inadequacy.

A second recommendation is negative: Do not attack UPPs with methods intended for more structured problems. This temptation is seductive because problem solvers crave the order that methods provide, and no strong methods are especially applicable to UPPs. One company tried to analyze a selling process using concepts from statistical process control. It discovered that sales were so variable that notions like in-control, out-of-control, common causes, and special causes were not useful in improving the process. UPPs can be addressed with cause-and-effect diagrams, force-field analysis, and other methods, but most of the thinking needed to solve this kind of problem cannot be encapsulated in a technique.

Three other prescriptions are even more pertinent to UPPs:

1. Use incentives to inspire improvement.
2. Develop expertise.
3. Add structure appropriately.

These will be discussed in more detail.

## Use Incentives to Inspire Improvement

*Incentives* is almost a fighting word in TQM, a center of controversy. Deming opposed performance incentives for workers on the grounds that they were unfair and demotivating, discouraged cooperation, and failed to address the causes of poor performance. On the other hand, academic research and practitioner experience indicate that well-designed incentive systems can yield performance improvements. A potent means of addressing UPPs, incentives reflect a push-down strategy: If management cannot solve a problem, it should incent others to do so, especially people familiar with the situation. Incentives spur the thought and attention needed for satisfactory performance.

When Windsor Export Supply, a division of Ford, found that large vans used to ship parts overseas were not being packed efficiently, they added performance incentives to the contract with their packing vendor. This led to significant improvements in van utilization. Incentives can motivate operators to make fewer errors in unstructured activities. Frequent departmental moves within IBM's Kingston, N.Y., facility gave rise to complaints about mistakes by moving contractors. IBM used statistical methods to determine an acceptable number of problems per move. Contractors were advised that they would be dropped from the bidding list if they exceeded this limit more than once. In twenty subsequent moves, problems virtually disappeared.

While incentives can cure UPPs, motivational factors can cause such problems. A case in point:

---

### case 8.3

A company was concerned about the accuracy of estimates buyers used when negotiating prices of purchased goods. The average estimate was more than 14 percent higher than the low bid from suppliers. This high-side bias was traced to the fact that company procedures required engineers to do more follow-up work on underestimates than on overestimates. Engineers avoided extra work by shifting their estimates upward.

---

Everything that goes on in an organization is affected by motivations. Managers must insure that motivations are aligned with effective performance.

## Develop Expertise

This recommendation applies to recurring tasks not specified by procedures—making a sales call, developing advertising copy, interviewing employment candidates. It is a learning strategy, one that determines the best way of accomplishing a task and teaches it to others. Intensive study is used to identify effective practices and task variations requiring variations in practice. Knowledge can be collected through interviews, group discussions, observational studies of task performance, and field experiments that compare different performance methods. As knowledge accumulates, it is organized into training programs.

In one implementation, a top-performing worker in a stocking factory trained others in her techniques. The approach used at the Louis Dreyfuss Distribution Center in Newark, Del., was more sophisticated. An employee who loaded rail cars with more drums than anyone else could not explain his technique. The company videotaped his activities and quickly identified the source of his success. A quality circle of pilots at Hawaiian Airlines noticed that pilots flying the same route used different amounts of fuel. By analyzing verbal reports of pilot behavior during flights, the circle identified fuel efficient flight methods and institutionalized these as standard practices. Fuel savings exceeded $2 million per year.

The expertise approach has been applied in customer support functions. Hewlett-Packard's experience is typical. Finding that support personnel solved the same problems over and over again, albeit for different customers, H-P set up two nationwide response centers, backed by sophisticated communications and computing technology. Now, when a customer calls in with a problem, support personnel retrieve a record of similar problems and how they were solved. Customer support functions are increasingly being served by expert systems that solve all but the most novel problems reported by customers.

## Add Structure Appropriately

A final recommendation follows from its predecessors: When best practices and effective solutions to UPPs have been identified, institutionalize them as standards. Having a tentative "one best way" of conducting at least part of a process is an improvement over personal discretion. The Hawaiian Airlines case illustrates what can be done. The pilots did not devise a complete procedure for flying, but they did establish procedures for parts of the process. Complex performances involve multiple activities, some of which are susceptible to procedures. Discretion granted to operators may exceed the real needs of the task. Tasks involving judgment cannot be fully proceduralized, but specific do's and don'ts can appropriately constrain performance.

In other cases, performance can be improved by establishing procedures for activities that support a core process. The Norand Corporation increased the speed and accuracy of production forecasts by standardizing reporting methods and formats for field sales input and by automatically loading customer order information into the system. With all such efforts, there is a danger of going too far and setting procedures that eliminate discretion needed to produce quality outputs. Thus, this prescription must be applied with care.

### NOTES

1. Harro von Senger, *The Book of Stratagems* (New York: Penguin, 1990).
2. The case is discussed in: Gerald F. Smith, "Heuristic Methods for the Analysis of Managerial Problems," *Omega* 18 (1990): 625–635.
3. Parasuraman, A., V. A. Zeithaml, and L. L. Berry, "A Conceptual Model of Service Quality and its Implications for Future Research," *Journal of Marketing* 49, no. 4 (1985): 41–50.
4. Evert Gummeson, "Truths and Myths in Service Quality," *Journal for Quality and Participation* 14, no. 4 (1991): 28–33.

# Efficiency Problems

---

## Chapter Outline

**Fundamentals**
> Relationship to Other Quality Problems
> Functional Demands

**Methods**
> Cost Reduction Strategies
> Problem Identification
> Eliminating Unnecessary Activities

**Prescriptions**
> Inputs
>> Equipment
>> Materials
>> People
>> Outside Services
>> Energy
>> Capital
>
> Activities
>> Unnecessary Activities
>> Timing of Activities
>> Search
>> Work Methods
>> Process Parameters
>
> Outputs
>> Amount
>> Variety
>> Waste
>> Free Goods

**Worker Safety**

---

Quality problems have traditionally been viewed as situations in which a product or service does not satisfy customer needs. This conceptualization leaves out many problems addressed by quality improvement efforts. A line of personal computers may be appealing to customers in all respects and yet be a persistent source of concern to the manufacturer, which is unable to earn a profit from its sales. Quality improvement programs have taken on issues of worker safety and working conditions, matters that do not involve customer needs. If quality is about satisfying user needs, why do quality improvement activities address situations in which user needs are not at issue?

Adopting a broader, stakeholder view of quality can resolve this anomaly. The stakeholder perspective underlies a category of quality problems termed *efficiency problems*, situations in which a system is not performing acceptably as regards the interests of its owners and operators. End users may be happy with system outputs, but if outputs are produced inefficiently or under hazardous working conditions, these problems must be solved.

In this chapter, the stakeholder perspective on quality is explained as part of defining the nature of efficiency problems. These are compared with other types of quality problems. They are also analyzed in terms of functional demands, the challenges such problems typically pose. The most important subset of efficiency problems—cost and productivity inadequacies—have been addressed by various techniques, discussed in the chapter. This subset is the target of an array of case-based prescriptions, presented in the chapter's longest section. The chapter concludes with a discussion of worker safety.

# Fundamentals

*Quality* is best defined as the goodness or excellence of some thing. It is assessed against accepted standards of merit for such things and in view of the interests of users and other stakeholders.[1] In market economies, the concept usually expresses consumer evaluations of a product's fitness for use. But quality can be ascribed to any entity—air, for instance—not just products for sale. And it can be assessed in terms of various standards and stakeholder perspectives, not just those of consumers. From a producer's perspective, a quality product is profitable in that it can be sold at a price exceeding its cost. This makes cost reduction an integral part of producers' quality improvement efforts. From a worker's perspective, a quality product is produced under safe, comfortable working conditions. These too are goals of quality improvement activity.

This view of quality legitimates the category of efficiency problems. It shifts attention from product users to other stakeholders, notably the producing organization and its workers. Figure 9.1 depicts this focus of attention. As indicated in the diagram, user needs are satisfied by system outputs, but the needs of other stakeholders are not. The most common efficiency problems are those in which production costs are high and/or output volumes are low. The category's name reflects the preponderance of such issues. Worker safety and working conditions are also important and are included in this class of problems.

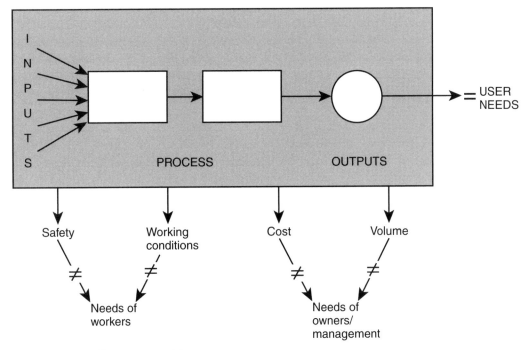

**Figure 9.1** Efficiency problems

## Relationship to Other Quality Problems

Whereas conformance problems involve unsatisfied needs of product users, efficiency problems address interests of other stakeholders. Unstructured performance problems can also reflect the needs of nonconsuming stakeholders, but UPPs are concerned with system effectiveness, not efficiency.

Efficiency and product design problems overlap. Product cost is a primary design consideration. Attempts to lower costs—say, by decreasing the thickness of a metal plate—can be conducted as part of design work or during subsequent cost reduction projects. A technique like value engineering can be viewed as a means of addressing both efficiency and product design problems. Though there is no clear demarcation line, especially regarding material costs, efficiency problems include issues unrelated to product design.

The border between efficiency and process design problems is even less clear. Inefficiencies often result in process redesign. Indeed, any change intended to improve efficiency could be viewed as process redesign. Thus, many topics discussed in this chapter could also be addressed in Chapter 11. In assigning topics between the two chapters, relatively narrow, isolated concerns were regarded as efficiency problems, while more far-reaching shortcomings were viewed as process design issues. For instance, the need to eliminate an unnecessary activity is an efficiency problem; the need to coordinate efforts of individuals or departments falls under process design.

## Functional Demands

In contrast with conformance problems, efficiency problems are rarely identified by talking to customers, who are usually not aware of or concerned with excessive production costs or unsafe working conditions. Employees play a crucial role in problem identification, since they often have firsthand knowledge of undesirable working conditions and inefficiencies. Safety problems are usually discovered in the wake of an accident or near-miss. Because efficiency can always be improved, there is a risk of overidentification and a need to target improvement efforts on activities offering the greatest potential betterment. Thus, goal setting plays a key role in PI. Benchmarking and other standards-development methods can be used to devise appropriate targets for cost and safety performance.

Given well-founded goals, problem definition is generic. This is how we are doing; there is what can reasonably be achieved. What must be done to get from here to there, to reduce costs, increase throughput, or improve safety by the indicated amount? The major definitional task is to develop an understanding of the system rich enough to reveal improvement opportunities when probed.

Diagnosis is the probing. It is different with efficiency problems since one is seeking the location or identity of inefficiencies and safety hazards rather than their causes. Finding significant improvement opportunities may be the critical task in solving efficiency problems. Improvement efforts can become so preoccupied with minor concerns that the big fish go unnoticed. Cost/benefit ratios are often assessed, formally or informally, for this purpose.

The other candidate for most critical task is devising changes that capture efficiencies without incurring offsetting losses. Sure, costs will go down if we use cheaper materials, but product quality might go down as well so we may be worse off than before. Yes, it might be safer to fabricate using this method, but will it take more time? One company tried to reduce the costs of its order-entry process. Orders submitted by sales representatives were validated for correctness. Viewing this validation step as unnecessary, the project team eliminated it. Their "improvement" yielded immediate results: Complaints from customers receiving products they had not ordered. Some gains are easily harvested, the proverbial low hanging fruit. Others entail intensive efforts to keep the system functioning effectively in the face of a proposed change.

Efficiency problems are generic; they will always be with us. Every organization can always strive to reduce its costs. Even low-cost producers who seem to have taken things as far as they can go can find improvement opportunities created by technological advances and changing customer needs.

## Methods

This section and the next focus on cost/productivity improvements, the most common efficiency problems and the category's eponymous core. To understand methods devised for solving such problems, imagine an ideal of perfectly efficient production. What would it be like? Basically, outputs would be produced instantaneously and *ex nihilo*, without inputs. Inputs are costly, so it is always more efficient to use less of them, and the limit of less is zero. Instantaneous production is ideal because of time-related costs. Time used to perform activities is costly and limits system throughput. Time spent by goods as work-in-process represents delays until costs are recovered through sales. Obviously, this ideal is unattainable, except for God, reputedly able to create something out of nothing, but even He needs six days for big jobs. Production activities require time and inputs, which are costly. To reduce costs, reduce the time and inputs used for production. Most techniques employ this strategy to solve efficiency problems.

## Cost Reduction Strategies

Though efficiency techniques start from a common foundation, they extend and operationalize it in different ways:

1. **Identify major cost items.** Locate time-consuming activities and expensive inputs, those offering the greatest potential for improvement.
2. **Reduce the cost of inputs.** Cost is a function of price and usage, either of which can be lowered.
3. **Eliminate activities.** Activities can be unnecessary if they serve no justifiable purpose or excessive if they are performed more than needed.
4. **Reduce errors.** The cost of mistakes includes amounts due to lost materials and wasted activities.
5. **Improve inputs and activities.** Learning and technological developments enable one to do more with less. One can learn from experience or from others.
6. **Reduce variety.** Variety slows activities and makes them more prone to error. It increases procurement costs, equipment maintenance costs, and inventory costs. Variety can be reduced through standardization.
7. **Reduce outputs.** Unnecessary outputs should be eliminated along with unneeded features of valued outputs.
8. **Increase outputs.** Economies of scale favor producing as much as possible, assuming all can be sold. This spreads overhead and reduces costs of unused capacity.

## Problem Identification

During production, many different costs are incurred, any of which could be excessive. Consequently, one challenge in addressing efficiency problems is to identify cost components offering the greatest potential savings. This is a traditional concern of cost accounting, a field that helps managers understand the costs and revenues associated with products and activities. Activity-based costing (ABC), a recent development in this field, is "a technique for accumulating cost for a given cost object that represents the total and true economic resources required or consumed by the object."[2] Another technique, OPTIM, developed at Westinghouse, graphically displays how time and cost accumulate during production, indicating where efficiencies can be realized.[3] Heuristics aid the identification of improvement opportunities: Look for piles of scrap and for idle workers or machines.

## Eliminating Unnecessary Activities

The most popular cost improvement methods seek to eliminate unnecessary activities. This can be done at several levels. On a micro level, one can identify and correct motion inefficiencies by workers performing repetitive tasks. Motion and time study is an industrial engineering technique for this purpose.[4] Of broader scope are methods identifying activities not essential to a process. One heuristic advises process analysts to look for activities that begin with *re*—rework, reposition, rearrange, for instance—viewing these as candidates for elimination. More far-reaching are methods targeting unnecessary tasks. Element analysis, often used in administrative departments, asks employees to record every task performed over a period of weeks. After a complete task inventory has been developed, individual elements are assessed in terms of need and value added.[5]

# Prescriptions

This section uses a framework based on the traditional input-activity-output description of a process to identify suggestions for improving organizational efficiency. The framework is depicted in Figure 9.2. Improvement suggestions organized by the framework have been identified through case analysis. The discussion cites trade-offs to consider in deciding whether an efficiency-seeking change should be made.

## Inputs

*Equipment.*   One common inefficiency is use of obsolete equipment. New equipment can quickly pay for itself through time savings. Time required for preemployment medical exams at an IBM facility was reduced from 74 to 40 minutes by installing new medical equipment. The nonavailability of nurses in a hospital was cured, in part, by switching from mercury to electronic thermometers. This turned a four-minute task into one requiring 40 seconds.

Obsolete equipment can increase waste and materials cost. By collecting data on wastage in a silicon chip cutting process, a division of Phillips Electronics justified

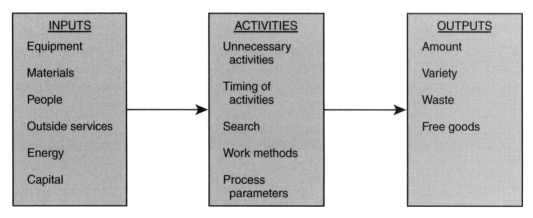

**Figure 9.2**   Cost improvement targets

the purchase of new cutting equipment. The following case illustrates more subtle inefficiencies due to inadequate equipment.

---

■ case **9.1**

International Packings Corporation manufactured a molded part at two plants, one having higher material usage rates. The more efficient plant had a weight specification range of 2.6–2.9 grams for the molding preform. The comparable specification range at the other plant was 2.9–3.3 grams. This specification had been adopted to insure that the molding equipment in the plant, older and less capable than its counterpart, would consistently produce acceptable parts.

---

Process adjustments like this can be made without considering their overall economics. It is possible that IPC's total costs were lower despite the inefficient use of materials, but the company would probably have profited from an equipment upgrade at its less efficient plant. Inaccurate measuring equipment can also yield higher costs. The Space Transportation Systems Division of Rockwell International found that postage expense could be lowered by purchasing a more accurate mail room scale.

Sometimes equipment is inappropriate, mismatched to task requirements. The order processing area of a mail order bookseller was an inefficient mess, with books stacked all over the floor. Workers eventually realized that the fault was with their work tables, which did not have lips to keep books from falling off during processing. Mismatches can occur when a temporary solution is perpetuated past the point of negative economic returns. The Norfolk Naval Shipyard used portable air compressors to service drydock operations. Annual savings exceeding $31,000 were realized when these were replaced by a permanent air compression system.

There may not be enough equipment. This results in bottlenecks, waiting time, and lost production. After documenting time spent by office workers waiting to use a personal computer, Universal Instruments Corporation purchased a second unit and saved $20,000 per year. The test department in a minicomputer manufacturer had a similar problem with long waiting times for users of a high-speed oscilloscope. The company purchased three new machines for $45,000, eliminating waiting time, reducing cycle time by one and one-half days, and achieving a 34 percent annual return on its investment.

Even when there is enough equipment, it may not be available due to inadequate controls. Small items—tools, gauges, and jigs—are prone to this problem because workers hoard them. After learning that one-third of setup time for machinery operations was wasted searching for fixtures and tools, a manufacturer established a central storage area for these items, saving 1700 labor hours per year. Responding to a similar situation in its engineering test area, another firm's technicians created color-coded tools and tool boards, assigning items to work areas. The company published a tool control procedure and had a monitor verify tool replacement at day's end.

Inefficiencies can occur if equipment is not used. A team from Ford investigated why vans used to ship parts overseas were not packed efficiently. It discovered that the packing vendor was not using rack slides Ford had designed to maximize packing volume. With computer systems and other complex devices, equipment capabilities often go unrecognized. The publications department of a software developer had trouble integrating electronic graphics into text material. Department members eventually realized that if artists saved artwork on the computer in a different way, its integration into texts was simple.

Sometimes efficiency can be improved by enhancing equipment capabilities, just as mechanics boost the performance of stock cars. In an aircraft assembly operation, one operator consistently met production quotas while others did not. His secret: He had rebuilt the motor in his power screwdriver. Equipment capabilities can be enhanced by making things portable. Workers at the Norfolk Naval Shipyard lost time shuttling between job sites and the shop to pick up tools. A quality circle designed portable work carts so tools could be moved to job sites in a single trip.

Equipment breakdowns are expensive due to repair/replacement costs and lost production time. Many breakdowns are preventable. In one year, a manufacturer replaced 1600 spindles on hand grinders. A third of the replacements occurred because workers struck locking nuts to loosen them. Giving workers a wrench for locking nut removal and improving spindle quality and design reduced breakage. A Japanese manufacturer had to reshape spotwelder tips after every 300 welds. Observing the operation, Shigeo Shingo noted that the tips were being slammed into parts to insure they did not move. Splitting the two functions—the welder did the welding, a clamp did the holding—extended tip use to more than 10,000 welds.

The decision to use expensive equipment poses a cost-quality trade-off. The age-old fatherly advice, "Only buy good tools," is generally sound. A quality circle at Hewlett-Packard found that workers spent two minutes an hour tightening soldering iron tips. By purchasing better irons, the company eliminated this inefficiency. Realizing that saw blades wore out too quickly, a team in a Ford plant recommended switching to a better blade, saving $14,000 a year and increasing sawing productivity by 800 percent. Sometimes cheaper is better, at least in economic terms. A firm that sews car seats improved efficiency by switching to cheaper, slower sewing machines less prone to breakdown and the throughput of which matched system demand. If inexpensive equipment is good enough, the cost-quality trade-off may favor its purchase.

As noted earlier, variety increases cost. Unneeded equipment variety creates operating and maintenance inefficiencies and adds costs for spare parts inventories. A French chemical supplier used nine models of pH measuring equipment. Significant savings were achieved when this menagerie was reduced to four models from two suppliers.

Efficiency can be improved by redesigning equipment to fit process needs. Workers at Rowntree Mackintosh, the British confectioner, redesigned a funnel used when candy was poured into tubes, reducing fill times by two seconds per tube.

Ingenuity is often displayed in the design of jigs, templates, and fixtures. At Japan Steel Works, a 26 percent reduction in time to assemble large chain links was achieved by developing a device that eliminated use of an overhead crane during assembly. Employees at another firm devised a fixture that improved the process for fabricating copper washers. The output of usable washers, originally 12 per hour, increased to 45.

Although jigs and fixtures are usually fabricated in-house, larger pieces of equipment pose a make vs. buy decision. The make option eliminates unneeded functions and saves idea costs and profits paid to outsiders. A Japanese company built a 300-ton press for $16,000, saving $36,000; it also constructed a $6000 bending machine that would have cost $20,000 if purchased outside. This option is attractive when it poses few challenges to in-house capabilities and when customization is needed. The Coors Brewing Company was wise to custom-make daily planners for employees. These scheduling books featured Coors' accounting schedule, cutoff dates, and other company-specific information. On the other hand, in-house production of equipment can be a distraction from the company's true business. This is why the Dana Corporation includes "Contain investment—buy, don't make" among "40 thoughts" stressed to employees.

**Materials.** Material costs are addressed by value engineering and other product design methods that minimize the amount and unit price of materials in a product. But devising minimal cost design specifications is only the first step toward achieving materials efficiencies. Other improvement opportunities remain. For instance, it may be inefficient to adopt universal, one-size-fits-all design standards if applications pose differing demands. When it realized that national standards for street paving thickness were excessive, given the area's climate and soil type, the city of Phoenix saved $1.2 million annually by using one less inch of pavement in street construction.

Sometimes product specifications are appropriate but materials are wasted because of process parameter settings. An Indian manufacturer of capacitors was losing market share due to stiff price competition. Its production process was set to produce outputs with a capacitance of 81.66, within the product's design range yet well above the target value of 77. Since capacitance is proportional to the amount of aluminum foil in the product, resetting the process at its target value enabled the company to reduce aluminum costs by 10 percent.

A similar situation occurred at Honda's plant in Marysville, Ohio. One paint line used more electrostatic coating pigment than the other. For three years this was explained away as a legitimate difference between lines. After an employee demonstrated that these explanations were spurious, studies verified that one line deposited a thicker layer of pigment on car bodies than the other and that temperature variation was the cause. Installation of an improved temperature control ended the waste of materials.

Materials like paint, glue, and lubricants are applied to a surface during a process. Consumption can be reduced if application is restricted to the area requiring coverage. The surface of stock used in a die-forming process was greased to lubricate it before applying pressure. Observing that lubricant was applied to stock that ended up as scrap, Shigeo Shingo redesigned the system so grease was sprayed from the top and bottom dies, reducing grease consumption by localizing its application. As he pointed out, "Why grease scrap metal?" In a similar case, a rural Japanese manufacturer of fountain pens received complaints from farmers because its process for painting pen caps polluted local water supplies. Noting that most paint went into the air, Shingo refined the process by precisely targeting sprayers and capturing excess pigment. This reduced paint consumption and eliminated the discharge of paint-contaminated water from the plant.

Many processes are inefficient in their use of secondary materials, often ignored by product design methods. Operators at a foundry used excessive amounts of expensive additives until heuristics were developed that identified amounts to be added to each melt. The consumption of machine oil used to cool blades and remove cuttings in machining operations can be reduced by more than 90 percent through magic cutting, spraying a high pressure oil mist to perform these functions.

As with equipment, materials purchasing decisions pose a cost-quality trade-off. Companies can find opportunities to use less expensive materials without compromising product performance. Unfortunately, many opportunities exist to make penny-wise, pound-foolish purchasing decisions. A shoe manufacturer experienced excessive sewing machine downtime because of thread breaks. The shop owner had purchased poor thread at bargain prices. Sometimes what is needed is ingenuity. The molded construction of the AV-8B Harrier, a Naval aircraft, made repairs expensive. A whole wing might have to be purchased for just one part. A team at the Cherry Point Naval Aviation Depot solved the problem by arranging for the manufacturer to ship rejects to Cherry Point, where they could be scavenged for replacement material.

Much excess material cost derives from shrinkage, damage, and spoilage. Shrinkage—material lost on its way through the process—typically reflects inadequate controls. Losses are greatest for materials of middling value, items not costly enough to justify inventory control mechanisms, but too costly to be left for indiscriminate use by employees. The Cherry Point Naval Aviation Depot spent too much on bearings because many people could order them and workers accumulated personal supplies. Breakage losses obviously are most serious for easily damaged materials. The cost reduction keys here are to improve packaging and materials handling practices, eliminating unnecessary handling. A manufacturer of printed wire boards incurred more than $100,000 in annual losses due to damaged materials. By redesigning its production process—using carts instead of tables and keeping materials at working height—the company reduced 16 handlings to 9, saving $18,000 annually in labor costs and $31,000 in scrap.

With perishable materials, spoilage is a concern. To reduce losses of a chilled potting compound that was unusable if its temperature rose above a certain point, a company streamlined and enforced usage procedures. Stock rotation is important, even when material does not seem perishable. A manufacturer's steel supply rusted despite application of a rust preventative. Materials handlers could not use first-in, first-out inventory methods with undated stock. By periodically changing the color of its rust preventative, the company date-stamped its inventory so stock could be rotated.

Beyond reducing costs of materials, efforts must be made to reduce costs that result from materials. Material variety is costly. The engineer who for no good reason consistently specified an unusual alloy in jobs increased his firm's purchasing and inventory management costs. Another example is a hospital, where surgical carts included rarely used supplies needing the same attention as frequently used items. At another manufacturer, a team redesigned a product to use only three screws with one type of head. The result was fewer bins in front of employees, fewer requests to replenish screw supplies, a need for only one powered screwdriver, a less cluttered work area, and shorter assembly time.

Weight of materials creates costs in airplanes and other transportation applications. An analogous loss was incurred during overseas facsimile transmissions of charts at Japan Steel Works' Hiroshima plant. Noting that transmissions took longer and thus were more costly when graph paper was used, clerical workers recommended that drawings be sent on unlined paper. Materials create inefficiencies if they are not tailored to process needs. At St. Agnes Hospital in Fond du Lac, Wis., admission packs were assembled by clerks who tore off sheets from pads of forms. The process was improved by string-wrapping forms so they did not have to be torn off pads.

Some materials pose a make vs. buy decision, and trade-offs are the same as for equipment. The Norfolk Naval Shipyard saved $6420 a year by fabricating wiper blades, an expensive item that was of low quality when purchased externally. Like equipment, materials can pose replace vs. repair decisions. The high cost of repairs, coupled with a throwaway culture, predisposes many toward replacement. Economics often favor repair. Army regulations listed Vulcan radomes as nonrepairable items to be replaced at $200 each in the event of hairline cracks on surfaces. After mechanics devised an effective repair procedure costing under $15 per unit, the regulation was changed, saving thousands of dollars annually.

***People.*** An obvious way to reduce labor costs is to reduce staffing levels. Downsizing reflects the following logic: Withdrawing a worker from each unit forces remaining people to work harder to keep up, so these people discover more efficient ways of performing tasks. This presumes that workers are motivated to keep up and that they can identify efficiencies. The remaining workers may feel overstressed and exploited and divest themselves of responsibility for meeting output goals. In those situations downsizing can be counterproductive. It is most likely to be beneficial if it reflects an analysis of system requirements. The Radiology Department at Mount Sinai Medical Center maintained a staff of transporters, people who used wheelchairs and stretchers to move patients around the facility. Demand for transporters was unpredictable, but by using historical data to develop a simulation model, the department reduced their number by two FTEs, realizing $30,000 in annual savings. The same analytical approach can be applied on a larger scale to achieve significant savings that are relatively undiluted by offsetting performance losses.

Traditional means of improving worker efficiency focus on personnel selection and training. Hire the right people for the job, people with the required knowledge, abilities, and attitudes. The Paul Revere Insurance Company saved $24,000 a year by rehiring its retirees to replace short-term workers contracted through temporary agencies. Training can cure knowledge and skill deficits. After receiving technical training, employees involved in a company's new product development process could develop and analyze proposals more quickly.

Tasks should be assigned to the lowest paid, but still qualified, people. The equivalent of using cheaper equipment or materials, this practice has comparable risks: Performance may suffer at the hands of the less skilled. The risk is manageable, and most workers perform some tasks that could be assigned to less well-paid coworkers. After studying skill requirements for engineering jobs, Westinghouse saved money by increasing technician head count and reducing engineer head count. A hospital reassigned the time-consuming prescription refill task from overburdened nurses to nonclinically trained staff members. Another hospital established a nurse's helper position, arranging for related classes to be taught at a local technical school. The cheapest workers are volunteers who work for free. Nonprofit organizations often use this resource.

Using inexpensive workers blends into another means of improving productivity: Provide support personnel. This insures that people spend their time doing the jobs they do best. At the Norfolk Naval Shipyard, high-paid mechanics lost time shuttling from waterfront work sites to pick up materials. The shipyard saved $53,000 a year by assigning a permanent employee to pick up and deliver materials to the waterfront. The Tennant Company devised a pull sheet listing tools needed for each job in production. Attendants pulled required tools from the tool crib, delivering them to operators' work stations when needed. The risk with this prescription is that the people being supported may not increase their output. The relatively easy tasks they were relieved of may have provided respite from core job demands.

A related strategy is to make operators self-sufficient, capable of performing incidental tasks that would otherwise require assistance. By training and empowering checkout personnel to authorize customer checks, supermarkets reduce customer waiting time and increase productivity. A computer system at the Cherry Point Naval Aviation Depot enabled artisans to order parts and speed up the process. Machine jam-ups at a Firestone Tire and Rubber plant resulted in 20- minute waits for maintenance personnel, until fasteners were changed so operators could remove cover plates and clear jam-ups themselves. A sawmill changed job classifications so equipment operators could oil and maintain machines, a standard practice in Japanese companies.

***Outside Services.*** Corporations increasingly use outside contractors to perform functions—such as information services, market research, and mailroom operations—previously performed internally. Contractors may have lower costs and more expertise than their customers. Outsourcing can achieve economies, but the practice deserves cost reduction attention. Standard economizing strategies are appropriate: Use low-cost providers for the required level of service quality. Negotiate lower rates by buying in bulk. In 1987, the Colonial Penn Insurance Company recruited workers from 23 temporary help agencies. In 1988, by negotiating a contract with a sole source supplier, the company reduced temporary help costs by a third, saving $458,000. Do not purchase unneeded services. Overnight delivery companies make a killing off people who absolutely, positively should have done the job in time to use regular mail. An office worker at Toyota found that special delivery mail often arrived no faster than regular mail, prompting a change in company practices.

One danger of outsourcing is the out of sight, out of mind trap. Because managers only see monthly bills—no people asking for raises, no requests for equipment—it is easy to forget about service costs and to overlook changes in supplier rates and offerings. The Paul Revere Insurance Company's practice of maintaining a zero balance in its many small checking accounts was a sound policy at one time. But after banks changed their terms in a way that favored maintaining defined minimum balances, the company's policy should have been revised. It was not, until an employee brought the issue to management's attention. Paul Revere had been losing $5000 a year by not keeping up-to-date with service terms offered by these providers.

It is also costly to adopt a broad-brush approach of letting someone else do it. Organizations should identify what outside providers have to offer and consider how responsibilities are best allocated between internal and external units. The New York State Cooperative Extension Service reduced postage costs by switching from standard mailings to a pouch system in which it consolidates weekly shipments for county and regional locations around the state and ships them via UPS. A manufacturer arranged to make drawings for its forging vendor to reduce their lead time. Helping one's suppliers be more efficient is a way of helping oneself.

The key to analyzing service outsourcing options is the same as make vs. buy decisions for materials and equipment: Who can do it cheapest and best? Special considerations—for instance, maintaining in-house capabilities—can be decisive. Another question is whether outside providers can deliver on their promises. Finding that its impeller balancing operation was more capable than those of suppliers, the Tennant Company brought the task in-house. After hiring an outside service to audit and pay its freight bills, Windsor Export Supply experienced an increase in late payments and carrier disputes. Though the contractor was capable, handoffs and logistical complications made it hard to perform the task externally. High transaction costs favor doing it yourself. Sometimes it is easier to keep your own calendar and do your own typing.

*Energy.* Since the oil price increases of the 1970s, energy consumption has been a prime target of cost reduction efforts by individuals and organizations. Substantial improvements have been achieved, but more can be done. Organizational efforts to conserve energy parallel those of individuals. The standard repertoire includes adding insulation to buildings and machinery, turning off lights, turning down thermostats, and eliminating and consolidating activities. Consumers save by purchasing energy-efficient automobiles and appliances; manufacturers save by using the most efficient equipment for the job. An Indian spinning mill used two different motors to power spinning frames. Finding that the smaller motor was more efficient, the company reduced power consumption 17 percent by only using these. Consumers have learned that tune-ups improve the fuel efficiency of their cars; companies rely on equipment maintenance to save energy. A Ford team fixed leaks in compressed air tanks to reduce power consumption.

Process analysis and the coordination of activities can save energy. At Century Rayon, an Indian textile manufacturer, twister cablers used to twist strands of yarn into a cord were the major power consuming machinery. An analysis of the twisting process revealed that power consumption was due to yarn tension, resulting in part from the weight of the traveler. Switching to a lighter traveler reduced power consumption by 23 percent in one twister and by 7 percent in another. Better planning of ladle heating time in a foundry to coordinate with planned pours also yielded energy savings.

Target energy applications so a minimum is employed. This is the principle behind using a reading lamp rather than an overhead light when working at one's desk. A Japanese firm reduced electricity consumption more than 30 percent by having individual controls for the 2000 fluorescent lights in a plant and by exhorting workers to turn off lights. Activities with energy implications should be scaled to minimize losses. A facility at the Norfolk Naval Shipyard lost heat when an overhead cargo door was opened to let people in and out of the building. By installing a smaller door for personnel, these losses were curtailed. The doors-within-doors on refrigerators are analogous.

Finally, challenge assumptions about energy requirements and update policies to reflect current costs. At a Nissan Chemical plant, thousands of high-voltage motors were constantly kept running with a low-level current to maintain insulator resistance. A team determined that an intermittent current would serve the same purpose and reduce annual electrical costs by $15,000. A Komatsu plant reduced power consumption 22 percent by shortening cycle time in a heat-treating operation. Another company heated soya bean oil in 12 and 15 ton vats to an operating temperature range of 110°C to 120°C. The 10° range had been established years earlier when energy was cheap. By lowering the range to 2° (110°C–112°C), the company reduced energy costs without affecting the process.

*Capital.* Capital costs are an oft overlooked source of savings. For many, contends Richardson, "capital is a costless 'free good' provided by senior management, and there is little incentive to reduce spending in this area."[6] Inventory and receivables draw management attention in most companies; other forms of capital do not. Case 3.3, about the Denver bank that unnecessarily kept $5.5 million in its vault overnight, is not atypical of capital management practices in some organizations.

One principle of capital cost reduction is centralization. Less capital is needed to maintain a centralized resource, be it inventory, equipment, or cash, than to maintain multiple units or stocks. Process requirements can make decentralization more economical overall, but do not assume automatically that decentralization serves legitimate process needs. Workers can do without the tools and parts accumulated in private hoards. Hitachi Denshi saved money by collecting office supplies employees had stashed away in work areas.

Like workforce, inventory can be downsized by fiat. The risk is that items will not be available to satisfy process or customer needs. Reductions should be based on careful analysis. Alpha Industries reduced inventory levels after developing better information regarding part lead times, reorder points, and reorder quantities. Another company used statistical methods to determine expected transit times for auto parts shipped from factories to customers across the country. This enabled reduction in inventory at field locations.

One inventory reduction strategy, applicable with products processed at various points in the value chain connecting ultimate suppliers with final customers, is to maintain inventory at the point in the value chain where product variety is least. Benetton dyes garments as the last step in its manufacturing process. In this way, the variegation of products into color groups can be matched to current demand for each color. Maintaining a single inventory of undyed sweaters is less costly than maintaining separate inventories for each color. A carpet manufacturer uses the same strategy, maintaining inventory at the value chain point with the fewest stock numbers.

Inefficient use of capital often shows up as excess capacity. A company has acquired more plant, equipment, personnel, and other resources than it can productively employ. Unused capacity can result from size mismatches in chunks of purchasable capacity. Though output requirements are 100 units per day, a task can only be performed by machines with a 70-unit daily capacity. To avoid underproduction, the company buys two units, accepting the excess capacity of 40 units. The company may find ways to put this capacity to work. An Indian manufacturer developed a jig so an underutilized lathe could be used for boring. The company achieved a 64 percent throughput increase in what had been a process bottleneck. Public works employees of the city of Herndon, Va., switched from a five-day to a four-day work schedule so refuse collection trucks could be used to collect recyclables.

Another inefficiency derives from one-sided activities, typically involving movement. One must transport something from Point A to Point B, but has nothing productive to do on the return trip. Honda formed Honda International Trading Company to increase backhauling on ships returning to Japan after delivering Honda products to the United States. On a smaller scale, a Japanese manufacturer redesigned a planer so it could cut on the return cycle. No longer "cutting the air," the machine's efficiency increased by 85 percent.

Efforts to employ excess capacity are vulnerable to "tail wagging the dog" mistakes. Companies in seasonal industries diversify into counterseasonal businesses, hoping to exploit off-season idle capacity. Many firms have suffered financial losses while learning that their idle capacity offered little competitive advantage in industries they did not understand. A similar mistake can be made by nondiversifying firms, as illustrated in Goldratt's book, *The Goal*.[7] Efficiency-minded managers put unused people and machines to work manufacturing products the company could not sell. Resource utilization rates go up, as do inventory carrying costs, the latter with greater bottom line impact.

## Activities

***Unnecessary Activities.*** Eliminating unnecessary activities is the cornerstone of most efficiency programs, but simply prescribing that such activities be eliminated is of little value. People need help identifying unnecessary activities, recognizing potential downsides of their elimination, and devising reductions that avoid adverse consequences. Figure 9.3 specifies the kinds of activities improvement efforts should focus on. It outlines the discussion that follows.

Activities creating products that no one uses should be eliminated. Such deletions offer pure cost savings undiminished by offsetting losses. For two years, a clerk

| General Activity | Specific Manifestations | Corrective Response |
|---|---|---|
| Activities creating products no one uses | Unneeded internal reports; unneeded product features | Discontinue; see if anyone complains |
| Inefficient information gathering | Unneeded information; duplicate information | Purge; use efficient collection methods |
| Unnecessary controls and authorizations | Obsolete requirements; false assumptions; trivial transactions; inconsistent requirements | Empower employees; audit periodically; eliminate activities that are not cost-justified |
| Unnecessary process monitoring and job tracking | Internal "CYA" requirements; frequent customer inquiries; thrashing | Discontinue; give customers direct access to information |
| Unnecessary testing and inspections | Obsolete requirements; improperly assigned tests; redundant tests | Upgrade process capability; discontinue tests that rarely find errors |
| Unnecessary motions | Lifting and lowering; excessive distance between tasks; inefficient process routing | Relocate activities; use carts; perform tasks on-site; integrate into natural work motion |
| Activities with reusable outputs | Repetitive information activities | Develop templates |
| Scrap removal | Activities that create waste | Localize, minimize, or eliminate waste |
| Activities that compensate for process inadequacies | Rework; extra activities | Eliminate mistakes; redesign and improve the process |
| Activities that must later be undone | Temporary results; "undoing" activities | Minimize; use methods that are easily undone |
| Activities initiated in response to one-time needs | No current rationale for activity | Discontinue |
| Activities that protect against rare events | Events have never occurred | Discontinue unless consequences are severe |
| Activities only needed in some cases | Overgeneralized performance of task | Restrict to appropriate cases; use cost-saving defaults |
| Oversized activities | Unnecessary subtasks | Eliminate excess; classification of characteristics |
| Overly frequent materials handling activities | Frequent replenishment or removal of materials | Add storage capacity |

**Figure 9.3** Unnecessary activities

at Toyota transcribed receiving slips and payment vouchers into a notebook. No one had ever asked to see the notebook and the original documents were available if needed. The worker saved 20 hours a month by discontinuing the activity. Since customers will not pay for something they do not need, the products most vulnerable to this pitfall are informational materials created for internal users. A regional office of an insurance company had long produced a series of reports, sending them to the home office where they were routinely filed and never used. Products or product features sold as part of a package should be evaluated; they may be parasitic, "free riding" on customers' needs for other parts of the offering. One way of finding out whether a product or activity can be eliminated is to discontinue it and see if anyone complains.

Even when useful products result, information gathering is often inefficient. Some information may not be needed at all, or it may have already been acquired. A quality circle in a hospital found that it took 25 minutes to prepare patient paperwork, largely because of duplication among reports. Redundancy can result from multiple organizational information systems when different departments maintain files concerning the same customers and transactions. Redundancies can be reduced by data management software. Acquire information by the most efficient means. Rather than order takers typing in customer information, a mail order company uses Caller Identification, a phone service feature, to strip information from incoming calls, automatically identifying callers from a customer list.

Excessive controls and authorizations drain process efficiency. Many companies persist in a controlling mind frame based on negative assumptions about employees. Controls can be enforced out of habit, after changes have made them obsolete. Florida Power and Light's accounting department sent checks for library vendors to the FPL library, which forwarded them to vendors. This added days to the payment cycle, prompting vendor complaints. The library had once recorded check numbers and mailing data. Changes in FPL's accounting system had long since made this unnecessary, but the check routing had never been revised. Some controls are established under mistaken assumptions. The employee separation process at the U.S. Bureau of Labor Statistics was prolonged by the need for signatures of two high-level managers, until the bureau learned that neither statutory nor administrative requirements mandated those signatures.

Some transactions are not significant enough to justify the costs of traditional controls. Take customer claims regarding shipments, for instance. Boise Cascade found that 83 percent of customer claims accounted for only one-third of total settlement costs. Most claims were too small to warrant Boise's intensive claims handling process. Boise streamlined procedures for handling small claims. Many firms follow Deming's advice: Pay small claims without question, but post-audit a sample of them.

Controls can be inconsistent, imposing tighter restrictions on low risks than on high ones. At one company, Finance department approval was required on any overhead expenditure, despite the fact that the same purchases could be made from petty cash without approval. Controls and authorizations should be assessed in cost/benefit terms: What do controls cost in terms of efficiency? Are these costs justified by prospective losses that controls plausibly prevent? Assessments often conclude that incurred inefficiencies are substantial, while potential losses are ephemeral. To determine if risks are real, relax controls temporarily. If the VP does not review these expenditures, do her subordinates abuse their autonomy?

A general antidote for excessive authorizations and controls is empowerment, delegating responsibility to employees. Dun and Bradstreet simplified its customer contracting process by allowing staff to approve contracts up to $5000. If approvals are needed, there are ways to lower their costs. An improvement team reduced the time needed for alteration notices to reach suppliers by requiring electronic sign-offs and colocating internal support activities to enhance coordination. After a study showed that a supervisor at Miles Laboratories made few revisions to the work of subordinates, his review was replaced with a periodic audit.

Unnecessary process monitoring and job tracking is another inefficiency. Excesses can result from intraorganizational factors, such as bickering among departments about who is responsible for delays, or can be a response to incessant customer inquiries, creating a thrashing effect: The more time spent answering questions about a job, the less time there is left to do it. By developing a system that made order processing data available to its sales department, which passed information along to customers, a Boise Cascade mill reduced time spent responding to customer requests for order information. The manufacturing department in another company was inundated with phoned requests to expedite orders, change orders, and provide order status reports. Once the company gave field offices read-only access to computer-based production control data, field-to-manufacturing phone calls declined by 80 percent. Reduce job tracking costs by giving customers easy access to job status information. Time spent handling inquiries can be used to get jobs out, so fewer customers will inquire about orders.

Testing and inspection are conceptually similar to authorizations. They are non–value-adding activities included in a process to protect against rare, but costly, events. The same cost-benefit trade-off applies when evaluating these activities. Since costs of shipping bad product to customers are substantial, the key consideration is the likelihood of doing so. Do tests and inspections turn up errors? If not, unless externally mandated or if an undetected error would be catastrophic, discontinue them. Every 30 minutes, Warner-Lambert conducted a battery of chemical tests on a product. Reviewing a year's worth of data, analysts concluded that hardness was the only troublesome product characteristic. Since hardness was checked elsewhere in the process, test frequency was reduced to four times daily.

Activities can persist even after they have been shown as unnecessary. Though a study demonstrated that maintenance inspection was not required for a part on a naval aircraft, the procedures manual was not updated and time continued to be spent on the unneeded task. One way to eliminate tests and inspections is to upgrade process capability. An ITT wire harness assembly operation included a destructive pull test costing the company $300,000 per year. By optimizing the process so weld splice strength exceeded the wire core strength, ITT could discontinue the pull test.

Be sure that required tests and inspections are properly located. It took 13 days to process incoming goods at the Tobyhanna Army Depot, largely because QC personnel were not always available to conduct inspections. Processing times dropped to one or two days when revised procedures allowed receiving inspections to be conducted by user departments, more qualified to decide if goods were acceptable.

Eliminate redundant tests and inspections. It may be necessary to inspect a product at multiple points in a process, but it is rarely wise to conduct back-to-back inspections on products with no interim processing. Doing so courts the "second checker" phenomenon: Each inspector relaxes, assuming the other will catch mistakes.

Shigeo Shingo noted that time is the shadow of motion.[8] To reduce time needed to perform a task, eliminate unnecessary motions. These range from macro—walking from one work station to another—to micro—positioning things so an operation can be performed. One heuristic is to keep items at working height as they flow through the process. Move materials on carts instead of pallets. Workers at Fasco Industries in Cassville, Mo., redesigned a process so parts trays did not have to be lifted from a conveyor to a welding station. The new process, in which trays flowed through the station, saved the company $55,000 a year and the backs of its employees. Personnel should also be kept at a constant height, rather than having to go up and down steps. A worker at Komatsu's Awazu Works wore herself out walking up and down steps between two machines more than 800 times a day. The company extended the floor, putting both machines on the same level. To minimize walking, L. L. Bean locates high-volume merchandise close to packing stations. Improvement teams at an insurance company moved filing cabinets closer to people who use them most.

Simplify the routing of items flowing through a process. An operation that repaired drums was simplified by having an assembler make needed repairs himself rather than transferring defective drums to another work station. Performing tasks on-site reduces routing. At the Cherry Point Naval Aviation Depot, a team implemented a program for reworking components close to aircraft, reducing routing, materials handling, and consequent damage and delays. Shingo reported several inventive means by which he economized on worker motion, including the following:

---

**case 9.2**

In a cut-tobacco packaging operation, glue was applied to packaging paper before it was sealed. When five sealed packages had accumulated, they were placed on a conveyor. Shingo proposed that each package be placed on a chute to the conveyor as soon as it was sealed, but the plant manager objected that the glue would not yet be dry. Shingo then recommended that each package be placed in a row leading to the chute. The row would hold five packages, allowing them to dry. When the sixth and subsequent packages were added, each would push the lead package down the chute to the conveyor.

---

This solution builds a queue of in-process work, allowing operators to move dry packages down the chute through their natural work motion.

Many jobs involving informational activities produce reusable outputs: A spreadsheet program developed for one task can be applied with modifications to others. Reuse offers economies. A division of the Beloit Corporation saved

$123,000 a year by developing a library of standard shapes for its CAD system. Inspectors for the city of Dallas used partially completed, machine-copied notices of violation, rather than writing notices from scratch for each case. Review processes to identify repetitions that can be eliminated in this way.

Scrap is a by-product of production; scrap removal is a non–value-adding task that can seem like a necessary evil. Evil, yes; necessary, maybe not. Scrap removal can be eliminated if waste is self-disposing. Or a company can make waste localized, minimized, or nonexistent. A machine operator in a Japanese firm spent too much time detaching metal chips, so a quality circle found a bit that made chips break off themselves. A molding operation was revised so sprue and flash were automatically removed from molded products. Another company maintained mold faces so they mated better and produced no flash. Sometimes the trick is to eliminate the problem without eliminating the waste. After cutting a part, a worker had to smooth rough edges, removing scrap that prevented proper positioning for the next operation. By making a gutter on the guide board to allow positioning despite rough edges, the factory reduced cycle time from 34 to 17 minutes.

Some activities compensate for process inadequacies. Improving the process eliminates these activities. The best-known situations of this kind involve rework: Correcting mistakes adds costs. Ford uses paint repair ovens to fix chips and scratches occurring during assembly. Fully trimmed vehicles are heated to temperatures exceeding 240° F. After learning that oven-processed vehicles had poor customer repair records, Ford undertook an extensive campaign to reduce the incidence of paint defects. Eliminate corrective activities by eliminating the mistakes that require them.

There are other process inadequacies. An activity may not do its job properly so additional work is needed. Operators at a Warner-Lambert plant devised complex blends of sublots of a material before drying to attain the desired bulk density. As it turned out, substantial variation across dryers was well documented in available data but had never prompted dryer adjustments or repairs. Once the dryers were fixed, there was no need to blend sublots of material. Adding an operation early in a process can eliminate a need for corrective action downstream. At Ford's Windsor Engine Plant #2, parts run through a washing unit rusted and had to be derusted. After a heated blow-off was installed on the washer to dry the parts, derusting was no longer necessary.

Some activities produce temporary results that must later be undone, such as a carpenter nailing in a 2 × 4 as a stopgap support. Ideally, one could dispense with temporary fixes and the consequent need to undo them. At a minimum, such tasks should be performed in a way that eases their reversal, as when carpenters use easily removed, double-headed nails. A quality circle at Bank of America improved a document handling process by insuring that staples were not used to hold documents together in temporary batches. A circle at Komatsu improved the process for painting dump trucks. Economies were achieved by removing, instead of covering, parts that were not to be painted, by making it easier to mask parts that could not be removed, and by delaying until after painting the installation of parts that could be attached later. In four months, the hours required for masking were reduced to 69 percent and the hours required for painting were reduced to 94 percent of previous averages.

Unnecessary activities accumulate as the residue of a system's history. Processing steps are initiated in response to one-time needs, but never discontinued. A company reacts to a past problem that never again poses a threat. While trying to improve the patient registration process, a team at the University of Colorado School of Medicine found that three versions of a patient health history questionnaire were being used. The standard questionnaire had been revised into three variations as part of a long-forgotten experiment, but no one had ever changed back. Activities can be performed to protect against rare events that might never happen. A Toyota worker, responsible for handling suggestions submitted by employees, had to date and time-stamp more than 2000 suggestions each month. This was done to protect against the possibility that the same idea would be submitted simultaneously by more than one employee. But this had never happened. Toyota saved eight hours a month by discontinuing stamping. Do not perform an activity to protect against a rare event unless the event's consequences are serious enough to justify related costs.

Some activities are needed, but not always. Reduce costs by restricting activities to appropriate cases. Responding to a problem with brushes in floor cleaning products that became unbalanced and vibrated, the Tennant Company added a brush balancing step to its production process. The company subsequently saved $56,000 by discontinuing the balancing of sweeper brushes, which never became unbalanced, and only balancing scrubbing machines that needed adjustment. The state of Colorado saved $60,000 a year by restricting the mailing of delinquency notices for late child support payments to the 1 percent of cases that truly needed the prompt. Dun and Bradstreet saved millions by switching from an annual contract renewal cycle with customers to an arrangement in which contracts were renewed automatically but could be terminated by customers at any time.

The D&B case illustrates the use of cost-saving defaults, a device employed by a firm that changed the credit review step in its order fulfillment process. Under the new policy, orders from regular customers are processed without a credit check, but these customers' credit standings are periodically reviewed. This also demonstrates how economies can be achieved by replacing constant monitoring with periodic audits.

Another possibility is to reduce the scope of an activity instead of performing it less often. A company learned serendipitously that the sludge treatment tank for a grinder worked best when filled to the three-fifths level. Hours were saved in tank filling and disposal time by changing to the lower water level. The typical Navy purchase order has 67 characters of identifying code, of which only seven are needed. Hours of data entry can be saved by shortening such items. Eliminate unneeded subtasks. Classification of characteristics eliminates inspection of unimportant attributes. One company saved $10,000 a year by discontinuing receiving inspections of the 38 percent of dimensions classified as of minor significance. Ford lightened the vehicle inspection load on dealers by reducing the list of items required for annotation on bills of lading from over 100 to just 18.

A final kind of unnecessary activity is materials handling conducted too frequently because of volume limitations. Imagine the time wasted if your car's fuel tank only held two gallons. When the Norfolk Naval Shipyard had a problem with oilers lacking the capacity required for daily oiling operations, it increased storage rack capacity to improve efficiency. By purchasing a compactor, the shipyard increased the capacity of trash removal operations, reducing the frequency of fork-lift and freight elevator utilization. An Indian textile mill increased loom shed efficiency by 6 percent by using larger capacity pirns, so looms could run longer between material replenishments.

*Timing of Activities.* Some inefficiencies result from the timing of activities, so that rescheduling results in savings. The most common of these situations involve peak load effects: Process performance is degraded because demand during certain periods exceeds capacity. If the company itself creates peak loads, reschedule activities to spread the load. Honeywell Information Systems in Lawrence, Mass., experienced loading dock delays because outgoing orders reached the freight elevator at the same time. Devising an elevator schedule resolved the problem. At Storage Technology Corporation, an informal tradition that made Friday the shipping day created untold hassles and mistakes, until the company arranged for European orders to ship on Wednesdays.

Peak load periods can be created by the natural timing of customer demand. One way of reducing consequent inefficiency is preprocessing, performing some activities during off-load hours. The Bursar's Office at the University of Wisconsin reduced waiting lines at the start of semesters by having students sign promissory notes early so they would not have to do so during the rush period. Another tactic is to reschedule discretionary activities not needed to service customer demand.

Inefficiencies can occur because of scheduling difficulties with time-sensitive or costly activities. Patients at a hospital complained that their food was cold by the time they got it. A project team found that nurses were often busy when food trays arrived. Rescheduling reduced the delay between receipt of food trays at the unit to their delivery at bedside from 13 to 5 minutes. Slow operating room turnaround at West Paces Ferry Hospital in Atlanta was improved by performing patient tests before the day of an operation. Preadmitting patients for tests helped the hospital increase the utilization rate of operating rooms.

Other timing-related inefficiencies derive from activity sequencing, in which the ordering of tasks may not be appropriate. At Decision Data Computer Corporation, changes in the ordering of assembly tasks for PC boards yielded processing time reductions of 2.5 minutes per board and production cost savings of $35,000. The internal customers of an insurance company's word processing center began dictation with information about the number of copies required. This makes sense if carbon copies are being produced, but that was not the case here. By having customers hold instructions regarding copies until the end of dictation, the center saved 30 seconds per letter. Automobile manufacturers traditionally mounted doors near the start of the final assembly line, before interior trim and fittings were installed. As a result, doors were constantly opened and closed to work on interiors, and parts racks had to be located further from lines to accommodate open doors. Some manufacturers now hang doors at the end of the assembly process or remove them during final assembly.

*Search.* Search, looking for things or information, is part of many processes but is often performed inefficiently. Search time and cost increase with the number of things one must look through to find the desired item. Accordingly, one principle of efficient search is to minimize the size of the search space. This principle was violated at Windsor Export Supply, a division of Ford, where a daily report of part numbers critical to the operations of overseas affiliates included hundreds of items, only 20 percent of which were truly critical. MIS reports and other information sources often include everything that could possibly matter, ignoring search costs.

Search efficiency can be compromised by a poorly organized search space. The large Coors plant in Golden, Colo., had excessive mail delivery costs because its mail stop numbering system lacked a rationale. One principle of organization is to segregate items on a usage basis, separating high and low volume items. To reduce search time, a Bank of America branch segregated open and closed account files. A quality circle at Westinghouse developed a 4-by-8-foot material identification chart so workers did not have to thumb through manuals to find out which solder, epoxy, or other material to use on a job. Finally, information needed for search must be readily available. Coors' employees did not know who to contact for in-house services until the company developed a directory listing 500 such services.

*Work Methods.* Work methods are a traditional target of cost reduction efforts, mainly through time and motion studies. In addition to economizing worker motions, such studies identify and correct activities that are physically demanding or disagreeable, require an unnatural posture, or call for great attention to detail. Other approaches merit attention as well. Use all of an activity, maximizing the output it can produce. Stacking gears on a jig to use the full stroke of a cutting machine helped a Japanese manufacturer increase output by 30 percent. Teaching and other information dissemination tasks are efficiently performed *en masse,* to a classroom of students rather than to individual learners. A banker was frustrated at having to spend hours with each person seeking a small business loan to explain the process, the bank's requirements, and business plan preparation. More efficient is the approach of providing applicants with printed materials and referring them to classes where they can acquire information as part of a group.

Even good rules have exceptions. Trying to get more out of each activity can be counterproductive. Sometimes less is more. In a factory, a hole-drilling operation was performed manually, since a worker could do the job in 20 seconds whereas a machine took 30. But machines only cost $1000. Having one operator run two machines increased productivity by 33 percent. An apparent sacrifice in processing speed improved efficiency.

Another principle is to use the most efficient method to perform each task. Large holes are more easily created by sawing than by drilling, since less material has to be removed. An Indian company found it easier to weigh out bromide paper sheets for customers than to count them. Weighing took one-fourth the time and was as accurate. Case 9.3 makes a similar point.

A related mistake is to use a standard method on a task that could be performed more efficiently by a less familiar approach. Psychologists call this **functional fixedness.** We stick with tried-and-true ways of doing things even though other methods could improve performance. For example, strict security measures govern maintenance work performed on presidential aircraft. When a fuel control component for such an aircraft was worked on at the Cherry Point Naval Aviation Depot, the item was locked in a cabinet in the "Clean Room" before lunch and again at night. The

---

■ case *9.3*

A machine tool manufacturer had a bottleneck in its polishing operation. Since six polishing machines running overtime could not keep up with the work, the company prepared to purchase a seventh. Shigeo Shingo observed that a milling operation, which preceded polishing, was leaving between 0.6 mm and 0.9 mm of material to be polished down. He noted that the milling operation had a 0.09 mm process capability. By having the milling machine remove more stock, polishing could be completed with fewer passes. Four of the six machines were no longer needed. The company had used the polishing operation to remove stock that should have been removed by milling.

---

component had to be dismantled and its parts inventoried each time this was done. This costly procedure was discontinued when people realized that security requirements would be satisfied by merely locking the Clean Room door any time the component was left unattended.

***Process Parameters.*** Every process is characterized by parameters denoting aspects of inputs, outputs, and activities. The most important are control variables that can be manipulated to achieve desired results. The level of process output is a control variable normally set to match product demand. Other parameters are adjusted in view of the output level and to achieve desired quality levels. Parameters can also be set to reduce costs.

Setting parameters involves trade-offs. Notwithstanding the truth in the claim that "quality is free," often it is not. Achieving defect-free products may reduce output levels, and it can cost more to use higher-quality ingredients in a product. The cost-quality trade-off must be managed intelligently. The trade-off was apparent in the waste extraction process at an Indian spinning mill. By extracting more foreign matter and short fibres from cotton, a mill can improve yarn strength and appearance, but at a cost in lost fibre and lower processing speed. This mill experimented to see if different waste extraction rates affected yarn quality. When no differences were observed in outputs, the mill adopted the most economical rate.

Another trade-off is between speed and accuracy. The faster a process runs, the more mistakes are made. When airlines implement tighter schedules with less layover time between connecting flights, incidents of lost baggage and missed customer connections increase. The spinning mill also faced a speed-accuracy trade-off: By increasing spindle speeds on frames processing yarn, it could increase output up to the point where gains are offset by losses due to yarn breakage and downtime. The mill had been running at a 10,400 rpm spindle speed, but experimented with a speed of 11,200 rpm. Observing no increase in breakage, it standardized on the higher speed, increasing production by 1800 pounds a month.

Other situations involve trading one cost for another, such as the cost of a tune-up versus higher fuel consumption in a car. Such a trade-off was mismanaged at the U.S. Army Depot in Sacramento, Calif. Broken steam traps, which can leak as much as $50 worth of steam a week, were not replaced so that a bulk order could be issued, saving $10 per trap. Since some traps were broken for as long as a year before being replaced, the $10 savings was offset by a loss of more than $2500.

Some operations pose a trade-off between cycle time and capacity. The operation can be run with large lots taking longer to process or with small ones completed more quickly. Demands of the next processing activity may be the deciding factor. At one company, the output of an operation that preheated mandrels was to be increased from 40 to 60 units per hour. The oven had a capacity of 40 mandrels, each of which had to be heated for 30 minutes. Operators had used lots of 20, keeping the oven full at all times, withdrawing a lot when needed. Since this approach would not work with the proposed 60 unit production rate, Shigeo Shingo devised an alternative: Split the oven into four parts, each containing a lot of 10. Withdraw and replace lots at 10-minute intervals, matching the production rate of one unit per minute, while allowing each mandrel to be heated the required 30 minutes. Reducing the lot size created a better match with the throughput rate.

Another of Shingo's cases offers a related lesson: At a confectionary, a syrup-melting process could not keep up with production needs. Workers had been packing 18-liter cans of syrup into an oven. Realizing that the oven's heat could not flow among the tightly packed cans, Shingo had cans arranged loosely in the oven and installed fans to circulate hot oven air. These changes reduced the operation's capacity per cycle by 40 percent, but cut cycle time by two-thirds, increasing melting capacity 180 percent. Sometimes the more efficient option is to be inefficient on one dimension of performance.

Some parameter settings can be fine-tuned through trial and error; others can be determined by reasoning things out. With extremely complex processes, conduct experiments to determine optimal settings. Campbell Soup used experiments to reduce variation and improve the speed of its can-filling operation, increasing filler speed by 100 percent and saving $85,000 per year. A wood products firm conducted experiments to improve efficiency of a pulping operation, achieving a 2 percent increase in process yield. Some processes are not understood well enough to enable optimization of process parameters. Not knowing which variables are important, experimentation is too expensive to be used effectively. Then process improvement can rely on a simple heuristic, evident in the following case:

■ **case 9.4**

A chemical producer assigned a team of consultants to work with a subsidiary manufacturing plastic-impregnated board used in graphic arts applications. The team found the subsidiary's rural plant to be a TQM manager's nightmare. Aging equipment, untrained employees, lack of process and product standards, and seat-of-the-pants management contributed to reject rates exceeding 20 percent. During production, paper was saturated with resin and cured for 10 days before final processing. By accident, a batch of saturated paper was processed after only a day of curing, with no adverse effects. When further study confirmed this result, procedures were changed so that all product was processed after a day of curing.

There were many opportunities to improve quality and efficiency in this plant, but the curing process stood out as a time-consuming operation. Lacking solid, data-based standards, it was smart to test existing practices by shifting parameters in cost-reducing directions. A general lesson is to focus on high cost parts of a process and, when standards are not well justified, to tweak process parameters in a cost-reducing direction to see if gains can be achieved without sacrificing quality.

## Outputs

*Amount.* Typically focused on process inputs and activities, cost reduction efforts should also attend to the outputs being produced. Obviously, producing outputs that no one wants is not wise. Produce outputs at a volume matching customer demand. This rule applies throughout the production process, not just for final goods. If output exceeds demand, the organization incurs inventory-related costs, including storage, breakage, obsolescence, and capital costs. If output falls short of demand, the company suffers from lost sales, unhappy customers, and the potential entry of new competitors. The basis for matching production to demand is an accurate sales forecast. Many forecasting techniques have been developed, but none is truly powerful when applied in dynamic market situations. Given the inherent limitations of forecasting, a complementary strategy is to improve one's knowledge of actual sales as they occur. By using information technology to inform suppliers of product sales, Wal-Mart insures that its shelves are quickly restocked and helps suppliers adjust production to match demand.

*Variety.* Output variety increases costs. Each item in a product line adds costs for inventory, equipment, expertise, and other inputs and activities needed for that item. Though reducing product variety is a powerful means of reducing costs, it can also reduce sales. Varied product lines satisfy varied customer needs. As Henry Ford discovered, insisting on one color, size, or configuration for all customers leads to competitive disaster. Nonetheless, some product variations may not generate enough sales to cover their costs. These should be discontinued. And there may be ways of making product variety less costly—for instance, using common components or not differentiating products until the last possible step in the value chain.

*Waste.* Waste refers to inputs consumed unnecessarily in a process or consumed but remaining behind after the final product goes out the door. Costs of unneeded inputs and disposal make waste expensive. It derives from many sources, so costs can be reduced in various ways. Breakage causes waste, especially with fragile items. Proper packaging and materials handling can reduce costs from this source. An Indian textile mill reduced yarn breakage losses by 40 percent through a program that trained employees in proper procedures, smoothed sharp edges on equipment, and cleaned equipment so control mechanisms were more effective.

Waste can result from process leakage, means by which work in process, materials, and other inputs slip out of the process flow. Procter and Gamble was concerned with the amount of a detergent it lost to the sewer. A study revealed that major culprits were faulty filters and pumps and spills during loading and unloading. Improved maintenance, equipment modifications, and worker training reduced waste by 58 percent. Liquids are not the only inputs that can leak from a process. Cleaners at a shipyard noticed much good material among the refuse, including nuts and bolts that they recycled back into production. A team at the Cherry Point Naval Aviation Depot found that mechanics discarded expensive bearings that were usable. Workers must be scrupulous in their usage of materials, and procedures for recovering losses should be instituted.

Containers often play a temporary role in the production process. They serve a purpose but are not part of the output that leaves the plant. Unless reused or recycled, such inputs create disposal costs. A software producer used pallets to bring materials to its packaging line for shipment. By switching to carts, it eliminated the need for boxes that had to be broken down and disposed of when empty.

Cleanup is another source of waste. Any step in a process can create a mess, but certain steps, such as painting, are messier than others, requiring additional inputs— soap and water or cleaning agents, for instance—for cleanup. Cleanup inputs are contaminated during the process and must be disposed of. Minimize the amount of necessary cleanup and, by implication, the volume of cleaning agents needed to do it. An ideal solution is to redesign the process to eliminate the need for cleanup. Shigeo Shingo did so for an engraving operation that used cutting oil to cool the engraving tool. A solvent was used to clean oil from metal parts before they were dipped in a plating tank. Shingo realized that compressed air could cool as well as oil and did not have to be cleaned up afterward.

If a company cannot avoid creating waste products, it should recycle or reuse them to reduce input and disposal costs. United Laboratories paid refuse fees to dispose of waste cardboard, but saved $1000 a month by recycling cardboard to another company, which picked it up free of charge. At another firm, cartons used to pack material were thrown away after being delivered to the place where the material was used. Returning empty cartons to their originating department reduced waste by 100 percent. Materials are not the only thing that can be recycled. Exxon uses cogeneration, recycling residual heat from one part of the production process to warm streams of material in another part.

Waste treatment and recovery operations often seem ancillary and are thus ignored even though many dollars can be lost as a result. This happened with the paper recovery operation at IBM's Poughkeepsie, N.Y., facility. When management got serious about paper recovery, it instituted refined sorting of paper and made careful sales of used paper to recycling mills. Earnings from paper recovery went from $30,000 to $200,000 annually. At a Warner-Lambert location, nonrecoverable bulk for a product increased from 232 pounds to 764 pounds per day over a three-month period. Inspection revealed a hole in the bag of a dust collector. Since a replacement bag was not available, $8000 worth of materials had been lost. Losses like this rarely happen on the main production line.

Because it can be expensive and dangerous, waste handling should be facilitated by special equipment. A division of Ciba-Geigy devised a mobile container for collecting solvent used to clean adhesives manufacturing machines. The container made it easier, cheaper, and safer to deal with this material. A quality circle at another manufacturer saved thousands of dollars and eliminated safety hazards by devising a solvent disposal system.

As the nuclear power industry will confirm, when dealing with sensitive materials, waste creates more waste and more costs. Any rags, water, or other substance that comes in contact with radioactive material is contaminated as a result and incurs waste disposal costs. Waste handling activities minimize contamination and segregate materials by the treatment required. These principles were applied by waste reduction task forces at Stanley-Bostitch, a Rhode Island manufacturer. One group reduced usage of an absorbent used to clean oil spills. It lowered the incidence of hydraulic leaks in machinery and purchased a portable liquid collection and dispensing unit to facilitate oil removal during machine changeovers. Another team segregated soap and water used to clean parts from waste oil and coolants with which they had been combined. Soap and water waste could be treated in-house; oil and coolants are regulated materials shipped off-site for expensive waste processing. The company tested replacements for trichloroethane, a solvent that is costly to use and dispose of. Change products and processes to replace inputs with high waste treatment costs with others more easily disposed of.

***Free Goods.*** While they have a universal appeal and are often given to customers to build goodwill, free goods are invariably overused. A product's price is a disciplinary mechanism which insures that the only people who buy the product are people who can benefit from it. When the price is zero, this discipline is gone and goods are wasted. Thus, when companies give products to internal or external customers, they should be careful that the gift is not a costly gesture yielding no benefit to users or themselves.

One form of free goods is *product giveaway:* Customers get more than they paid for. This is important for products sold by weight or volume since giveaway increases manufacturing costs. Companies reduce variability in packaging processes to give customers everything they pay for but nothing more. Giveaway is also troublesome in services involving the consumption of materials, especially if customers derive no benefit from the excess. At Spa Resorts Hawaiian, north of Tokyo, the soy sauce provided with a meal is measured to the milliliter to satisfy diners without creating waste. Waitresses in a Matsushita plant cafeteria studied lunch period tea consumption, computed average consumption for each table, and served different amounts of tea to reflect each table's usage. Their efforts reduced tea consumption by 50 percent and earned them Matsushita's Presidential Gold Medal. This award was not given for the savings—their study may well have cost more than it saved—but for the cost-reducing mentality that these workers demonstrated.

Organizations often offer free goods to internal users. When departments and divisions do not pay for legal, informational, or other in-house services, they overuse those services. Auditors at a company found that half the MIS reports delivered to manufacturing managers were not used. The company changed its policy, requiring users to pay for information services previously charged to a general administrative fund.

Though customer relations can be improved if some products or services are provided free of charge, it may not be wise to advertise freebies. A team at Colonial Penn, an insurance company, found that the firm spent $10 apiece issuing free duplicate policies to customers. The costs of this gesture had burgeoned because a form letter invited customers to ask for a duplicate policy and sales representatives offered the service in telephone solicitations. High costs induced Colonial Penn to discontinue the offer.

If free goods are provided for customer relations purposes, make sure the offering yields the most bang for the buck. An international hotel chain provided guests a complimentary basket of fruit, placing baskets in advance in rooms covered by reservations. Unfortunately, the perishable product went to waste if a room was not occupied that evening. By changing its procedure so fruit was only delivered to the rooms of guests that had checked in, the hotel reduced fruit costs from $6196 to $409 during a three-month period.

## Worker Safety

After decades of indifference, industrial societies have come to regard workplace safety as a matter of utmost importance. It seems tragically absurd that people should lose their lives while trying to make a living. Society is becoming much less tolerant of lives lost and injuries incurred unnecessarily in this way.

Three steps are involved in improving workplace safety. First, identify hazards. Second, assess the nature and severity of hazards, prioritizing them for remedial attention. Finally, reduce or eliminate hazards, consistent with other goals.

There is no analytical, sit-at-your-desk way to identify all safety hazards. We know certain things are dangerous: sharp edges, moving objects, explosive and flammable materials, and people and heavy things at great heights. Beyond attending to salient risks, we have no analytical means of identifying all the ways someone could get hurt in even the most innocuous workplace. Consequently, the primary resource in identifying safety hazards is experience, our own and the experiences of others. The U.S. Occupational Safety and Health Administration (OSHA) reflects a societal attempt to learn in this way. For most companies, their own past experiences suggest current hazards. Thus, the primary strategy of workplace safety programs is to identify past accidents and incidents and build an experience base that can direct corrective action. Finding that flight attendants were its highest risk group in terms of accidents and insurance premiums, Hawaiian Airlines collected data on accidents, flight conditions, locations of injury occurrences, and time lost due to injuries.

Such efforts are somewhat after the fact. More proactive programs try to identify hazardous conditions before an accident occurs. The Kashina Steel Works of Sumitomo Metal Industries encourages anyone who sees a near-miss or potential accident cause to write it up for discussion at a quality circle meeting. As a result, the facility had gone two years without accidents of any kind. Another Japanese plant, the Chiba Factory of Furukawa Electric Company, had no accidents for seven years. Chiba workers use a what-if method, imagining how accidents might occur, what their causes would be, and what preventive measures could be implemented. Similar programs have been initiated at American companies like DuPont and Florida Power and Light.

The second step in safety improvement programs is more analytical. The causes of accidents and safety incidents must be determined and identified hazards must be evaluated and ranked in order of seriousness. Management Oversight and Risk Tree Analysis (MORT), a technique developed for nuclear power plants,[9] offers a framework for accident/incident analysis. MORT assumes that an accident was caused by management oversight or omission or by a risk that management accepted consciously, though perhaps unwisely. Workers at Toyota's Motomachi Plant developed a formula to use in evaluating hazards. Multiplying the expected degree of injury by the number of people who had near-accidents by the number of predictable accident sites yields a point total for a hazard. The workers computed a total of 387 points for hazards in their area, with gasoline leaks identified as most serious. A safety improvement program eliminated virtually all hazard points.

Safety is a lot like ethics: Knowing the right thing to do is one matter, and doing it is quite another. The second presumes but does not necessarily follow from the first. Identifying and evaluating safety hazards puts one in a position to take corrective action, but action is not necessarily taken. Safety can be costly, slowing process throughput or requiring capital expenditures. Safety can also be a hassle, witness the blade guards and other protective devices removed by workers who just want to get the job done. An agency like OSHA can prompt organizations and employees to give safety its proper due, but ultimately individuals and organizations must insure that reasonable safety precautions are taken.

One target of improvement efforts is unsafe work practices. Employees of an airplane manufacturer were hammering fingers while fabricating certain parts; devising a new fixture solved the problem. Managers at another company investigated upon learning that the most common on-the-job injury was sprained fingers. They found that machine operators moved heavy metal blocks by putting their fingers in small holes near the top of the block. Rods had been used to move blocks, but they were in short supply. By making rods available to all who needed them, the company reduced the incidence of sprained fingers.

Equipment is another safety factor. Equipment that can make unsafe manual activities, such as lifting heavy objects, easier should be readily available. A team at Stanadyne found that workers manually torqued plugs, causing carpel tunnel syndrome. Providing operators with holding fixtures and air torque guns made the operation easier, safer, and more efficient. Position equipment controls to promote safe operation. Switches on large presses force operators to have both hands outside the danger zone during machine operation. At Toyota, a single worker operates multiple presses, the switch for each located at its successor so the worker is safely positioned when the operating cycle begins. Danger and safety interlocks require operators to complete one motion before moving to the next.

A final means of improving safety is to increase worker attention. Carelessness is the mother of many accidents. Safety awareness programs, publicizing the number of accident-free days, and repeated exhortations by managers and workers promote and sustain high levels of employee attention to safety. Florida Power and Light went further: The company placed drawings of tombstones in places where accidents had occurred.

Every company has room to reduce costs and to improve workplace safety. Attempts to do so should be conducted with the company's broader position in mind, as illustrated in this case:

■ **case** *9.5*

"After several years of depressed order books, a small shipyard received an influx of orders that ensured full capacity operation for at least two years. Late delivery of the vessels under construction could wipe out any profits on the order. The company had been surviving by implementing a cost-management strategy that stressed minimizing direct costs and cash outflows.

Two months after the orders were received, it was apparent that the yard was already falling behind schedule. When executives reviewed the situation they found that their managers and supervisors were still operating under the old cost-management style. Materials were being ordered on a hand-to-mouth basis, which meant that workers were frequently waiting for delivery and not putting in needed overtime.

Having recognized this problem, the senior executives spent the next three months changing the focus of cost management away from direct costs to those associated with delays, lost production time, and late delivery. Cost-management symbols were changed, rewards were offered for ideas that increased the build rate, task forces were formed to develop approaches to reduce lead times, and an on-time/on-budget bonus was developed for the entire work force."[10]

Efficiency-improvement efforts can be short-sighted if pursued at the expense of larger objectives, notably that of satisfying customers.

## NOTES

1. The stakeholder view of quality is discussed in: Gerald F. Smith, "The Meaning of Quality," *Total Quality Management* 4 (1993): 235–244.
2. Ostrenga, Michael R., Terrance R. Ozan, Robert D. McIlhattan, and Marcus D. Harwood, *The Ernst & Young Guide to Total Cost Management* (New York: John Wiley, 1992).
3. Edward Sullivan, "OPTIM: Linking Cost, Time, and Quality," *Quality Progress* 19, no. 4 (1986): 52–55.
4. Marvin E. Mundel, *Motion and Time Study: Improving Productivity,* 6th ed. (Englewood Cliffs, N.J.: Prentice Hall, 1985).
5. Peter R. Richardson, *Cost Containment* (New York: Free Press, 1988).
6. See note 5.
7. Eliyahu M. Goldratt, *The Goal* (Croton-on-Hudson, N.Y.: Noah River Press, 1992).
8. Shigeo Shingo, *The Sayings of Shigeo Shingo: Key Strategies for Plant Improvement* (Cambridge, Mass.: Productivity Press, 1987).
9. Wilson, Paul F., Larry D. Dell, and Gaylord F. Anderson, *Root Cause Analysis: A Tool for Total Quality Management* (Milwaukee: ASQC Quality Press, 1993).
10. See note 5.

# Product Design Problems

This chapter shifts our attention from performance problems to design problems. Performance problems, discussed in the three preceding chapters, are situations in which an existing system is not performing acceptably. Design problems, addressed in this chapter and the next, are situations in which a new system must be created or an existing system remade.

Some professions, notably architecture and engineering, view themselves as design fields. Management has historically seen itself as a decision-making field, paying scant attention to design. Organizational life encompasses numerous design activities, from the development of new products and services to the design of organizational structures, information systems, and incentive programs. Inadequate organizational processes may have been ignored for so long because few managers saw themselves as designers or viewed processes as things to be designed.

Total quality management has helped change those views by placing business process improvement on the agenda of every manager. Moving quality improvement efforts upstream led TQM to a concern with product design, this chapter's topic. Within product design, TQM has focused on the challenge of identifying customer needs. It has paid little attention to the inventive efforts of individual designers. This allocation of attention is mirrored in the chapter's contents.

The chapter begins with a discussion of design as background for an understanding of product design. Product design problems are discussed in terms of the functional demands they pose and in relationship to other types of quality problems. Design methods are reviewed, with most attention focused on techniques featured in TQM practice. The chapter's final section offers prescriptions, illustrated by cases, for improving product design.

# Design

**Design** involves making something, a system or artifact, when the making is not from an existing plan. Design problems can be understood in terms of five conceptual elements: goals, constraints, alternatives, representations, and solutions. Relationships among these are depicted in Figure 10.1.[*1]

## Goals

Unsatisfied needs motivate design activity, instigating design efforts and providing criteria for the evaluation of design outputs. Design goals reflect human physiological needs (such as food and warmth), needs arising from social interaction (the coordination of drivers on a freeway), aesthetic interests, and other issues. In modern societies, many artifacts perform functions that connect only remotely to human needs. A bushing in the engine mount of an airplane enables the plane to fly, to transport people, and thereby to satisfy social needs. But the bushing is designed in light of its specific function, oblivious to the remote social purposes it serves.

---

*The content of this section is an adaptation of material copyrighted in 1993 by IEEE. Adapted and reprinted, with permission, from *IEEE Transactions on Systems, Man, and Cybernetics* 23, no. 5, September/October 1993: 1209–1219.

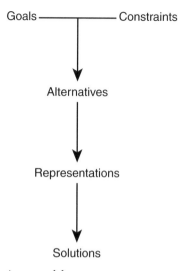

**Figure 10.1**   Elements of design problems

Goal identification is a major challenge in design. If unmet goals are to be addressed by designed systems, they must be recognized by designers. Designers cannot introspectively determine all relevant needs and customers cannot be relied on to express them. Customers do not always know what they want, especially when they do not know what possibilities are available. It can be difficult to determine how a designed system will affect other parties. What if the noise created by snowmobiles inspires legislation restricting their use? Design work usually starts from an incomplete specification of goals, which is augmented during the design process. As design proceeds, goals come to light and are translated into system specifications. Indeed, design can be viewed as a series of translations—from user goals into product functions, then into its causal structure, and finally into the product's form.

## Constraints

Design problems require the creation of something new. Human imagination can generate possibilities, but this capacity and the alternatives it creates must be disciplined by feasibility considerations. Constraints serve this purpose, limiting alternatives in light of practical demands. Goals are constraining since only options that promise goal satisfaction will be considered. Goals indicate desirability; constraints express feasibility.

Constraints are of two kinds. **Internal constraints** reflect facts of nature, technological capabilities, and the evolving demands of the artifact (Part *A* must fit with Part *B* for instance). **External constraints** come from product users, other stakeholders (such as building codes), and the environments in which designed artifacts must function. An electrical appliance must be compatible with household power supplies. Constraints can be hard or soft, more or less firm.

Like goals, constraints cannot all be identified at the outset of design. Internal coherence constraints deriving from the problem's partial solution are identified when the designer recognizes commitments entailed by the emerging design. Other constraints come to mind through experience or by analyzing the inadequacies of proposed solutions. Identifying constraints is not the only challenge. To be innovative, designers must determine which constraints can be shifted or ignored.

## Alternatives

Alternatives are solution possibilities the designer generates and considers. They range from high-level design concepts for the overall system to proposals for minor components. Whereas alternatives in decision problems are known or can be discovered through search, design alternatives must be created. Alternative generation is the most distinctive and critical functional demand posed by design problem solving.

Methods for generating alternatives vary in the extent to which they rely on reasoned analysis, experiential knowledge, and creative imagination. Most analytical approaches assume that goals and constraints are known. Such methods typically rely on decomposition, viewing design as a search for simple objects, such as bolts, shafts, and gears, that can be combined in constraint-satisfying configurations. Another approach focuses on the designer's experiential knowledge; designers generate alternatives by recalling similar problems and solutions that were effective in those cases. A designer's education can be viewed as a matter of accumulating a mental inventory of **design prototypes,** stock solutions that can be adapted to current problems. An architect might learn the housing styles and floor plans used for private dwellings. Finally, alternative generation can be viewed as a nonanalytical creative process that moves beyond the bounds of experience.

In design, evaluation of alternatives proceeds hand in hand with their generation. Because evaluation enables discovery of unrecognized goals and constraints, it promotes the generation of better alternatives. An evaluated alternative might be rejected immediately or, if it has promise, the designer can decompose it, identifying subproblems to resolve as part of the option's development. Because evaluation is fallible, inadequacies may not be discovered until an artifact fails during use. For this reason, failure and the study thereof are vehicles for progress in design disciplines.

## Representations

A representation is a depiction of something else. Representations are the language of design, a partially verbal, mostly visual system of symbols. Since the change from traditional trial-and-error methods of artifact creation, design has become the production of representations. Rather than making the artifact, designers create a representation, a plan communicating specifications to those who make the product. Composers create scores, process designers create flowcharts, and product designers create three-dimensional views of the intended product.

Representations not only communicate design intentions, they facilitate the design process. Diagrams allow one to see the implications of choices made during design. They disclose unrecognized constraints and help designers maintain system coherence. Most design methods are representational devices allowing information to be depicted in new and useful ways. Designers use multiple representations during a project, each portraying aspects of the envisioned artifact that merit attention at that stage. As the design process moves toward completion, representations become more inclusive and comprehensive. They enforce a higher degree of fit among the object's components; dimensions are specified with greater precision.

## Solutions

The solution to a design problem is a system or, more typically, a representation in a conventional specification language that enables system construction. Solutions can be very different and remote from statements of the original problem. The problem involves a need (such as warmth), whereas the solution specifies an artifact (a house), the design process having made numerous translations getting from one to the other. Design solutions are so complex that it is hard to validate their effectiveness. Designers do not know whether a proposed solution will work until a physical prototype is constructed and tested. Most design problems have many acceptable solutions. Solution search ends when an acceptable alternative is successfully implemented. Though an optimal solution may exist, it is unlikely to be found.

The complexity of design solutions explains the importance of decomposition in the design process. Designers cannot mentally envision an entire, fully detailed solution—say, a new chair—in one swoop. Solutions are developed in stages, working from high-level concepts for the artifact down to precise specifications for its components. At each level, the designer faces new, but smaller, design problems with the challenge to make it or break it: Design a solution for the current problem or decompose into subproblems and try again. Because components function as an integrated whole, subproblems cannot be solved in isolation. Each partial solution must fit the emerging solution for the overall problem.

The existence of many acceptable solutions for design problems creates an opportunity for the influence of designer discretion and values. This influence is apparent in architecture, where aesthetics are an essential part of design. Engineering design is dominated by functionality and offers less latitude for designer discretion. The design of organizations and business processes is more like engineering than architecture in this respect.

# Product Design

The quality movement has been concerned with two kinds of design problems: process and product design. Process design involves devising a set of activities to convert inputs into desired outputs. Product design is a matter of creating artifacts that satisfy user needs. Though the two are distinct problem types, there are overlaps. Consider services. A car wash designs its service to satisfy customer needs and markets that service like other commercial products. Yet the service is a set of activities, a process. Services are both fish and fowl, creations of product and process design work. There are other hybrids as well. Organizational programs—cost reduction, government antipoverty programs—are complex configurations of structures and processes that entail both process and product design work for their creation. This book makes the customary distinction between process and product design, discussing the latter in the present chapter.

## Relationship to Other Quality Problems

Conformance problems are often attributed to product design inadequacies. A study of 850 field failures of electronic equipment found that 43 percent were due to engineering design. Pushing quality improvement upstream in the production process leads to a focus on product design. There is not much sense in disciplining production to comply with product specifications that do not reflect customer needs. Conformance problems can be reduced if products are designed for manufacturing and with mistake-proofing features that prevent production errors.

Product design is less closely related to unstructured performance problems. The discussion of that category (Chapter 8) included an analysis of services. As noted, services are a hybrid, the development of which includes both product and process design considerations.

Efficiency problems are closely affiliated with product design. Though only a small portion of product costs are spent on design, design decisions determine 70 percent of those costs. A major impact is on the cost of materials. Techniques like value analysis eliminate unnecessary materials without compromising product functionality. Just as poor product design can lead to manufacturing errors and conformance problems, it can also increase machining and assembly costs, creating inefficiencies.

The most important relationship between product and process design concerns manufactured products. The design of such products has strong implications for the processes by which they are produced. As a result, product design is increasingly affected by production process considerations.

In summary, product design is often a cause of efficiency and conformance problems. The product design process has been expanded to address such issues, primarily by taking production process design into account.

## Functional Demands

Product development is a critical success factor for most organizations, especially those in dynamic, high technology industries. As a result, product design is an institutionalized organizational function, an activity requiring no special stimulus for its initiation. Companies constantly look for ways to improve existing products and to invent new products satisfying market needs. Product design problems are identified through customer feedback, monitoring of competitor activities, and surveillance of technological developments.

Product design problems are defined through activities that specify the product inadequacy or opportunity. This requirements determination, conducted as the front-end to design work typically results in a product design specification or brief. Definitional efforts vary, depending on whether a contract-led or market-led product is involved. The former are defined by formal statements of customer requirements, while requirements for the latter must be determined from scratch. This necessitates studies of the market to determine customer needs and of existing products, available technologies, patents, licenses, and organizational capabilities to determine relevant constraints. Improper problem definition creates huge opportunity costs as scarce product development resources are squandered on undeserving projects.

The functional heart of product design problem solving is design itself. This is largely a matter of generating and evaluating alternatives, repeatedly and at varying levels of generality—system, subsystem, and component. Design is invention that can employ analytic methods, the recollection of past experience, or the creation of fundamentally new things.

## The Product Design Process

Viewed narrowly, product design is what designers do in translating a design brief into product specifications adequate for production purposes. These activities have been differentiated into phases. One account distinguishes between **conceptual** and **detail design.** The former outputs a design concept, engineered to a level establishing its validity. Detail design continues engineering through subsystem and component levels, resolving subproblems and yielding a complete set of product specifications.

Another account, prominent in the quality literature, sees design as a three-stage process:

1. **System design,** which establishes the overall design concept
2. **Parameter design,** which sets nominal or target values of product dimensions and other attributes
3. **Allowance** or **tolerance design,** which sets acceptable ranges of variation around nominal values

Design is affected by the nature of the product: Custom-made products, such as office buildings, entail extensive system design work; established, high-volume manufactured goods, such as brooms, do not. It has been argued that, in comparison with their Japanese counterparts, American engineers devote more attention to system design at the expense of parameter design. If true, this may reflect a Japanese strategy of optimizing parameter settings for proven product concepts. There is also evidence that tolerance design is often performed by haphazard, seat-of-the-pants methods.

A hallmark of the design process is the need to incorporate numerous considerations in the artifact: intended performance capabilities; product cost, size, weight, materials, appearance, and life span; quality and reliability; safety; ergonomics; competitive offerings; company and market constraints; patents and legal issues; political and social implications; industry standards; expected production volumes; production processes; manufacturing facilities; testing requirements; packaging and shipping requirements; product installation; documentation; shelf life; any environment the product might encounter during its production, sale, or use; maintenance needs; and product disposal after its service life has expired.[2] These motivate the "design for . . ." prescriptions found in the literature.

Because no individual designer could understand and accommodate all these factors, the product design process has come to be viewed more broadly. Product design encompasses the efforts of market researchers who determine customer needs, legal experts who investigate patents, production personnel who insure manufacturability, and other parties who bring specialized bodies of knowledge to the design effort. The most important contributions bring the voice of the customer to bear on the intended product. This is the aspect of product design most intensively addressed by TQM.

# Product Design Methods

There are many design methods. Several fields of professional practice, notably architecture and engineering, are centrally concerned with design and have developed design methodologies. Design lends itself to methods-based improvement. It is a complex activity encompassing tasks performed over an extended period of time. There are numerous opportunities for techniques to improve on intuitive performance. In addition, design results in the creation of a structured, systemic artifact. Methods rely on structure and are more applicable when such is the goal of problem solving.

Design methods can be differentiated in terms of the parts or aspects of design they address and the strategies they employ. Some methods are concerned with requirements determination, others with conceptual design, and so forth. The best methods are powerful for certain parts of design. Their power derives from the use of effective strategies, the other basis for differentiating methods. Strategies include decomposition, conceptual translation, identification of interrelationships, and learning from experience.

Five design methods, or families of methods, of importance for quality problem solving will be reviewed in detail. Thereafter, other methods will be cited in a discussion organized around elements of the design process.

## Quality Function Deployment (QFD)

This technique, which originated in Japan's Kobe Shipyard in 1972, is the quality movement's most significant contribution to product design. The method has been described as a set of planning and communication routines that facilitate cooperation between marketing, design, and manufacturing during the design process.[3] QFD enacts a series of translations from customer needs to product characteristics and ultimately to manufacturing procedures. Customer needs are deployed or operationalized as production process instructions that will produce outputs with desired characteristics.

The QFD process centers on a set of matrices, the first being the House of Quality (Figure 10.2). The uppermost rows of this matrix (indicated as *A* in the figure) denote customer needs regarding the product in question. Determined by user feedback or market research, these needs must present a complete and accurate account of customer desires for the product. Needs can be ranked or weighted to indicate their importance (*B*). The right-hand side of the House (*C*) incorporates the needs in a competitive analysis comparing the product with leading competitors. This part of the matrix can identify sources of competitive advantage, high priority needs not satisfied by existing products.

The columns or vertical dimension of the House of Quality are defined by product characteristics affecting customer needs (*D*). In the case of a car door, customers'

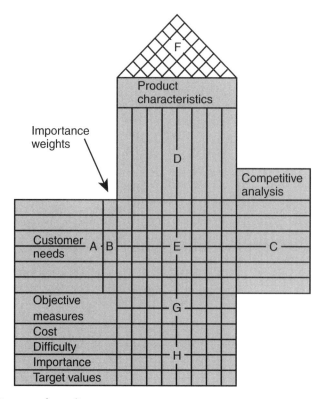

**Figure 10.2** House of quality

desire for a door that is easy to close is affected by door seal resistance. Interactions between customer needs and product characteristics can be positive or negative and of varying strength, indications to this effect being recorded in the body of the matrix (*E*). Thus, the House's center depicts relationships between customer needs and product characteristics that could be adjusted to satisfy those needs.

Additions to the core matrix accommodate other considerations. Product characteristics defining columns can interact—for instance, increases in component strength imply weight increases—and those interactions are recorded in the House's "roof" (*F*). Objective measures of product characteristics for one's own and competing products are entered in rows at the bottom of the matrix (*G*). These are augmented with target values for design activity and, optionally, with estimates of the cost, difficulty, and importance of achieving those targets (*H*). The lowest part of the House records design goals developed through QFD.

Though the House of Quality is the technique's most familiar creation, the QFD process does not end with its construction. Changes in product characteristics must be translated into changes in subsystems and components. Other matrices are constructed to this end. These changes in turn must be carried through to the production process. Process plans and controls are reviewed in light of changes to product parameters. Again, specialized matrices effect the desired translations. The final deployment is to procedures and instructions used by operators making the product. QFD encompasses production process design in a product design methodology.

QFD has been widely applied. Eaton Corporation's Controls Division used it to design a new blend door actuator, an air conditioning control mechanism. Compared to a similar product developed several years earlier, the QFD-inspired design was 30 percent smaller, had better mounting flexibility, reduced the noise specification from 50 to 38 decibels, reduced engineering expenses by 50 percent and drafting expenses by 20 percent, and sold at half the price. The Tokyo Juki Kogyo Company used QFD to achieve a competitive advantage with a line of sewing machines. Market studies revealed customer dissatisfaction over the difficulty of handling cloth at the start of sewing. QFD translated this concern into a focus on the product's bed cross-section and holding height characteristics. The redesigned product was an instant success.

The power of QFD derives from its use of matrices as translation devices that transform one thing into another. *Whats* become *hows,* which become the *whats* of another translation. Design is a transformation process—from needs to functions to form—so QFD is suited to its task. On the other hand, the method does not penetrate the work of designers themselves. QFD brings the voice of the customer to bear on design and alters production processes in light of design changes, but it does not generate design concepts, integrate components into wholes, or direct other core tasks of designers. QFD is applicable in situations of incremental design, where existing products must be improved rather than replaced by new product concepts. It will not create a Sony Walkman but these limitations do not negate the method's value. QFD offers a powerful framework for integrating marketing, design, and manufacturing concerns in the product design process.

## Design for Manufacturing

Several design methods, sometimes called the *design-fors,* emphasize particular criteria of good design. Each design-for is a loose collection of methods and heuristics with a common focus—for instance, product cost, safety, or disposability. By packaging heuristics under a common label, a design-for makes its criterion more salient to designers and provides a kit of practical tools for achieving that criterion.

Design for Manufacturing (DFM) is a leading design-for. Its concern is that products can be manufactured efficiently and effectively. Reflecting the nature of the manufacturing process—parts are purchased or made and assembled into wholes—DFM consists of two elements: design for piece-part producibility (DFP) and design for assembly (DFA).

Design for producibility is more difficult and diverse. Many parts must be made, and different production processes can be employed. Designers must consider the capabilities of the firm's workforce and equipment. Failure to do so can result in fiasco: A drug company had an industrial designer create new bottles and caps for a product, but the proposed teardrop-shaped container could not be produced by the company's existing machinery or by anything it tried to purchase or create. The company was forced to abandon the bottles and related marketing campaign.

The most powerful DFP heuristics, shared with DFA, are to reduce the number of parts in a product and to use generic parts if possible. This simplifies manufacturing and lowers purchasing and service costs. Screws and other fasteners can be eliminated by designing parts that snap together. Designers try to reduce the need for jigs and fixtures during production. Products with common jigging fixtures are devised so production is not disrupted by model changeovers.

Design for assembly includes the choice of assembly method—manual, robotic, high-speed automatic—and heuristics making the product more easily assembled by a given method. An example of a well-known heuristic is to design parts with bevels around holes to make insertion easier and with mistake-proofing features to prevent assembly errors. A product might be designed so parts are only added from one direction, reducing the need to turn the product over during assembly. Motorola used design for manufacturing methods to redesign a battery charger, reducing assembly time by 94 percent, assembly defects by 50 percent, parts by 85 percent, and direct material cost by 50 percent. IBM redesigned its Proprinter with 79 percent fewer parts and an assembly time of three minutes, down from 90 minutes for the previous design. NCR redesigned an electronic cash register so its 15 parts (down from 75) could be assembled in under two minutes by a blindfolded worker.

Design for manufacturing overlaps with **ergonomics,** designing products to be compatible with the capabilities of their human users. Though ergonomic considerations typically reflect the needs and abilities of consumers, they can also bring worker capabilities to bear on the design of products and production processes. Mazda's production line tilts cars so workers can reach in to perform tasks without straining or injuring themselves. Workers at Ford's Louisville plant stood in a pit under the assembly line, using heavy torque wrenches to tighten nuts on bolts holding the cargo box to the truck frame. They suggested mounting nuts on the frame so bolts could be tightened from above, making the operation easier and less error prone.

Design for manufacturing is also related to **concurrent** or **simultaneous engineering,** the parallel development of a product and its manufacturing process. Though process design inevitably lags behind product design, concurrent engineering shortens product development cycles. It insures that uncertainties about the producibility of components are quickly resolved. Concurrent engineering promotes DFM by keeping manufacturing concerns at the forefront of designers' attention.

As collections of heuristics, design for manufacturing and other design-fors seem vulnerable to charges that they lack the power of formal methods. Such complaints are not justified. Most of the heuristics have a successful track record. Moreover, these aspects of design have not been addressed by formal techniques and arguably cannot be, given the variety and complexity of related tasks. A more valid concern is the potential for imbalance, the risk that manufacturing, safety, or another factor receives excessive attention during design and dominates other considerations. Imbalances can occur within a method if one heuristic takes unreasoned precedence over others. Volkswagen avoided this mistake with the rule of reducing the number of parts. VW engineers found that the use of an *extra* frame part allowed car engines to be installed by hydraulic arms in 26 seconds, an activity that had required several assemblers working a minute or more.

# Design for Reliability and Maintainability

Reliability and maintainability, topics of other design-fors, are concerned with a product's useful life, the period during which it is expected to satisfy user needs. Design for reliability (DFR) devises products with long service lives rarely interrupted by breakdowns. Design for maintainability focuses on the ease of performing preventive maintenance and repairing products after breakdowns.

Design for reliability lends itself to structured methods. The reliability of a product reflects reliabilities of its parts. Statistical estimates for these can be developed from historical data. Thus, meantime between failure and other product reliability measures can be computed from a decompositional analysis using failure probabilities for parts. The nature and conditions of product use—the duty cycle and external environment—must be factored into a reliability assessment. With worst-case analysis, designers predict product performance under extreme conditions. Failure Mode and Effects Analysis (FMEA) identifies things that can go wrong with a product and their effects on its performance.

Designers use various means to improve product reliability. Minimize the number of parts. Use parts with records of reliable performance. Improve "weak link" parts that are critical to performance. Strengthen weak links by derating, using parts intended for more demanding applications. Build in redundancy, back-up functions that maintain performance if a part fails.

The importance of design for maintainability is recognized by every car owner who has tried to replace an impossibly positioned oil filter. This design-for reduces the maintenance required by products, increases the ease with which maintenance can be performed, and facilitates repairs when products break down. Automobiles that go 100,000 miles before scheduled maintenance demonstrate progress toward the first goal. Repairability can be improved by modular design so that repair personnel need only identify the faulty module, perhaps replacing it in the field. Another heuristic is to make failure-prone components accessible for easy replacement. After talks with insurance companies, Ford engraved marks on suspension towers in Taurus and Sable models, facilitating front-end realignment after accidents. More and more products have self-contained computerized diagnostics, a design for maintainability device.

DFR methods are vulnerable to the usual pitfalls of quantitative techniques—for instance, the tendency to overvalue reliability models constructed on a base that includes unreliable estimates of component failure probabilities. As with all design-fors, judgment must be used in trading off design goals. Reliability and maintainability are means of extending a product's service life. One strategy might reasonably be favored over the other in the design of a given product.

# Value Analysis

Product cost is a key design criterion, the related design-for going by the names *value analysis* and *value engineering*. Though the terms are used interchangeably, strictly speaking value engineering (VE) is the cost-conscious design of new products, and value analysis (VA) is the cost-saving redesign of existing products. They use the same techniques and heuristics.

One tool of VA/VE is the functional analysis system technique (FAST) diagram developed by Miles.[4] FAST diagrams decompose product functions from primary functions the product must perform to secondary functions that may not be necessary. Functions can be correlated with a cost analysis, disclosing nonessential high-cost functions that can be eliminated. Designers search for less costly ways of performing required functions. One can eliminate components, replace expensive parts and materials with cheaper substitutes, relax tolerances, and redesign parts to reduce manufacturing costs.

One company redesigned a resistor terminal board. The original design had 30,000 tapped holes into which machine screws were threaded. The new design used drilled holes and thread-cutting screws. Left- and right-hand parts were replaced by common items. Carryovers from an earlier design, 40,000 crimp washers were eliminated. A Japanese manufacturer reduced the cost of an electronics product by loosening tolerances on parts, eliminating two production operations, and identifying eight parts that could be purchased as standard catalog items rather than as custom parts.

Even more than other design-fors, value analysis must be used with discretion. Cost reduction is a constant quest in organizations, and it is all too easy to save money by means that degrade quality and have other adverse effects. VA/VE users must recognize the trade-offs this technique entails.

## Taguchi Methods

The influential work of Japanese engineer Genichi Taguchi is partly methodological, partly philosophical, and wholly concerned with improving product design as a means of improving quality.[5] Taguchi's ideas express three themes. The first and most philosophical posits a loss function relating to products, claiming that all variation around target values of product parameters results in a loss to society. Taguchi condemns the use of specification limits as criteria for product quality. "Being in spec" is not enough since any deviation from target values creates a social loss. Organizations must minimize these losses. Evidence supports Taguchi's claim that variation around target values degrades product performance. His concern with social costs contrasts with the usual bottom-line preoccupation of corporations.

The notion of *robust design* is the second defining theme of Taguchi's work. Variation is bad and should be reduced. Moreover, designers should create products that are insensitive or robust to different sources of variation: inputs, the manufacturing process, and conditions of use. This requires that designers understand sources of variation and how those sources affect product performance. Often, Taguchi claims, one can set certain design variables to achieve robustness, using others to center product parameters on target values. Robust design is the heart of Taguchi's contribution to design methodology. It focuses on parameter and tolerance design for the few variables that strongly affect product performance.

Taguchi's third theme is the design of experiments that efficiently provide information concerning optimal settings of product parameters. This is the most technical and controversial part of Taguchi's work and the least pertinent to our purposes.

Some statisticians question whether Taguchi's experimental design techniques are new, and whether what is new is an improvement over existing approaches.

Controversies notwithstanding, Taguchi's robust design method has had considerable applied success. A Japanese tile manufacturer had a kiln with positional temperature variations affecting the quality of tiles. Design engineers identified seven controllable factors affecting tile quality. Research indicated that a change in limestone content would reduce product defects from 30 percent to less than 1 percent and allow elimination of a costly ingredient. Thus, controlling one variable (limestone content) made product quality insensitive to variation in another (kiln temperature), creating production economies (elimination of the costly ingredient) as a bonus.

The first theme of Taguchi's work, minimizing variation around target values, has been influential, though in a nebulous, philosophical way. The third theme, his experimental design methodology, has ardent supporters and opponents. Robust design, the second theme, is applicable to the detail stage of design. Its power derives from the emphasis placed on understanding how key variables affect product performance. The method exploits the facts that all designs contain much that is arbitrary and that unused degrees of freedom offer opportunities to improve product performance.

Figure 10.3 summarizes the strengths and limitations of these methods.

## Other Methods

Less familiar to quality practitioners are design methods developed in fields like architecture and engineering.[6] A sample of these is reported below. This discussion, organized by stages of the design process, highlights strategies employed by the techniques.

***Requirements Determination.***   This is the task of developing a design brief or specification, a statement of customer needs and real-world constraints the product must satisfy. Task performance requires communicating with customers and other product stakeholders and analyzing existing products. Requirements determination methods structure the information obtained, usually hierarchically. Such structures prompt identification of unrecognized requirements. Like QFD, these methods enable translations from one conceptual level to another, making requirements operational for design purposes.

**Objective trees,** a requirements determination method, develops a hierarchical structure of needs, high-level objectives at the top expanding into specific product goals. The tree, developed through interaction with customers, clarifies and operationalizes objectives and translates ends into means for their attainment. Another method, **function analysis,** translates product functions into subfunctions. The method helps bound the problem by determining which capabilities to include in the artifact. For instance, should a camera include automatic film loading? **Block diagrams** depict interactions among functions, suggesting viable subsets. A final technique, the **performance specification method,** focuses on desired product performance. What level of performance must the product achieve for each important

| Method/Practice | Applications | Strengths | Weaknesses |
| --- | --- | --- | --- |
| Quality Function Deployment | Translating customer needs into product characteristics and production processes. | Rigorous, systematic, and comprehensive; a powerful means of improving existing products. | Does not generate design concepts; not very helpful with the design of innovative new products. |
| Design for Manufacturing | Designing parts and products that can be easily produced and assembled. | A collection of proven heuristic practices that can be readily incorporated into product design. | Not a well-specified, systematic technique; risk that related concerns dominate other design considerations. |
| Design for Reliability and Maintainability | Designing products with long service lives and that can be easily maintained and repaired. | Combines heuristic practices with structured methods based on statistical analysis. | Danger of relying too much on quantitative methods; risk that related concerns dominate other design considerations. |
| Value Analysis | Identifying essential product functions and cost-effective ways of performing them. | A systematic decompositional method; fairly general and operational. | Danger that product quality is compromised in pursuit of cost reduction. |
| Taguchi Methods | Designing products that are insensitive to different sources of variation; design of cost-efficient experiments. | Powerful means of setting optimal parameters and tolerances during the detail stage of design. | Does not generate design concepts; disagreements about the value of experimental design methods. |

Figure 10.3   Overview of product design methods

attribute? Defining the product more or less broadly—a means of transportation vs. a bicycle—allows performance specifications to be set at different levels of generality. This method can serve as an extension of objective trees, translating subgoals into performance requirements.

***Conceptual Design.*** Using requirements stated in the design brief, conceptual design generates design concepts, high-level solutions to the problem. These are explored and the most promising are selected for further development. Conceptual design requires creativity in the generation of alternatives and a critical, unbiased, evaluative capacity for selecting the best. Designers use standard creativity techniques and other specific-for-design means of generating and evaluating alternatives.

The **morphological chart** is an analytical creativity technique of special relevance to product design. The product's essential functions and features are specified. For each, different means by which it could be achieved are identified. For instance, an automobile must include a stopping function, achieved by drum brakes, disc brakes, and sundry other means. These ingredients are combined in a grid with product functions/features listed in rows on the left, the means to each being entered in spaces to its right. A completed grid suggests numerous product alternatives, combinations of means for satisfying essential functions and features, only some of which are feasible. A designer can explore the grid to discover viable product options. Based on decomposition, morphological charts are a systematic way of generating designs for products that can be characterized in terms of discrete functions and features. **Reverse engineering,** deconstructing competitor products to identify their components and modes of functioning, can be used to develop morphological charts.

Evaluation of design alternatives is aided by the method of **controlled convergence.**[7] This technique also uses a matrix with rows defined by evaluative criteria and columns by product concepts. The existing product design or favored concept is included as a benchmark. Matrix entries indicate how other concepts compare to the benchmark on each criterion, either better, worse, or the same as the benchmark. Partial evaluation scores are summed at the bottom of the matrix, and promising concepts have more pluses than minuses. During evaluation, designers suggest new product concepts as they discover means of overcoming negatives assigned to current options. The high scoring concept that emerges from this process is used as a benchmark for another iteration. The cycle repeats until a dominant product concept is established. Controlled convergence uses decomposition and exploits the fact that thinking about an option's inadequacies promotes generation of improved alternatives.

***Detail Design.*** As the time-consuming grunt work of design, detail design converts a viable product concept into specifications for subsystems and components. It includes parameter and tolerance design. Designers identify standard parts to perform functions or design new parts serving those purposes. Attention is given to interactions among parts, all of which must cohere in a working whole. Designers set dimensions and other parameters for parts to optimize achievement of design goals.

Techniques help designers manage interrelationships among parts. The **interaction matrix** is a systematic way of identifying connections between parts of a product. The matrix lists all parts along its vertical and horizontal dimensions with entries in cells denoting interactions between indicated parts. A more sophisticated technique, **AIDA** uses a matrix to identify compatible sets of solutions to design sub-problems. Similar to a morphological chart, AIDA is helpful when the chosen design concept does not specify how to perform needed functions and why achieving one function may be incompatible with means of achieving others.

Tolerances can be developed with the aid of **realistic tolerance parallelogram plots,**[8] scatter diagrams indicating relationships between parameter values and product performance. Tolerances are set so acceptable performance is highly likely to be achieved by products meeting specification limits. A final tool takes account of the fact that product attributes do not affect customer satisfaction equally. **Classification of characteristics** rates dimensions and other attributes in terms of importance: critical, major, and minor. These ratings, recorded on blueprints and other documentation, allow manufacturing personnel to direct their attention appropriately.

# Prescriptions

The rules and procedures contained in design methods can be augmented with advice culled from design practice. This section offers case-based prescriptions organized around major elements of the design process.

## Requirements Determination

TQM's major focus regarding product design has been on the identification of customer needs. Find out what your customers want. This advice has been offered so frequently that it comes off as a truism, obviously worth doing but not something one needs to think about. This is unfortunate, for the task of determining customer needs can be difficult. Moreover, it is only part of product requirements determination.

To determine customer needs, identify actual and potential product users. Segment the market into groups of customers based, for instance, on different product applications. All customers are desirable, but some market segments are vital for product success. Extra effort must be made to identify and satisfy special needs they might have. A newspaper concluded that advertisers were a critical category of customers. Recognizing their concern with keeping ad copy up-to-date, often through last-minute changes, the paper revamped its operation so late ad copy could be handled effectively.

The primary means of determining customer needs is to communicate with customers. One avenue is market research, such as surveying parts of the customer population. Sales/service call analysis is another method. Sony identifies problems with TV sets by studying service tickets written up by repair specialists. The least formal approach, simply talking with customers, can be the most effective. Discussions with customers led a car wax manufacturer to reconsider the formulation and name of its product. The company thought a glossy finish was the key to customers' hearts. It learned that users view a wax's beading properties, how water rolls off the surface, as the best indicator of performance. Consider the following case:

---

■ **case** *10.1*

A paper mill losing sales due to poor quality and service had representatives visit customers to discuss their needs. The company learned how its late deliveries could shut down customers' plants and how product defects created costs and poor quality for customers. It discovered that customers' equipment was affected by the mill's paper-winding procedure. Wound one way, paper moved smoothly through the process; wound the other way, nothing worked right. The mill could wind paper either way just as easily, but had not known that the direction made a difference to customers. After studying a customer's operations, a mill operator proposed that the mill produce a slightly thinner paper that would satisfy customer needs while giving the mill a price advantage its competitors could not match.

---

Talking with customers is a necessary, but not sufficient, step in determining their needs. Customers do not always know what they want, and their expressed needs may not reflect true needs. Though this seems to suggest that customers are idiots—How could they not know what they want?—there are less pejorative explanations. For even simple products, interactions between product, user, and conditions of use are so complex that people cannot anticipate what they will like and dislike about a product until they use it. This is true of managers asked to state requirements for a new information system and of drivers queried about the ideal vehicular ash tray.

Another factor is that people cannot say what they want if they have no idea what they can have. Customers do not know what technology has made possible. Their needs are often expressed in terms of existing means of performing a function, rather than the general goal. Women consistently expressed a need for hairnets, until hair spray proved to be an effective way of holding hair in place. Needs can be biased by mistaken beliefs or associations. The grocer Stew Leonard sold wrapped fresh fish until the company realized that customers believed unwrapped fish to be fresher.

Even if customers recognize their true product needs, there is a risk that these will be garbled when translated into product specifications. A manufacturer of abrasive cloth lost market share because its product specifications did not reflect customers' concern with cost. IBM's National Service Division redesigned its service delivery process when it realized it perceived quality differently from customers. Customers' primary concern, when experiencing system downtime, was rapid restoration of normal operations. The true quality characteristics valued by customers must be completely and accurately embodied in the substitute quality characteristics expressed in product specifications.

In light of these challenges, what can be done beyond talking to customers to determine their needs? The most valuable step is to study the product in use and the system in which the product is involved. To reiterate Chapter 3's advice regarding problem identification: Go to Gemba, where the action takes place. Map the product user's system with process flow diagrams to find product improvement opportunities like these:[9] conditions of product use different from design assumptions; user activities that are disagreeable, inconvenient, or mistake prone; ways in which product use falls short of its capabilities; product alterations by users to suit their needs; system functions that can be incorporated into the product; and ways of improving product compatibility with the system of use. Personnel at the First National Bank of Chicago, which processes corporate tax payments for the IRS, visited the IRS processing center to see how their "product" was used. Noticing how boxes of remittance information were filed, the bankers changed from labeling boxes on top to labeling box fronts so contents could be identified more easily. In the early 1970s, Canon's consumer research indicated that people were satisfied with their cameras. By studying negatives at film processors and finding overexposed initial frames, Canon learned that users had trouble loading cameras. This led the company to develop a highly successful product featuring automatic film loading.

Incorporate customer use in the product development process. Toy manufacturers have playrooms in which new products undergo the acid test: Will kids play with it, and does the product survive the experience? An adult version of this exists in the software industry. IBM has a software partners lab where customers evaluate software being developed. Most software companies place products in customer installations for in-use evaluation before market rollout. General Electric surveyed the first 1000 purchasers of a dishwasher, making product and process design changes as a result. One innovative aspect of Ford's design process for the Taurus was making prototypes available to customers, Ford employees, and suppliers who offered design recommendations.

For out-of-the-ordinary customers with special needs, simulate their experience with the product. A bookstore owner pretended to be both an extra large and extra small customer to assess the adequacy of his store's layout. See what options customers purchase and make popular options standard features in future models. See what freebies customers take advantage of. Marriott Hotels stopped providing complimentary bath crystals, which guests did not use, and offered free cable TV service, which they did. Using reverse engineering, analyze competitors' products to find characteristics suggesting customer needs that they, but not you, have recognized. Look for product weaknesses that can be exploited by your offering. Before entering the economy hotel business, a hotel chain had researchers stay at competing hotels over six months to evaluate the services provided.

But customer needs are only part of a product's requirements. Design must also consider the product's environment of use. Customers do not specifically want related characteristics, but the product will not function effectively if they are not provided. Even Japanese manufacturers, noted for product design, have been tripped up by overlooked environment-of-use considerations. Some of the first Japanese cars exported to North America experienced severe rusting because of exposure to road salt, which is not used in Japan. Cameras exported to an Asian country were afflicted by mold growing inside lenses, a mold peculiar to that area. A Japanese television manufacturer had high defect rates with products exported to Canada. Its TVs, designed to endure temperatures as low as −25°C, could not withstand the −40°C temperatures common in Canadian warehouses. Designers must consider all environments the product might encounter.

Beyond determining product requirements, one must insure that they are satisfied in the final product. When designers do not meet known requirements, it is usually for want of technical means. For instance, there may be no existing motor both small and powerful enough for the application. But nontechnical failures can occur as well. One is the mistake of assuming that a response to a known product inadequacy was successful. When a customer survey indicated that a washing machine caused excessive tangling of clothes, the manufacturer noted that the failing had been fixed in a new model. Yet owners of new models complained as frequently. The design change had not cured the problem. Customer requirements can simply be overlooked. A purchase order required a manufacturer to provide product test data according to customer specifications. After the requirement was omitted from the work order, 50 units were shipped. All were rejected by the customer and returned to the manufacturer at its expense for completion of contract requirements.

## Conceptual Design

Conceptual design is the heart of the design process and the target of most design methods and theories. It has been largely ignored by quality management, perhaps because a concern for improving quality provides little leverage in generating design concepts.

Design activity is initiated for two reasons: to develop new products and to improve existing ones. The purpose pursued affects the process. When new products are developed, design is a wide-open activity and the key challenge is to generate innovative design concepts. When existing products are improved, conceptual design is more constrained, guided by the current product and focused on overcoming its inadequacies. Ideas are narrower in scope and can often be lifted from competing products. Detail design assumes more prominence.

As noted earlier, designers draw on three resources in their search for new product ideas: analysis, experience, and creativity. In fact, creativity techniques employ all three. Methods that decompose things into parts and attributes are analytical, checklists using tried-and-true prompts draw on experience, and methods requiring analogical or associative thinking are creative in the traditional sense. The characteristic weakness of the latter is non-operationality. Telling a designer to generate analogies or to think associatively is little more useful than the injunction to be creative. Experiential and analytical approaches to conceptual design offer more help.

New product ideas can come from direct experience, as with the company trying to develop an inexpensive cabinet for a TV. A design team member noticed a plastic wastebasket of the right size and shape in a store window. The basket was adapted for use as a TV cabinet. Experience can be more generalized, taking the form of design prototypes, standard ways of performing certain functions. Just as an engineer considers a small set of structural forms in designing a bridge, a product designer mentally reviews known means of performing product functions. Understood in this light, conceptual design is the task of assembling compatible sets of prototypes into effective wholes.

The kicker here is that the set of prototypes, or means of performing functions, expands through technological advances. If technology generates new means fast enough, conceptual design becomes an effort to adapt and apply emerging capabilities to the satisfaction of customer needs. The use of microprocessors and information technology in new products and services exemplifies this technology-driven aspect of conceptual design.

The potential for an analytical approach to conceptual design has been demonstrated by Robert Weber. His book, *Forks, Phonographs, and Hot Air Balloons,*[10] argues that intelligible principles and heuristics underlie invention. One heuristic is to add or delete functions vis-á-vis existing products. Another is to join products into new ones. The Swiss Army Knife joins many simple tools. Joins are facilitated if the elements have shared properties. The clock radio combines appliances sharing an electronic base. It is smart to join devices that are complementary, or used in the same context. A version of this heuristic is to join devices that undo the other's action, such as a pencil and eraser or the claw hammer. Weber's work exposes the informal logic hidden within effective designs.

Other heuristics for conceptual design can be gleaned from the quality literature. Associated with several design-fors is advice to design products to minimize trouble spots. Part-to-part interfaces are an example. Difficulties welding together halves of a lamp fixture prompted Alkco Lighting to redesign the parts as a single piece. The Tennant Company's success in reducing oil leaks from hydraulic joints in floor cleaning machines can be attributed to product redesigns that eliminated joints. When products are redesigned to correct inadequacies, the effort must be based on sound problem diagnosis. Ford's attempts to improve speedometers and a remote fuel door system succeeded because project teams talked to customers and assembly workers and reviewed quality reports and warranty claims to find out what was wrong.

Computer and information technology (IT) is a bountiful resource for new product concepts. Sensors and microprocessors make high-value products, such as cars, copiers, and computers, self-diagnosing. IT can support user design and customization of products, as in systems for creating personal greeting cards and devising paint color schemes for houses. A cardboard manufacturer provided customers with microcomputers and CAD software, enabling them to design packaging and submit orders.

Among the mistakes to avoid in conceptual design is failure to consider human factors, how users are likely to behave. A computer system at Windsor Export Supply was plagued with slow response times, inciting users to repeatedly hit command keys. This reentered data, overloaded the system, and evoked more dysfunctional responses from frustrated users. After users were taught to suppress their natural urges, this poorly designed system functioned adequately. Donald Norman offers a litany of human factors horror stories and counteracting design principles.[11] Another pitfall, deriving from the practice of using established concepts and components in new designs, is carryover of failure-prone features. At a copier manufacturer, the 10 leading field failure modes remained virtually unaltered through several model changes. Many companies are lax in diagnosing and correcting field failures and in including related improvement targets as part of product redesign projects.

Troubles with products often inspire hurried, undisciplined redesign work. Superficial fixes can have side effects worse than the original problem. A printed circuit board used by a consumer products firm charred due to heat radiating from a resistor, causing the product to fail. The problem resulted from a previous design change that had not been thought through carefully enough. Another pitfall is designing unneeded functionality into a product. Excess bells and whistles cause consumers to balk at high prices. Also, products used for many things or over a wide range of conditions are rarely as effective as those that do one thing well. A company's attempt to market an all-temperature detergent in Japan ended in disaster. The Japanese, who wash clothes in cold water, may have inferred that an all-temperature detergent could not be as effective in cold water as products designed solely for that purpose.

## Detail Design

Detail design has received more attention from TQM than conceptual design. It is more prominent in the redesign of existing products, and TQM has focused on redesigning products in response to customer dissatisfaction.

Much prevailing design wisdom is implemented during detail design: reduce the number of parts and parts vendors, use proven standard parts, and configure products in terms of replaceable modules. These prescriptions map into focused heuristics. Recognizing ways in which redundancy exists can eliminate unnecessary parts. One company saved millions by eliminating a subassembly part. The discontinued piece followed the actions of two other parts in producing the product's operating states. Changing the shapes of the two parts allowed elimination of the third.

When off-the-shelf parts cannot be used, new ones must be devised, requiring parameter design. Despite the many factors taken into account, designers can have considerable discretion regarding such product parameters as material thickness or hole locations. Some parameters allow discretion though performance implications come to light if parameter settings are not adequate. In the late '70s, Mercury Marine experienced a 10 percent to 12 percent barb fitting breakage rate on cylinder blocks purchased from a vendor. A study disclosed a thin section vulnerable to stress where the fitting joined the block. Moving the fitting so it junctured where the block was thicker solved the problem. By not taking into account the stress that fitting-related activities impose on the product, the designer had not used available degrees of freedom.

Trade-offs are frequent. For instance, thicker metal is sturdier but more costly. Taguchi methods are the most powerful means of establishing optimal parameter settings, but less sophisticated techniques can be effective. Whereas Taguchi and other experimental design techniques create new data to determine cause-effect relationships, statistical regression is a much less expensive means of finding such relationships in existing data. An Indian manufacturer used regression to study parameter-performance relationships for transistors it manufactured. The studies led to revised specifications that increased process yield from 59 percent to 80 percent. When such techniques are not used, parameter settings may be governed by the designer's attitude toward risk. Aggressive engineers cut back on safety margins, exposing products to premature failure when they encounter demanding conditions. Their conservative colleagues overengineer, creating products that last 20 years but are technologically obsolete in 10.

Related to parameter design is tolerancing, setting ranges within which dimensions can vary around target values. Quality experts agree that tolerances are not always developed in a defensible way. Analytical methods establish tolerances that balance cost, quality, and other considerations. Designers resort instead to published standards, precedents, bargaining, and seat-of-the-pants judgment. Worst-case analysis, a widely used technique, results in overly tight tolerances if designers do not recognize that interacting dimensions are unlikely to be simultaneously at extreme values.

Ignoring the fact that parameters are not equally important, designers may set demanding tolerances for noncritical characteristics. A company's line of attache cases had an excessive gap between metal edge strips. A quality engineer studied product dimensions and tolerances that could affect this characteristic. Only one dimension had a discernible effect. When that dimension and tolerance were adjusted, the problem disappeared. Designers often ignore **cost of tolerance,** the expense of holding parameter values within a range. Manufacturers end up with tight tolerances loosely enforced, a resolution that shields engineers from blame, gets product out the door, but leaves the company and its customers worse off than they might have been.

The inadequacies of prevailing tolerancing practices are well recognized, as are the cures.

1. Determine which product parameters and tolerances are truly critical.
2. Develop cost of tolerance data for parameters that must be controlled.
3. Use statistical tolerancing methods to develop valid tolerances. This includes the use of computer simulation to study interacting dimensions. Dimensional variability usually allows related tolerances to be looser than would be prescribed by a worst-case analysis.
4. Finally, open up noncritical tolerances to reduce production costs.

Other advice on detail design is to design products and processes in a way that establishes product traceability. This is increasingly important in a regulatory environment where malfunctions can trigger product recalls. Parts used in a product must be appropriate for the intended application. A push-button switch used in an airborne navigation system suffered repeated failures. The switch had not been tested for vibration or humidity and was not sealed. In fact, the part was intended for the home appliance market.

Finally, a lesson lies in the story of Ford's bumper shims. Ford designed cars with a shim, a piece of metal something like a washer, that allowed adjustments to be made so bumpers fit car bodies. The company subsequently discovered that Japanese cars do not have a shim. Japanese manufacturers force processes to be controlled so bumpers fit perfectly. Bumper shims, like inventory, are slack or buffering devices that make things easier but at the same time retard progress toward perfection. Though product designs may include such buffers, the goal should be to eliminate them.

## Process Management

Companies try to make the product design process faster and more efficient. Speed is measured by the time required to transform a market need into a product offering. Efficiency is reflected in the absence of aborted projects and expenditures not leading to successful products. Both objectives are supported by efforts to improve coordination between product design and other organizational functions, notably marketing and manufacturing.

Process design methods, discussed in the next chapter, can shorten the product design process. Such methods were applied when AT&T's Power System business unit reduced prototyping time for a product line. Selling a customized product, the unit took an average of 53 days to design a prototype in response to a customer order. To reduce this time, AT&T emphasized constructing applications around standard product platforms. Dedicated design teams were established with team members working together in the same bullpen on a project. Handoffs and meetings were eliminated. Each team member did his or her own documentation, rather than having it done by technical writers. As a result, prototyping time was reduced to five days.

Parallelism, conducting activities simultaneously (as with concurrent engineering), speeds the design process and improves coordination. Whether or not activities are conducted in parallel, marketing, manufacturing, and other functions should participate throughout design. A comparative study of American and Japanese manufacturers noted that at U.S. companies, manufacturing was not involved in product design until after prototype development. By contrast, Japanese manufacturing functions participated throughout the design process. In one company, a proposed design change was not submitted for evaluation to other groups potentially affected by it. After spending thousands of dollars implementing the change, an engineer discovered that the new design required a major revision of another component. The original design had to be reinstated. Time and money lost in the redesign effort would have been saved by better interdepartmental coordination.

**Design reviews** are a means of controlling the design process. Reviews are periodic meetings during which a project's progress is evaluated against its completion schedule, contract requirements, customer specifications, cost targets, and technical objectives. Another control regime, **configuration management,** insures that designs are documented and that revisions to established configurations are authorized and recorded so product specifications remain up-to-date.

Involving manufacturing early in the design process can avoid scale-up difficulties. In a chemical company, a new process devised by a scientist in the laboratory could not be implemented at production scale because of the need to handle gases at high pressure, something not done in the lab. Production designs of products differ from prototype designs in the need to simplify manufacturing processes, reduce material costs, standardize in relation to existing products, and use available production facilities.[12] If adjustments cannot be made, an appealing prototype may have to be scrapped.

A final suggestion is to develop a capacity for organizational learning. Mechanisms for *design experience retention* include design standards manuals, checklists of considerations in design projects, and usage and failure data banks. The last of these was implemented at Electrolux AB, where field engineers transmit data on defects back to product engineers, helping them weed out bad designs and parts.

## NOTES

1. The material in this section is adapted from: Gerald F. Smith and Glenn J. Browne, "Conceptual Foundations of Design Problem Solving," *IEEE Transactions on Systems, Man, and Cybernetics* 23 (1993): 1209–1219.
2. Stuart Pugh, *Total Design* (Reading, Mass.: Addison-Wesley, 1991).
3. John R. Hauser and Don Clausing, "The House of Quality," *Harvard Business Review*, May-June 1988: 63–73.
4. L. D. Miles, *Techniques of Value Analysis and Engineering*, 2nd ed. (New York: McGraw-Hill, 1972).
5. Taguchi's work is described in: Berton Gunter, "A Perspective on the Taguchi Methods," *Quality Progress* 20, no. 6 (1987): 44–52.
6. Most of these methods are drawn from: Nigel Cross, *Engineering Design Methods* (Chichester, England: John Wiley & Sons, 1989); and J. Christopher Jones, *Design Methods: Seeds of Human Futures* (New York: John Wiley & Sons, 1981).
7. See note 2.
8. Keki R. Bhote, *World Class Quality: Using Design of Experiments to Make It Happen* (New York: Amacom, 1991).
9. Frank M. Gryna, "Field Intelligence," sec. 12 in *Juran's Quality Control Handbook*, 4th ed., Joseph M. Juran and Frank M. Gryna, eds. (New York: McGraw-Hill, 1988).
10. Robert J. Weber, *Forks, Phonographs, and Hot Air Balloons: A Field Guide to Inventive Thinking* (New York: Oxford University Press, 1992).
11. Donald A. Norman, *The Psychology of Everyday Things* (New York: Basic Books, 1988).
12. Frank M. Gryna, "Product Development," sec. 13 in *Juran's Quality Control Handbook*, 4th ed., Joseph M. Juran and Frank M. Gryna, eds. (New York: McGraw-Hill, 1988).

# Process Design Problems

---

## Chapter Outline

### Fundamentals
Relationship to Other Quality Problems
Functional Demands
Types of Processes
The Process Design Process

### Process Design Methods
Flowcharts
Process Analysis
Reengineering
Benchmarking
Soft Systems Methodology (SSM)
Other Techniques

### Prescriptions
Process Flow and Layout
Input Screening and Control
Processing Alternatives
Exception Handling
Task Assignment and Scheduling
Setup
Coordination of Activities
Consolidation of Activities
Process Triggers
Process Interruptions and Delays
Process Monitoring and Control (PM&C)
Centralization/Decentralization

Standards and Procedures
Information
Information Technology (IT)
Automation

A process is an organized set of activities aimed at achieving a goal. Process design is the task of devising processes that achieve their goals. If all processes were correctly designed, there would be few problems of any kind. Admittedly, things sometimes get done on the fly, without direction from a predesigned process. Problems can occur if a well-designed process encounters circumstances that could not have been anticipated. However, especially in organizations, where most tasks are recurring, process design is the nearest thing to a problem-solving panacea.

TQM has long recognized the importance of organizational processes and process design. This recognition was expressed by statistical process control, which shifted attention from the end of the line to the processes by which defective products get to the end of the line. TQM's process orientation has been deepened by reengineering and other process improvement methods.

If TQM has led, the management profession has lagged in recognizing the significance of processes. Until, say, ten years ago, few managers paid attention to organizational processes. Manufacturing processes were left to industrial engineers, while administrative and other processes fended for themselves. Business schools taught managers to make decisions, saying nothing about process design. Things are different today. The design and improvement of organizational processes is a key management responsibility.

The chapter begins with a discussion of general issues regarding process design. This leads into a review and assessment of process design methods, notably reengineering. The last and longest section presents case-based prescriptions for process design.

# Fundamentals

A process design problem exists when a new process must be created or an existing process substantially revised. Since many organizational problems eventuate in process changes, no sharp line demarcates process design from other types of quality problems.

## Relationship to Other Quality Problems

Efficiency problems are closely related to process design problems, the two categories blending imperceptibly together. The typical efficiency problem is a situation of unsatisfactory performance regarding cost. Problem solving can lead to process changes. Situations with only local effects—unneeded activities—have been treated as efficiency problems. Situations with broader impact—poor coordination among operators—are discussed as part of process design.

Conformance problems have a similar relationship to process design, but here the occurrence of defects motivates process changes. In most conformance problems, the relevant process is not problematic. Rather, activities are not performed as intended, as when an assembler fails to follow procedures. In some cases, the process is inadequate—procedures may be outdated, for instance—so process design changes are called for.

Unstructured performance problems (UPPs) involve activities that are not well specified by procedures, such as knowledge work and service delivery. Related processes are variable and informal. UPPs give rise to process design problems if performance can be improved by structuring activities. A company might require customer contact personnel to follow a protocol. Establishing procedures may or may not be the way to solve a UPP.

Product design is connected to process design in two ways. A product design must be deployed into the design of a process by which the product will be manufactured. Process design follows product design. Second, because the design of new products is critical for competitive success, the product design process is often targeted for improvement efforts. Companies use process design methods to devise better ways of designing new products.

## Functional Demands

For a long time, process design problems were identified almost exclusively via other concerns. Diagnoses of conformance and efficiency problems indicated process inadequacies, motivating process design effort. This has changed. Companies are more conscious of their processes and of the need to improve them. Process design is being institutionalized, much like product design, as a critical organizational function deserving unremitting attention. In the future, process design problems will be identified less reactively and more as a result of ongoing improvement efforts.

Problem definition is an underdeveloped part of process design. With product design, problem definition centered on requirements determination, creating a design brief. Requirements determination is important with process design, but less informative. Customer needs regarding outputs only weakly designate the process by which outputs are produced. In addition to establishing process requirements, problem definition should determine how the existing process, if there is one, works. This is accomplished through studies of the process. Problem definition should investigate how the process is performed in other organizations. Benchmarking is the key technique for this task. A final part of defining the problem is to develop an appreciation of what is possible. Benchmarking can determine achievable performance levels, and research into pertinent technologies will suggest means for achieving those goals.

Generating and evaluating design alternatives is the key functional demand in process design problem solving. Alternative generation is affected by the nature of the process and by whether an existing process is being revised or a new process created. These issues are discussed in greater depth.

## Types of Processes

The nature of processes in general and the characteristics of the process in question drive process design. Whereas products are static things, processes occur over time.

This suggests the use of a linear, start-to-finish design strategy, an approach not possible with products. Processes are not physical things. They are described by flowcharts, instructions, and task assignments rather than by blueprints and 3-D views. Process design produces a different kind of output than product design.

Processes differ in the outputs they produce. Some yield physical outputs (gears), while others produce states (order fulfillment) or ideas (corporate strategies). Tangible outputs make it easier to determine if a design alternative delivers desired results. Processes also differ in the extent to which they can be structured or defined. Some repetitive processes functioning in a stable environment can be highly specified. Other processes—conducting a sales call or employment interview—must be flexible, shaped by the needs of the situation. Finally, some processes address generic tasks performed in many organizations. There may be **process prototypes,** tried-and-true ways of performing such tasks. Experienced designers know the prototypes and adapt them to fit different situations.

## The Process Design Process

Process design is strongly affected by whether one is designing a new process or redesigning an existing process. This distinction is featured in the reengineering literature, which denotes the two tasks as process innovation and process improvement respectively. When revising an existing process, that process must be thoroughly studied and understood. Failing to do so risks adoption of proposals that do not accommodate legitimate needs and constraints. On the other hand, focusing too strongly on the current process can result in anchoring, seeing it as the only way to do the job, so that only minor changes are proposed. The redesign of a process relies implicitly on a notion of the ideal process that always produces perfect outputs instantaneously without the need for inputs. Designers eliminate unnecessary activities, reduce time needed to perform tasks, and replace unreliable operations with ones that are consistently successful.

Process design is more challenging when a new process must be created. Many reengineering proponents endorse a start-from-scratch, "green field" approach, even when an existing process is in place. They claim, justifiably, that it can yield more innovative processes and more substantial improvements. Unfortunately, proponents of start-from-scratch design offer scant aid in the task of generating design alternatives. Exhortations to be creative and to develop a "process vision" are not very helpful.

There are viable strategies and tactics for developing new process designs. If the process yields a consumer product or other output that is strongly shaped by user needs, these needs can inform process design. Product drives process. As in Quality Function Deployment, a designer can map product characteristics needed to satisfy user needs into process activities producing desired outputs. Process prototypes, proven ways of achieving common design objectives, are resources for generating design alternatives. These serve the same role as high-level design concepts in product design.

Process design is often conducted as a form of means-ends analysis in which high-level process requirements are decomposed into specific steps for achieving those ends. The sequential nature of the process can be exploited by working forward from the initial state or backward from the desired output, or by identifying intermediate states the process necessarily passes through. For instance, given that management approval is required as part of a capital investment process, what activities must be performed before approval is sought and which should be performed thereafter?

# Process Design Methods

Process design methods share characteristics with their product design counterparts. One commonality is the use of design prototypes: Process and product designers both rely on knowledge of standard solutions to recurring design problems. Both disciplines use the copy-cat strategy: See how someone else has solved a design task, and appropriate ideas that might help with one's own problem. Product designers call it *reverse engineering;* benchmarking is the process design version.

Several differences separate the two sets of methods. Whereas product design methods promote top-down elaboration of design concepts into detailed product specifications, process design techniques encourage working from start to finish. The conceptual translations made during product design, from user needs to product functions to product structure and form, are less apparent in process design. There is no process design counterpart of QFD, a technique based on conceptual translation.

Five process design methods—flowcharts, process analysis, reengineering, benchmarking, and Soft Systems Methodology—are discussed in depth. Other techniques are noted to provide a comprehensive view of the process design toolbox.

## Flowcharts

As stated in the last chapter, representations are the language of design, the medium within which designers work, the vehicles by which their creations are communicated to others. Flowcharts are the representational core of process design, the *lingua franca* of the trade. They are less a design method than a tool used within design methods.[1]

Flowcharts depict existing processes so they can be understood and improved. New process designs are represented with flowcharts to facilitate evaluation of proposals and to provide documentation needed for implementing changes. Apart from process improvement efforts, having a flowchart gives operators an understanding of how their work fits in the overall process, increasing their sense of process ownership and control.

Flowcharts have been around for as long as people have thought carefully about processes. Their most extensive use is in the development of computer programs. Flowcharting techniques and conventions have been devised in various fields. Quality practitioners have drawn from these to create a flowcharting methodology suited to the design of organizational processes. This methodology encompasses several diagrammatic variations. The most widely used flowchart is the familiar block diagram, which depicts activities with labeled boxes, using arrows to show their sequencing through time. Figure 11.1 is typical, depicting the process by which a municipality's broken vehicles are repaired and returned to service.[2] When the physical movement of materials from one workstation to another is an important activity, diagrams can overlay the process flow on a map of the workplace. Doing so increases the visibility of transport activities, suggesting opportunities to reduce them. Flowcharts also can be structured to highlight the individual or department responsible for an activity, as in Figure 11.2, which depicts a billing process.[3] Other

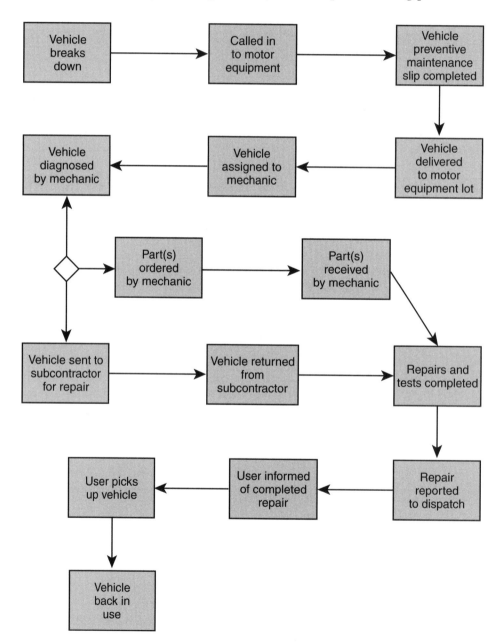

**Figure 11.1** Block diagram flowchart

diagrams list process activities on a sheet of paper, from top to bottom in order of occurrence, along with pertinent information, such as the kind of activity, who performs it, equipment used, duration, and distance traveled.

Flowcharts are usually developed by groups consisting of process managers and operators, but potentially including suppliers, customers, and other parties. Such groups inevitably discover that seemingly simple processes are quite complex. Using a group facilitates identification of inconsiderable process steps, process variations employed in special circumstances, and ancillary flows of information and authority. Constructing a flowchart can take days, even weeks for major organizational processes. The completed flowchart is used to evaluate the necessity and order of process steps. By highlighting delays, inspections, and non–value-adding activities, by denoting rarely used process variations, and by indicating activities consuming the most resources, flowcharts facilitate analysis of existing processes and the design of better ones.

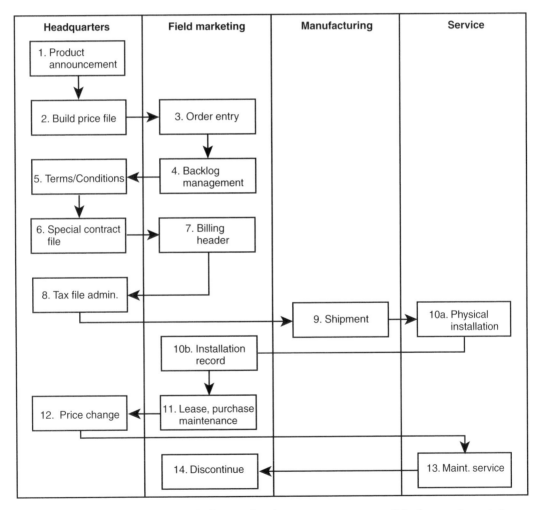

**Figure 11.2**  Flowchart highlighting the department responsible for each activity

The major pitfall of flowcharts—the danger that the map becomes the territory—is shared with other representational devices. Just as people can mistake an organization chart for the organization, they can regard a flowchart as the process. All representations are simplifications. The most elaborate flowchart omits aspects of the process that could be critical from an improvement standpoint. No flowchart captures everything an experienced operator knows about the process nor all that could be learned from careful observation. Flowcharts are not substitutes for other sources of knowledge.

## Process Analysis

The quality movement's most significant contribution to process design goes by many names, including business process improvement, process flow analysis, activity analysis, and business process analysis. Beneath the variations in terminology is a widely used, fairly standardized method for improving business processes.[4]

The goal of process analysis is to improve the performance of existing processes. Though it can result in substantial changes, process analysis starts from an existing process. It does not create processes anew. The method's core activities are as follows:

1. Study and document the current process.
2. Analyze the process and propose improvements.
3. Implement process changes and process management activities.

Different authors embellish these activities in different ways.

To conduct a process analysis, first identify business processes needing improvement. Designate process owners, people held responsible for process performance. Establish improvement teams. A team will study the current process until it is thoroughly understood by means of a *process walk-through,* a formal investigation relying on disciplined observation and interviews with operators. The team sets process boundaries and identifies process activities, variations, and interfaces. Its accumulated knowledge is typically represented in a flowchart. Process performance measures must be established and/or reviewed as baseline performance data is developed.

The second core activity of process analysis—analyzing the process and proposing improvements—is heuristic in nature, with informal techniques supporting some tasks. Cost, cycle time, and value-added analyses indicate process activities offering the greatest potential improvement. Each activity must be analyzed as to how it should be performed and who should do it. Team members search for opportunities to eliminate activities, simplify them, combine them, and improve their sequencing. They look for ways to error-proof and standardize the process. These efforts might identify quick fixes that can be easily implemented. Most process analysis methods incorporate identified changes in a revised version of the current process. Some urge improvement teams to consider radical new process designs that use new information technology and require major organizational changes.

These efforts culminate in the delineation of a compatible set of changes or specification of a fundamentally new process. Following feasibility tests, proposed changes are implemented. Implementation is usually a major undertaking that can fail due to resistance and error. Process analysis recognizes these vulnerabilities and endorses traditional countermeasures: careful implementation planning, top management support, and employee involvement and communication. Process analysis offers one other contribution, the notion of process management. It argues that processes must be consciously managed and their performance continually monitored and improved.

Process analysis has limitations, notably its focus on existing processes. Reengineering proponents have argued, with cause, that TQM's process improvement efforts are too conservative, anchored on current processes. Process analysis rarely exploits the potential of information technology. It provides no real support for high-level conceptual design, as team members use flaws in existing processes to trigger redesign efforts. In summary, process analysis is a useful tool for improving existing processes, but not an effective means of designing new ones.

## Reengineering

If *quality management* was the foremost business buzzword of the 1980s, *reengineering* enjoyed that status during the first half of the '90s. Reengineering is not entirely new (Nothing is!), but it is a significant development in management practice.[5] Reengineering effects a lesser, though substantial, advance over process design as conceived by TQM. Although reengineering can be encompassed under the quality improvement umbrella, it was developed by information technology (IT), not TQM, professionals. At the same time, attempts by reengineering proponents to differentiate it from TQM, to position reengineering as TQM's successor, should be regarded as a marketing tactic in the unending battle for management's attention and consulting fees.

Viewed as a process design method, reengineering has two salient characteristics. First, it adopts a clean slate, start-from-scratch approach, even when a viable process is in place. Second, it makes extensive use of information technology in devising radical new process designs. In essence, reengineering is the application of existing and emerging IT means to organizational process ends. It unites means and ends that had not previously been conjoined because managers did not think much about processes and did not know much about IT.

At both its front and back ends, the reengineering process looks like any other program for organizational change. It begins with the need to secure top management support, to identify organizational processes in need of improvement, to establish process ownership and project teams. After a new process has been designed comes the usual implementation demands: thorough planning, careful testing, reaffirmation of management support, phased rollout, sensitivity to those affected by the change, institutionalization of the new process, and continuous monitoring of its performance.

The unique elements of reengineering occur in the middle, when process designs are developed. In keeping with a clean slate approach to design, project teams study existing processes but are cautioned against analyzing them too deeply so as not to become anchored on current ways of doing things. This is good advice, though it leaves designers with the task of devising fundamentally new processes. They cannot simply identify flaws in the current process and propose targeted corrections.

How do reengineering gurus and methods respond to this challenge? Davenport exhorts team members to create a "process vision," but says little about how this might be done. He admits that "there is less to say about the design phase of process innovation" and describes design activity as "largely a matter of having a group of intelligent, creative people review the information collected . . . and synthesize it into a new process."[6] This is a copout. Hammer and his associates are more helpful. In the *Harvard Business Review* article that inaugurated the craze, Hammer cited principles of reengineering—for instance, organize around outcomes, not tasks—that can guide design efforts.[7] Hammer and Champy identified themes commonly encountered in reengineered processes (such as workers making decisions), traditional rules that can be broken by modern IT (that field personnel can send and receive information wherever they are, for instance), and symptoms of reengineering opportunities (complexity, exceptions, and special cases reflecting accretion onto a simple base process).[8] Hammer and Stanton stressed the need to challenge assumptions governing existing processes and conceive new process designs that ignore invalid assumptions.[9] These heuristics are complemented by less useful calls for creativity and critical thinking. Arguably, most of the conceptual design work required in reengineering projects is accomplished by recognition of process prototypes. Experienced reengineers know means by which common organizational processes— order fulfillment, for instance—can be performed. They devise new processes by adapting proven means to current demands.

Like any program that fosters significant organizational change, reengineering has had successes and failures. The latter can often be attributed to such "usual suspects" as inadequate management support or lack of user involvement. Many failures presumably result from design errors, say, the use of untested or inappropriate technology. Continued experience will yield higher success rates, since reengineering is fundamentally sound. It exploits the enormous potential of information technology for improving organizational activities. Its insistence on clean slate design is unwise and wasteful, as some proponents have recognized, but it answers a need to move beyond the conservative process analysis approach endorsed by TQM. Though reengineering has not developed a powerful method for high-level conceptual design, experience will provide process prototypes and heuristic practices to support this task.

## Benchmarking

Benchmarking came into prominence in the late 1980s and quickly established itself as a valuable addition to the standard managerial toolbox.[10] As noted in Chapter 3, benchmarking is in part a problem identification technique that uses data on world-class performers to develop goals against which organizational performance can be assessed. Even more, benchmarking is a process design method. Project teams determine how world-class performers achieve their performance levels and emulate their methods, adapting them to the needs of the target organization. Thus, benchmarking employs a copycat strategy. Though challenges can be encountered during its implementation, the strategy is straightforward and needs no explication.

Because of its copycat strategy, benchmarking has been criticized as being "just a tool for catching up, not for jumping way ahead" of competitors.[11] This criticism has less force when benchmarking reaches beyond industry boundaries to world-class process analogues in other fields. Even then, benchmarking reproduces, but does not advance, the state of the art. The criticism's flaw is its assumption that state-of-the-art processes can routinely be improved upon. Reengineering enthusiasts might claim to do so, but such claims are vastly overblown: Rather than creating radical new process designs, most reengineering efforts employ established process prototypes. Since no design method consistently improves on the state of the art, there are no grounds for denigrating a method that advances processes to the current cutting edge.

## Soft Systems Methodology (SSM)

Less widely known and applied, Soft Systems Methodology is an interesting, systems-based process design technique developed by Peter Checkland.[12] It can be used for organizational design and for the design of organizational processes. SSM consists of seven stages.

1. Enter and explore the problem situation.
2. Develop an account of the problem.
3. Shift attention from the problem situation to human activity systems involved in it, and formulate *root definitions* of one or more of these systems. A root definition is a concise statement of key system characteristics, such as customers, products, owners, and transformations.
4. Elaborate each definition into a conceptual model of the system, a detailed specification of activities the system must perform to achieve its goals.
5. Compare these conceptual models to the problematic situation.
6. Identify feasible and desirable real-world changes.
7. Implement selected changes.

Steps 3 and 4 are the keys to SSM. They generate conceptual models of systems pertinent to the problem situation that can be compared to the problematic system itself. Applied mostly in the United Kingdom, SSM has been used as part of business process redesign efforts.

Checkland ascribes SSM's effectiveness to the power of the systems concepts it employs. Arguably, if SSM is effective, it is for other reasons. The technique is based on abstraction, a sound problem-solving strategy. Used in some creativity techniques, abstraction keeps problem solvers from becoming bogged down in the current situation by forcing them to move away from that situation, though not entirely. A conceptual linkage is maintained. In SSM, the root definition developed during Step 3 is connected to the original problem but is so abstract that it can be elaborated in Step 4 without evoking recollections of the problem. SSM practitioners can design processes not anchored on their flawed organizational counterparts.

## Other Techniques

Other process design methods employ other strategies. The Kokai watch technique, discussed in Chapter 3 as a problem identification method, is based on direct observation.[13] The method has a small group of people—operators, managers, outsiders—observe a process. Group members write down improvement opportunities that come to mind. The group discusses these ideas among themselves and later with process operators, yielding a set of proposed changes. Given its focus on the current process, Kokai watch is not a vehicle for creating innovative process designs. Nonetheless, it is easy to implement and can produce substantial improvements.

Like SSM, many process design methods are based on systems concepts. A system is a purposeful whole with parts that function and interact to promote achievement of overall goals. Since products and processes are systems (but then, what is not a system?), systems concepts have been incorporated into design methods. In some, systems concepts perform useful work. For instance, input-process-output analysis uses these elements of a system to direct process design.[14] In other methods, systems concepts add no real value, merely a veneer of intellectual respectability.

One of the critical challenges in design, especially when replacing an existing process, is that designers recognize legitimate goals and constraints embodied in the current process without allowing their thinking to become dominated by that process. The abstraction strategy used by SSM is one way of navigating this dilemma. Another way exploits the fact that process design is typically undertaken by project teams. Split the team into two groups, a requirements group responsible for understanding and documenting the current process and a design group that proposes innovative design concepts. After working awhile, the requirements group, consisting primarily of people who know the current process, can draft a concise statement of process requirements and pass it on to the design group. These people, more aware of relevant process technologies, generate and develop design concepts satisfying the requirements. As conceptual design moves into detail design, the two groups can reunite so in-depth knowledge of process requirements is brought to bear in evaluating and improving design proposals. Like the abstraction strategy, this approach keeps knowledge of the way things are from smothering imagination of how they might be.

The strengths and limitations of the major process design methods are summarized in Figure 11.3.

## Prescriptions

The tremendous performance benefits achieved through process design suggest that powerful problem-solving methods are at work. This is not true. For the most part, process design benefits result from informal heuristics. Some of the heuristics are general and well-known; others are less familiar and more narrow in application. This section, organized around process design topics, presents an array of prescriptions illustrated by case applications.

| Method/Practice | Applications | Strengths | Weaknesses |
|---|---|---|---|
| Flowchart | Graphically depicting the activities, sequence, and elements of a process. | Highly general and flexible; powerful visual support for process analysis and improvement. | Danger that the map becomes the territory; no diagram includes everything of importance. |
| Process Analysis | Improving the performance of existing processes. | Reasonably general; a useful collection of heuristics and informal techniques that can be adapted to different situations. | Strong focus on existing processes can result in anchoring; little support for conceptual design. |
| Reengineering | Designing new processes that are substantial improvements over their current counterparts. | Clean slate approach can be highly effective; exploits the power of modern information technology. | Little support for conceptual design; risks and disruptions not always justified by results. |
| Benchmarking | Identifying and adapting best-practice processes to current organizational needs. | Quite general, applicable to most organizational processes; can bring processes to current state of the art. | Implementation challenges can be significant; a copycat strategy that rarely delivers radical new process designs. |
| Soft Systems Methodology | Redesigning processes and systems in light of performance inadequacies. | Fairly general; abstraction strategy keeps one aware of, but not tied to, the existing system. | Not widely known or applied; some steps are not operational; systems concepts are oversold. |

**Figure 11.3** Overview of process design methods

## Process Flow and Layout

Production processes are traditionally classified in terms of three types of process flow:

1. **Line.** Line flow processes, as in assembly lines and oil refineries, involve sequences of operations making large volumes of standardized outputs.
2. **Intermittent.** Intermittent flow processes produce outputs in batches. Also called job shops, they allow flexibility to fit the needs of different orders.
3. **Project.** Project operations produce relatively unique outputs, such as ships, one at a time.

One goal of process design, especially for manufacturing processes, is to minimize inventory. Much inventory exists as work in process in intermittent flow processes. To reduce this, intermittent processes can be converted to line processes, replacing batch processing with flows of material through the workplace. In a company producing television cabinets on two lines, Shigeo Shingo noted that a single saw fed batches of output to both lines. Though the saw's operating rate was under 40 percent, Shingo arranged for a second saw to be purchased so pure line processes could be established. This enabled sawing and planing to be combined in each line, eliminating the need for a worker. It also shortened the production cycle and reduced in-process inventory. Shingo made similar changes at the Tokai Iron Works, where machines had been grouped by type and production was in batches. Arranging machines by product flow and using a conveyor to carry work in process through the plant resulted in a 200 percent productivity increase. Use line flow processes if possible, especially when inventory costs are significant.

The process employed affects facility layout. Most line flow processes require a fixed layout, intermittent processes are less constraining, while project operations are configured to meet the needs of individual orders. The spatial arrangement of activities has significant performance effects. The efficiency of a loom shed in a spinning mill increased from 79.0 percent to 86.5 percent after blocks of looms were reconfigured.

One layout improvement goal is travel distance reduction. The *string method* can help streamline repetitive processes. On a flow diagram map of the work area, use string to trace the movement of work in process from one work station to another. By varying routings and work station locations, one can identify process designs needing less string, hence less travel distance. When activities are not performed in a standard sequence, reduce distances of frequent trips. Locate tools, jigs, filing cabinets, and other resources near people who use them. Arrange activities to eliminate unnecessary trips. By moving timers to the machines they controlled, the Firestone Tire and Rubber plant in Albany, Ga., eliminated 15 timer adjustment trips per machine per shift, saving $8800 annually.

Distance reduction is important for interorganizational activities, as you can see in the competitive advantage enjoyed by suppliers located near their customers. Geographic proximity reduces transportation costs and improves communication among process participants. Ford's Windsor Export Supply division was dissatisfied with the processing of freight bills by an outside audit service. Bringing the process in-house reduced geographic dispersion and increased communication among processors. Processing errors and cycle times dropped dramatically.

There may be a trade-off to manage if concentration of activities results in congestion. Operators and activities compete for space, interfering with each other and degrading system performance. Faculty mailboxes in a high school were located near the office so secretaries could easily distribute mail. Faculty members picking up their mail exacerbated morning crowding in the office. Moving mailboxes to the faculty lounge solved the problem. Position activities to avoid spatial conflicts, especially during peak load periods. The Bursar's Office at the University of Wisconsin established satellite payment locations for some student transactions during the start-of-semester rush. Dispersed service facilities allow customers to avoid long lines and confusion attendant on a central processing location. But the dispersion strategy will not work if many customers have multiple transactions requiring them to travel from one service location to another. Providing customers with the convenience of one-stop shopping takes precedence in the positioning of service activities.

## Input Screening and Control

Processes do not function effectively unless inputs are appropriate in kind, quantity, and quality. Input screening and control mechanisms must be designed into the process. The most familiar are inspections of incoming materials and selection and training regimes experienced by new employees. Informational inputs are usually the most troublesome.

Job instructions may be incomplete. Work submitted to a word processing pool was delayed by illegible and incomplete job request forms. In another company, orders entered by salespeople could not be processed because of missing or inconsistent information. Inadequate inputs must be detected quickly and corrected or withdrawn from the process. Be sure that input forms are concise and easy to understand and that people submitting inputs have been trained. Persistently faulty inputs should be returned to originators to inform them of mistakes and motivate better performance. This prescription requires careful implementation with external customers who can take their business elsewhere.

In service processes, customers can be inputs. Most people brush their teeth before dental appointments, but many enter service processes without information needed for transactions. Service providers can prepare customers for processing by providing instructions beforehand. Outpatient registration inefficiencies at a hospital were corrected by giving customers checklists preparing them for the process. The Social Security Administration's Atlanta office reduced claims processing time by 60 days and saved $351,000 annually by asking claimants to bring medical records along when filing claims. Some customer deficiencies can be corrected as they wait to be processed. The University of Wisconsin Bursar's Office gave replacement bills to students, waiting in payment lines, who had forgotten their tuition statements.

Triage is sorting performed during input screening. Popularized by the TV series "M.A.S.H.," the term is often associated with emergency medical facilities where patients are sorted so those needing immediate attention are served first. Urgency is one sorting criterion, but triage can be performed for other reasons as well. Inputs should be triaged for acceptability, so inadequate inputs do not waste time waiting to be processed. A utility's processing of customer applications for rebates improved when it used a checksheet to screen incoming applications, immediately returning the 50 percent that were incomplete. Paralleling the medical triage of patients who cannot be saved, inputs can be sorted to avoid wasting resources on unlikely prospects. This strategy keeps most job applicants from getting interviews. It was used at a refinery to cull out marginal engineering projects, so attention was available for promising proposals.

Some processes involve multiple participants, each acting relatively independently. Making all participants aware of a job when it enters the system facilitates preparation so processors are ready to perform tasks when the job gets to them. The Cherry Point Naval Aviation Depot reduced turnaround time on aircraft engine repairs by bringing shop members together when an engine was disassembled so each shop could immediately order needed parts. Front-end awareness and involvement smoothes approval processes. Avco Aerostructures instituted a system of "run-bys" for improvement projects. These secured early buy-in and participation by affected departments, helping reduce the proposal-to-implementation cycle from 226 days to an average of 64 days.

## Processing Alternatives

Few processes produce the same outputs from the same inputs via the same activities on every cycle. Rather, processes encompass variations and include different ways of producing outputs. Variations reflect differing inputs (such as the chemical composition of crude oil received at a refinery), requirements of different customers (customizing activities in a furniture factory, for instance), and contingencies that arise during processing (machine breakdowns forcing revised routings of the process flow). Processing alternatives must be recognized and included in the process flowchart. Designers should identify split-points at which process alternatives diverge and the proportion of output produced by each.

Three basic strategies for handling variation in cases are:

1. Distinct processing alternatives take parts of the transaction stream. This approach is used for major variants that occur frequently.
2. Subroutines or conditional branches are added to a core process. These address less substantial variants.
3. Individual cases are handled as exceptions, one-of-a-kind occurrences processed on the fly with no prespecified procedure.

This subsection addresses the high-end, processing alternatives approach, while the next considers the low-end, exception handling strategy. Each blends into the middling, process subroutine option.

Variation forces designers to decide whether to use a single complex process or several simple ones. Hammer and Champy argue that organizational processes become overcomplicated by provisions for special cases, claiming it is better to have several simple processes with a front-end split-point deciding which to use in each case.[15] In contrast, when Dun and Bradstreet's customer contracting process was reengineered, separate processes for three different contract types were replaced by a single flexible process, contributing to major reductions in cycle time. There is no right answer to the one vs. many question. The deciding factor is the degree of process overlap for different cases: If overlap is high—all cases undergo many common activities—use a standard process with variations. If overlap is low, use distinct processing alternatives.

Processing alternatives serve various needs. Different processes may suit different customer groups. The Meriter Hospital in Madison, Wis., relieved congestion at its outpatient registration desk by allowing series patients, those visiting the hospital on a regular basis, to register in their appointment areas. The New York City Probation Department classified probationers on the basis of predicted recidivism. It changed its processes so that low-risk people simply have to report in, whereas high-risk probationers are carefully monitored and receive a variety of special services. Different processes can be used for different transaction sizes, as with loan approvals in banks. Transaction complexity is also pertinent. Reengineering the credit approval process at IBM Credit exploited the fact that few transactions were truly complex and most were simple enough to be processed by one person. Splitting processes on this basis allows skilled processors to focus on cases that really need their attention.

Once processing alternatives have been devised, criteria for case assignments must be defined and enforced. Processing alternatives may have different costs for the organization, different implications for operators, and different benefits for customers. These differences can prompt unwarranted use of an option, as the following case illustrates.

---

■ case *11.1*

The West Paces Ferry Hospital in Atlanta experienced excessive numbers of caesarean sections (c-sections) in its maternity ward. The c-section, a special purpose delivery method, is far more expensive than vaginal birth. Investigation by a project team revealed that 13 percent of c-sections were to mothers who previously had the operation. This practice, called "repeat c-section," had once been necessary for medical reasons. Improved surgical practices now made it possible for women who had had c-sections to deliver subsequent babies vaginally. Being unaware of this change and afraid of having a vaginal delivery, many patients continued to request and receive repeat c-sections.

---

In this case, customers were motivated, primarily by fear, to select an expensive processing alternative that they typically did not have to pay for. The hospital's failure to update its sorting criteria to reflect obsolescence of the repeat c-section rule and to educate patients on the benefits of vaginal delivery resulted in excessive use of the alternative.

Notably vulnerable to overuse is the fast-track process, or expediting. Users compensate for their mistakes and tardiness by insisting on expedited handling of their transactions. The use of express mail is a version of this. More harmful are abuses like those experienced at a word processing pool in the Wisconsin State Department of Revenue, where half of all typing requests were designated as rush jobs. At a company that sells built-to-order products, 85 percent of orders were entered into the production control system late, requiring expediting to meet promised delivery dates. Fast-track processing alternatives are expensive, disrupt normal operations, and, if overused, lose the speed that makes them distinctive. If all jobs are expedited, none are, not even the ones deserving this treatment. Organizations must enforce rigorous controls on the use of fast-track processes.

Unneeded processing options should be eliminated, as they are costly to maintain and foster confusion and duplication. If there is more than one way of doing something, some people will do it every which way to make sure the job gets done. Others will not do it at all, figuring it has already been done. Lab test turnaround time in a hospital was excessive, in part because the lab was often notified three or more times—by computer entry, telephone, and pocket pager—that a test had been ordered. Another hospital lost revenue due to problems with documentation and billing for medications because multiple charging systems allowed items to be charged in six different ways. Processing alternatives can live on after their original purpose has disappeared, creating extra costs.

All processing activities are not required for all cases. Do not force every job to undergo operations that can be targeted more selectively. The State of Wisconsin's Department of Revenue found that many tax returns claiming refunds could be diverted from the normal processing stream. This reduced average turnaround time by two weeks. The discharge process at Holston Valley Hospital in Kingsport, Tenn., was slowed by a policy requiring a hospital employee to escort discharged patients to a waiting vehicle. This policy, adopted to keep semiambulatory people from collapsing as they left the hospital, was revised so only those needing help were required to use it.

## Exception Handling

Judgment must be used in deciding whether to treat infrequent variations as exceptions or to handle them with special-purpose subroutines. The second approach risks cluttering up the core process at a loss in efficiency. On the other hand, it can be time consuming to handle exceptions on a case-by-case basis. If process designers opt to have cases handled as exceptions, they can make this less burdensome by establishing a dedicated exception-handling function. In some factories, special orders are filled by designated individuals using dedicated pieces of equipment. When a division of Honeywell responded to problems created by incorrect routings of correspondence and telephone calls, it made full-time coordinators responsible for handling such communications. This allows the development of expertise, since even exceptions exhibit commonalities over time.

If exceptions are diverted from the main processing stream but handled by regular operators, take care that these unusual cases are not lost or ignored. This happens because operators focus on everyday tasks. Special cases, once out of sight, are quickly out of mind as well. Delays in processing customer complaint information at Miles Laboratories resulted when incomplete forms were held prior to data entry and then forgotten. Ford found that cars left plants with low engine oil levels because they had been diverted for rework and did not undergo the normal oil fillage procedure. Special cases require special care so they receive all required activities.

When exceptions result from errors, the exception-handling burden can be addressed by reducing the incidence of errors. Boeing Military Airplanes uses "withhold tags" to mark inadequate vendor parts that get into its production process. When the company realized it was spending $5 million to deal with each year's average of 12,000 tags, it initiated a rigorous supplier relations program to improve the quality of purchased parts.

More often, exceptions reflect special customer needs. If exceptionality is anathema in high volume production processes, it is accepted without question by job shop customizers. Here there may be opportunities to improve performance by identifying commonalities in the stream of seemingly unique jobs. Reengineering succeeded in Federal Mogul's sample development process when engineers realized that most new product designs were variations of past designs and that work went faster if commonalities were exploited. Becton Dickinson improved customer service on special orders by adding special-product types to its standard product line. The number of special orders filled per year declined from 700 to 200, saving the company $55,000 in order-filling costs. Some exceptions are best handled as normal transactions.

Indeed, there are cases where norms of exceptionality should be reversed so that standard practice is replaced by one previously regarded as exceptional. The Baptist Memorial Hospital in Atlanta activated television and telephone service in patient's rooms upon request. Time lags in doing so prompted patient complaints. Considering that 93 percent of patients wanted the services, the hospital changed its policy and now disconnects them only if a patient asks.

## Task Assignment and Scheduling

This topic encompasses several issues:

1. Managing the inflow of jobs to the processing system.
2. Determining who is responsible for processing activities. This is done at three different levels:
   a. organizational
   b. departmental
   c. individual
3. Assigning jobs to process operators.
4. Determining the sequence of activities.
5. Scheduling orders.

Many of these issues are addressed in operations management texts. Some are resolved in real time on a case-by-case basis, with process designers only offering general guidelines for their resolution.

The inflow of cases to the system is determined by customer demand. This is less true for make-to-stock manufacturing systems. The process must be designed to match capacity with demand, minimizing idle capacity and avoiding backlogs of unfinished orders. Forecasts provide information about customer demand, but even if forecasts were perfectly reliable, it would be difficult to match capacity to demand. The latter is variable, the former inflexible. If processes get jobs from organizational subunits, performance can be improved through intraorganizational coordination. A quality circle at the Veteran's Medical Center in Albany, N.Y., found that 25 hours a month were spent waiting for patients to arrive for X-rays. Better scheduling improved coordination between departments, eliminating waiting time.

Extreme variation in job inflow is the bane of process efficiency. Peak loads should be anticipated and smoothed. At the *Tallahassee Democrat*, a Florida newspaper, advertising salespeople were given faxes and car phones so they could transmit sales orders throughout the day rather than dumping them on the ad makeup department at day's end. Dun and Bradstreet uses telecommunications technology to transfer special customer requests among its offices, smoothing demand bulges at individual locations.

Process managers must insure that adequate capacity is maintained at all times. This can be troublesome for service processes during break and lunch periods. When a survey revealed that a bank's customers disliked waiting for phone calls to be answered, the bank investigated and found that delays occurred during lunch periods when only one operator was on duty. By rescheduling lunch shifts and giving a clerk part-time operator responsibilities, the bank had at least two operators at all times, reducing the number of waiting calls.

In determining who will perform processing activities, the dominant consideration is who can do the best job. Assignments must be made at organizational, departmental, and individual levels. The first kind of assignment, a make vs. buy decision, reflects an assessment of how responsibilities should be allocated across members of the value chain. The **value chain** concept denotes the complete set of organizations involved in transforming raw materials into a final product and selling it to customers. A manufacturer began to buy steel from a service center that cut bars to size, replacing its internal cutting operation with the vendor's more efficient process. Reengineering its production process led Coca-Cola-Schweppes of Great Britain to manufacture plastic bottles in its plant rather than purchasing from outside. Other organizations may perform activities for free. By assigning different post office box numbers to departments, organizations shift mail sorting from their mail rooms to the postal service.

Assigning activities to organizational subunits can be complicated by turf wars. Departments fight for some tasks and the attendant resources, while avoiding others and the related headaches. Again, who can do the best job? A hospital that had trouble maintaining adequately stocked top-up carts (portable supply centers) solved the problem by transferring cart responsibility from its transportation department to the stores department. Knowledge of inventory was more important than experience with wheels.

When there are no task experts, other factors come into play. A hospital lost revenue because of inadequate marketing of private rooms. Nurses had been responsible for selling this service to patients. By reassigning the task to admitting personnel, the hospital increased its revenue and nursing staff morale. It is rarely wise to ask overburdened professionals to perform a task for which they have no special qualifications. Even if relevant expertise exists, task assignment may be dominated by other considerations. If individual case knowledge outweighs task expertise, each operator should perform multiple tasks for a case rather than having each case addressed by many task experts.

Assigning activities to people and departments is a prerequisite for the third of the five issues addressed in this subsection: assigning individual cases. Who will perform this activity on this order? Assuming all workers are qualified, jobs should be assigned to level the workload. Morale will plummet if some workers get too much work while others get too little or only the easy jobs. Again, however, assignments can veer from this norm when other considerations are prominent. Whirlpool routes customer service calls to the representative who last dealt with that customer, knowing that case familiarity is the key to an effective response.

If employees have flexibility in deciding what to work on next, the process design must insure that appropriate selection criteria are used. Workers at a Signetics plant selected jobs for processing, doing so in a way that maximized piece transfers from their stations, a measure of individual performance. Since this led to suboptimal performance for the process, management devised a new measure that provided appropriate worker incentives. Note that management motivated employees to make selections that were good for the company rather than telling workers what jobs to select.

Finally comes the question of "When?" When should activities be performed during a process, and when should particular jobs be done? The sequencing of activities is often constrained by technical factors. Workers cannot start on B until A has been completed. If degrees of freedom exist, they are used to smooth task-to-task interfaces. Some jobs—making deliveries in a truck, for instance—consist of tasks that can be sequenced at will. Process designers provide operators with resources, such as routing software, for making intelligent sequencing decisions. L. L. Bean's order processing function uses a computer-based short interval scheduling system: A small number of orders are accumulated, sorted, and scheduled by computer, which generates routes pickers use to collect items for that cluster.

Dispatching rules—as in the commonplace first come, first served—determine which job next enters the system. If operators can select from a pool of jobs waiting to be processed, certain heuristics apply. Perform demanding tasks when at your physical and mental peak. Avoid procrastinating indefinitely on difficult or distasteful jobs. Perform time-sensitive tasks as soon as possible. To shorten the time needed to acquire publications, library staff at Florida Power and Light process publication requests at the start of each day.

## Setup

Setup refers to tasks performed in preparation for processing. Front-end work, once done, may not have to be redone until the process starts producing a different output. Historically, because setup was time consuming and costly, organizations used long production runs. Spreading setup costs over thousands of outputs reduced costs on a per unit basis. But this practice conflicts with consumer preferences for product variety. Companies could either have short production runs with high setup costs or use long production runs, making products that would be inventoried until sold. Both options are costly.

A way out of this dilemma was discovered by the Japanese, not surprisingly in the auto industry, where consumers desire many models, inventory carrying costs are high, and production setups are massive undertakings. The solution, developed by Shigeo Shingo, was to drastically reduce setup time. Shingo devised a set of heuristics, collectively termed Single Minute Exchange of Dies (SMED), enabling Toyota to reduce setup times by several orders of magnitude.[16] SMED techniques have spread throughout the auto industry and elsewhere. After Ford adopted SMED, presses that had required five to seven days to change could be switched in a few hours.

One source of SMED's effectiveness is the distinction between **internal** and **external setup.** Internal setup activities are performed on the production line; they create downtime for part or all of the process. External setup, conducted off-line, does not interfere with normal processing. SMED replaces internal with external setup to reduce process downtime. A Kokai watch team at Bridgestone (USA) noticed that a worker changing a die had trouble looking up information. His gloves made it hard to turn pages. The team recommended that paperwork be completed as much as possible before the die change. Victory Memorial Hospital in Waukegan, Ill., reduced waiting time in its emergency department by having the triage nurse initiate the patient specimen process when assessing patients with urinary tract infections. This reduced the wait for lab results so physicians could make diagnoses more quickly. Because hospital operating rooms are expensive facilities, external setup should replace internal preparation. West Paces Ferry Hospital in Atlanta reduced delays in operating room admissions by preadmitting patients for tests and paperwork the day before a scheduled operation. Another hospital performed two additional operations a week as a result of better procedures for preparing instrument tables. Previously, 70 percent of tables were improperly prepared, causing delays while nurses searched for equipment.

Another SMED strategy is to facilitate positioning and other adjustments made during setups. Well-designed fixtures allow adjustments to be performed as part of external setup. Replace bolts and screws, fasteners having an infinite number of settings, with clamps or pins that only permit prescribed settings. Bridgestone (USA) reduced setup times for tire molds by 95 percent in this way. Visual cues on the workpiece, machines, and floor ease adjustments and other setup tasks. A. O. Smith devised standard markings and color-coded charts reducing model-to-model changeover times for truck frames.

Reduce the number of things to be changed as part of changeovers. The trick here is standardization. Shingo standardized die heights by attaching blocks to smaller dies. A fast-food chain had raw materials for all grille items produced to the same thickness. Grille heat settings never had to be changed and cooking times were equalized, reducing over- and undercooking. Eliminate differences between outputs to reduce setup tasks. Harley-Davidson simplified changeovers between two crankpins by revising an oil hole angle. One had been at 45°, the other at 48°, a difference that made no difference for product functionality, but a world of difference for setups.

Just as using common parts reduces changeovers, so does consolidating jobs. Workers at the Square D Company wanted to reduce the solvent used to clean paint sprayers after color changes. By gathering information on job colors, they were able to collect jobs by color, reduce the number of changeovers, and save solvent and changeover time. Another cause of changeovers is job switching, setting aside unfinished jobs to work on others. Knowledge workers incur excessive mental setup costs in this way, taking time to get up to speed on new transactions. A refinery's process for handling engineering projects was improved by reducing switching from one project to another by drafters, checkers, and engineers.

## Coordination of Activities

Coordination failures occur because organizations consist of multiple units and individuals, each not knowing what others are doing. Different units may work at cross-purposes, or their efforts aren't integrated to the extent required for success. Activities within a process must be coordinated, some activities must be coordinated across processes, and coordination must often occur across organizational boundaries.

Coordination is in part a question of timing. At the Norfolk Naval Shipyard, machinery compartments were seldom ready for required inspections. This created work disruptions for other compartments. By assigning a crew to make sure all compartments were prepared for inspections, the shipyard saved more than $138,000 annually.

Poor coordination can be manifested through duplication. If the right hand does not know what the left is doing, both can end up doing the same thing. This often happens with data collection. A process improvement project at Dun and Bradstreet disclosed that analysts repeated work done by screeners. Analysts did not realize how thoroughly screeners checked for identification errors and consequently made the same checks themselves. Duplications can be prevented by developing clear task assignments and educating process participants on the activities of others.

Another coordination failure involves poorly designed interfaces between activities when the outputs of one do not match input requirements of its successor. This occurs when operators do not understand downstream requirements. The critical care unit in a Canadian hospital performed an additional procedure on patients transferred from the emergency room because ER did not provide the required type of IV hook-up site. Processors may not always provide needed instructions, especially for special cases. Nineteen percent of customer returns to a consumer durables manufacturer occurred because salespeople did not notify manufacturing and engineering of changes required for special orders.

Inadequate instructions reflect a broader lack of communication. Operators do not notify others that activities have been completed. Until a new discharge form was developed, a hospital's admitting unit, cashier, and pharmacy were notified of only 25 percent of patient discharges. Non-notifications caused inaccurate bed counts and failure to arrange payments. At another hospital, patients waited an extra half hour in the emergency room because the critical care unit was not prenotified of, and consequently could not prepare for, impending transfers. Communication may be initiated by media that are too slow. A company's process for issuing design changes to suppliers was slowed by the internal mail system. The use of electronic sign-offs reduced throughput time considerably.

Poor communication can show up as a failure to notify process participants early enough during job processing. Audit reports produced by the U.S. General Accounting Office are reviewed by as many as 29 people outside the original work team, so it typically takes six months for GAO findings to be published. When a project team tried to speed the process, its first step was to establish preliminary review sessions where reviewers could discuss ongoing audit work and offer suggestions about methods and report findings.

The need to coordinate activities extends beyond process boundaries. Seemingly unrelated activities can be complementary or conflicting; in either case, coordination benefits can be realized. A trucking company had a line haul driver traveling nightly from Florence, S.C., to Hazelhurst, Ga., and another traveling the same route at the same time in the opposite direction. The company saved thousands of dollars by arranging for drivers to meet at the route's midpoint, switch vehicles, and head home. Ford held meetings between its treasury personnel and consumer finance people. The latter learned how to adjust consumer loan periods to reduce Ford's financing costs. Intraorganizational coordination cured crowded hallways in a school when three grades of students rushed to classes. Letting one class out a minute later eliminated the problem.

If coordination is needed across process boundaries, it is also needed across organizational boundaries, especially with the growth of cooperation among value chain members. Information technology has a leading role in this regard, providing fast, detailed information that allows suppliers to adjust production in light of actual demand and enables customers to monitor the status of orders. An integrated circuit manufacturer locked its customers into an arrangement synchronizing its manufacturing capacity with their daily product usage. Coordination between the manufacturer and its customers allowed the former to eliminate order status reports and other overhead activities, saving money for all.

Coordination failures reconfirm established wisdom about organizational processes. In addition to identifying a process owner, points of contact should be designated so participants can use them to coordinate activities. Responsibilities should be clearly delineated. NCR found that process changes on assembly lines in its Wichita facility were not communicated because no one was assigned that responsibility. A log was created to record changes and lead people were made responsible for communicating them to workers.

## Consolidation of Activities

One response to coordination problems is to reduce process handoffs by consolidating activities. Consolidation is a reaction to overspecialization. Since Adam Smith, specialization has been viewed as the key to productivity improvement: Workers should perform specialized tasks at which they are proficient due to repetition. While specialization has benefits, it also has costs. It results in fragmented processes involving numerous operator-to-operator handoffs, processes that require strong integrating mechanisms. Process designers have learned that the costs of specialization can outweigh the benefits and that many processes can be improved by consolidating activities. The traditional argument against consolidation—workers lack knowledge needed to perform multiple activities—may be inapplicable or can be countered through information technology.

The major benefit of consolidating activities is elimination of setup time—not the time needed to prepare a machine for a job, but **mental setup,** the time an operator needs to learn enough about a case to perform required tasks. Mental setup is significant in knowledge work where standard procedures are less decisive for task performance than characteristics of the case. Thus, it made sense for AT&T Power Systems to have product design team members write their own documentation rather than handing the task off to technical writers. Knowledge of the product is more important for the task than knowledge of documentation writing. Mental setup time was saved when Mutual Benefit Life reengineered its processing of insurance applications, replacing a system that involved 19 people per application with one in which a single case manager performs all activities.

Consolidation can be a way of employing unused capacity. Transportation companies consolidate shipments to minimize empty space in vehicles. Workers are given added tasks to occupy idle time. Task consolidation eliminates transportation costs. The New York City Department of Parks and Recreation removed dead trees with a process involving three separate teams. Over a period of days, each traveled to where a tree had to be removed, performed its tasks, and went to the next site. The department increased productivity by establishing multifunctional teams that performed all tree removal activities in a single visit to a job site.

Consolidation can also reduce cycle time. In a Japanese plant, one worker ran 14 cutting machines, manually starting each for each operating cycle. Noting that the machines finished their operations well before being restarted, Shigeo Shingo arranged for installation of one-touch startup buttons for two sets of seven machines. Consolidating 14 startups into two reduced the cycle time from 35 to 4.2 seconds.

A final economy of consolidation is the opportunity to avoid redoing partially completed tasks. The continuous casting of steel improves over traditional ingot processing methods by eliminating the need to reheat the metal: Form molten steel into desired shapes when it is first heated, so metal does not have to be reheated for forming later. When redesigning a special requests process, Dun and Bradstreet noticed that customers were called by analysts and later contacted by trade callers needing references. Contacting someone by telephone is an uncertain, time-consuming task that is undone once the party hangs up. The company arranged for analysts to collect information on customer references so only one call was needed.

In addition to providing economies, consolidation improves task performance. Fragmented tasks are vulnerable to duplication and oversight. Different operators do not know what has and has not been done. Consolidation reduces coordination errors. When the Tennant Company investigated mistakes in the packing of overseas parts shipments, it concluded that the packing process was poorly organized, with weak communication among involved work groups. Making one person responsible for each order improved shipment accuracy.

Consolidation can increase worker satisfaction. The demotivating effects of repetitive tasks are well known. Industrial psychologists argue that many jobs should be enlarged by increasing the range of activities. A telephone company used a process consisting of 17 operations, each performed by a designated worker, to compile telephone books. When it switched to a process in which each worker performed all tasks for a directory, errors, overtime, absenteeism, and turnover declined. A typewriter manufacturer assigned one operator to plate carriage end covers and another to buff them. When the company realized each operator could learn the other's job, it made each person responsible for producing half the covers. Doing so made the work more interesting, eliminated finger-pointing that accompanied defects, and inspired a spirit of friendly competition between workers.

A final beneficiary of task consolidation is the customer. Consolidating customer contact functions enables one-stop shopping, giving each customer a single contact person in the organization. This can be the person who has processed the customer's case as at Mutual Benefit Life. Or it can be a full-service customer representative knowledgeable in all aspects of the product. The *Tallahassee Democrat* established an Advertising Customer Service Department where advertisers deal with one person for all ad-related activities. The Nashua Corporation did the same in its Office Products Division, eliminating specialized positions in customer service, order entry, product management, and credit. Nashua reduced order cycle time from three days to one hour, achieving a 95 percent reduction in errors and a 20 percent annual productivity increase. One-stop-shopping eliminates chains of telephone call transfers and waits in different lines to perform different transactions. Machinists at the Norfolk Naval Shipyard spent five to ten minutes standing in different tool room lines waiting for different tools. Combining tool room windows so one stop satisfied all requests saved the shipyard $200,000 per year.

The benefits of task consolidation have led some to endorse case-based processing. Rather than performing one task or function for many cases, operators should perform many tasks for relatively few cases. The ideal is that a single operator completes all tasks required by a case. This advice is often valid, but not always. Some processes should be performed by task specialists. Others are better served by generalists handling complete cases. A prerequisite for case-based processing is that individuals can perform a wide range of activities. But even if workers can perform all activities for a case, they should not do so unless the benefits of a case-based approach outweigh its costs. Consider the following situation:

## case *11.2*

The Water and Gas Group of Schlumberger Industries (UK) changed from a traditional flow line to cell-based production in which work teams assembled complete meters from start to finish. Shortly after implementation, rejects increased from 0.07 percent to 1.91 percent. Investigation revealed mistakes in two areas, each involving a task previously performed by highly trained workers. Because problems had not been experienced in those tasks for years, the company underestimated the skill required for effective performance.

In this situation, case-based processing offers no benefits to customers and no savings of mental setup time. There is little case-specific knowledge but much task-specific knowledge, which the company failed to recognize. Case-based processing is an antidote to excesses of specialization and yields substantial gains when case-specific knowledge is critical for process performance. However, it is not a universally appropriate process design strategy.

## Process Triggers

Process triggers are events and conditions that initiate processes and their activities. The most common trigger is arrival of a customer, order, or job to be processed. Activities within a process are triggered by arrival of work-in-process from the previous station. Designers decide what triggers to employ in a process, insuring that they are easily noticed and properly timed.

Processes triggered by customer arrivals must deal with unpredictability. Organizations make arrivals more predictable by requiring customers to provide advance notification. Physicians ask customers to make appointments, and restaurants require reservations. When customer arrivals are unscheduled, a service representative, who has probably been working on another task, must be alerted to take the order. Drive-through restaurants use bell hoses to announce arrivals. A task force at Burger King repositioned hoses so ordertakers would be ready to greet customers just as they arrived at the display menu. A trigger must be properly timed: too early and the notification may be forgotten, too late and the customer has to wait.

Increased cooperation among organizational members of value chains has forced process designers to reconsider customary triggers for purchasing, payment, and other processes. Existing triggers are often based on conservative legal and accounting practices intended to protect organizational assets. Such triggers can be too cumbersome for contemporary needs, and their defensive character is out of place in the context of well-established organizational relationships. Process triggers reflecting a more collaborative world view should be adopted.

For instance, Ford's reengineered accounts payable system used a different trigger for vendor payment. Payment had been prompted by receipt of an invoice. After redesign, payment was triggered by receipt of goods. The change reduced document sorting and matching performed to authorize payments. Bell Atlantic redesigned its process for providing telephone service to corporate customers. Traditionally, service connection was not triggered until Bell acquired billing and other information. After redesign, service was connected once it was technically possible, and billing information was gathered thereafter. The old trigger was safer from a legal standpoint, but there is little risk with this group of customers. By responding to customer needs, the new trigger is better for the company from a competitive standpoint.

## Process Interruptions and Delays

Processes thrive on continuity, establishing and maintaining a rhythm of activities. Disruption breeds error. The pattern of motion is lost, and people and machines struggle to reachieve an active equilibrium. The filling operation in a food processing plant had stable fill weights when operating continuously but erratic weights when the process was disrupted by problems with other systems. Disruptions and delays plague knowledge work, undoing mental setups. It is hard enough to write a book, but to do so with an open office door would be impossible.

Delays can be caused by bottlenecks, points in the process where throughput slows and backlogs form. The standard response is to increase the capacity of bottleneck operations. Disruptions and delays also result from poor planning if the process is not prepared to run smoothly from start to finish. Poor planning and preparation for inspection of incoming electronic components caused average inspection times of 20 days at an Indian manufacturer, resulting in production bottlenecks and delays. Process changes, including finalizing test standards, arranging for documents, and planning for test facilities, reduced the average inspection time to five days. At a Hewlett-Packard plant, in-process work was frequently pulled from production because kits used to build products were incomplete. The problem was alleviated when only complete kits were allowed to enter the process. Activities may not be initiated at appropriate times, extending the critical path and creating delays. A company took years to create new products because Manufacturing Engineering was not involved until design work was complete.

Disruptions occur if jobs are set aside for ones with higher priority. At Naval Station Mayport in Florida, customer dissatisfaction with the time needed to complete programming projects prompted data processing managers to investigate. They found that programmers were often called away on troubleshooting tasks, disrupting their project work. After adoption of a flexi-place plan in which programmers could work at home for a week writing programs, the backlog of programming requests was eliminated. Processing of employee suggestions at Boeing's Defense and Space Group was slow because this task always seemed less important than others. Among the remedies were to designate individuals to handle firefighting tasks, establish better dispatching rules so jobs get done before they become urgent, strictly enforce expediting criteria to block bogus gate-crashers, and set aside time for low priority tasks that might be crowded out of the work week.

Some interruptions, such as breaks and lunch periods, are normal. The most that can be done is to ease predictable stops and starts, by allowing knowledge workers to break at task-convenient times, for instance. Other interruptions—machine breakdowns, power outages, and injuries—are unforeseeable. Their frequency can be reduced by preventive maintenance, job safety, and other programs addressing their causes.

This mirrors general advice for dealing with process disruptions and delays: Monitor the incidence of events over time, diagnose their causes, and devise remedies targeted to those causes. Process designers should consider how to design continuity into processes and how to make processes resilient in the face of disruptions. Insulate processes from outside disturbances. You would not have telephones at work stations, exposing process continuity to the depredations of telemarketing campaigns.

## Process Monitoring and Control (PM&C)

The ideal process has no monitoring and control activities. Inputs are invariably converted into desired outputs, so there is no need to monitor the process or adjust its parameters. PM&C are non–value-adding activities. As such, they are often targeted for elimination by process improvement efforts. Dropping an inspection is a way to save money and reduce cycle time. It can also lead to disaster. Processes do not always run as intended so, value-adding or not, process monitoring and control activities are needed.

Unnecessary PM&C tends to be found in fragmented processes. Why? Departments keep logs and make inspections to protect themselves from other organization members. "The order was on schedule when it left our department," and so forth. To identify unnecessary PM&C, designers must determine when such activities are truly needed. Once a need is identified, designers should consider how PM&C can best be performed. These assessments can change as a process matures—fewer mistakes are made, workers become more capable of self-inspection.

Since PM&C protects against poor performance, its need is driven by the cost and likelihood of poor performance. Some processes—airline maintenance, for instance—are monitored because health and safety implications make any breakdown potentially catastrophic. Processes with more mundane impacts are monitored because of a history of getting off track. PM&C is often excessive for noncritical processes with solid performance records. If a failure would not have catastrophic implications and if few problems are detected by existing PM&C efforts, reduce monitoring and control.

If PM&C is worth doing, it is worth doing well, in a way that provides reliable information. Accurate measurements made by up-to-date methods replace qualitative "feels" with quantitative readings where possible. Controls should insure that deviations are corrected and that the process holds to its intended course.

Other PM&C issues are addressed by process designers as well. Can workers be relied on to self-inspect their output, should that task be assigned to their successors in the process, or should full-time inspectors be used? Perhaps inspections can be automated. Is continuous inspection needed or would periodic audits suffice? Auto insurers have reduced the need for adjustors in claims processing by sending claimants to approved body shops and paying for whatever needs to be done. Companies review body shop charges periodically, dropping those that overcharge.

When PM&C is done as part of employee performance monitoring, care must be taken to insure that employees do not "game" the system to make themselves look good at the expense of the organization and its customers. After redesigning its credit granting process, IBM Credit found that employees achieved near-perfect compliance with performance standards, though average order completion times were longer than ever. Employees conveniently discovered errors on bid requests so they could be sent back for rework. As a result, troublesome jobs were excluded from individual performance evaluations.

## Centralization/Decentralization

A perennial issue addressed by organizational design is the extent to which authority should be centralized in a single top management group or decentralized geographically and among lower level employees. Centralization offers improved coordination, consistency, and economies of scale. School principals in Sullivan County, Tenn., called the same few substitute teachers, necessitating additional phone calls.

Adopting a centralized calling process eliminated duplication and spread the work to more substitutes. Decentralized decision making increases the organization's responsiveness to local needs. It increases employee responsibility and commitment, improving performance.

Centralization/decentralization is an important process design issue. Not surprisingly, given its support for worker involvement, the quality movement favors decentralization. Dun and Bradstreet's redesigned customer contracting process allows staff to approve contracts up to $5,000. Information technology permits hybrid centralized/decentralized operations, whereby management can decentralize authority but remain informed of and able to control activities throughout the organization. IT can also preserve scale economies in a decentralized operation. Hewlett-Packard has a decentralized purchasing system but uses a central database of purchasing transactions to negotiate vendor contracts and volume discounts.

Centralization/decentralization is also an issue with shared resources. Some tools used by many workers are too expensive to provide to each. Tools can be kept in a central location to maintain control, wasting time workers spend getting them when needed. Or control can be decentralized. One company reduced congestion and walking distances by decentralizing the control of gauges to the work areas using them most. Gauge checkout times fell from 15 minutes to less than 3. When a shared resource is informational, IT can create multiple versions. The IRS Service Center in Cincinnati used a three-ring binder to announce job openings. Only one person could use the binder at a time and announcements were often removed by the overzealous. These problems were cured by a computer-based system allowing users to view announcements simultaneously from different terminals. This solution was needed at the Williams Family Medicine Center in Denver, where a single appointment register forced nurses and patients to wait 15 minutes on the phone before appointments could be made.

If a resource is shared by multiple users, process designers must avoid Tragedy of the Commons situations. This occurs when some parties use the resource excessively, so it is overused and deteriorates. Typing pools are vulnerable as are sales forces serving multiple product divisions. Process designers must insure that resource availability is adequate to user needs and that utilization rules prevent parties from appropriating more than their proper share of the resource.

## Standards and Procedures

A process change in a foundry required melters to use scales to weigh amounts of metal to be poured. After using scales for a while, some melters went back to their former look-and-feel ways of estimating amounts. This is a common phenomenon in which comfort, not performance, drives process evolution. Even changes that make things easier for operators are reversed because habitual ways are easiest in the short run. Cross-functional processes atrophy because departments and functions pursue their own interests at the expense of process performance. To counter these tendencies, processes must be institutionalized, acquiring durable identities and definitions. Standards and procedures are means of doing this. Like product blueprints, they document the process and give it a concrete reality.

Process design includes the task of devising process standards and procedures. Lacking such, things do not get done or are done in different ways, mostly wrong. Some of the inadequacies in Digital Semiconductor's sales forecasting process were attributed to the fact that the Marketing, Materials, and Finance departments used different definitions for key terms and data elements. After a manufacturer developed standard testing procedures, rejections of gear boxes due to noise declined from 56 percent to 17 percent of production. Hoffmann-La Roche was plagued by mistakes and oversights occurring when temporary workers filled in for absent secretarial and support staff. The company solved the problem by developing a handbook for each employee's position and for general office procedures.

Standards and procedures must be consistent throughout the process. They must be enforced and communicated to process participants. One company suffered from incorrect assembly of parts, until a quality circle devised a better way of communicating specifications changes. They put up signs by work tables and prepared checklists of changes that workers had to read before going on duty. Documentation must be reviewed periodically and purged of outdated specifications. A manufacturer found that its maintenance department lacked parts because a former manager established strict replenishment policies that had not been rescinded. A review of Ford's process for handling dealer claims regarding damaged vehicles disclosed a process bloated by special procedures added in response to specific needs and disruptions.

## Information

Some processes, such as sales forecasting, produce informational outputs; every process creates and depends on a collateral information flow mirroring its parent. Processes involve multiple participants. Information communicates intentions, activities, and accomplishments among these agents. Process design includes the design of related information flows.

Information is collected from customers initiating a process. Information gathering must be complete and efficient. Customers should not be asked to provide the same information several times. If needed information is lacking, further contacts must be arranged or processors will rely on guesses about what customers want. A well-designed data collection protocol prevents such errors. Similar concerns apply to an organization's relations with suppliers. A manufacturer of aircraft instruments had problems with a control panel supplier until the company realized its procurement drawings were unclear.

Information, in the form of instructions, is required by operators who tailor activities to specific processing needs. To prevent disruptions, this information should be easy to find and interpret. Westinghouse used 4 × 8-foot material identification charts to display data so workers did not have to thumb through manuals. Upstream processors should anticipate and satisfy downstream information needs. Nurses at the University of Colorado School of Medicine spent extra hours handling prescription refills because physicians did not provide clear refill instructions in medical records. The flow of information across departmental boundaries is often troublesome. Because customer service representatives at Metroweb, a Cincinnati printer, were not producing acceptable layout sheets, the prepress department did not know how to prepare jobs for printing. By getting together to discuss the issue, people from different departments learned what information was needed to process orders.

Information must be made available to customers. Manuals show how products should be assembled and operated. Customer complaints indicate that these instructions are not always inadequate. Customers often want order status information to facilitate planning and reassure them that their order is progressing. A hospital improved its processing of physical plant requisitions by sending periodic progress reports to initiating departments. Boise Cascade speeded customer pickup of orders with a computer-based system that allowed sales representatives to inform customers of scheduled pickup dates.

Though instructions are the most common process-related information, others should be noted. Information is used for product identification, which is critical in the event of recalls or other needs to trace product origins. Records confirm that processing activities were performed. Check sheets direct and document aircraft maintenance inspections. The Meriter Hospital in Madison, Wisc., lost revenue due to poor documentation of medications administered by its intensive care unit. A revamped process, including new forms, policies, and procedures, generated annual savings of $54,000.

Informal informational activities are vulnerable to omissions and oversights. Formal activities rely on the design of appropriate forms that collect all and only needed information. Good forms are easy to understand and complete. Just as forms should not collect unneeded data, the information systems surrounding a process should not provide users with unneeded information.

The prescription to consolidate activities to reduce handoffs and mental setup suggests that informational activities be performed by operators rather than staff specialists. There are exceptions to this rule. Expert operators should not disrupt processing to take counts or handle administrative tasks that could be completed by less skilled personnel.

Information should be shared with customers, suppliers, and other process partners. This builds trust and is essential for coordination. By adopting a collaborative relationship with construction vendors, a relationship in which information was shared and an agreed-on cost analysis system resolved disputes, the Ford Motor Company achieved quicker resolution of disagreements concerning construction projects.

## Information Technology (IT)

IT, which includes computer and communications technology, has been part of organizational life for over 40 years. Its importance has burgeoned during the past decade, to the point where IT has a strategic role in many companies. IT is a vital part of business process design, a technological means enabling development of processes that are orders of magnitude better than their predecessors. Some argue that process design should begin with an assessment of IT capabilities rather than an analysis of the current process. Assuredly, process designers must be aware of what IT can do. The following are among the most significant capabilities of information technology in organizational processes.

Computers can solve structured organizational problems. Scheduling and routing problems are routinely solved by mathematical techniques implemented through software packages. Ore-Ida saved $700,000 annually with automated order consolidation and motor carrier selection software. Computers aid in solving semistructured problems, running decision support software that provides access to databases and computational routines. Expert systems technology extends this capacity. The reengineering of Mutual Benefit Life's applications processing system relied on PC-based workstations running expert systems. By expanding the knowledge of case managers, these systems enabled the company to replace a fragmented process of specialized operators with one involving autonomous case managers. In some applications, expert systems replace human operators. American Express uses the technology to authorize credit card purchases; Progressive Insurance employs it in making risk assessments of automobile drivers. As part of a reengineering project, Intermountain Health Care in Salt Lake City, Utah, developed an expert system that serves as an antibiotic consultant, reviewing patient medical records to determine if a proposed drug might have harmful side effects. This system recommends the best antibiotic 94 percent of the time, compared to 77 percent for doctors working without it. It has saved $900,000 in adverse drug reaction costs.

Modern communications technology allows high-speed transmission of huge amounts of data. Authorizations can be secured electronically rather than by mail. A Japanese manufacturer replaced its purchasing system with an IT-based counterpart. Pallets of goods now include plastic cards with magnetic strips. As pallets are used, cards are read electronically to report material usage, instigate reorders, and initiate the payment process. Rapid data communication eliminates geographic distance as a constraint on process design. When salespeople began using faxes and phones to transmit ad copy, Knight-Ridder smoothed the load on its advertising department and improved customer service. Dun and Bradstreet electronically transferred special customer requests to offices best able to respond to them.

IT allows information to be shared. Electronic databases permit multiple simultaneous access, and electronic copies can be created and sent effortlessly. Ford's reengineered accounts payable system uses electronic documents instantaneously available to anyone who needs them and matchable without manual sorting. Computer-based scheduling and appointment systems permit simultaneous access by many parties. No one has to wait while someone else is using the appointment book.

IT enables tracking of goods and vehicles. Federal Express scans a package up to 10 times before delivery so it can locate missing packages and respond to customer inquiries. Railroads use satellite systems to track the locations of trains. Scanning technology, the bar code readers used in supermarkets, provides fast, direct pickup of information in electronic form. UPS drivers have electronic clipboards; consignee signatures provide next-day confirmation to shippers that packages were received.

Due to the range of information communicated, IT allows closer contact between remote process participants. A firm used teleconferencing to reduce its product development cycle by six months, conducting weekly discussions impractical to hold in person. Interactive videodisks can augment a company's contact with customers. A potential side effect of this capacity is disintermediation, replacing human intermediaries, such as brokers or agents, with direct company-to-customer contact. Travel agencies are threatened as airlines make it easier for PC owners to make flight reservations.

Another effect of the data-handling capacity of IT is the ability to customize service delivery. Otis Elevator's system provides service technicians with data on the problem and the unit's repair history by the time they reach the site. Florida Power and Light developed a similar system to support service personnel responding to customer calls. The concept applies to individual customers. The Ritz-Carlton Hotel maintains an electronic record of individual service preferences of guests, using this to customize service at its facilities.

Finally, by doing things for process participants, IT frees time for other tasks. By providing sales representatives with portable computers, printers, and cell phones, Hewlett-Packard enabled them to spend less time on paperwork and more with customers. These efforts can backfire. Spreadsheet software, intended to release planners and analysts from number crunching so they could do more thinking, may have had the opposite effect.

## Automation

To automate a task is to have it performed without human intervention. Automation can be accomplished in many ways and for many reasons. One reason for automating is to reduce cycle time, to make a process go faster. Automating data transfer activities in a forecasting process reduced cycle time from 75 to 8 days. Automation frees operators for the performance of other tasks. A manufacturer of automotive fabrics devised controls so sewing machines stopped automatically when jobs were done. Each machine had been operated by a worker; after the change, one worker could operate a dozen machines, moving from one to another, removing completed work and initiating a new job at each.

Automation reduces errors and oversights. Globe Metallurgical used a computer to calculate ladle additions during refining, improving on the accuracy of manual computations. Globe also automated the weighing and dispensing of additives, relieving workers of dangerous tasks. Thus, another reason for automating is to eliminate tasks that are uncomfortable, unsafe, or otherwise noxious to workers.

Recurring tasks can be automated as can tasks performed in special circumstances. The latter are prime candidates for automation if they are easily overlooked. Workers may not notice if a system is running out of an input; automated shutdowns prevent spoiled operations. A company's painting process had to shut down because of clogs after the filtering system ran out of paper. The problem was fixed by a photoelectric eye-based shutoff that stopped the process when paper ran out. Unnoticed stoppages of a conveyor caused damage at the Norfolk Naval Shipyard until an alarm system was installed notifying workers of stoppages. Sensors can detect precursors of shutdown conditions, so corrective action is taken before it is too late. Ford devised a sound detection system that monitored drill vibration, shutting off a drilling machine before bits broke. Firestone Tire and Rubber used an electric eye to detect material not feeding properly into a cutting operation, stopping the process before jam-ups occur. The system saved $5,100 a year.

These cases suggest ways in which activities can be automated. They range in sophistication and expense from industrial robots at one end to simple mechanical devices at the other. Shingo describes two of the latter:[17] a pair of rubber rollers mounted on a conveyor automatically positioned biscuits face-up as they moved through a process, and stoppers aligned rods so they did not fall as they slid down a chute. Another way of automating a task is by piggybacking, consolidating it with a task that is already automated. When Ohio Bell Telephone had problems with one of the 4000 computer production jobs run each day, operators had to contact the programmer responsible for the job. Inaccurate information on the user ID list prevented calls from getting through, leading to lost time and missed deadlines. By integrating its ID list into an existing database, the company automated list updating and maintenance, reducing the incidence of stalled jobs.

The "discovery" of business processes has been one of the most significant developments in management thinking during the past several decades. Now comes the task of turning this awareness into effective programs for process improvement and innovation. In addition to assessing existing programs, this chapter has suggested a rich, heuristic approach to process design.

## NOTES

1. Flowcharting is explained in: Dianne Galloway, *Mapping Work Processes* (Milwaukee: ASQC Quality Press, 1994).
2. Figure 11.1 is taken from: Hunter, William G., Janet K. O'Neill, and Carol Wallen, "Doing More With Less in the Public Sector," *Quality Progress* 20, no. 7 (1987): 19–26.
3. Figure 11.2 is taken from: Edward J. Kane, "IBM's Quality Focus on the Business Process," *Quality Progress* 19, no. 4 (1986): 24–33.
4. See, for instance: H. James Harrington, *Business Process Improvement* (New York: McGraw-Hill, 1991); and Geary A. Rummler and Alan P. Brache, *Improving Performance* (San Francisco: Jossey-Bass, 1990).
5. Reengineering is discussed in: Thomas H. Davenport, *Process Innovation: Reengineering Work Through Information Technology* (Boston: Harvard Business School Press, 1993); and Michael Hammer and James Champy, *Reengineering the Corporation: A Manifesto for Business Revolution* (New York: HarperCollins, 1993).
6. See note 5.
7. Michael Hammer, "Reengineering Work: Don't Automate, Obliterate," *Harvard Business Review* August/September 1990, 104–122.
8. See note 5.
9. Michael Hammer and Steven A. Stanton, *The Reengineering Revolution: A Handbook* (New York: HarperCollins, 1995).
10. Robert C. Camp, *Benchmarking* (Milwaukee: ASQC Quality Press, 1989).
11. See note 5.
12. Peter Checkland, *Systems Thinking, Systems Practice* (Chichester, England: John Wiley & Sons, 1981).
13. Mary Walton, *Deming Management at Work* (New York: Perigee, 1990).

14. E. H. Melan, "Process Management in Service and Administrative Operations," *Quality Progress* 18, no. 6 (1985): 52–59.
15. See note 5.
16. Shigeo Shingo, *A Study of the Toyota Production System from an Industrial Engineering Viewpoint* (Cambridge, Mass.: Productivity Press, 1989).
17. Shigeo Shingo, *The Sayings of Shigeo Shingo: Key Strategies for Plant Improvement* (Cambridge, Mass.: Productivity Press, 1987).

# chapter 12

# Looking Back, Looking Ahead

---

## Chapter Outline

Lessons Learned

Case-Based QPS: An Assessment

Redirecting Research

---

Three topics are addressed in this brief concluding chapter. First, important themes that recur throughout the foregoing chapters are identified. This highlights and reinforces the book's major findings. Second, case-based QPS, the methodology underlying much of the book's content, is evaluated. What has it delivered? What more could be achieved? Finally, I offer some thoughts regarding future research on quality problem solving. There is a need for additional work in this area, but the need requires a reorientation of traditional academic research practices.

## Lessons Learned

This book contains hundreds of pieces of problem-solving advice, especially in the last five problem-driven chapters. Most of the advice has limited domains of applicability. In addition, some general lessons reappear, explicitly or implicitly, throughout these pages. These recurring themes constitute the book's major claims or findings. They are, it is hoped, what the reader will take away and remember, over and beyond particular suggestions. Six broad lessons or themes, summarized in Figure 12.1, are discussed.

The book's most general claim concerns the term *problem solving*. The issue was discussed in Chapter 1 and is implicit in all that followed. Against the customary view that problem solving is what you do when things go wrong, a broader notion

1. Problem solving is thinking done to improve things.
2. There are different types of problems, and recognizing a problem's type is critical for solving it.
3. Problem-solving functions provide a useful way of conceptualizing and improving thinking.
4. There are no strong general methods for solving quality problems.
5. Analyzing the situation, thinking carefully about the problem, is a key to effective problem solving.
6. Past experience provides the most useful knowledge for solving problems.

**Figure 12.1**   Lessons learned

was endorsed. Problem solving is thinking done to achieve one's goals, to improve things. It is action-oriented thought. On this account, problem solving is an integral part of quality management, of management in general, and of life in general. It is important because it is, or can be, effective: Good thinking improves the chances of achieving one's goals.

A second claim: There are different types of problems and recognizing a problem's type is critical for solving it. Everyone acknowledges that problems are not all the same. Yet problem solvers rarely consider what kind of situation they are dealing with, as one can see in the tendency to employ popular methods—cause-and-effect diagrams, for instance—in situations to which they do not pertain. This failing can be attributed in large part to the lack of well-known, usefully defined problem types. The book addresses that lack by identifying five types of quality problems. These represent the preponderance of situations that quality improvement activities confront. The identified types of quality problems were essential to the book's exposition, structuring most of its content. This demonstrates the value of problem types: They organize knowledge in categories that can be mapped onto the situations we encounter. When solving a problem, first determine what kind of problem it is.

A related lesson, evident in Chapters 3 through 6, is the importance of problem-solving functions. These tasks or demands encompass most of the mental work of problem solving. They index knowledge and techniques used to perform that work. The book focused on four functions: problem identification, problem definition, diagnosis, and alternative generation. Some functions apply to all problems, while others only pertain to certain situations. After identifying the type of problem to be addressed, a problem solver should determine the functional demands it poses. This aids recollection of pertinent knowledge and techniques.

A fourth finding is that there are no strong general methods for solving quality problems. The existing arsenal of methods includes powerful, but specialized, techniques. Statistical process control is an example. It also includes methods—the PDCA cycle, for instance—that are highly general but lack power and/or operationality. No technique combines high levels of generality, power, and operationality, because trade-offs among these characteristics are inevitable. Thus, problem solvers should not expect "silver bullet" solution methods to be discovered. Future method-ological developments within QPS will be much like the past or, if anything, less pro-ductive. Some new methods will be proposed, but it is unlikely that the future will offer substantial advances beyond the current state of the art. Ten years from now, people solving quality problems will rely mostly on techniques used today.

Accepting the limited value of problem-solving methods, where can one turn for assistance and support? This book argues that human analytical abilities provide a substantial and largely untapped problem-solving resource. People are constantly enjoined to think critically and creatively, but they have never been taught to think analytically about problems. By analyzing the elements and relationships that consti-tute a situation, identifying problem types and structures, and exploring a problem's distinctive features and demands, problem solvers can surface solution possibilities inherent in or serendipitous to the situation. Some problems offer more to analysis than others, but thinking carefully about the problem is always a good move.

The other indispensable problem-solving resource is experience. Previous encounters with similar situations, by oneself or others, suggest things to try and mistakes to avoid in the current confrontation. Experience complements problem analysis. Thinking about the problem evokes relevant experiential knowledge. Those problems offering the least to an analytical approach are most susceptible to an experiential one. The usual failing of this problem-solving strategy is nonopera-tionality: People are told to acquire experience. That may be good advice, but it is no help in the short run. This failing is remedied by efforts to capture and compile experiences of many people. By collecting the experiences of operators, maintenance workers, and customer service representatives, an organization can create valuable problem-solving tools. The book's final lesson is that past experience can be the key to solving problems. Experience should be acquired from a broad base and orga-nized to support recurring problem-solving activities.

## Case-Based QPS: An Assessment

Case-based QPS is an attempt to learn from experience. It has been implemented throughout the book, especially in Chapters 7 through 11. This section evaluates what has been done.

This book probably represents the most far-reaching effort of its kind. Its case base of 719 cases drawn from 242 sources is large, though certainly not the largest. Existing case-based reasoning systems and formal organizational compilations of lessons learned from experience assuredly include many with larger case bases. But this implementation of case-based QPS is noteworthy for two reasons. First, its domain is broader than those addressed by CBR or organizational learning systems. These typically concern a particular product line, production system, or narrowly defined field of practice, such as the diagnosis of lung diseases. The current effort covers the full range of organizational problems addressed by quality management. Breadth of coverage and the relative lack of domain structure created challenges in organizing lessons drawn from cases. Second, the current effort is concerned with deriving lessons from the cases studied. Most CBR systems simply cite cases of apparent relevance to the problem situation, allowing users to find pertinent insights. At the other extreme, books written for managers typically use cases to illustrate prescriptions drawn from other sources. This book is distinctive in its attempt to directly extract useful knowledge from a case base.

Notwithstanding the scope of the current endeavor, more could have been done. The case base could have been expanded by a more comprehensive review of published sources of practitioner experiences with quality problems. In addition, access to unpublished sources, including company records and files of consulting firms, would have enabled the case base to grow by several orders of magnitude. Would a larger inventory of experience have affected the book's content? Probably not much. It is unlikely that many major lessons not already included in these chapters would have been discovered. The 700 tries, represented by the current case base, probably caught most of the big fish. An expanded case base would disclose many small and midrange prescriptions not reported in these pages. These might have added substance to the coverage of certain topics, but there is a limit to what can be done in a single book. With its broad scope, this book could not have developed many topics in greater depth without running up against normal page restrictions for a work of this kind.

Viewing this book as a representative, but by no means definitive, implementation of case-based QPS, how must that methodology be evaluated? Is it useful? Do its products deserve the attention of practitioners?

An assessment of case-based QPS must begin by acknowledging that some lessons learned from case analysis are trite for most, if not all, readers. But then experience is repetitive, often teaching us what we already know. For instance, eliminating unnecessary activities is a well-known way of reducing costs. Such lessons could have been dropped from the text at the risk of leaving a few readers uninformed and with a loss of narrative flow and coherence. The trite lessons are usually generalities under which lie more informative specifics. Thus, one kind of unnecessary activity to look for is work done to protect against occurrences of rare but noncatastrophic events. While writing the book I was continually disheartened at having to include things already said, many times and with better words, by others. Consolation came with the belief that these commonplaces had to be repeated, that they were concisely expressed, and that the book's original content repaid readers for their attention.

Looking past its truisms, I believe there is much here that will be useful to many readers—not necessarily to consultants and expert practitioners who make a living solving quality problems, but to the larger audience of managers, workers, and students interested or sporadically involved in organizational improvement efforts. Case-based QPS provides these people with a comprehensive, accessible set of experience-based advice. Individual and group problem solving can be enhanced by this resource. I suspect quality experts can also learn from these pages, though not so much as novices.

Much problem-solving expertise is situation-specific. It lies in knowing the ins and outs of an administrative process, why a machine tends to break down, what aspects of a software product give users the most trouble. A book written for a general audience cannot include this kind of knowledge. Fortunately, experience offers lessons that generalize across problem situations, these being the target of case-based QPS. As noted earlier, an expanded set of QPS cases could be developed. These would enable identification of lessons beyond those included in the book. Presumably most of the general lessons have been identified. And, at some point, narrowly targeted heuristics shade into situation-specific advice that does not merit publication to a general audience. But a more complete set of cases might provide material to justify individual volumes on, say, diagnosis, conformance problems, efficiency problems, and process design.

In summary, case-based QPS is a viable means of extracting insights from reports of past problem-solving experiences. These insights must be fit into an organizing framework to be accessible to users. The current implementation is in a traditional textual medium; a computer-based system could be used. The resulting body of knowledge will not include situation-specific information that is often crucial for solving problems. It will not much exceed, if at all, the problem-solving knowledge of experienced consultants and other experts in a field. But it will in many respects match their expertise. A consultant has this knowledge and can apply it to problem situations. This book makes the knowledge available to readers who must themselves apply it to particular situations. Of course, the book costs less and will always be there when needed.

## Redirecting Research

The kind of applied problem-solving research featured in this book is rarely conducted in business schools. It is not reported in academic journals on management, including the research literature on quality management, such as *Quality Management Journal*. Indeed, this kind of work would be out of place in almost every behavioral or social science (BSS) field, pure or applied.

This anomaly does not result from accident or oversight. Rather, it derives from a deep mismatch between traditional goals of academic research and the inherent demands of practice. This mismatch has been expressed as one of rigor versus relevance, but it is far more profound. Scientists seek truth, hoping to add to our stock of highly validated knowledge claims. Practitioners pursue practical goals; they want knowledge that can be used. Invalid knowledge claims are not useful, but—here's the rub!—valid claims may not be either. BSS researchers propose and test theories of near-universal generality expressed in abstract theoretical terms. In contrast, practice requires knowledge that can be effectively applied in specific situations. Generality is fine, but not if achieved at a loss in operationality and power in particular applications.

Scientists are obsessed with avoiding error. They adopt rigorous research methods—formal proofs, tight experimental controls, large replicated studies, peer reviews—to minimize the chances that untrue claims are accepted as true. Practitioners are less demanding on this count. They want knowledge that will improve on current ways of doing things and they want it now, not in some far-off future when claims have been conclusively established. Practitioners know the truth of pragmatism, that practical outcomes are the ultimate test of knowledge.

They are prepared to try what is plausibly effective, knowing that results will winnow out error.

Because of their concern with rigor, most scientists study causal relationships between a small number of carefully defined variables pertaining to a phenomenon. They assume that narrowly targeted investigations accumulate toward an understanding of that phenomenon and that understanding benefits practice. However, the variables scientists study may not connect to the real world. Research findings often do not accumulate toward understanding, much less one that practitioners could apply. Most BSS research, including research conducted in business schools, will never, and could never, have an identifiable impact on practice.

The gap between research and practice has been acknowledged and lamented by many in the academy. On the other hand, some deny that BSS research is irrelevant to practice. They point, for instance, to modeling methodologies used to solve practical problems. Cognitive science has improved teaching methods and the design of man-machine systems. Research in finance has changed financial management practices and the design of financial instruments. Other examples of effective applications can be cited. Yet for each research program that delivers useful results, 20 or more fail to make an impact on practice. The applicability of some scientific knowledge should increase our concern that the large majority goes unused.

Recent developments within the field of management demonstrate how little academic research contributes to practice. Management has changed considerably during the past decades, but the major changes were invariably inspired by practitioners. Total Quality Management grew out of the work of Deming, Juran, and the Japanese. People at Xerox developed benchmarking. Reengineering was initiated by quasi-academic consultants who published their findings in practitioner journals. Academic research had no role in the revolutionary improvements in production methods achieved by the Japanese. Management scholars would be hard-pressed to name any research-based development as significant as these.

Some insist that this is merely a communication problem: Research findings are useful, but practitioners are not aware of them. This explanation is implausible in a society where published results of academic research are available in hundreds of libraries, where the profit motive impels individuals and organizations to find useful knowledge, and where educational programs introduce practitioners to academic research. How many people in your organization read BSS journals? Assuredly, if the knowledge in those journals was useful, it would be used.

Most behavioral and social scientists are committed to the pursuit of knowledge for its own sake. They want their work to have practical value, but are more concerned that it offer a true account of reality. However, philosophers of science deny that we can establish the truth about reality. If this applies to the physical sciences, where there is a hard, physical reality to be known, it is even more pertinent to BSS domains, where reality is conceptual and changing. How could one know that a theory of such phenomena was correct? A focus on theoretical truth might be justified if we could achieve truth and know when we found it. We cannot. Choosing truth over practical results, BSS researchers end up with neither.

It could be alleged that the gap between research and practice is unfortunate but inevitable. This is not true. Some fields have redirected their research efforts to be responsive to practitioner concerns. Public administration, a field closely related to business management, has turned toward practice. This is evident in books like *Reinventing Government*.[1] It proposes guidelines for effective practice derived from implementations rather than academic theories. Developments in another field, artificial intelligence, provide intellectual support for the turn toward practice. AI researchers initially believed that intelligent behavior was based on strong general principles, such as might be expressed in scientific theories. The inadequacies of this assumption forced researchers to view intelligent behavior as dependent on domain-specific knowledge and heuristics. Expert systems reflect this perspective. Many of these are grounded in knowledge of individual cases, hence case-based reasoning systems.

Science can be allied with practice, but doing so requires fundamental changes. BSS researchers must give up their obsession with abstract theories. They must relax requirements for rigor to accommodate legitimate practical considerations. Scientists must start with a focus on problems faced by practitioners and constantly assess the relevance of their work to those problems. They must recognize new, practice-oriented research methodologies. And the academy must respect and honor research results that forswear generality for the sake of applicational power.

This book represents one form of practice-driven research. It is not the kind of product traditionally produced or endorsed by academia. It is, I believe, a research product of value to practitioners. For other products of this kind or other forms of practice-driven research to be created, the academy must change. It will not do so on its own. Perhaps the voice of the customer, of practitioners who are the potential consumers of applied behavioral and social science research, can inspire the needed changes.

## NOTES

1. David Osborne and Ted Gaebler, *Reinventing Government* (New York: Penguin, 1992).

# appendix A

# Sources of Cases

Cases used in writing this book were drawn from the books, journals, and conference proceedings cited below. References for specific cases can be obtained by writing the author at the Department of Management, College of Business Administration, University of Northern Iowa, Cedar Falls, Iowa 50614-0125, or by an e-mail message to Jerry.Smith@uni.edu.

*ASQC Annual Quality Congress Transactions*
Ralph J. Barra, *Putting Quality Circles to Work* (New York: McGraw-Hill, 1983).
Keki R. Bhote, *World Class Quality: Using Design of Experiments to Make it Happen* (New York: AMACOM, 1991).
Soren Bisgaard, "The Quality Detective: A Case Study," Report #32, Center for Quality and Productivity Improvement, University of Wisconsin–Madison, Madison, Wis., 1988.
Vernon M. Buehler and Y. Krishna Shetty, eds., *Productivity Improvement: Case Studies of Proven Practice* (New York: AMACOM, 1981).
Robert C. Camp, *Benchmarking* (Milwaukee: ASQC Quality Press, 1989).
Frank Caropreso, ed., *Making Total Quality Happen,* The Conference Board, Report #937, New York, 1990.
Marlene Caroselli, *Total Quality Transformation: Optimizing Mission, Methods, and Management* (Amherst, Mass.: Human Resource Development Press, 1991).
Crocker, Olga L., Cyril Charney, and Johnny Sik Leung Chiu, *Quality Circles* (New York: Mentor, 1984).
Philip B. Crosby, *Quality Without Tears* (New York: McGraw-Hill, 1984).
Thomas H. Davenport, *Process Innovation: Reengineering Work Through Information Technology* (Boston: Harvard Business School Press, 1993).
W. Edwards Deming, *Out of the Crisis* (Cambridge: MIT Center for Advanced Engineering Study, 1986).

*Enterprise Reengineering*

*Fortune*

Ryuji Fukuda, *Managerial Engineering* (Stamford, Conn.: Productivity, Inc., 1983).

Howard S. Gitlow, *Planning for Quality, Productivity, and Competitive Position* (Homewood, Ill.: Dow Jones-Irwin, 1990).

Frank M. Gryna, Jr., *Quality Circles: A Team Approach to Problem Solving* (New York: AMACOM, 1981).

Hale, Roger L., Douglas R. Hoelscher, and Ronald E. Kowal, *Quest for Quality* (Minneapolis: Tennant Company, 1989).

Michael Hammer and James Champy, *Reengineering the Corporation: A Manifesto for Business Revolution* (New York: HarperCollins, 1993).

Michael Hammer and Steven A. Stanton, *The Reengineering Revolution: A Handbook* (New York: Harper Collins, 1995).

H. James Harrington, *Excellence: The IBM Way* (Milwaukee: ASQC Quality Press, 1988).

*Harvard Business Review*

David Hutchins, *Quality Circles Handbook* (London: Nichols, 1985).

Masaaki Imai, *Kaizen: The Key to Japan's Competitive Success* (New York: McGraw-Hill, 1986).

*Industrial Engineering*

Sud Ingle, *Quality Circles Master Quide* (Englewood Cliffs, N.J.: Prentice Hall, 1982).

Sud and Nima Ingle, *Quality Circles in Service Industries* (Englewood Cliffs, N.J.: Prentice Hall, 1983).

*International Journal of Quality and Reliability Management*

Johansson, Henry J., Patrick McHugh, A. John Pendlebury, and William A. Wheeler III, *Business Process Reengineering: Breakpoint Strategies for Market Dominance* (Chichester, England: John Wiley & Sons, 1993).

*Journal of Business Strategy*

*Journal of Creative Behavior*

*Journal of Quality and Participation*

J. M. Juran, *Managerial Breakthrough* (New York: McGraw-Hill, 1964).

J. M. Juran, *Juran on Quality by Design* (New York: Free Press, 1992).

Joseph M. Juran and Frank M. Gryna, Jr., eds., *Juran's Quality Control Handbook*, 4th ed. (New York: McGraw-Hill, 1988).

Kenneth Kivenko, *Quality Control for Management* (Englewood Cliffs, N.J.: Prentice Hall, 1984).

Peter J. Kolesar, "The Mess at Plastron: A Case History of an SPC Startup," Working Paper, The Deming Center for Quality Management, Graduate School of Business, Columbia University, 1993.

*Management Review*

William L. Mohr and Harriet Mohr, *Quality Circles: Changing Images of People at Work* (Reading, Mass.: Addison-Wesley, 1983).

*National Productivity Review*

Masao Nemoto, *Total Quality Control for Management* (Englewood Cliffs, N.J.: Prentice Hall, 1987).

*Newsweek*

J. S. Oakland, ed., *Total Quality Management: Proceedings of the 2nd International Conference* (Bedford, England: Springer-Verlag, 1989).

David Osborne and Ted Gaebler, *Reinventing Government* (New York: Penguin Books, 1992).

Donald E. Peterson and John Hillkirk, *A Better Idea* (Boston: Houghton Mifflin, 1991).

C. R. Prasad, ed., *Statistical Quality Control and Operational Research* (Calcutta: Indian Statistical Institute, 1982).

*Problem-Driven Case Studies in Quality Improvement*, Third Annual Symposium, Center for Quality and Productivity Improvement, University of Wisconsin–Madison, 1991.

*Public Administration Review*

*Quality and Reliability Engineering International*

*Quality Circles Journal*

*Quality Control Circles at Work* (Tokyo: Asian Productivity Organization, 1984).

*Quality Forum*

*The Quality Imperative* (New York: McGraw-Hill, 1994).

*Quality Observer*

*Quality Progress*

Peter R. Richardson, *Cost Containment* (New York: Free Press, 1988).

George D. Robson, *Continuous Process Improvement* (New York: Free Press, 1991).

Mike Robson, *Quality Circles: A Practical Guide*, 2nd ed. (Aldershot, England: Gower, 1988).

A. C. Rosander, *Applications of Quality Control in the Service Industries* (New York: Marcel Dekker, 1985).

Joel C. Ross and William C. Ross, *Japanese Quality Circles and Productivity* (Reston, Va.: Reston Publishing Company, 1982).

Naoto Sasaki and David Hutchins, eds., *The Japanese Approach to Product Quality* (Oxford, England: Pergamon Press, 1984).

William W. Scherkenback, *The Deming Route to Quality and Productivity* (Washington, D.C.: CEEPress Books, 1986).

Richard J. Schonberger, *World Class Manufacturing* (New York: Free Press, 1986).

L. William Seidman and Steven L. Skancke, *Productivity: The American Advantage* (New York: Simon and Schuster, 1989).

Y. K. Shetty and Vernon M. Buehler, eds., *Productivity and Quality Through People* (Westport, Conn.: Quorum Books, 1985).

Y. K. Shetty and Vernon M. Buehler, eds., *Quality, Productivity, and Innovation* (New York: Elsevier, 1987).

Y. K. Shetty and Vernon M. Buehler, eds., *Competing Through Productivity and Quality* (Cambridge, Mass.: Productivity Press, 1988).

Shigeo Shingo, *The Sayings of Shigeo Shingo: Key Strategies for Plant Improvement* (Cambridge, Mass.: Productivity Press, 1987).

Shigeo Shingo, *A Study of the Toyota Production System from an Industrial Engineering Viewpoint* (Cambridge, Mass.: Productivity Press, 1989).

Shigeo Shingo, *The Shingo Production Management System* (Cambridge, Mass.: Productivity Press, 1992).

Jay W. Spechler, ed., *Managing Quality in America's Most Admired Companies* (San Francisco: Berret-Koehler Publishers, 1993).

*Target*

James Teboul, *Managing Quality Dynamics* (London: Prentice Hall, 1991).

*Total Quality Management*

Patrick L. Townsend, *Commit to Quality* (New York: John Wiley & Sons, 1990).

*TQM Magazine*

*Transactions of the Association for Quality and Participation's Annual Spring Conference and Resource Mart*

*Wall Street Journal*

Mary Walton, *The Deming Management Method* (New York: Perigee Books, 1986).

Mary Walton, *Deming Management at Work* (New York: Perigee Books, 1990).

# Index